FORGOTTEN IDEAS,
NEGLECTED PIONEERS

FORGOTTEN IDEAS, NEGLECTED PIONEERS:
Richard Semon and the Story of Memory

Daniel L. Schacter
Harvard University
Cambridge, MA

USA	Publishing Office:	PSYCHOLOGY PRESS *A member of the Taylor & Francis Group* 325 Chestnut Street Philadelphia, PA 19106 Tel: (215) 625-8900 Fax: (215) 625-2940
	Distribution Center:	PSYCHOLOGY PRESS *A member of the Taylor & Francis Group* 7625 Empire Drive Florence, KY 41042 Tel: 1 (800) 634-7064 Fax: 1 (800) 248-4724
UK		PSYCHOLOGY PRESS *A member of the Taylor & Francis Group* 27 Church Road Hove E. Sussex, BN3 2FA Tel.: +44 (0) 1273 207411 Fax: +44 (0) 1273 205612

FORGOTTEN IDEAS, NEGLECTED PIONEERS: Richard Semon and the Story of Memory

1 2 3 4 5 6 7 8 9 0

Printed by Sheridan Books, Ann Arbor, MI, 2001.
Cover design by Nancy Abbott.

A CIP catalog record for this book is available from the British Library.
∞ The paper in this publication meets the requirements of the ANSI Standard Z39.48-1984 (Permanence of Paper)

Library of Congress Cataloging-in-Publication Data
Schacter, Daniel L.
   Forgotten ideas, neglected pioneers : Richard Semon and the story of memory /
Daniel L. Schacter.
     p. cm.
   Includes bibliographical references and index.
   ISBN 1-84169-052-X (alk. paper)
   1. Semon, Richard Wolfgang, 1859–1918. 2. Memory. I. Title.

BF371 .S355 2001
153.1′2′092--dc21

2001018920
CIP

ISBN: 1-84169-052-X (paper)

In memory of my father,
Philip Schacter

Contents

Preface

Although I did not know it at the time, this book was conceived on a rainy afternoon in March, 1977, when Eric Eich and I, both graduate students in experimental psychology at the University of Toronto, discussed the usefulness of the term "ecphory" in the analysis of human memory. About a year later, after becoming familiar with the imaginative work and dramatic life of the inventor of the term—Richard Semon—I decided to write this book. The resulting monograph is a blend of biographical, historical, and psychological materials, and has two major purposes: To tell a story, and to examine substantive issues in the history and psychology of science that are related to the story.

Several of the issue-oriented chapters investigate little explored areas in the history of scientific thinking about memory, including Semon's contributions to memory theory. I anticipate that these chapters will be primarily of interest to cognitive psychologists, although they are also relevant to historians and scientists concerned with the interaction between psychology and evolutionary biology. Other chapters address wide-ranging problems in the psychology of science that have not yet received serious attention. I hope that my treatment of these problems is sufficiently broad to interest readers from many areas of psychology, as well as from cognate disciplines such as history and sociology of science. The discussion of all these issues, however, is preceded by the story of a rather remarkable life that I suspect will appeal to readers with diverse backgrounds.

Acknowledgments

The undertaking and completion of this book has been made possible by help from numerous individuals and institutions. My research was initially supported by a National Science Foundation Predoctoral Fellowship, and then by an Ontario Graduate Scholarship. I also gratefully acknowledge the support my research received from Natural Sciences and Engineering Research Council of Canada Grant No. A8632 awarded to Endel Tulving. Work on the book was initiated during my stay at the Department of Experimental Psychology, Oxford University, in 1978: I thank all of the members of the department who made my time at Oxford so enjoyable.

The staff at the Bodlean Library, Oxford, and Robarts Library, University of Toronto, frequently aided my efforts by locating materials that were difficult to find. The Bavarian State Library in Munich permitted me to inspect and make copies of letters written from Ernst Haeckel to Richard Semon. I owe a special debt of gratitude to Professor Huldrych Koelbing and the rest of the staff at the Institute of the History of Medicine in Zurich. Professor Koelbing gave me access to the Institute's collection of letters written from Richard Semon to August Forel, and encouraged my research in a spirit of scholarship that I will always remember fondly. Mrs. Majorie Semon graciously assented to spend an afternoon with me discussing what she knew about the Semon family, and also permitted me to reproduce her photographs of Sir Felix Semon.

Many of the source materials for this book were in German. Agnes Kocsis aided my work by doing excellent translations of the numerous (and frequently illegible) letters written by Semon to Forel, and by Haeckel to Semon. The other translations from the German are my own, but it should go without saying that I am responsible for all of the translations in this book. I also extend my thanks to Hugo Stöckel of the International Summer Courses in Mayrhofen, Austria, a master teacher who vastly improved my ability to read German during a delightful month in his summer course.

My ideas about the book have developed and changed during the course of conversations with numerous colleagues: I thank them collectively because the list is a long one. Part or all of the manuscript has been read and commented upon by Eric Eich, Lawrence Erlbaum, John Furedy, Agnes Kocsis, Middian Kurland, Michele Stampp, Endel Tulving, and Polly Winsor. Many of their comments and criticisms have helped me to structurally, substantively, and stylistically improve the manuscript. I am, of course, alone responsible for the final contents of the book. Several of my debts should be individually acknowledged. Michele Stampp provided extensive emotional and practical support during the later phases of this project, and also contributed useful comments and questions about the manuscript. I owe many thanks to Lawrence Erlbaum, who has taken a keen interest in the book since its inception; he has been a source of both encouragement and incisive editorial guidance. Endel Tulving has contributed to this project in many ways: By having faith in my ability to complete the book and also do a satisfactory Ph.D. thesis; by aiding my research efforts during the past several years in ways too numerous to list; and by taking the time to carefully read the entire manuscript and discuss it at length with me. I am deeply appreciative of all of his efforts. Finally, I feel somehow compelled to thank Wolfgang Amadeus Mozart for his twenty-seven piano concertos. They constituted endlessly interesting contexts for the pursuit of much of the work.

Daniel L. Schacter
Toronto, Ontario

Foreword

Among the smartest people in psychology and related sciences are graduate students. And, along with the rest of humanity, they are getting smarter year by year, as specified by the well-known Flynn effect. Thus it has come to be that, especially as they get close to the end of their pre-doctoral careers, ready to be called 'doctors,' they know, or at least think they know, everything. That is, everything that is worth knowing. Whatever they do not know, by definition, is not worth knowing.

These smart people know what is important in the world of science and what is not. This latter category clearly includes history of psychology, and indeed history of anything. The important problems and ideas that matter originated some five or ten years before the budding scientists themselves entered graduate school. Whatever little happened earlier in the past is unimportant and immaterial, and not worth wasting any time on. History is for old folks, aging full professors who have nothing better to do than to amuse themselves with irrelevancies. Whatever these oldies say or write on the antiquities can be safely ignored, because it possibly cannot make any difference in the real world, here and now, and perhaps tomorrow. (I happen to be privy to these kinds of beliefs of most eager young researchers not only because I have seen quite a few in my life but also because, a long time ago, I was one myself.)

This volume, about a bit of the history of memory research, reaches back a hundred years into the past. Its author, Daniel Schacter, probably is thought to be old by his own graduate students. (Old age, as everyone knows, begins fifteen years from where one oneself is on the scale.) Schacter is a full professor at Harvard, and currently Chairman of the Department of Psychology. He is also one of the most eminent and renowned memory researchers in the world today, known and admired for his many creative experimental, clinical, and theoretical contributions to the science of memory.

So, what would we expect our astute graduate students to do about this book? Clearly, if they want to be cool, and remain true to their convictions, they would not care whether they know about it or not, and certainly they would not want to read it even if they accidentally came into contact with it, despite the fame of the author. If he is writing about history, he himself may be a part of the past, but why should we bother with anything that is not of the real world, one that exists here and now?

Suppose someone tells these young people that the book was actually written by one of their own, by another graduate student. What would happen then? Would their curiosity be aroused? Would they prick up their ears?

But surely, the first thing they would do is to have the matter clarified. What does it mean, "suppose"? Why should we suppose something that is not so? Here is a book whose author is a world- famous scientist nearly fifty years old, that is, of advanced years. Why would anyone want to suppose anything else about its possible authorship? Surely it was not written by one of Professor Schacter's graduate students? We know that they must be smart, too, and that means they are not dumb, and that means they would not waste any of their time on history. And surely Harvard professors would not hire graduate students as ghost writers, and then publish the fruits of the students' labors under their own name? Or would they?

The point of this Foreword is to reveal to the world one of the secrets about this book that would not be apparent without such revelation.

This book in fact was written by a graduate student. Over twenty years ago, Daniel Schacter, while he was working towards his doctorate at the University of Toronto, wrote a book-length monograph under the cryptic title of "Stranger Behind the Engram," clarified somewhat by its subtitle: "Theories of Memory and the Psychology of Science." He wrote it at the same time that he was doing experimental research on his dissertation, on a topic totally unrelated to the topic of the monograph. (His dissertation was entitled "Feeling of knowing and the expression of knowledge from episodic memory" and was eventually published in the Journal of Experimental Psychology: Learning Memory and Cognition in 1983.) "Stranger Behind the Engram" was published by Lawrence Erlbaum Associates about the same time that Schacter received his degree. After several highly positive reviews of the book, and glowing person-to-person recommendations in the small circle of aficionados of memory research, it was quickly sold out, and has remained a collector's item ever since.

The present volume is a re-issue of the "Stranger Behind the Engram." The idea of the re-issue originated with another "oldie," Henry ("Roddy") Roediger, who however, as another exception to the general rule, *was* interested in history even in his younger days, and who, even more important for the present venture, is an Advisory Editor at Psychology Press and in that role persuaded the Editors to have Schacter's book reprinted. The book's reappearance should put an end to the frustration of the many people who have been looking in vain for Schacter's early book in book stores and on the Internet, as well as to Roediger's own growing impatience with people continually wanting to borrow his precious copy of the "Stranger."

The title has been changed to "Forgotten Ideas, Neglected Pioneers: Richard Semon and the Story of Memory," to better alert the reader what the book is about. Also, an Appendix has been added, a reprint of an article from the *Journal of Verbal Learning and Verbal Behavior* that Schacter, with a little help from his fellow student Eric Eich and his research supervisor at the time, had published several years before the "Stranger" book. The reader of the book, in several places, is advised to go to that article for a bit more detail on Semon's theory of memory than is described in the book, and the inclusion of a copy of the article in the volume makes it easy to follow these suggestions.

Except for these two minor changes—the title and the added Appendix— the book is the same as it was in 1982. What kind of a book is it? It is not easily classified, and to get graduate students to read it, one should perhaps not even try to classify it. The title, of course, hints at the contents. A part of it tells a fascinating story of Richard Semon, a brilliant German biologist who lived a dramatic life around the turn of the century, and whose insightful ideas about memory, unmercifully too far ahead of their time, remained unappreciated by most of the contemporary 'experts.' Another part analyzes the general phenom- enon of neglect of great scientific ideas that Semon's case so strikingly repre- sents. Why do scientists, objective and dispassionate seekers of truth about na- ture (in abstract theory), not appreciate when one of their own adds a bit to such truth? In pondering the issue of such unfortunate real scientists, and com- paring it with that of scientific 'cranks,' Schacter comes up with an original, revealing interpretation of his own, in terms of the mathematical theory of sig- nal detection. But there is very much more to it all, of course.

The whole gripping story, lucidly told, beautifully written, coupled with an admirably dispassionate treatment of a subject that would be easy to sensation- alize, exhibits the kind of wisdom and maturity, balance of judgment and psy- chological insight, that one rarely finds in younger people, anywhere, at any time. Amazing!

I and my wife Ruth had the rare pleasure of watching the young phenom- enon named Daniel Schacter—the talented and disciplined self-taught histo- rian, psychologist, and sociologist of science—with both awe and affection. We witnessed his love affairs, both scientific and romantic; we empathized with him in his passion for classical music and love of the game of golf; we admired, after appropriate testing, his knowledge of the German language that he had acquired, starting from scratch, in a summer school in Salzburg in 1978 (he wanted to read the material for his Semon book in the original); and we listened with fascination to his stories of visits to faraway libraries, archives, and private homes of people connected with the story of Richard Semon.

In the new book, Ruth Tulving has made sure that Maria Semon's name appears in the Index, along with the names of a number of others who were overlooked in the first edition. She has also helped to correct some typographi- cal errors.

I consider it my most pleasant duty to highly recommend the book to gradu- ate students of all stripes. You do not have to be a future psychologist, or a cognitive neuroscientist. You do not even have to be in any kind of science. As a graduate student, you should read the book, and think about who wrote it. Also reflect on what you find out about neglected creative intellectuals—one day you may be one, or feel that you are one! I recommend the book even more strongly to all others who are interested in memory, the history of ideas, or the human element in the making of science. Indeed it is recommended to anyone who is curious about the rich and interesting world in which we live. This is a remarkable book, about a remarkable intellectual figure from the past, by a remarkable young man, who has become a remarkable intellectual figure in our time.

Read, think, admire, be amazed, and enjoy!

Endel Tulving
Toronto
February 2001

About the Author

*D*r. Daniel Schacter is Professor and Chair of Psychology at Harvard University. He studies the psychological and biological aspects of human memory and amnesia, emphasizing the distinction between conscious and nonconscious forms of memory, and the mechanisms involved in memory distortion and forgetting.

Schacter has published over 200 scientific articles and chapters. His 1996 book, *Searching for Memory*, was named a New York Times Book Review Notable Book of the Year, one of Library Journal's Best Science and Technology Books of the Year, and received the William James Book Award from the American Psychological Association. Schacter recently published *The Seven Sins of Memory* (2001).

Schacter has received numerous awards for his research, including the Troland Research Award from the National Academy of Sciences and a Guggenheim Fellowship. He is a member of the Society of Experimental Psychologists and the American Academy of Arts and Sciences.

Schacter lives in Newton, Massachusetts, with his wife, Susan, and his two daughters, Hannah and Emily.

1

Introduction

*T*he treasures of the past are often cloaked in improbable disguises. Intellectual detectives investigating the mysteries of antiquity—archeologists, paleontologists, and historians are some of the most persistent—eventually learn that they cannot afford to overlook the unexpected but intriguing clues that point their explorations in previously unplanned directions. A clay cup and perfume bottle found by archeologists off the coast of Italy ultimately led to major advances in understanding colonization patterns of the early Greeks; seemingly innocuous bits of information have also triggered surprising revelations in other domains. As with the Grecian cup and bottle, the clues that gave rise to this book were unanticipated but irresistibly suggestive. They pointed to a little-known scientific figure from the past, and intimated that a cache of intellectual riches was hidden behind the deceptive veneer of the stranger's obscurity.

The stranger was a German biologist named Richard Semon. Semon wrote, in the first decade of the 20th-century, two books on the psychology of memory that are virtually unknown to modern memory researchers.[1] My interest in him was aroused by several references to his work that suggested that Semon's ideas merited more attention than they had received. Kurt Koffka, the eminent Gestalt psychologist, provided one of the initial hints. Koffka alluded to Semon's theory of memory in a footnote tucked away within his massive *Principles of Gestalt Psychology:* "I refrain from giving a survey of Semon's theory and from discussing how far it agrees with the one here presented and how far it is different. . . . I must add, however, that this omission is not due to a lack of

---

1. The sole scholarly investigation of Semon's work that I could find was a doctoral dissertation submitted to the Medical History Institute at the University of Zurich (Schatzmann, 1968). The opening line of this monograph confirmed my opinion regarding Semon's historical obscurity: "Richard Semon is today almost completely unknown (p. 4)."

appreciation of Semon's great achievement (1935, p. 598)." Koffka's acclaim was matched by homage from the prominent neuroanatomist J. Z. Young, who asserted that "many modern ideas on the subject [of memory] go back to Richard Semon (1965, p. 288)" Erwin Schrödinger further heightened the aura of mystery surrounding Semon. This Nobel Prize winning physicist wondered why a physiological model of Semon's memory theory had not been developed, "important though it would be for the advancement of our knowledge (1964, p. 14)." Semon's work also received enthusiastic advocacy from no less a figure than Bertrand Russell, who devoted an entire chapter of his 1921 treatise, *The Analysis of Mind*, to the presentation of Semon's theory. He flatly stated that "The best writer on mnemic phenomena known to me is Richard Semon (1921, p. 83)."

As a student of human memory with a keen interest in the history of the field, I was perplexed by these testimonies to a man whose ideas have had no detectable influence on modern memory research. If Semon's work was not sufficiently important to have attracted the attention of memory researchers, why did the likes of Russell and Schrödinger praise him with such enthusiasm?

I spent some time exploring possible answers to this question; the investigation yielded an intellectual harvest that exceeded my expectations. The first discovery was that the claims of Koffka, Russell, Schrödinger, and Young concerning the importance of Semon's work seemed entirely justified: His innovative ideas anticipated numerous developments in recent memory research. In fact, Semon coined one of the best known terms in psychology—the word "engram"[2]—although few are aware that he originated the term. I also became convinced that Semon's analysis of memory could not be properly grasped without a thorough understanding of the intellectual contexts in psychology and biology from which his ideas derived. These contexts turned out to be as intriguing, and almost as unknown, as Semon's work itself. In addition, my attempts to understand why Semon's ideas had gone unrecognized for so many years led me to investigate other cases of scientists whose work was ignored for lengthy periods of time. Consideration of these cases raised basic questions about the recognition and neglect of ideas in science, and also provided a broader perspective on the fate of Semon's work.

In these initial explorations, then, I confronted a variety of historical and psychological problems that were relevant to, but more general than, the investigation of Semon's work itself. As my involvement with the case deepened, I became increasingly curious about the circumstances of Semon's personal life: What sort of man was Richard Semon? Where did he live? Under whom did he study? How did he respond to the neglect of his work? Answers to these ques-

---

2. The term "engram" is roughly equivalent to the notion of "memory trace." The numerous historical misconceptions of the genesis and meaning of this term, as well as its role in Semon's theorizing, are explored in Section II of the book.

tions emerged slowly, over time, as I uncovered and fit together the various pieces of Semon's life. Although not all of the pieces could be found, and some of them were difficult to understand, it became clear to me that an extraordinary human drama had been played out during the fifty-nine years of Richard Semon's existence. The drama seemed sufficiently abundant in personalities, adventure, romance—and ultimately, tragedy—to render it comparable to a play or novel that is not entirely believable.

This book grew out of my initial investigations. The book is concerned both with the tale of Richard Semon's life, and with the historical and psychological issues raised by his work. By telling Semon's story in conjunction with the analysis of more general intellectual issues, I hope to place each of these pursuits in a richer context than would be possible if they were treated separately. In the first part of the book, we follow Richard Semon's evolving personal odyssey through its labyrinthine course, including various subplots, twists, and turns. In the second part, our attention shifts to Semon's biological and psychological work. We explore in some depth the historical contexts that constitute the relevant background to his work; we also confront a number of key questions in the psychology of science that emerge from consideration of the reception of Semon's work by the scientific community. Before we begin this polymorphic journey, however, it will be useful to delineate both the major characters in the story and the broader questions that are confronted during the course of the book.

STORY AND CHARACTERS

Although this book contains much biographical material, it is not intended to be a comprehensive biography of Richard Semon. My primary intent in the biographical section of the book is to recapture the many different facets of Semon's life; all relevant historical, cultural, and familial contexts are used. Thus I pay more attention to the characters and issues surrounding Semon's story than one usually finds in a traditional biography, and less attention to filling in the missing bits and pieces of Semon's life than would a professional biographer. Indeed, there is a great deal of biographical information about some parts of Semon's life, but relatively little about others. One of the problems encountered when writing about an unknown scientist such as Semon is that the wealth of information preserved about major figures like Darwin, Freud, or Einstein is simply not available. Where the biographical record is spotty—and there are numerous such places—I have attempted to smooth the gaps by drawing attention to relevant cultural and situational contexts.

A number of fascinating characters played major parts in Semon's life. Several of these characters—his mentor Ernst Haeckel, his friend and scientific ally August Forel, and his wife Maria—influenced Semon in important ways and formed part of the fabric of his life for long periods of time. I extensively consider both Haeckel and Forel: They are among the most interesting figures in late 19th- and early 20th-century science, and their role in Semon's life is best understood in the context of their own personalities and achievements. As for Maria Semon, although she influenced the direction of her husband's life in a dramatic fashion, little is known about her as a person; the fragmentary bits of information that are available surface during the course of the story.

I also pay some attention to Semon's family. The plight of his parents, Simon and Henrietta, is explored in the early chapters; the impressive triumphs and ultimate downfall of his brother Felix occupy our attention at other points. I argue at the conclusion of the first section of the book that consideration of the experiences of Simon, Henrietta, and Felix Semon may increase our under- standing of Richard Semon. It should be noted, however, that I make no at- tempt to offer psychoanalytic or other psychodynamic interpretations of Semon's actions, words, or intentions. To be sure, I analyze where appropriate any clues to Semon's personality that are provided by various sources; but my emphasis is on psychological description rather than psychodynamic explanation.

ISSUES: HISTORY AND PSYCHOLOGY OF SCIENCE

The issues confronted during the course of this book can be broadly catego- rized as (1) those pertaining to history—more specifically, to scientific theoriz- ing about memory in late 19th- and early 20th-century psychology and evolu- tionary biology; and (2) those concerning the role of various psychological processes in the pursuit of science. Let us consider each of these topics in turn.

Beyond the Freud and Darwin "Industries"

Richard Semon was trained as a marine zoologist in the 1880s, pursued ana- tomical and evolutionary research during the 1890s, and wrote two books dur- ing the first decade of the 20th-century that approached problems of memory with conceptual tools that were provided both by psychology and by evolution- ary biology. Since the contexts from which these two books emerged will be central to our later examinations of Semon's work, it seems important to com- ment upon modern perspectives on the psychology and evolutionary biology of Semon's time.

I want to make a strong claim about our historical understanding of this epoch: It is dominated by the lengthy shadows cast by two men, Charles Dar-

---

3. I am, of course, defining the "epoch" of Darwin and Freud in a broad sense. Darwin preceded Freud by a full scientific generation, and they cannot be regarded as con- temporaries. But there is an extensive temporal intersection between the historical spheres of influence of these two men, dating roughly from 1880 to 1920. I refer to that period as the age that has been dominated by attention to the work and influ- ence of Darwin and Freud.

win and Sigmund Freud.[3] Darwin, as the father of evolutionary biology, and Freud, as the father of psychoanalysis, have commanded our attention in a way that is rivaled by few figures from the scientific past. Although they may seem like whimsical labels, the "Darwin Industry" and the "Freud Industry" have very real existences; the number of scholars whose bread is buttered by the study of these two giants of science is impressive. The matter can be most simply illuminated quantitatively. Consider the number of books listed under the subject headings "Sigmund Freud" and "Charles Darwin" in a recent catalogue of a large university library.[4] Freud accounts for 202 entries; Darwin, a somewhat more modest 90. What of other figures in psychology and evolutionary biology of that time? Wilhelm Wundt, the father of experimental psychology, is mentioned in seven entries; Edward Bradford Titchener, the influential Cornell psychologist, accounts for even less with two; and John B. Watson, the founder of Behaviorism, registers a paltry one. The picture is similar in evolutionary biology. Ernst Haeckel, a major figure in his day, is represented by 14 entries in the subject index; August Weismann, one of the most respected neo-Darwinian theorists of his time, is barely visible with two entries; and Alfred Russell Wallace, co-founder of the theory of evolution and natural selection with Darwin, accounts for six entries.

There is one sense in which the historical domination of Darwin and Freud is neither surprising nor inappropriate.[5] They exerted profound effects both in and beyond their respective fields—certainly none of the other figures listed above wielded such pervasive influence—and the enormous consequences of their work have rendered almost every aspect of their lives an object of intense scrutiny. But a price has been paid for all this attention, because there is a limit to the number of questions of *contemporary* consequence that can be posed about the life and work of these great scientists. Precisely because their influence has been so massive, studies of Darwin and Freud inform us about the conditions that contribute to the making of one kind of scientist—a hugely successful one. But not all scientists are hugely successful, and not all the important lessons of history can be gleaned from the scrutiny of those who are. One of the major purposes of this book is to demonstrate that the study of an historically unknown scientist can raise important questions about the nature and function of the scientific enterprise, questions not encountered in analyses of triumphant historical figures. Of course, this is not to say that continued study of highly influential figures such as Darwin and Freud will prove entirely unrewarding, but it is to suggest that new lessons may be learned by searching beyond their imposing historical shadows.

---

4. I consulted the 1980 catalogue of the Robarts Library at the University of Toronto.
5. Clearly, my case is to some extent overstated. One need only read a few issues of the *Journal of the History of the Behavioral Sciences* or the *Journal of the History of Biology* to realize that specialist historians do pay attention to late 19th- and early 20th-century figures other than Darwin and Freud. But even here, Darwin and Freud command a disproportionate share of attention.

A second consequence of the attention paid to Darwin and Freud is that other interesting figures from their era have been overlooked. Whatever their influence, Darwin and Freud were by no means the only creative psychologists or evolutionary biologists at work in their time—quite the contrary. The more one studies the evolutionary biologists and psychologists of the late 19th- and early 20th-centuries, the more one is impressed by the intellectual richness of the epoch; the sheer number of original thinkers who were active in each field is impressive. However, too many of the period's most creative minds have been neglected in the rush to study Darwin and Freud. Such figures are frequently given no more than cursory mention as background characters in studies principally concerned with the two great men. Fortunately, the light has begun to dawn, and some of the important thinkers obscured in the shadows cast by Darwin and Freud are now receiving appropriate credit for their unique contributions. The theories of James Mark Baldwin, the psychologist from Toronto, Princeton, and Johns Hopkins who promulgated important ideas in both psychology and evolutionary biology, have been brought to light in recent work (Broughton & Freeman-Moir, 1981; Ross & Kerst, 1978); the ideas of Wilhelm Fliess, long considered an ancillary curiosity to the Freud story, have received serious treatment in Sulloway's (1979) revealing book; and Gould's (1977) study has taken a long second look at the ideas of evolutionary biologists such as Haeckel, Alpheus Hyatt, and Edward Drinker Cope. One hopes and expects that more such thinkers will be considered in future analyses of this bountiful intellectual epoch. Innovative scientists such as Morton Prince, Pierre Janet, Ernst Meumann, August Forel, George John Romanes, Wilhelm Roux, Théodule Ribot, and Thomas Laycock, to name just a few, have more to teach us than can be communicated in a footnote to the next biography of Darwin and Freud.

One of the purposes of the present book is to contribute to the understanding of the fertile turn-of-the-century era, and some of the foregoing names appear in the following pages. But Richard Semon is the central character of this exercise in intellectual archeology. His ideas, absorbing in their own right, also serve to illuminate some important but little known features of the psychology and evolutionary biology of the time. As we proceed, I hope to show that Semon's work, and the contexts in which it occurred, are related in an interactive manner. Semon's efforts lead us to examine the relevant context, and the insights garnered while exploring that context contribute to a more refined appreciation of Semon's work and its reception. It should be kept in mind that no attempt is made here to lionize Semon as a cruelly misunderstood scientific hero, or to elevate him into a class with Darwin or Freud. Their insights have had profound effects on both science and society; Semon has had no such effects. As stated earlier, however, that is one reason why Semon's work is such a potentially rich source of questions that are not usually posed in analyses of major historical figures.

Just as our study of Semon's work requires an understanding of the key features of the intellectual contexts that are relevant to it, consideration of the neglect of his ideas about memory, and Semon's psychological responses to that neglect, leads us to some engrossing problems in the psychology of science. Let us now explore some of the salient background to these problems.

The Human Scientist

> The scientist is a man who wears a white coat and works in a laboratory. . . . He is a dedicated man who works not for money or fame or self-glory, but . . . for the benefit of mankind and the welfare of his country . . . The scientist is a brain. He spends his days indoors, in a laboratory, pouring things from one test tube into another. His work is uninteresting, dull, monotonous, tedious, time consuming.

It is unlikely that many practicing scientists would recognize themselves in the above characterization, but the image of dour white-coated men was reported by many subjects in Mead and Metraux's (1957, p. 387) study of high school students' attitudes toward scientists. Although it is tempting to regard such descriptions as harmless statements born of benign naiveté, it should be remembered that similar notions have long typified the psychological conception of the scientist among large segments of the lay public, as well as in some sectors of the intellectual community. The image of a cold, dispassionate searcher after truth—somehow immunized against the intrusion of annoying human traits such as bias and egoism—has been temporally resilient. Although students of behavior such as Lawrence Kubie (1954) have long called for a more realistic appraisal of the psychological forces that enter into the pursuit of scientific truth, the storybook image of the cooly detached scientist has wilted only during the past decade: The scientist has finally been brought out of the closet as a human being.

This change of perspective can be traced to several sources. First, and perhaps foremost, has been the explosion of research in the rapidly developing sociology of science. Sociologically-based analyses of science are found in the early work of George Sarton (1931) and Alfred North Whitehead (1919) among others, but the major figure behind the recent surge of interest is, unquestionably, Robert K. Merton. Merton's myriad applications of sociological theory to the scientific enterprise have placed the pursuit of science in a broad social perspective. The important topics broached by Merton have included revealing analyses of reward systems in science, the role of social recognition in scientific communication, and the social norms that underly scientists' conduct (Merton, 1973). These and other crucial issues have also been confronted in the subsequent research of sociologists working within the tradition established by Merton. The significance of this sociological research—some of which will be considered later in the book—is that it has elucidated the continuity between scientists' behavior and other forms of human social behavior. When science is viewed as a dynamic social enterprise that shares many features in common with other social processes, the image of the machine-like man in the laboratory fades rapidly.

A second key reason for the development of a psychologically more sophisticated view of the scientist is found in the influential analyses of Thomas S.

Kuhn. Kuhn's major work, *The Structure of Scientific Revolutions*, and his major conceptual innovation, the paradigm, have achieved wide recognition. They will be introduced in Chapter 10, but for now it is sufficient to note that Kuhn's ideas have sparked widespread interest—and controversy—concerning the role of such psychological processes as bias, commitment, and selective perception in the pursuit of scientific knowledge. As in the case of Merton and the sociologists, the "detached" scientist has no place in the Kuhnian framework; he has been replaced by a psychologically active and complex human being.

A third possible influence on the changing image of the scientist is found in popular monographs such as James D. Watson's *The Double Helix* (1968). Watson's book, which described the series of events that led to the discovery of the structure of DNA, graphically depicted the behavior of scientists in a way that few outsiders were familiar with: The scientists in Watson's account were competitive, jealous, and occasionally petty people whose scientific pursuits did not seem segregated from their ambitions and biases. Watson's essay has been followed by two more monographs that provide similarly revealing glimpses into various aspects of the egos and rivalries that made the DNA hunt such a psychologically interesting one (Judson, 1979; Sayre, 1975). A number of other recently popular works have also placed the pursuit of science in an unambiguously human context (e.g., Feuer, 1974; Koestler, 1959, 1971).

The above noted influences have helped to replace the image of the sterile figure in the white coat with a more diversified and interesting person coping with a complex human situation in an intensely personal manner. We too shall leave behind the storybook images. One of the most absorbing aspects of Richard Semon's story concerns the interrelations among his work, the reasons for its neglect, and Semon's psychological reaction in the face of indifference from the scientific community. These relationships lead us to confront two problems in the psychology of science: (1) the factors affecting the recognition versus the neglect of new ideas; and (2) the reaction of isolated scientists to the indifference encountered by their work. Our extensive explorations of these problems serve to broaden our understanding of Semon's scientific and psychological status.

It may be worth noting that the psychology of science—in sharp contrast to the flourishing sociology of science—has remained a theoretically impoverished area. Others have commented upon this discouraging circumstance (Mahoney, 1976), and it is not immediately apparent why psychologists have so far made such a modest contribution to the understanding of *homo scientus*. Although Kuhn himself relied heavily on psychological constructs in *The Structure of Scientific Revolutions*, these ideas have not been systematically developed by psychologists (for exceptions, see McDonagh, 1976; Weimer, 1974b). This seems particularly ironic in light of the potentially crucial role that psychologists might play in the analysis of the scientific process. The chapters in this book that deal with the psychology of science are no more than prefatory attempts to delineate and explore key issues and problems. One of their purposes, however, is to encourage further theoretical activity in this area on the part of psychologists.

PART I
THE STORY

1

THE STORY

2

Roots of the Drama

*H*istory is dotted by certain years that seem imbued with special significance. Many of these years—1066, 1492, and 1914 are prominent examples—acquire landmark status because of dramatic episodes that powerfully influence subsequent events. Other years initially suggest no great events or crucial developments, and their significance is appreciated only when they are examined in cross-section. These years are defined by a spectrum of events and have their impact when considered in toto. One of those years was 1859. Though most would be hard pressed to name more than one or two of its highlights, Gasman (1971, p. xi) labeled 1859 the *"annus mirabilis"* of 19th century European intellectual history, and Barzun (1958, p. 20) acknowledged its status as a "pivotal year." Let us consider the diverse intellectual landmarks that originated in 1859: Darwin's *Origin of Species*, Marx's *Critique of Political Economy*, Dickens' *Tale of Two Cities*, John Stuart Mill's *"On Liberty,"* and Sir William Hamilton's *Lectures on Metaphysics and Logic* all appeared in the same year that Pasteur discovered micro-organisms and Wagner composed *Tristan and Isolde*. But 1859 was distinguished not only by the work of mature intellects, it was also the year that shaped the course of future decades: Kaiser Wilhelm II and Theodore Roosevelt, Henri Bergson and John Dewey, Pierre Curie and Svante Arrhenius, and Sir Arthur Conan Doyle and A. E. Housman were notable pairs of politicians, philosophers, scientists, and writers born in 1859. Italy was unified under Garibaldi in 1859, the John Brown incident at Harper's Ferry took place in the same year, and the central figure of another drama first saw the light of day when Alfred Dreyfus was born on October 19, 1859.

The weighty creations and portentous births of 1859 may serve either to augment or reduce the significance of Richard Wolfgang Semon's birth in Berlin on August 22nd of that remarkable year. Yet some of these events proved to be more than just interesting bits of historical context that define Semon's year of birth. Darwin's *Origin* played a critical role in the young Semon's choice of career, and the Kaiser's foreign policies contributed in a dramatic way to Semon's ultimate demise. But other, less well-known events had an equally decisive impact. The year 1859 witnessed the reawakening of German nationalism, aroused from a "decade of uneasy slumber (Pflanze, 1963, p. 127)." The rise of that nationalistic tide intimately affected the way in which Semon lived and the manner in which he died. And although 1859 merely signaled the beginning of the new nationalism to most Germans, for some the vision of a unified Germany taking its rightful place as the master of Europe was already fully formed. For one young man of 25, travels in Italy during that country's period of unification elicited a virtual eruption of emotion for the Fatherland. On October 16, 1859 he wrote home in an agitated state of mind: "It had to be heard all over Italy and Sicily, in the majestic environment of Naples, as well as on the glorious plains of Palermo, among the quarries of Syracuse, as well as on the peak of Aetna: *Deutschland, Deutschland, über alles, über alles in der Welt! Ich bin ein Deutscher, will ein Deutscher sein!* (Gasman, 1971, p. 3)"[1] The young man was Ernst Haeckel, who within 15 years would become the most influential biologist in Germany. He would soon after become Richard Semon's mentor; and the emotional brand of patriotism that Haeckel first expressed in 1859 constituted an essential ingredient of a personality that left a permanent impression on Semon. However, let us retreat from Semon's year of birth and its confluence of significant developments; other salient events occurred in years prior to 1859.

BEGINNINGS

When Simon Joseph Semon came to Berlin in 1852, he had every reason to believe that the most prosperous period of his life was about to unfold.[2] Born a Prussian Jew, he had successfully endured a difficult, laborious youth, and established early in life an association with the highly reputable Danzig banking house of Max and Heinrich Behrend. A kind man who was liked by many, Simon's fortunes rose quickly in the Behrend House, and he attained at an early age a position of high rank. He soon felt sufficiently confident of his status and financial assets to contemplate marriage. The prestige enjoyed by the Behrend House assured Simon a place in the upper echelons of Jewish society, and there he met his wife. On the surface, Henrietta Aschenheim differed markedly from her future husband. As stiffly formal as Simon was conciliatory, and as humorless as Simon was jocular, she had thoroughly mastered all the mannerisms and affec-

---

1. The part of the quote that is in German translates roughly as follows: "Germany, Germany, everywhere, everywhere in the world! I am a German and will always be a German!"
2. Most of our information on the Semon family background derives from *The Autobiography of Sir Felix Semon* (1926). The biographical sketch of Richard Semon that was published by his friend Otto Lubarsch (Lubarsch, 1920) tells us much about Semon's adolescent experiences, but does not provide much insight into his parents' personalities.

tations that were expected of a "society girl" reared in a German boarding school during the 1830s. Yet warmth and kindness lie hidden behind the veneer of coolness and propriety, and Simon Semon must have detected this before marrying her. Their first child was born in Danzig, but three years after Felix Semon's birth on December 8, 1849, they felt sufficiently prosperous to move to Berlin.

The Berlin of 1852 was still a far cry from the *Weltstadt* (World-City) of the early 20th-century, and most of the features that marked the Prussian capital during Richard Semon's childhood could already be found. To be sure, the city had outgrown the characterization of "mediocre" (Masur, 1970, p. 20) that accurately described it at the time of Friedrich Wilhelm I's death in 1740. Under the subsequent rule of Friedrich the Great, the political status of the city rose considerably, and some of its most prominent architectural landmarks were built: the spectacular Fredericianum Forum, and, in a huge nearby square, the Opera House, Hedwigskirche, and Prince Henry's Palace. Although these structures preserved the late Baroque and early Rococco spirit of the period, they were more muted than contemporary architecture in Munich or Vienna, and reflected traditional Prussian restraint. The Brandenburg Gate, built in 1793, and the classical architecture of Carl Friedrich Schinkel, were even more conspicuous embodiments of the Prussian mode.

Prussian restraint dominated not only the city's architecture but its inhabitants as well; as one historian noted, "Berlin society still adhered to the old order established when Prussia was not a state that had an army but an army that had a state (Masur, 1970, p. 149)." A reactionary wave following the failed revolution of 1848 heightened the atmosphere of provincial Prussianism when Simon and Henrietta arrived in Berlin. Still, the city was rapidly growing—the population had doubled to 400,000 between 1815 and 1848, reaching nearly 700,000 by 1865 (Masur, pp. 42–49)—and it was soon to embark upon 20 years of swift economic development. The 1850s were prosperous years in Berlin, and for a while it seemed that Simon Semon's financial rise would continue unabated. The family's lifestyle reflected his success. Shortly after the birth of daughter Anna, they left their modest Berlin home for a larger one, and, by the time Richard was born, they had moved into a stately residence in a prestigious neighborhood. Simon's prosperity enabled the couple to become part of Jewish Berlin's social élite, and his wife relished the opportunity. For a Prussian Jewess with a proper social upbringing nothing could be more desirable than membership in the Berlin élite. Affluent Jews had found a modicum of acceptance in Berlin since the 18th century days of Moses Mendelssohn. In spite of sporadic outbreaks of anti-Semitism, the special cosmopolitan qualities that comprised the "Berlin-Jewish spirit" enabled the city to remain a center for Jewish social and intellectual activity (Gay, 1978). Henrietta Semon's enthusiastic involvement in the upper social circles led to an obsessive concern with her standing in the select group, a concern that did not go unnoticed by her eldest son:

> She had a peculiar dread of the 'opinion of the world.' Socially, only the *élite* of the Jewish Society of Berlin were of any importance to her. The 'opinion

of the world' meant, for my poor mother, nothing more or less than the gossip of a few elderly ladies of 'good' Jewish families, whom she herself had selected as supreme judges. How much did I suffer during my boyhood from these 'good families'! Everything in our house was carefully arranged to suit these selected few. No Countess with sixteen ancestors in unbroken lineage could have guarded more severely against the invasion of her sacrosanct circle by people of unequal birth. What happened outside this interested her but little (Semon, 1926, p. 18).

Problems of a more practical nature soon perturbed the Semons' affluent lifestyle. Without warning, the Behrend House—ranked among the most stable financial establishments in Prussia—went into bankruptcy in 1866. Although Simon quickly regrouped after the collapse and found work as a broker at the stock exchange, the family had to relinquish their impressive home and move to much humbler lodgings in the western section of Berlin. Simon managed to secure a reasonable income for the next few years, but when disaster struck again in 1870 the effects were more drastic. With the outbreak of the Franco-Prussian war, stocks depreciated and Simon suffered major losses. He could not, however, bear to inform the family of his financial difficulties; instead, Simon tried to spare them by concealing the depressing reality of the situation. His strategy did not work for long. The economic crash of 1873, intensified his problems, and after he had dissipated the last of his meager reserves, Simon made a desperate final attempt to salvage his financial condition by speculating. He failed dismally. The secret could be hidden no longer, and the once proud banker from Danzig had to turn to relatives and friends to help cover his losses.

As might be expected, Simon's financial woes deeply disturbed his wife. Yet somewhere inside the woman who so feared the opinion of her world were reserves of strength and loyalty. When Henrietta finally learned of Simon's fiscal chaos, she submitted to its consequences with surprising equanimity and remained loyal to her husband throughout the trauma. Their final dark years together were spent in a small flat, where Simon succumbed to apoplexy on their wedding anniversary in 1883. After Simon's death, Henrietta felt it her duty to help pay off the numerous debts that he had left. The years of struggle continued, and as she reached her 80s Henrietta suffered from severe progressive senile dementia. Felix recalled the sad sight of the woman whose manners remained "as carefully chosen and obliging as ever (Semon, 1926, p. 19)" at the same time as her cognitive apparatus rapidly deteriorated; Richard watched in distress as "her personality completely altered (Semon to Forel, 9–28–09)" within the span of a few short years. After daughter Anna died in 1906, she hardly missed her; and when Henrietta herself passed on in 1909 at the age of 84, it was a blessing for her and the family. For both Richard and Felix, the last years of their parents were difficult to watch. They had no way of knowing that their own final days would be similar.

Richard, barely seven when the first of his father's misfortunes struck, could not have fully understood the significance of his family's move from their grand home. Yet with the failure of Simon's strategy of concealment, the adolescent Semon became ever-more aware of his family's changing status. And just as his early years saw radical alterations in his family's life, they also witnessed sweeping changes in his country's life, transformations that helped to shape Semon's perception of the world. The reign of Friedrich Wilhelm IV had come to a functional end in 1857 when the Emperor suffered a stroke; his brother Wilhelm I became Prince Regent in 1858 and ultimately succeeded to the throne in 1861. The striking differences between the two have often been noted— Friedrich Wilhelm's sensitive, artistic nature sharply contrasted with Wilhelm's harsh, militaristic qualities—and many have speculated that Germany's fate in the 19th century might have differed considerably had Friedrich Wilhelm held the crown for just a few more years. Such was not the case, and the so-called "New Age" of nationalism in Prussia and Germany took shape under the rule of the man who "was a true representative of the old Prussia which, he felt, rested on the four pillars of monarchy, army, bureaucracy and nobility (Feuchtwanger, 1970, p. 174)." When Wilhelm appointed Bismarck to the post of Prussian Prime Minister in 1862, he insured that the cause of German nationalism would be pursued in a manner that assigned priority to Prussia and the preservation of Prussian hegemony. It was Bismark who negotiated the great Prussian military successes of the 1860s, making good on his famous statement of 1862 that "The great questions of the day will not be settled by speeches and the resolutions of majorities—that was the great mistake from 1848 to 1849—but by blood and iron (Taylor, 1976, p. 108.)"

Yet these conquests, which resulted in the establishment of the North German Confederation, were only a prelude to the military venture that Bismarck knew he could use as a final step to the formation of a unified Germany under Prussian control—a war with France. He realized that the success of a Franco-Prussian war as a tool of Prussian-style nationalism critically depended upon the "impression which the origin of the war makes on us and others. It is important that we be the attacked party (Hamerow, 1969, p. 387)." Bismarck hoped that his countrymen's perception of aggression on the part of the despised French enemy would rally their fighting spirit. His strategy worked. The outbursts of nationalistic sentiment and the desire to protect the endangered Fatherland that spewed forth from Germans of various backgrounds transcended their own rivalries and quarrels. Even in Bavaria, traditionally an opponent of Prussian militarism, support for the war was enthusiastic. In Prussia, excitement reached a fever pitch, and 21-year-old Felix Semon's perception of the heady spirit on the day that France declared war attests to the success of Bismarck's manipulation:

> Nobody outside Germany, at that time, can imagine the excitement, the enthusiasm of those days. . . . Every German interpreted the sudden conflict as the inevitable clash with the 'arch-enemy', who . . . as recently as in our grandparents' time had inflicted upon us the deepest humiliation in the history of Prussia.

> I happened to be in Berlin's main street, Unter den Linden, on the day when King Wilhelm returned from Ems, and was an eye-witness of his reception. I have never seen such enthusiasm. It seemed as if the fundamental note of the feeling was genuinely serious, almost religious (Semon, 1926, pp. 42–43).

When Felix returned home, "deeply moved by this historical scene," he discussed with the family exactly what his military role should be; that he would join the army was not questioned. Even Henrietta was swept away by the patriotic fervor. She joined the nursing corps in a volunteer capacity, and eventually received a medal for her efforts. For Richard, one month short of his 12th birthday, these great events were frustrating as well as inspiring. A burgeoning patriot, he could hardly be pleased that he was too young to serve the Fatherland.

The eventual Prussian victory was greeted with ecstasy in the homeland. Paris had fallen, Alsace-Lorraine belonged to Germany once again, and Napoleon III and the Second Empire had been defeated. For Felix, it meant an end to the long strain of battle and the glory of a victor's return. On the great day of military celebrations and parades in Berlin, Felix arranged for Richard and the family to witness the festivities from a friend's apartment overlooking the Brandenburg Gate. Following a royal review, Felix rode as leader of his squadron's left flank as thousands of soldiers marched into the city on a hot summer's day. The long march was filled with memorable scenes, but for the youthful soldier and part-time composer:

> the climax of the whole day . . . was reached at the moment when our Regimental Band passed through the Brandenburg Gate, playing my St. Quentin March . . . and when, debouching from the Gate into the Pariser Platz, we were received with overwhelming jubilation, hurrahs, and waving of pocket handkerchiefs from the immense crowd which covered the tribunes, the windows, and the roofs of the big square (Semon, 1926, p. 54–55).

Participation in the momentous event impressed Felix greatly. For the younger Richard, perched in a window bay overlooking the drama, the mere opportunity to witness such an historic occasion must have been overwhelming. As we trace Semon's developing nationalism, we would do well to remember the emotional power of the events he experienced in those days preceding German unification.

The victory that the Semons and countless thousands celebrated on that spirited summer's day ushered in a new era of German politics. With unification completed, Wilhelm I was crowned Emperor of the German Empire in 1871. Bismarck, however, negotiated the unification, and Bismarck directed Germany's tremendous expansion of power during the next 20 years. Richard's enthusiasm for Bismarck's vigorous brand of German nationalism led a childhood friend to describe him as "a spirited admirer of Bismarck (Lubarsch, 1920, p. xx)." The roots of this respect may have grown from the scenes he observed

FIGURE 1. Felix Semon as a young member of the Prussian Army.

overlooking the Brandenberg Gate. The victory march, however, was not an isolated experience for the adolescent Semon. The 1870s marked the beginning of Berlin's ascent to its eventual rank as a *Weltstadt*, and excitement pervaded the new first city of the German Empire. The spirit driving Berlin's evolving sense of significance is well captured in Rudolf Mosse's pronouncement upon launching his newspaper, *Berliner Tagesblatt*, in 1871:

> At a time when the eyes of the world look upon Berlin, we present to the public the *Berliner Tagesblatt*. The capital of Prussia has become the capital of Germany; the royal city of Prussia, the imperial city of Germany. As Paris . . . was France, so Berlin will and must become Germany, a metropolis, a world city. . . . We must be inspired by the thought that he who writes for Berlin, writes for the civilized world (Masur, 1970, p. 70).

For Semon, the great developments of the 1870s took on added dimensions of immediacy and importance through his associations at the *Gymnasium*, that unique German institution of secondary school education. Richard attended the newly constructed Kaiser Wilhelm Gymnasium; his experiences there powerfully influenced the subsequent course of his life. It was at the Gymnasium that Semon first met Otto Lubarsch, who remained a close friend for over 40 years. Semon and Lubarsch shared many adolescent experiences together, and it is through Lubarsch that we receive most of our glimpses into Semon's life at the Gymnasium.

The students of the Kaiser Wilhelm Gymnasium were sons of eminent public figures, well-known not only in Berlin, but in Prussia and Germany as well. Richard could count among his friends the sons of the statesmen and soldiers who were responsible for the major developments of the day, so the events themselves seemed all the more real and alive. The frequent opportunity to meet face-to-face with these great men further enhanced Semon's sense of involvement with ongoing events of historical significance. The Gymnasium itself heartily endorsed the new nationalistic spirit. Such a heady atmosphere deeply affected impressionable young minds, and, as Lubarsch put it, "the youth in this great time were seized by the spirit of the Fatherland, which continued for their whole life (1920, p. xiii)."

In addition to cultivating such long lasting patriotic zeal, the Gymnasium also emphasized the old Prussian values of duty and discipline. The classical German Gymnasium had long been identified with a military-like rigor in its approach to education. With the liberal revolution of 1848, however, a more humanistic attitude briefly prevailed. But after the failure of the revolution, 17th-century disciplinary methods rode the reactionary wave that swept the country back into prominence. They remained the most conspicuous feature of the classical Gymnasium until the educational reforms of the late 19th-century (Learned, 1914). Many who attended Gymnasium during these years looked back upon the days of drill and discipline with distaste; Einstein's hatred of the Gymnasium's formal rigor is not atypical (Clark, 1971, p. 31). For Semon, the experience left a mixed impression. On the one hand, he resented the excessively repressive methods of the Gymnasium. He sharply criticized its drill tactics in a letter to his friend August Forel (12–27–04), and recounted the painful marks they left upon his youth. Lubarsch, too, recalled Semon's disgust with the pettiness of "small minds" (1920, p. xiii) that he encountered at the Gymnasium. Yet at another level the disciplinarians of the Gymnasium left their mark upon young Richard. Lubarsch recalled the great value that Semon, throughout his life, attached to a "stricter sense of duty and more spartan discipline (1920, p. xiii)." When the two old friends met just months before Semon's death, Richard still firmly maintained that the old Prussian virtues were of vital importance to the German people. The juxtaposition—sometimes conflict—of Semon the humanist with Semon the Prussian traditionalist is crucial to our story.

Semon's adolescence was not, however, limited to patriotic enthusiasm and rigorous discipline. Simon and Henrietta's cultural interests permeated the household, at least in the years preceding Simon's financial ruin. These interests were supplemented by the rich intellectual atmosphere at the Gymnasium. The school of statesmen's sons included the offspring of prominent artists, publishers, and professors. Consequently, Semon was exposed to a broad spectrum of intellectual pursuits; and as Lubarsch emphasized, it was his precocious schoolmates, rather than his teachers, who provided most of the intellectual stimulation. Semon's developing musical preferences—he especially admired Schumann—were complemented by intensive reading of contemporaries such as Gottfried Keller, Gustav Freytag, and Conrad Meyer, as well as the Greek poets. These and other interests, however, all took a back seat to his most consuming passion: Semon became addicted to science. It is not clear just how the adolescent Semon turned toward *die Naturwissenschaft*. Neither of his parents were scientifically inclined, and the subject had not yet attained a respectable status in the classical Gymnasium (Learned, 1914). Perhaps his older brother Felix's developing interest in medicine played some part. In any case, Semon had read the major works of Darwin and Haeckel well before leaving the Gymnasium. As most of his schoolmates decided between the pursuit of such professions as law, journalism, and politics, the magic of the new evolutionary biology espoused by Darwin and Haeckel made Richard's choice a simple one. The aspiring biologist set up elaborate terrariums and aquariums at home, filling them with the most exotic reptiles or amphibians that he could find. He expressed a special fondness for his pet Axolotl, and Lubarsch remembers Semon's pride in showing off his prize specimen to his friends.

Unfortunately, Semon's interests did not coincide with the program prescribed at the Gymnasium. He detested grammar and spent little time on the subject—the single most emphasized topic at the Gymnasium. Though mathematically talented, he often became so caught up in seeking the most creative solution to a problem that he failed to complete his assignments. And the ideas espoused by Darwin that so captivated Semon found no place in the tradition-laden curriculum of the Gymnasium. No surprise, then, that Semon's teachers thought him an ungifted, clumsy student. Yet the boy characterized as "intellectually awkward" (Lubarsch, p. xvii) by the drill sergeants of the Gymnasium was one of the few students who passed the difficult *Reifeprüfung* that controlled entry to the German universities. For a young man ignited by the spark of biological science, there was only one place in Germany to go in the fall of 1879: to Jena, and to Haeckel.

3

Haeckel, Monism,
and the Dilemma
of the German Jew

M ajor changes awaited Semon in Jena. He had so far known only the fastpaced, cosmopolitan lifestyle that characterized virtually every aspect of existence in Berlin. But neither the bustle of Unter den Linden nor the spartan majesty of the Brandenburg Gate were to be found in the small Thuringian town nestled in the mountains of the Saale river valley. Jena, though, offered a natural beauty and serene pace of life that immediately appealed to the displaced Berliner. Semon, an avid hiker and mountainclimber, frequently visited the nearby limestone mountains and thoroughly enjoyed the emphasis on outdoor, physical activity in his new rural environment. The locale that he would later affectionately refer to as his "ancient German town (Semon, 1899, p. 71)" also possessed a rich cultural tradition. The University housed some of Germany's most creative minds when it was a center of German romanticism and *Naturphilosophie* at the close of the 18th century. Schiller, Fichte, Hegel, Schelling, and Oken all held teaching posts at Jena, and Goethe, at work in nearby Weimar, maintained a lasting affection for the University and spent much time there (see Steinmetz, 1958). There were, to be sure, some bitter memories associated with the city: No German could think of Jena without being painfully reminded of Napoleon's conquest there in 1806.

The Jena tradition also included deeply embedded nationalistic sentiments that pleased the youth who had personally witnessed the euphoria of unification in Berlin. Friedrich Ludwig ('Father') Jahn turned to Jena as "the most nationalistic of all German universities (Snyder, 1969, p. 29)" when he formed the first of the *Burschenschaften*—patriotic student organizations that celebrated old German traditions with the aim of achieving a new national synthesis—in 1815. The original Jena association blossomed into the larger *Allgemeine deutsche*

Burschenschaft by 1818, and the spirit of the Jena student body remained avidly nationalistic in subsequent years.

Jena had much to offer a student with Semon's inclinations, and the traditions of romanticism and nationalism, in combination with its idyllic setting, heightened his appreciation of the bucolic University existence. But these were only a few of the important influences operating in Semon's life. In order to understand one of the most potent forces that he encountered there, we must turn to the imposing figure of Ernst Heinrich Philipp August Haeckel.

THE ORACLE OF JENA

By the time Semon arrived in Jena, Haeckel had established himself in the first-rank of German biologists. His fame largely stemmed from his activity as the most energetic apostle of Darwinism in Germany—or for that matter, anywhere else. Haeckel's unbounded zeal for Darwinian theory had turned Jena into an important European center for evolutionary research. Eager young students considered it the highest privilege to study with the great man of German biology. Semon, as we shall later observe, was markedly affected by the captivating force of his mentor's personality, and this is why we now turn our attention to Haeckel and his various scientific, philosophical, and religious doctrines before directly considering his effect on Semon.

Haeckel ranks as one of the most fascinating and bizarre characters in 19th-century science. Modern opinion concerning the value of Haeckel's scientific work varies widely. Although Holton (1978, p. 127) praised him as a "splendid biologist" and admired the "grand, Teutonic sweep (p. 128)" of Haeckel's wide ranging theories, Biddiss (1977) scorned "the aberrations of Ernst Haeckel (p. 20)," offering him as "an excellent example of travesty (p. 52)," who engaged in "scientific fantasy (p. 89)." Yet even amidst Haeckel's often bombastic extrapolations from Darwinian theory, one can see his love of science and his willingness, in the face of bitter opposition, to defend what he believed were irrefutable truths.

Born at Potsdam in 1834, Haeckel studied under such prominent biological mentors as Matthew Jacob Schleiden, one of the early developers of cell theory, and Johannes Müller, the great Berlin physiologist. His first major scientific contribution—considered by some to be his most important—concerned the structure and behavior of the marine organisms Radiolaria. However, just before he published the work in 1862, Haeckel encountered a book that permanently altered his scientific thinking and dictated the subsequent direction of his career. Many young naturalists read the German edition of Darwin's *Origin of Species* when it first appeared in 1860; few were converted to the evolutionary thesis as quickly as Haeckel. It has been suggested that a severe crisis of faith that Haeckel experienced just prior to reading Darwin might account for the passion with which he embraced the message of the *Origin:* Darwinian theory provided Haeckel with a potential means of grasping anew the whole meaning of existence (Bölsche, 1906, pp. 133–135).

Whatever the source of his inspiration, Haeckel's fervent espousal of evolution by natural selection was consistently tinged with conjectures concerning the social and religious implications of evolutionary theory. These conjectures were a good deal more extreme than Darwin himself ever ventured; they cast the issues surrounding Darwinian theory in black-and-white, all-or-none terms that divided the world into believers and non-believers. Haeckel's most complete statement of his Darwinian views is found in *Generealle Morphologie* (1866), a detailed volume concerned with numerous areas of zoology that may have been his last important scientific effort. In it are the two ingredients essential to Haeckelian Darwinism: his philosophy of Monism and the biogenetic law. Haeckel believed that Darwinian theory provided the key to constructing a unified, monistic view of the cosmos in which many phenomena could be explained on a mechanical basis within a cohesive theoretical framework. He argued that all manifestations of life—ranging from the simplest one-celled organism, to the individual human being, to society as a whole—were amenable to similar analyses based on principles of the new evolutionary doctrine. Haeckel abolished traditional dualistic distinctions from his system—oppositions of organic and inorganic, spirit and matter—and labeled his new philosophy *Monism:*

> By this we unambiguously express our conviction that there lives 'one spirit in all things,' and that the whole cognisable world is constituted, and has been developed in accordance with one common fundamental law. We emphasize by it, in particular, the essential unity of inorganic and organic nature, the latter having been evolved from the former only at a relatively late period (1903, p. 3).

The "fundamental law" Haeckel alluded to was the one idea he cherished above all others. It dominated the field of evolutionary biology in the second half of the 19th century, and was known as the biogenetic law: Ontogeny is the short and rapid recapitulation of phylogeny. The idea that each developing organism quickly passes through or recapitulates the salient phases of its racial history was not originated by Haeckel. It had a long history, stated in various forms by different authors. However, as Gould (1977) pointed out, Haeckel was the first to firmly tie the notion of recapitulation to the new evolutionary doctrines. Haeckel argued that phylogenesis mechanically *caused* ontogenesis, and held that anatomical correspondences between the early stages of ontogenesis and the mature stages of phylogenetically more primitive forms (e.g., the observation of gill-slits in the human embryo) provided the key to understanding evolution.

Generealle Morphologie, then, highlighted the fundamental ingredients of Haeckel's scientific creed: Darwinism, Monism, and the biogenetic law. During his remaining 50 years, Haeckel added no fundamentally new ideas to these three, nor did he alter or develop them in any significant fashion. Rather, Haeckel devoted most of his considerable energies to popularizing the proposals—which he regarded as established truths—put forward in *Generealle Morphologie*. It is here that Haeckel wielded his greatest influence. *Natürliche Schöpfungsgeschichte* (1868; translated as *The History of Creation*) and *Anthropogenie* (1874; translated as *The Evolution of Man*) were his first successful popularizations of evolutionary doctrine. He produced his most spectacular popular success in the closing year of the 19th century when he wrote *Die Welträtsel* (1899; translated as *The Riddle of the Universe*). One of the most widely read scientific works of all-time, the book sold over 100,000 copies within a year of its publication and was eventually translated into 25 languages (Gasman, 1971, p. 14; Haeckel, 1904, p. vii). On the basis of these and other popular treatises, Haeckel's influence extended far beyond the scientific arena; one historian went so far as to argue that, "there are probably not many personalities who have so powerfully influenced the development of human culture—and that, too, in many different spheres—as Haeckel (Nordenskiöld, 1929, p. 505)."

For Haeckel, the issues at stake were more than just parts of a scientific jigsaw puzzle whose proper arrangement required empirical investigation. Haeckel viewed himself as a noble representative of evolutionary theory and Monism, engaged in a life-and-death struggle with forces of darkness represented by the Church. The outcome of the struggle, he believed, would be crucial in deciding the intellectual future of mankind:

> In the mighty 'war of culture', affecting as it does the whole history of the world, and in which we may well deem it an honour to take part, no better ally than Anthropogenie [evolutionary theory] can, it seems to me, be brought to the assistance of struggling truth. The history of evolution is the heavy artillery in the struggle for truth. Whole ranks of dualistic sophisms fall before the monistic philosophy, as before the chain shot of artillery, and the proud structure of the Roman hierarchy, that mighty stronghold of infallible dogmatism, falls like a house of cards. Whole libraries of church wisdom and false philosophy melt away as soon as they are seen in the light afforded by the history of evolution (Haeckel, 1879, Vol. I, pp. xxii–xxiii).

Haeckel's commitment to preaching the evolutionary truth bore much fruit. As noted by Fothergill (1952) and Montgomery (1974), the warm reception that Darwinism enjoyed in Germany can be traced largely to Haeckel. After the battle for evolutionary theory had been won, at least some of his contemporaries gratefully acknowledged Haeckel's role in the victory: "above all it was Haeckel, who, in energy, eagerness for battle, and knowledge may be placed side by side with Huxley. . . . Haeckel has contributed more than anyone else to the spread of the Darwinian doctrine (Schwalbe, 1910, pp. 130–131)."

However, Haeckel's contributions were probably more than offset by his dogmatic style and propensity for unwarranted speculation. Haeckel saw only two sides to any issue: his view and the wrong view. He conveniently identified all of his opponents with the sinister forces of ignorance represented by the

FIGURE 2. Ernst Haeckel at 80.

Church. For those scientists who balked at his visions of the new evolutionary doctrine, Haeckel expressed only contempt:

> It is a question of that profound and irreconcilable opposition between knowledge and faith, between a real knowledge of nature and alleged 'revelation'. . . . These heated partisans may continue to attack and calumniate

my person as they will; they will not hurt the sacred cause of truth in which I labor (Haeckel, 1904, pp. viii–ix).

Haeckel's righteous reference to the "sacred cause of truth" is particularly ironic since, as Charles Singer puts it, "He habitually perverted scientific truth to make certain of his doctrines more easily assimilable (1959, p. 488)." Haeckel confidently informed his readers that the major problems of life had been solved by science. He saw no limits to the domain of scientific knowledge and ridiculed those who did.[1] The epistemological naiveté and excessive claims found in many of Haeckel's popular works provoked severe criticisms within the professional community. One of his harshest critics was the philosopher Friedrich Paulsen, who abhorred Haeckel's crude philosophical style and was troubled by its spectacular popular success:

I have read this book with burning shame over the condition of the general and philosophical education of our people. It is painful that such a book was possible, that it could have been written, edited, sold, read, pondered and believed by a people who possess a Kant, a Goethe, and a Schopenhauer (cited in Gasman, 1971, p. 14).

Haeckel's prestige within the biological community declined sharply during the first decade of the 20th century. When he reviewed the status of Darwinian theory in 1907, American biologist Vernon Kellogg argued that the recent backlash against *Darwinismus* could be largely attributed to Haeckel's "daring and reckless speculative development of certain phases of evolutionary thought." Further, Kellogg contended that Haeckel's ideas had become "the object of a curiously bitter and often-expressed contempt in German biological circles (1907, p. 130)." Such criticism also reflected the field's changing orientation—changes that Haeckel remained entirely out of step with. For instance, in the early years of the 20th century, Haeckel's most cherished creation—the biogenetic law— was abandoned. As Gould (1977, Chap. 6) has pointed out, the law was not discarded because of empirical contradictions. Rather, Haeckel's bold speculative schemes simply became irrelevant to the concerns of experimental embryology. The new emphasis on the fine-grain of experimental detail left little room

---

1. The extent of Haeckel's epistemological arrogance is revealed in his dispute with the eminent physiologist Emil DuBois-Reymond. In 1880, DuBois-Reymond delivered an influential paper to the Berlin Academy of Sciences in which he elucidated seven "world-enigmas" that he believed science could probably not solve: (1) the nature of matter and force; (2) the origin of motion; (3) the origin of life; (4) the orderly arrangement of nature; (5) the origin of sensation and consciousness; (6) rational thought and speech; (7) freedom of the will. Haeckel (1929) blithely claimed that his Monistic philosophy had solved enigmas 1, 2, and 5; "our modern history of evolution" solved enigmas 3, 4, and 6; and enigma 7 "is not an object for critical, scientific inquiry (1929, pp. 12–13)." Such flamboyant speculation hardly qualifies as rigid adherence to the "sacred cause of truth."

for baroque generalizations such as those put forward by Haeckel. Consigned to the role of "harmless elder statesman (Gould, p. 197)," Haeckel responded in typically bellicose fashion by portraying the new field in a caustic light: "The modern province of experimental or mechanical embryology is especially marred by these useless and perverse experiments (1904, p. 9)." Haeckel's declining scientific status is of interest not only in our characterization of him, but will also help us to understand some of the difficulties that Semon had with his own work.

Before considering Haeckel's influence on Semon, it may be useful to depict one of the most remarkable aspects of Haeckel's personality—his proclivity for a mystical variety of German Romanticism. Haeckel presented himself as the embodiment of materialistic rationalism, so it seems unlikely that he would display any such tendencies. Yet several historians have claimed that a pronounced romantic tendency tinged with irrational qualities formed an essential part of Haeckel's thought, coexisting with his Darwinian and positivistic views (Gasman, 1971; Nordenskiöld, 1929). This claim seems fully justified. Consider first his idiosyncratic brand of Monism. Haeckel referred to his Monistic teachings interchangeably as his "Monistic science," "Monistic philosophy"—and "Monistic religion." Monism constituted more than an approach to science for Haeckel; it offered a complete vision of life. In place of the personal Deity that Haeckel believed evolutionary science had discredited, he substituted a pantheistic "Monistic religion" based upon nature worship and idolatry of science.[2] The German Monist League that Haeckel founded in 1906 enthusiastically developed his 'theological' teachings. Haeckel and the Monists advocated sun worship in place of traditional prayer ("Sun worship seems to the modern scientist to be the best of all forms of theism, and the one which may be most easily reconciled with modern Monism [Haeckel, 1929, p. 229]."), and invoked the rituals of pre-Christian pagan Germanic religions in favor of the 'perverted' Judeo-Christian traditions. The almost surreal vision expressed by Haeckel's religion is also conveyed by his own work as an illustrator. Haeckel rejected the painstaking efforts of accurate reproduction in favor of extravagant, ornamental designs that depicted Nature in a strangely deified manner. The complete volume that he devoted to his artistic renderings of Nature (*Kunstform der Natur*) is characterized by these surreal qualities: "the fantastic and bizarre look of the unfamiliar flora and fauna, transform them in the direction of disquieting, even

---

2. The romantic spirit of Haeckel's flowery prose is difficult to capture in words other than his own:

Blind and insensible have the great majority of mankind hitherto wandered through this glorious wonderland of a world; a sickly and unnatural theology has made it as repulsive as a "vale of tears." But now, at last, it is given to it to show that a true knowledge of nature affords a full satisfaction and inexhaustible nourishment not only for its searching understanding but also for its yearning spirit (1903, pp. 85–86).

nightmarish representations . . . the essential strangeness of the plates reveal a mystical, decadent, and demonic vision of Nature (Gasman, 1971, p. 74)."

Haeckel's affinity for the quasi-mystical furnishes clear links with a treasured past and a disastrous future. On the one hand, Haeckel's Monism bears a striking similarity to the romantic view of nature offered at the beginning of the 19th century by the *Naturphilosophen* at Jena. Schelling, Oken, Meckel, and others in the movement engaged in a pantheistic Nature-worship. They also sought grand cosmic principles in much the same broadly speculative manner displayed by Haeckel in the *Welträtsel* (see Gode-Von Asch, 1941; Nordenskiöld, 1929). Indeed, Johann Wolfgang von Goethe, a figure who worked closely with and markedly influenced many of the *Naturphilosophen,* exerted a profound influence on Haeckel's romantic tendencies.[3]

However large their influence, the humanistic views of man advanced by many of the German romantics were not faithfully extended by Haeckel and many of his followers. Haeckel's romantic view of nature converged with his extreme brand of German nationalism to elevate the Aryan race to a privileged place in the biological universe (see Gasman, 1971). In connection with his forceful Social Darwinism and admitted anti-Semitism, the overtly racist teachings of Haeckel and the Monists later served as scientific justification for the doctrines of National Socialism. This theme will be noted again in the next section of the book when we consider its relation to one of the great crises in Richard Semon's life, but let us first describe Haeckel's influence on Semon's scientific development.

One of the keys to understanding Haeckel's effect on Semon's life and work is to appreciate the hypnotic influence that Haeckel exercised over almost all of his students. One only needs to read the idolatrous biography of Haeckel written by his pupil Wilhelm Bölsche (1906) to see the awe with which Haeckel's followers regarded him. Bölsche cast Haeckel as the daring high priest of evolutionary science, a Teutonic warrior who shattered the illusions of weaker men in his noble—and successful—quest for truth. The romantic image of the brave young Haeckel taking on the jaded establishment of science is conveyed in Bölsche's description of Haeckel's pro-evolutionary talk at the Scientific Congress of 1863: "Haeckel, young and handsome, was an embodiment of the *mens sana in corpore sano*. He rose above the grey heads of science, as the type of the young, fresh, brilliant generation (1906, pp. 146–147)." Haeckel, in fact, represented a God-like figure to many of his followers. Heinrich Schmidt, one of Haeckel's most devoted students, contended that "Haeckel is in fact the great-

---

3. Haeckel frequently acknowledged that his Monism owed many of its principal features to Goethe's monistic "God-Nature"—an identification of spirit and matter. Haeckel closed his preface to *The Wonders of Life* with the following lines from "our greatest German natural philosopher (1904, p. xiv)": "What greater thing in life can man achieve, than that God-Nature be revealed to him?" Haeckel prefaced *Anthrópogenie* by the complete text of Goethe's poems "Prometheus" and "Faust," and deferential references to Goethe can be found throughout his work.

est theologian the world has ever seen (Gasman, 1971. p. 15)," while another admirer predicted that "Generations will pass, new ones will arise, nations will fall, thrones will topple, but the wise old genius of Jena will outlast all (Gasman, p. 16)." A collection of similar statements can be found in the volume of adoring testimonies dedicated to Haeckel in honor of the aging prophet's 80th birthday (Schmidt, 1914).

Semon was not immune to Haeckel's influence. He went to Jena to study with the great man, and within a year of his apprenticeship became one of Haeckel's favorite pupils. Despite various later disagreements, the bond between mentor and student was never broken. When a sick and isolated Haeckel wrote to Semon in 1918, he expressed appreciation for his student's fidelity: "thank your for all the love that you have given me over the last 40 years as a loyal and grateful pupil (a rare thing) (Haeckel to Semon, 4–2–18)." Given their warm personal relations, it is not surprising that the young man adopted so many of his formidable mentor's scientific doctrines. Semon reflected upon Haeckel's qualities in his contribution to the testimonial volume: "He is not only a superior researcher, but a man whose devotion to the highest goals and whose idealism...had to rouse and inspire the minds of his students (Semon, 1914, p. 221)." For Semon, the significant truth that Haeckel preached was Monism— not only in the pursuit of science but also in the conduct of life: "Haeckel has remained true to this ideal through his older years . . . consequently he has blended life and research into a living unity so that one can identify him as a practicing Monist; he has had a powerful influence upon me (1914, p. 221)." Semon neither shared Haeckel's propensity for the quasimystical, nor adopted the Aryan oriented Social Darwinism that so many of Haeckel's followers wholeheartedly endorsed. In fact, he eventually condemned Haeckel's extreme German militarism at the outbreak of World War I. But for Semon as for Haeckel, Monism constituted a complete approach to life that eventually acquired the status of religious faith.

It is in the Monistic approach to the study of nature that Haeckel most pronouncedly affected Semon. For Semon, Monism meant searching for unity in nature. By combining the insights of different scientific disciplines, he hoped to capture the unified essence of nature that the Monistic doctrine promised was hidden behind man's artificial distinctions. One of the peculiar ironies that we will encounter in Semon's work is that the same Monistic orientation partially contributed to his scientific downfall—owing to his views on the mechanisms of heredity—and to his strikingly original contributions to the theory of human memory.

Although Semon's adherence to Monism probably constitutes his largest scientific debt to Haeckel, we can find clear instances of Haeckel's influence at almost every level of Semon's scientific work. The major biological questions that haunted Semon throughout his career were problems of development: What laws govern the growth of the embryo, the youthful organism, or entire species and races? It is the theme of development that unites his early research on marine life of the Mediterranean (Semon, 1887), his investigations on his Australian expedition (Semon, 1899), and his later attempts to formulate a synthetic framework that accounted for all aspects of organic change (Semon, 1904). Such a theme is precisely what we would expect from a disciple of Haeckel. Haeckelian influence is evident even in other areas of Semon's work. Semon's belief in the inheritance of acquired characteristics, his analogy between the mechanisms of memory and heredity, and his proclivity for inventing new—and frequently bizarre—scientific terminology can be traced to Haeckel. The details of these intriguing correspondences will become clearer later in the book. My purpose in mentioning them now is to convey a sense of Haeckel's multiple influences on his young pupil. We will see just how far those influences may have extended when we seek the causes of a decision that temporarily plunged Semon's life into chaos.

Throughout his Jena years, Semon maintained the fiery enthusiasm for physical activity that he had first cultivated as a youth in Berlin. He and Lubarsch had hiked together extensively, and Semon's love of the outdoor life blossomed in pastoral Jena—and in the shadow of Haeckel. In Haeckel, Semon saw how sport and science could be forged into high adventure. Part of Haeckel's mystique derived from his vaunted reputation as a traveller who pursued research on grand expeditions in far-off lands. It was during Semon's days in Jena that Haeckel made his celebrated journey to India and Ceylon (Haeckel, 1883). About this time, Semon began to wonder if he could partake in a similar expedition. He could not, like Haeckel, command the necessary funds to initiate his own voyage, but he could participate in someone else's expedition. The only questions were who and how. Semon could not yet resolve the first problem, but in response to the second he took steps that he felt sure would increase his usefulness to any explorer: He became a doctor. The decision to pursue a medical degree had immediate consequences. He took temporary leave of Jena in the winter of 1882 to study medicine at Heidelberg, where he worked with the noted cell-biologist Otto Bütschli. Semon had scant desire to practice medicine—his commitment to research remained firm—but anything that brought him closer to an expedition seemed well worth the effort. Semon passed the State Medical Examination in 1884, and received a medical license in 1885. The young doctor then excitedly set out in search of an explorer who could use him. He quickly found one. But there were dark clouds gathering over another part of his world.

THE CONVERSION: CAUSES AND CONTEXTS

During his tenure at Jena, Semon came to grips with more than just his scientific identity. He also had to face the fact that he was a Jew, and Jewishness was not easy to face amidst the blatant anti-Semitism of Germany in the 1880s. Different Jews dealt with their Jewishness in different ways; Semon reacted by converting to Christianity in 1885. The decision was an agonizing one, and sufficiently important to merit our careful attention: A man does not abandon his religion without revealing important clues about the deepest wellsprings of his personality. It is also a decision whose implications cannot be properly grasped without penetrating the complex of familial, cultural, and personal influences. Accordingly, let us examine the prevailing attitude towards Jews during Semon's youth in Berlin, the psychology of late 19th-century Jews, and Haeckel's views of the Jewish problem before directly considering Semon's conversion.

German Jews endured periodic outbursts of anti-Semitism throughout the 19th century, so they were relieved that Bismarck's constitution of 1869 granted them equal political and civil rights. With the realization of the German Empire in 1871, Jewish rights became Imperial Law. For a family such as the Semons, then, the grand victory march that they proudly watched Felix lead through the Brandenburg Gate had double meaning: Their country was victorious and unified, and they, as Jews, could claim full rights of citizenship. But the halcyon days following unification were disappointingly brief: The subsequent wave of anti-Semitism was the most vituperous and protracted expression of Jew-hatred witnessed in 19th century Germany. The economic crash of 1873 precipitated the latest outburst. With the economy of the newly-formed Reich in a shambles, the burden of blame was placed squarely upon the runaway speculators at the Berlin exchange: "The culprit was the Jew, that alien parasite who represented 90 percent of all speculators on the stock exchange (Schorsh, 1972, p. 36)." Simon Semon was one of those speculators, and his position among the much-abused Jewish brokers likely exposed the Semon family to the full bitterness of the new anti-Semitism.

Berlin, in fact, emerged as a center for the new anti-Semitism; we should keep in mind that Semon spent his formative years in an atmosphere charged with growing anti-Jewish feeling. And Berlin provided the setting for the events of 1879, a watershed year for German anti-Semitism in which Jew-hatred received legitimization from the highest echelons of German society. First came Adolph Stoecker. On September 19, 1879—just one month before Semon left Berlin for Jena—the court chaplain of Wilhelm I launched a blistering public attack on German Jewry. The prestige of Stoecker's office conferred upon his polemics a respectability not enjoyed by previous anti-Semites. Only the intellectual elite remained unimpressed by Stoecker's harangues, but this circumstance quickly changed. Less than two months after Stoecker's initial attack, Heinrich von Treitschke, one of the great names in German academia and Professor of History at the University of Berlin, cast his lot with the anti-Semites. Treitschke's stance gave anti-Semitism a new legitimacy in the German universities and contributed to the appearance of the notorious "Anti-Semitic Petition" of 1880. This document demanded emancipation from Jewish influence by restriction of Jewish rights; 225,000 Germans signed the petition (Dawidowicz, 1977, p. 65).

The reactions of German Jewry were not only fascinating—and somewhat disturbing—they also furnish insights into Semon's apostasy. In spite of the open and virulent anti-Semitism of the 1870s and 1880s, German Jewry did little to organize a systematic defense (Schorsch, 1972). The reason for German Jews' relatively passive stance towards anti-Semitism is found in their self-concept.

German Jews identified themselves primarily as Germans and desperately wished that their countrymen would accept them as such (Gay, 1978; Tal, 1975). German Jews felt more bewildered and disappointed than angered by the outbursts of anti-Semitism. They had ardently advocated national unity, fought enthusiastically for the Fatherland in the wars of the 1860s, and harbored deep pride in their Germanic cultural heritage. Now their patriotic love went "pathetically unrequited (Gay, 1978, p. 162)." German Jewry had learned that flaunting their Jewishness would not earn them entry into German society; assimilation represented the only possible route. The long struggle for emancipation "decisively affected the self-esteem and self-image of the German Jew. He had not failed to grasp the message that his admission into society demanded the suppression of every external trace of Jewishness (Schorsch, p. 1)." To openly resist anti-Semitism would require of the German Jew the act that he most abhorred: A public affirmation of his Jewishness. Hence many Jews simply hoped the anti-Semitism of the 1880s would fade, labeling it a phase that Germans would surely outgrow. But they did not. Finally, in 1893, an organized defense group was formed to combat anti-Semitism (see Lamberti, 1978; Schorsch, 1972).

The problem of conversion became inextricably linked with the dynamics of the Jewish psyche in the 1880s. To be sure, conversion constituted a real problem. The rate of apostasy in Prussia alone nearly doubled from about 100 annually for the period 1822–1840 to nearly 200 annually for 1841–1880 (Reinharz, 1975, p. 8), and it rose even more steeply in the 1880s (Schorsch, 1972, p. 138). There were many causes for conversion. Some used it as an entry to professions that would otherwise be closed to them; some fell in love with Christians; others hated their Jewishness and sought to identify completely as Germans. But one fact remained clear: Jews who chose to remain Jews despised the apostates. In fact, one prominent defense organization waged a public war against apostasy: "Committed to the revival of self-respect, the Centralverein soon came to label the apostate as the most dangerous enemy to Jewish survival in Germany (Schorsch, pp. 138–139)."

We shall return to the psychology of apostasy when more directly discussing its relation to Semon's conversion, but we shall first sketch Ernst Haeckel's view of the Jewish position in German society. Haeckel, an admitted anti-Semite, articulated ideas that were similar to those of other avowed anti-Semites who leaned heavily upon the tenets of Social Darwinism to justify their assertions that Jews represented inferior racial stock.[4] Haeckel believed that the Jews themselves were responsible for anti-Semitic feeling. How else, he argued, could such sentiments have persisted throughout history?[5] He thought that the con-

---

4. Some of the most prominent of these racial anti-Semites—Houston Stewart Chamberlain, Julius Langebehn, and Paul LaGarde—also relied on mystical notions of a noble German *Volk* to justify their anti-Semitism. For penetrating analyses of the German Volkish movement, see Mosse (1964) and Stern (1961).
5. See Gasman (1971, pp. 157–159) for a more extensive discussion of Haeckel's anti-Semitism and its possible sources.

temporary anti-Semitism was an entirely justified reaction of the German people to a foreign influence. Anti-Semitism did not constitute a religious problem, Haeckel contended, but rather represented a national and racial one. He believed that the new national consciousness of Germany justifiably heightened Jewish alienation from the German way of life. Given Haeckel's tendency to Romantic irrationalism and his enthusiasm for Social Darwinism, it is not surprising to learn that several of his students—most notably Ludwig Woltmann and Willibald Hentschel[6]—articulated strongly anti-Semitic views that drew upon both of these traditions. However, in light of Haeckel's stated opinion that anti-Semitism constituted a racial problem, it is surprising to learn that Haeckel endorsed Jewish efforts to assimilate and convert. He asserted that if the Jews completely ceased to exist as a separate group, they could serve the Fatherland and live as patriots:[7]

> It must be understood that the German people will no longer tolerate the strange ways of Jewish life, and their desire is to deprive the Jews of all that is specifically Jewish and to convert them to German habits and customs so that they will resemble the people among whom they live in all respects (cited in Gasman, 1971, p. 158).

Let us now directly examine Semon's reasons for conversion. Most of our information on Semon's apostasy comes from his friend Otto Lubarsch, who corresponded with Semon about the decision. Lubarsch held that Semon's conversion was widely misunderstood. He did it not for religious reasons, claimed Lubarsch, but rather national ones. Semon felt no "inner relationships" (*innerliche Beziehungen*; Lubarsch, 1920, p. xx) to Judaism. But he did feel an intense loyalty to the German state—characterized by Lubarsch as "evangelical Prussianism (p. xx)"—and he converted in order to express his patriotism more faithfully. Evidence from various sectors of Semon's life points toward the same conclusion. First, consider brother Felix's sentiments about Judaism. Felix was not a practicing Jew, and felt no strong attachment to his religion: "Venerable as appears to me the creed of my ancestors . . . I can never accustom myself to the

---

6. Ludwig Woltmann, who studied with Haeckel in the 1890s, became a vociferous proponent of Aryan racial superiority. He was awarded a prize for his contribution to an essay competition on the subject of "racial hygiene" that included Haeckel on the panel (Poliakov, 1974, pp. 294–297). In his *Politische Anthropologie* (1906), which uses a quote from Haeckel as its frontispiece, Woltmann attempted to establish German racial superiority on the basis of evolutionary theory. He committed suicide in 1906 at the age of 36. Another ex-Haeckel student, Willibald Hentschel, proposed the creation of a Volkish colony in which an Aryan nobility would be created by selective breeding along Darwinian lines. He later proposed the creation of a Germanic religious order, the "Artamanen Bund," named after the ancient German deity "Artam" (Mosse, 1964, p. 116).
7. Most racial anti-Semites, however, believed that conversion could do little to ameliorate the Jews' biologically engrained flaws (Tal, 1975, Chap. 3).

rigid formalism of its rites (1926, p. 33)." Noting the career difficulties often posed by the practice of Judaism, Felix decided as a young man not to impose his religion on his own children: "I therefore vowed to myself to bring them up in the State religion of their native land, and to leave it to themselves to form their own opinions. I have faithfully kept that vow (1926, p. 34)." Though Felix himself never formally converted, he did baptize his three sons. Felix's testimony rather strongly suggests that Simon and Henrietta did not inculcate any profound sense of Jewishness in their children. It is not surprising, then, that Richard did not experience any *innerliche Beziehungen* to his ancestral faith.

Next, let us remember the *Zeitgeist* of the culture in which Richard matured. These were the heady days of unification: Nationalism was the ideal that excited the young students of the Kaiser Wilhelm Gymnasium and Bismarck was their idol. Young Semon embraced this idea and worshipped the national hero just as his schoolmates did. When we recall the general trend of German Jewry to repress purposefully all signs of their Jewishness—and Simon and Henrietta do not appear to have been conspicuous exceptions to this rule—then we should not be surprised that Semon found a deeper emotional identification with Germany than with Judaism. But many young Jews experienced the excitement of unification and many felt a powerful commitment to the Fatherland; much fewer followed the road to apostasy. What, then, distinguished Semon from his numerous patriotic contemporaries who chose to remain Jews? It is quite likely that the answer can be found in his life at Jena.

In 1879 Semon left an area with the largest Jewish population in Germany—Berlin alone included 54,000 Jews—for a comparative desert of Jewry in Jena. Anti-Semitic sentiment had deep roots in the Jena tradition. The *Burschenschaften* that originated at Jena specifically denied entry to Jewish students, and prominent members of the University already endorsed anti-Semitic views early in the 19th-century (Kohn, 1960, pp. 87–98). In addition, Semon initiated his studies at a time when German university students were among the most feverish proponents of anti-Semitism: "Often the first bitter experience of prejudice for a young Jewish student accompanied his entrance into the university, and unable to cope with its organized character, he desperately concealed his Jewish identity (Schorsch, 1972, p. 72)." By the mid-1880s, life for Jewish university students had become so difficult that the first Jewish fraternities were formed as a defense weapon:

> In the face of such overwhelming odds the Jewish undergraduate is bound to lose self-confidence and it is easy to understand that he will lose heart and give up the fight. But there is more to it. Jewish depravity is put forth in anti-Semitic propaganda with such conviction and zeal that the young Jew himself begins to doubt the righteousness of his cause and the right of Jewry to exist at all (Reinharz, 1975, p. 30).

Semon, then, attended university during a difficult period for Jewish students; the openly anti-Semitic atmosphere may well have pushed him further along the road to apostasy. Yet for the probable key to understanding his conversion, we must turn again to Haeckel. We have already observed that Semon came under the spell of Haeckelian hypnosis. He did not, to be sure, subscribe to Haeckel's peculiar brand of racial ideology. But he personally testified to Haeckel's "powerful influence" on him, and the striking parallels between the form and content of Semon's scientific pursuits and Haeckel's teachings also point to a marked effect of mentor on pupil. Haeckel, too, was a fervent nationalist—recall his cries of *Deutschland, Deutschland, über alles* in 1859—which no doubt increased the patriotic Semon's identification with him. And as we have just seen, Haeckel openly professed his anti-Semitic views while allowing assimilation as the one road to salvation for a suitably enlightened Jew. Given this setting it seems plausible that Semon's conversion was partially motivated by a desire to please his mentor.[8] In addition, Haeckel provided an alternative faith—Monism—to which Semon most assuredly did feel a spiritual relationship: Semon aspired to conduct his life in accordance with the Monistic principles set forth by Haeckel. It should not be surprising, then, that Semon discarded a faith for which he felt little in favor of one that provided a meaningful framework for his life.

But the story of Semon's conversion does not end there. In order to complete the tale, we must also consider the practical realities that confronted a young Jewish scientist in 1885, and then plunge into the psychology of Jewish self-hatred. The prospects that confronted the aspiring Jewish academics of Semon's generation were not encouraging. Although a disproportionately large number of German Jews held academic positions—particularly scientific ones—advancement proved exceedingly difficult. The following statistics, dating to the years 1909–1910, are revealing. At a time when Jews comprised approximately 1% of the German population, 12% of the university instructors (the lowest rung on the German academic ladder) were Jewish. Less than 3% of the full professors, however, were Jews (Ringer, 1969, p. 136). But when apostates are included, the percentage of Jewish instructors rises to 19% and the percentage of full professors grows to 7% (Ringer, p. 136). The list of scientific converts is a long one, and contains some eminent names; George Cantor, Fritz Haber, Leopold Kronecker, and George Simmel are a few of the better known. Of course, not all Jews converted in order to attain the prized professorship, and

---

8. In considering Semon's position as a Jewish disciple of an outspoken anti-Semite whom he admired, it is instructive to note another case that included a similar relationship. Hermann Levi (see Gay, 1978, Chap. 4) was the most accomplished Jewish conductor in Wilhelmian Germany. Yet for the better part of his career he permitted himself to be abused by one of Germany's most passionate anti-Semites—his mentor, Richard Wagner. Levi conducted many of Wagner's important works at Bayreuth, and basked in the praise of the master. But he also willingly endured Wagner's frequent reminders that Levi could not escape his "tragic flaw." Levi responded by reaffirming his love for the Fatherland and expressing an anti-Semitism of his own. It is unlikely that Semon's relationship with Haeckel ever reached the pathological extremes found in the Levi-Wagner case; there is certainly no evidence to show it. But the resemblances between the two cases suggest that similar dynamics may have been common to both.

Einstein and Freud are the best known of those who did not repudiate their Jewishness.

Lubarsch claimed that career prospects played little role in Semon's decision to convert: "External concerns such as a career did not come into play for him; it was a graver, painstakingly reflected upon step, which was all the more courageous in that time, since its natural motives were misunderstood by Jews and Christians (p. xx)." Semon's attachment to Monistic principles, his deep-felt nationalism, and corresponding lack of enthusiasm for Judaism all point away from career concerns as a major component of his apostasy. In addition, Semon's response to a later life crisis (Chap. 4, pp. 54–57) strongly suggests that he did not place the advancement of his career over his personal life. But given the tenor of the times, we must acknowledge the possibility that career concerns influenced Semon's decision.

The final dimension of Semon's conversion is related to a particularly painful feature of the German Jewish psyche: the self-hatred that many of the apostates expressed by their conversions. The term *Selbsthass* (self-hatred) was coined by Theodor Lessing in 1930. However, there is abundant evidence of the phenomenon in 19th-century Germany. The self-haters expressed this sentiment in numerous ways; as Kurt Lewin remarked, "There is an almost endless variety of forms which Jewish self-hatred may take (1948, p. 187)." Some went as far as to vote for anti-Semitic candidates and publicly endorse anti-Semitism in order to assert their Germanness (Gay, 1978, pp. 196–197), and others launched scathing attacks on Jewry that betrayed a fundamental lack of Jewish self-respect (Kahn, 1968). Still others went further. For instance, Otto Weininger (a disciple of Freud) expressed his contempt for Judaism and his infatuation with Nordic-Aryan qualities in his book *Geschlecht und Character (Sex and Character)*. Weininger desperately hoped to turn himself into an Aryan by conversion; when he realized that he could not escape his "indelible Jewishness (Gay, p. 196)" he shot himself at the age of 23 (Abrahamsen, 1946).

Semon never publicly displayed his distaste for Judaism, but he informed Lubarsch of it numerous times. The form of his antipathy bears the classical trademark of self-hatred. Semon expressed a "marked aversion" (*ausgesprochene Abneigung*) toward Judaism, recalls Lubarsch, and felt a particular disdain for "big-city Judaism" (*grosstädtisches Judentum*; 1920, p. xx). Of course, Semon himself was a product of "big-city Judaism," and this is why the label of self-hatred seems at least partially appropriate. The possible roots of such sentiment are not difficult to spot. Recall the reaction of Felix Semon to his mother's obsessive concern with the opinions of Jewish society, and her ordering of the household to please these "big-city Jews": "How much did I suffer during my boyhood from these 'good families'!" There is no reason to believe that Richard did not respond in a similar manner. Then there was Simon. He was a broker at the Berlin exchange, and Jewish stockbrokers were targets of abuse and ridicule after the crash of 1873. Certainly this circumstance could not have contributed to a healthy Jewish self-image in his son. Of course, we do not know if these familial influences are responsible for Semon's dislike of his own heritage; but there must be some reasons for it, and they seem likely candidates.

In the final analysis, what we make of Richard Semon's conversion depends largely on what we focus upon. If we concentrate on the cultural context of his time, we can regard Semon as another instance of the German Jew's tendency to identify himself more as a German than as a Jew. If we see his conversion as one manifestation of his devotion to Monistic principles, then we may admire the courage he displayed in taking an unpopular step: "Jews generally despised their baptized bretheren as renegades. Christians despised them as opportunists. Converts, seeking to win by moving from one camp to another, lost in both (Gay, 1978, p. 98)." If we find in Semon's apostasy elements of weakness and self-hatred, or a pathetic attempt to please his mentor, then we may feel sympathy for him. All these factors played some role in a complex and agonizing *decision*. Semon later faced decisions of similar—or greater—magnitude. He made them in ways that irrevocably altered the shape of his life.

4

Journey and Exile

After he finally decided to convert, Semon again devoted his energies to the exciting prospect of joining a research expedition. The man who finally took him on was Robert Flegel, a well known German explorer about to embark on an extensive journey through Africa to the recesses of the Benue and Niger Rivers. This was exactly what Semon had hoped for: He could learn the adventurer's art from an experienced master on a trip through exotic lands that bore all the signs of high adventure in the grand Haeckelian style.

Before departing for Africa, Semon visited with older brother Felix, who had settled in London after earning his medical degree and now practiced laryngology. Richard's buoyant spirit impressed Felix, who remembered his brother as a "picture of health (1926, p. 139)" on the eve of departure. When the expedition left for Lagos on April 6, 1885, both Flegel and Semon were full of confidence. But trouble was not long in brewing, and the difficulties were of an international variety. The Flegel expedition temporally coincided with Germany's sudden and spectacular entry into imperialistic pursuits. Though Germany had traditionally left colonial ventures to the English and Dutch, Bismarck made a dramatic first play for colonies in 1884. German entry into the hotly contested "scramble for Africa" yielded immediate territorial gains. They established German South-West Africa in 1884, and German East Africa in 1885 (Taylor, 1970). This burst of activity, however, created new tensions with England, and problems for Flegel. The English National African Company, suspecting that Flegel's journey was motivated by other than purely scientific concerns, attempted to block the expedition's progress. Their efforts proved sufficiently bothersome to command time consuming defensive measures from Flegel, Semon, and the rest of the crew that seriously undermined their progress. The worst, however, had not yet arrived. When malaria struck the adventurers, it spared nobody on board. Semon's case became particularly severe. He hovered near death for days, and when Flegel ordered his return to Europe at the end of July, Semon felt so weak that they feared to take him off the ship. After recovering some of his strength on the return journey, Richard suffered a violent relapse upon arriving in London; Felix, shocked at the sight of his feverish brother, called it "the worst form of quotidian malaria that I have ever seen (1926, p. 139)." Richard remained in London for his convalescence, still too weak to be overly concerned about the disastrous end to his much anticipated journey.

Richard's illness of 1885 did, however, provide a welcome opportunity for him to spend some time with Felix; the two had not seen much of each other since Felix's departure from Berlin. Felix Semon had engineered an impressive series of personal triumphs during his 10 years of residence in London. Most important was his emerging position as the leading laryngologist in Britain. When Felix decided to practice laryngology in 1875, the field was a struggling young specialty that enjoyed scant prestige in the eyes of the British medical profession. But Felix Semon's scientific research and attempts to organize fellow laryngologists contributed to a new respectability for laryngology by the mid-1880s. Felix's most well known scientific contribution, which concerned the pathology of the abductor and adductor muscles that control the position of the vocal cord in the larynx, is familiar to modern laryngologists as "Semon's Law": In progressive lesions of the recurrent laryngeal nerve, the abductors are paralyzed before the adductors (Semon, 1881).[1] Felix's research efforts were complemented by his energetic advocacy of laryngology's special place in the medical profession. In 1881, Felix's efforts earned laryngology a separate section at the International Medical Congress; in 1884, he created his own journal. Published in German, the *Internationales Centralblatt für Laryngologie* first appeared on July 1, 1884 with Felix as its editor. The journal quickly acquired an excellent reputation as a focal point of laryngological thought and experiment. It also provided a forum for its outspoken editor to expound his influential ideas concerning the advancement and direction of laryngology. Felix's views became so characteristic of his beloved journal that its name was eventually changed to *Semon's Internationales Centralblatt für Laryngologie*. Felix's star had risen sufficiently high by 1885 that he was entrusted with the treatment of ex-Prime Minister Gladstone just before his malaria-stricken brother arrived from Africa.

Richard Semon enjoyed the time spent with Felix during his month-long convalescence in London. Although he could not conceal his disappointment that the African expedition had been a scientific failure, Semon was thankful that he had survived a potentially fatal disease. He returned to Jena in good health, but never felt entirely free from the effects of his encounter with malaria. Symptoms recurred from time to time, and as late as 1912 Semon complained to his friend August Forel that the old problems had returned to bother

---

1. History has passed a mixed verdict on the validity of Semon's Law. Some modern laryngologists still attest to its clinical (Hall & Colman, 1973) and theoretical (Huizinga, 1966) usefulness, but experimental studies of laryngeal neurology have tended to discredit Semon's Law (Clerf & Baltzell, 1953; Kolby & Haugen, 1970). Indeed, Wyke and Kirchner (1976, p. 546) called it "one of the historic myths of laryngology."

him. Others also noted the residual effects of his tropical illness. Felix, for instance, maintained that his brother "throughout life retained a certain degree of irritability as a legacy from the disease (1926, p. 139)." But even his brief tenure with the explorer Flegel yielded some lasting benefits. He picked up many useful pointers concerning life in the wild and the organization of a large-scale expedition that later helped him on his own, more successful, research journey.

Shortly after his return to Jena in August 1885, Semon arranged for an extended period of study at the well known Naples Zoological Station. The time was profitably spent. He collected valuable data for his medical dissertation (his interests focused upon the morphology and ontogeny of starfish and sea-snails), and further strengthened his weakened body in the restful Naples environment. Semon returned to Jena in winter 1886, and submitted—successfully—a dissertation based upon his Naples research.

Semon experienced particular satisfaction when a research appointment at Jena's Anatomical Institute immediately followed. The Institute, under the leadership of eminent zoologist Oskar Hertwig, and infused by Haeckel's zeal for evolutionary theory, abounded in new ideas and approaches that promised to extend the frontiers of the emerging science of evolutionary biology. Semon's own research concerning problems of ontogeny rapidly progressed at the Institute (e.g., Semon. 1887, 1888, 1891). His productivity was acknowledged when he qualified as *Privadozent* in 1887 and then received an associate Professorship in early 1891. The research was exciting; his rank at the Institute steadily improved; he further cultivated his affection for the tradition-laden town of Jena. Yet in spite of all these positive forces, he felt an undeniable restlessness gnawing at him: The explorer's urge could not be suppressed. Semon had not successfully overcome his chagrin that the African expedition had turned sour, and still wished to make amends for that frustrating episode. In addition, the romantic image of the naturalist-traveller, represented by Haeckel as well as by Semon's scientific heroes Darwin and Alfred Russell Wallace, appealed enormously to him. By the spring of 1890, he had developed a plan for a journey that would match Haeckel's exploits in Ceylon, Darwin's adventure in South America, or Wallace's expedition through the Malayan Archipelago. Semon's target was Australia. Australia was the land of "missing-links," and evolutionists were hopeful that some of the conspicuous transitional gaps between species that plagued Darwinian theory could be filled-in by judicious search for them. Eugene DuBois sent shock waves through the scientific world about this time with his discovery of *Pithecanthropus erectus*—the "Java man" that many regarded as a theoretically decisive missing-link (e.g., Eisley, 1961, pp. 279–285). Semon's interest in developmental problems provided further incentive to go: "of eminent importance, moreover, is the study of the embryological development of these 'missing-links' (Semon, 1899, p. 2)."

He revealed his plan to Haeckel, who enthusiastically assented and immediately attempted to find financial support for Semon's project. He had little trouble. Paul von Ritter, a wealthy researcher with interest in evolutionary problems, consented to provide the expedition with most of the prodigious financial backing it would require. By the spring of 1891, the preparations were completed. When Semon left Jena on June 13th, he felt intoxicated by the enticing prospects of the unknown and determined to see this expedition through to a successful conclusion.

The Australian journey is of special interest to us for two reasons. First, the expedition was a scientific success that substantially contributed to Semon's rising zoological reputation in the 1890s. Second and more important, his detailed account of the journey (Semon, 1899) provides a wealth of insights into Semon as a human being. His experiences in Australia reveal an energetic, spontaneous man who was sensitive to the people and environment around him. And his excursion into the unknown preserves an irrepressible spirit of high adventure—one that is no less appealing to us today than it was to Semon in 1891.

IN SEARCH OF CERATODUS

The trip that lay ahead was an imposing one. If he kept to his timetable, Semon would be isolated from familiar culture and surroundings for nearly two years; perhaps he thought of this when he set aside a few weeks to say farewell to his favorite spots in Europe. After climbing in the Alps, relaxing amidst Northern Italy's mountain lakes, and touring the coast of the Tyrrhenian Sea, he juxtaposed the beauty of the old world with the intrigue of the new as he awaited departure in Genoa: "Nothing, I am sure, exists that deserves to be compared to these gems in the garment of the world. But cannot the charm accompanying the research of the peculiar and the unknown vie with the delight afforded by the enjoyment of absolute beauty (1899, p. 3)?"

Semon arrived in Queensland—which occupies the northeastern section of Australia—after a long and dull ocean voyage. What kinds of creatures had drawn him to this remote part of the world? The major attraction was unquestionably *Ceratodus forstieri*, popularly known as the Australian lungfish. Ceratodus comprised a special constellation of intriguing features for the marine zoologist with evolutionary inclinations. Anatomically, the most interesting aspect of the "rather sluggish, purely freshwater animal, with very large scales, small eyes, remarkable cockscomb-shaped crushing teeth, and fringed fins (Whitely, 1940, p. 239)" resides in the name by which it is popularly known. Ceratodus breathes not only through gills, but can also surface and inhale air into its celebrated lung. Ceratodus had hardly been studied at the time of Semon's journey—it was first discovered by naturalists in 1870 (Whitely, 1940)—and the developmental processes that Semon wished to inspect remained unexamined. Ceratodus also posed a particularly fascinating evolutionary problem. Though teeth remains found in Europe, North America, Asia, and Africa testified to its existence in prior geological epochs, and fossil remains indicated that it once lived in most parts of Australia, by 1891 Ceratodus could be found in only a few rivers of the Queensland bush. What had brought about this peculiar evolutionary circumstance? Semon hoped to shed some light on this question by observing the lungfish in its natural habitat.

Though the study of Ceratodus clearly comprised Semon's primary scientific goal, it was not his sole objective. He could hardly venture to Australia without wishing to study the continent's most famous fauna, and he indeed planned to collect developmental data concerning possums, kangaroos, and the other pouched mammals known as marsupials. Here, too, were interesting evolutionary problems. How had the marsupials, once spread throughout Europe, become isolated in Australia? Wallace had put forward various theories to account for this circumstance, but Semon relished the idea of examining the conditions of marsupial life and development for himself. Equally fascinating were the monotremes: Mammals such as the duck-billed platypus and echidnas (spiny anteaters) who are distinguished from other mammals by their reproductive capacity to lay eggs (see Barrett, 1947). With visions of the zoological Eldorado before him, Semon first settled in the small Queensland town of Gayndah before heading out to the bush: "only a brother naturalist will sympathize with me, when I own that an almost solemn feeling overcame me as, on starting from the little station of Maryborough, on the morning of 24th August, I began my pilgrimage to land sacred to the zoologist (1899, p. 15)."

Semon's first task in Gayndah was to secure the services of enough men to assist his scientific collections in the bush. He was fortunate to meet Edward Dahlke, a native German who had spent most of his life in Queensland. Dahlke had mastered the survival tactics required by life in the bush and understood the patterns of animal life found in the Queensland wild. But Dahlke was merely a guide. Semon also needed hunters and collectors, and he turned to the native aborigine population in search of them. An acquaintance in Brisbane put him in contact with a native who acted as an agent between Semon and the aborigines. Everything went smoothly at first: Semon had little trouble rounding up sufficient numbers of natives to partake in the collection of his specimens. However, he encountered some potential difficulties upon meeting with Mrs. Catherine Corry. The elderly Mrs. Corry lived in a "miserable roadside inn" near the eventual site of Semon's camp; what disturbed him was her reputation as a liquor dealer for the aborigines. Semon knew that alcohol could be used to motivate his assistants; he had brought along several bottles of rum for that specific purpose. But he was warned by English acquaintances that such favors had to be strictly controlled, and Mrs. Corry's willingness to sell the natives everything they could pay for alerted Semon to possible dangers.

Not overly concerned by such warnings, Semon turned his attention to the alluring Australian fauna once camp was constructed along the Burnett River. He devoted the early morning hours to stalking the fabled duck-billed platypus, and sent the blacks in search of echidnas and marsupials. Semon was enthusiastic during these first days of bush life, and decided to share his excitement with the aborigines by rewarding productivity with cash. The tactic paid handsome dividends—in the beginning. A spirited competition arose among his helpers, and they provided Semon with more material than he could dissect, examine, and conserve each day. He had not yet entirely adjusted to his aboriginal companions—"They had set up their camp about a mile from my own, as I wished, for various reasons, to keep them at a certain distance (1899, p. 139)"—but he enjoyed learning about their customs and admired their spontaneous behavior.

Collections were proceeding so smoothly that Semon decided to leave camp for several days and visit some friends in nearby Coonambula. Whatever the initial excitement of bush life, he already dearly missed the trappings of culture taken for granted at home. The absence of intellectual stimulation from his fellow campers led him to hunger for "above all, the intercourse and conversation with pleasant and refined persons (p. 49)." Several relaxed evenings of absorbing discourse provided welcome nourishment, and Semon rode back to camp in particularly high spirits. All the more disconcerting, then, when Dahlke met him with a pained expression on his face. Semon hopefully asked if all had gone well; Dahlke's answer quickly dispelled his optimism: "All the camp is drunk since yesterday . . . most of them are so stiff that they can't move and Johnny has nearly beaten his wife to death (p. 55)." Semon's heart sank as he remembered the warning he had been given. He soon learned the details of the episode:

> On Sunday morning two of the blacks, happy possessors of horses, had set out for Mundubbers with the greatest part of the wages paid by me on Saturday. There dwelt worthy Mrs. Corry, like the bad witch in the fairy tale, and from her they had purchased four bottles of abominable rum for heavy money. . . . The best of the thing was that the two ambassadors had already got totally drunk in the course of their ride, and had arrived in the camp in a perfectly senseless condition, having lost one of the precious bottles by the way. This, however, was found by some children sent out to look for it. And now all the camp, men, women, and children had sent themselves about the speedy consumption of the sweet poison, which has not its equal in taste or effect (1899, p. 55).

Though he clearly perceived the humor in the situation, Semon was also exasperated by the natives' drinking spree. But he blamed himself for the comical predicament, and refused to punish the blacks for doing what he had been warned about.

The adjustment to bush life, however, required not only tolerance of his capricious companions; the physical environment also had to be mastered. Though a veteran camper, Semon had not previously encountered anything like the dense scrub of the Australian bush, and he received a baptism of fire during a harrowing two-day escapade when he was lost alone in the bush. It took some time for Semon to assimilate such unsettling experiences, but he soon felt truly at ease with his environment for the first time since his arrival. The long periods of solitary observation and hunting were no longer threatening; instead, they promoted a sense of inner tranquility. Semon became increasingly intoxicated by the isolation that he found in the bush. In view of the major role that isolation—of a much different variety—played in his later years, Semon's introspections concerning his solitude in the bush are of special interest:

> It is very difficult to find solitude to such perfection upon earth nowadays, and I had never known anything like it before. . . . The immense Australian bush offers *genuine* solitude, by allowing a man to exist in its interior as it pleases him, without his undergoing any dangers or difficulties by being alone. Such solitude cannot be compared with the sort which the stranger experiences when staying in a great metropolis, the language of which is unknown to him, still less with the terrible loneliness of a prisoner in his cell. At first the solitude of which I speak was new . . . to me, and it used to bring me lonely hours and a sense of abandonment, but I finally felt it like a great and mightly revelation, a thing as vivid and intense as the witnessing of the most varied scenes amongst foreign lands and nations. It gives a man time and a chance to look into his innermost self, to see himself, not as he appears in the eyes of his neighbours, but in his relation to great, ever-creating, ever-destroying Nature. No other circumstances favour an intimate relationship with Nature like this, the living free and alone among her works, without a house, without any vestige of human culture, without any human society (1899, pp. 77–75).

As the Australian weather warmed in the first days of November, the first Ceratodus eggs were finally spotted. The harvest was small, and Semon suspected that one female was responsible for the few eggs that his searchers had found. But spawning time had just begun, and as long as no fish were removed from the river, he felt confident that his take would increase. Suddenly, however, the eggs were no longer to be found. The dramatic disappearance of the prized specimen initially perplexed Semon. He then discovered an annoyingly simple answer: The natives had gone fishing behind his back and dined on their prize catch—a tasty female Ceratodus. The river supplied no more spawn for Semon's collection.

The aborigine's behavior deeply disturbed Semon; their irresponsibility had seriously undermined his most important scientific activity. Because of the unauthorized fishing trip, Semon had to seek a new camp on the Burnett that would yield a reasonable harvest of eggs. The growing tension led to open conflict, and within days the ephemeral natives had disappeared in the bush: "The great rum affair at the beginning had incited their discontent, and the sameness of their occupation, the perpetual searching for animals, began now, after three months to pall upon them. . . . This results from their perfect independence. . . . I must own that I rather admired them for it (1899, pp. 100–101)."

Stripped of this necessary support, Semon sent his companion Dahlke back to Gayndah in search of help. He decided to engage white men this time ("To engage other blacks would have been impossible, for they held together like burs, (p. 102)"), and felt particularly pleased when Dahlke returned in the company of two able-bodied German workers. Semon had in the meantime located a promising new campsite on the Burnett. The hunt for Ceratodus eggs had to

FIGURE 3. Richard Semon in Australia.

commence immediately: It was already late November, and only weeks remained in the spawning season. Semon enjoyed his capable new assistants, the river seemed rich in Ceratodus, and no obstacles to success were evident. Then came the floods.

When the rain first started, the men were able to hunt in spite of it. Instead of relenting, however, the showers became consistently torrential; days of rain turned into weeks of downpour, and the river rose at an alarmingly rapid rate. Semon's prime concern initially centered on potential damage to Ceratodus spawn. The force of the rushing river had washed away many of the water plants that harbored the eggs at a time when collections remained short of his goal. This concern was soon replaced by fears that the men would not survive the flood. Trees collapsed in the area of the vulnerable campsite, the rising river came dangerously close to it, and the men could no longer seek desperately needed provisions:

> Hitherto we had been able to swim through the river on horseback, and thus procure meat from Coonambula. This now grew impossible, as neither man nor horse would have been able to cross the raging floods without being swept away and crushed by the trees whirling along the waves. Consequently, we had to resign ourselves to being cut off from the world, and had to begin to handle our only food, the salt meat, rather sparingly (p. 110).

The rains did not relent. A temporary brightening in early December was followed by even more violent thunderstorms, the river was within 10 feet of camp, and supplies were exhausted. Action had to be taken, and there was only one way to reach the outside world. Though the Burnett could not be crossed, the Boyne River, a short distance from camp, seemed passable—at great risk. Semon volunteered for the dangerous task. He made the trip to Cooranga without serious difficulty and procured the necessary provisions. But he returned in the midst of frightening hailstorms and collapsing trees, struggling hard to safely reach camp. The distended Burnett had reached its peak; Semon described it as "a gigantic stream of nearly a mile in breadth and about seventy feet in depth, the muddy waters of which, with its loads of drift-wood, rolled along with immense power and rapidity, the air perpetually resounding with the rushing, grinding, and foaming of the raging river (p. 113)." The camp harbored numerous stranded travellers, and Semon offered them hospitality in spite of the shortage of food. Although their prospects remained bleak for several days, the rains finally relented and the river began to subside.

Though he had escaped major physical damage, Semon soberly assessed his scientific prospects in the wake of the flood. Inspection of the Burnett confirmed his worst fears: The Ceratodus spawn had vanished. Trying not to panic, he decided to seek Ceratodus eggs upstream, where the flood waters had probably not done so much damage. The strategy failed, however, because the fish did not inhabit those sections of the river high enough to escape serious flood damage. Semon trudged back to camp a depressed man. His first campsite proved an impoverished source of eggs, the blacks had eaten the one female that did produce some offspring, and now the floods washed away all traces of Ceratodus spawn with little time remaining in the mating season. To further complicate matters, Semon was scheduled to leave Australia in just a few weeks. A final effort to uncover the elusive spawn proved futile, and by mid-January it became clear that the mating season had long passed. Semon then decided to break camp. Though disappointed that he had collected few Ceratodus spawn, he reminded himself of his successes—collection of marsupials and monotremes had gone well—and resolutely set off for the next stop on his journey.

But he became obsessed by the Ceratodus failure. Memories of the abortive African expedition returned to haunt him, and intensified his discomfiture in face of this latest fiasco: "I felt that the insufficiency of my success would depress me for years to come (1899, p. 135)." Then he realized that another option was open to him: He could rearrange his schedule and return to the Burnett next Autumn. Such a maneuver would curtail his stay elsewhere, but the peace of mind it would bring seemed worth almost any price. He balked at the plan several times, fearing that a failure on the second attempt "would have been still more depressing and shameful than on the first (p. 136)." However, he chided his anxiety as "cowardly," and with a sense of relief and self-respect banished all doubt that he would journey back to the Burnett in the fall.

The months from February to April 1892 were enjoyably spent in the Torres Straits, which separate Australia from New Guinea. Graceful mountains, variegated flora, and agreeable weather combined to make Semon's research on the anatomy of local aquatic life exceedingly pleasant. He left for New Guinea (Papua) in early April refreshed by this respite from adversity. His time here, too, was spent productively and peacefully. Scientifically, Semon's attention focused upon some interesting local varieties of sea-life as well as the Papuan echidnas, but his efforts were not as intense as in Queensland. Consequently, he had more time to observe and partake in Papuan cultural life.

The native Papuans fascinated Semon from the day of his arrival. Their spontaneous and joyful personalities resembled the Queensland aborigines; their love of art, however, distinguished the Papuans from all the other natives who Semon had observed. Artistic creativity permeated the culture. Ornaments and decorations were characterized by a dazzling diversity of patterns, and even functional objects—axes, combs, or pipes—bore distinctive and intricate designs. Semon was impressed by the depth of the Papuans' artistic consciousness; it seemed to him more genuine than the contrived artistic values that he frequently observed in fellow Europeans. But Semon's admiration for Papuan artistic sensitivity did not obscure his dissatisfaction with other aspects of the culture. For one, he detested their conduct of warfare—consisting chiefly of "cowardly assault (1899, p. 394)"—and though he appreciated the spontaneous nature of this "sunny and childlike race," he could not always hide his disapproval of their lax work habits. Nor was Semon particularly fond of the Papuans' often deficient personal hygiene. He dreaded engaging in one of the most revered greeting ceremonies—rubbing noses—because this activity was acutely unpleasant when his ceremonial partner was "a Papuan, given to the chewing of betel and ignorant of the existence of soap and towel. Still in some parts of New Guinea it is impossible to avoid rubbing noses with dozens of aborigines (p. 357)."

What he later called "the halcyon days" in New Guinea ended all too soon. Fall would soon arrive; excitement and fear engulfed him as he set out on the long trip back to the Burnett in search of Ceratodus.

Semon contacted Dahlke before returning to the bush, so when he finally arrived at Gayndah in July 1892 most preparations had already been made. One serious problem remained unsolved: Did he dare to rehire the blacks as hunters? Many of the old crew turned up in Gayndah to offer their help, and, conveniently repressing memories of past difficulties, Semon again engaged their services. This time the expedition ran smoothly from the start. Marsupial collections were so plentiful that Semon constructed a tanning yard to convert the skins of excess possums into furs. By mid-August the amount of data he had gathered concerning the development of echidnas exceeded even his boldest expectations. But the tension slowly mounted as the Ceratodus spawning season approached. Semon again attempted to motivate the aborigines by establishing a cash award for the first person to bring back satisfactory eggs. Maximal efforts were needed, and they were needed immediately; there would be no further chances should this attempt fail. Several discouraging days passed without success, and Semon tried to suppress his growing anxiety. September 16th was the watershed. On that evening, "Mackenzie came towards me with a radiant face, bringing three eggs he had just found (1899, p. 194)." Semon became jubilant during the next few days, as his hunters brought back over 700 Ceratodus spawn. The decision to return had been the correct one, and he could finally relax now that the major purpose of the journey had been spectacularly fulfilled.

With the scientific part of his expedition largely completed, Semon could leave Queensland content that he had procured everything he wanted. When the long journey home began, he relished the opportunity to travel as a tourist through the plains of India and into the Himalayan mountains. Much like Haeckel in years before him, Semon returned home triumphant from mysterious lands with many stories of the unknown to tell. Familiar sights, though, were welcomed by the exhausted adventurer: "Spring was reigning in all its radiance over the plains of Italy, spring, that charming season unknown in the tropics, bade me a laughing welcome to dear old Germany (1899, p. 535)."

SEMON IN AUSTRALIA: SOME PSYCHOLOGICAL PERSPECTIVES

I noted earlier that the Australian expedition interests us because it tells much about Semon as a person. The picture that emerges from this journey is a deeply human one. We have observed a man excited by the unknown but often frustrated by it; appreciative of people culturally different from himself, yet sometimes exasperated by them; passionately committed to the successful execution of his work, though not always able to immediately achieve it. Semon's profound appreciation of solitude and persistence in the face of discouraging circumstances also help to enrich our perspective on him as a man attempting to understand and influence the world around him.

His experiences during the Australian journey also reveal a dualism in Semon's character, an ever-present schism that displayed itself in various fashions throughout his life. This is the conflict between what I will call the "Germanic man" and the "Universal man." The 'Germanic man' is the "evangelical Prussian," the man who forsakes his religion in favor of his country, holds German culture and people above all others, and deeply loves the Fatherland. Our forays into Semon's childhood and subsequent tenure with Haeckel have elucidated some of the possible bases of the 'Germanic man' in his psychological make-up. One does not have to search long for evidence of 'Germanic man' in his account of the Australian journey. Semon's nationalistic sentiments are displayed in many ways; his longing for "my dear German soil (1899, p. 130)" and obvious pleasure in returning to "dear old Germany (p. 535)" are just a few of Semon's affectionate references to the Fatherland. His romantic German self-concept surfaces in the Preface to his travel account: "May these pages go out into the world...a token of faithful memory to my numerous friends in the East, and of gratitude for their noble support of the German wanderer (p. viii)."

Semon's Germanic pride displays itself even more conspicuously when he engages in protracted—and seemingly inappropriate—discussions of issues related to Germany in the travel account. For instance, in reporting his first encounter with Dahlke, one of the few German colonists in Queensland, he launched into a lengthy discussion of the merits of German colonists. Semon noted proudly that "Several British Australians of sound judgment have assured me that the modest, industrious, and thrifty German colonists are hardly equalled, and decidedly not surpassed by any other European nation (p. 22)." He then defended the maligned ability of Germans to rule colonies despite the contrary evidence: "I have always contradicted the far-spread prejudice that Germans are not fit to govern a colony, and consider it false and unreasonable, although, I am sorry to say, facts seem to justify it so far (p. 23)." Still, he foresaw a bright future for German colonists, noting that "We hope yet to show that not only German farmers and merchants, but that also the agents of the German Government can vie with the colonists of any other nation (p. 23)." As a final illustration of the "Germanic man' in Semon's character, let us consider the value that Semon attached to the traditional Prussian values of duty and discipline. The following episode is revealing. Shortly after his return to the Burnett, the camp became inundated by a swarm of ants. Semon attempted to rid the camp of the invaders by sprinkling bits of potassic cyanide over their nest. He expected the colony to disappear by the next day. Instead, he encountered a shocking scene that elicited his deepest respect:

How astonished I was when I found the whole surface of the heap strewn with dead ants like a battlefield. The pieces of cyanide, however, had totally disappeared! More than one half of the community had met death in this desperate struggle, but still the death-defying courage of the heroic little creatures had succeeded in removing the fatal poison, the touch of which must have been just as disagreeable to them as it was dangerous. Recklessly neglecting their own safety, they had carried it off little by little, covering every step with a corpse. . . . The considerably reduced little people enjoyed unmolested from that day the possession of their courageously defended home. For the heroism of these insects—which far surpasses what any other creature, including even man, has ever shown in the way of self-sacrifice and loyalty—had made such an impression on me that I gave up my campaign, and henceforward I bore with many an outrage from my neighbours rather than destroy the valiant beings whose courage I had not been able to crush (1899, pp. 147–148).

A sense of duty, indeed, that even the most spartan Prussian would find awesome.

"Germanic man," however, constituted only part of Semon's personality; it co-existed with the part of him that I have labeled "Universal man." This is the Semon whose interests transcend national boundaries, and whose appreciation of human qualities is not confined to traditional German virtues. We repeatedly encounter this component of his personality in the Australian journey. Consider first his attitude toward the blacks. Despite their various misadventures and his trepidation upon first meeting them, Semon attempted to understand the aborigines on their own terms. He admired their spontaneity, their knowledge of the local animals, and their dexterous hunting abilities. Though he claimed that the intelligence of the Australians was "far inferior to that of any other wild people that I have met (1899, p. 217)," he vociferously argued against the common European prejudice that the aborigines more closely resembled apes than men: "The Australians are no link between monkeys and men, but human creatures through and through (p. 206)."

In his travels through New Guinea and the Malayan Archipelago, the "Universal man" emerges even more clearly. The blush of a Papuan girl photographed for the first time, or the concern of a Papuan mother for her children, impressed Semon as examples of fundamental qualities shared by all human beings—German or otherwise. During his stay in Java he reflected that "I have ever been struck by the identity of the more fundamental human characteristics. Love and hatred, self-devotion and selfishness, fill almost alike the heart of the Australian savage and of the classic Greek (p. 437)." In closing his account of the great research expedition, Semon expressed the overriding conviction that he carried with him after its termination:

the certainty that the main factors of life and character, that the mainsprings of action are the same in Australians and Germans, in men and women all over the world . . . the same passions, failings, and virtues repeat themselves with endless variations, and that one Great Theme, transposed into a variety of keys, may be heard wherever human beings live, love, and hate (p. 536).

Although he was exhausted after almost two years in the wild, Semon found little time for rest upon his return to Jena. He now faced the formidable problems of collating and analyzing the vast amount of data he had brought back from Australia. This imposing task, however, clearly could not be handled by just one person—or for that matter by ten. A massive collaborative effort would be needed, so Semon formed an editorial committee consisting of Haeckel, colleague Max Fürbringer, and himself to oversee distribution of the materials to appropriate persons. The diversity of the data required participation by specialists in numerous fields. Invertebrate and vertebrate zoologists, embryologists, physiologists, anatomists, evolutionary biologists, and histologists all contributed to the analysis of Semon's numerous specimens. The work required time and money. Paul von Ritter, whose support had financed the expedition, again provided necessary funds, and the Jena-based publisher Gustav Fischer agreed to underwrite a large portion of the costs of publishing the collective analyses of Semon's data.

The first volume of *Semon's Zoologische Forschungsreisen in Australien und dem Malaiischen Archipel* appeared in late 1893; the last of the six volumes did not appear until 1913, a full 20 years after analyses of the data were initiated. The sheer quantity of effort expended upon the research is impressive. Seventy-seven scientists contributed a total of 112 articles—including many by Semon himself—to the massive folio volumes, which totaled 5407 pages and included 1810 illustrations as well as 343 tables. Their efforts were fruitful. Among 2021 varieties of fauna that Semon had collected, the researchers managed to identify 207 new species and 24 new genera (Fürbringer, 1913). Their analyses also shed new light on morphological, ontogenetical, physiological, and evolutionary processes in Ceratodus, marsupials, and monotremes, insights that have been acknowledged by modern zoologists (Butler, 1967; Müller, 1969; Johansen, Lenfant, & Grigg, 1966; Dowd, 1966).

Preparation of this colossal enterprise fully occupied Semon for several years following 1893. The work was well received by the scientific community (e.g., MacGregor, 1897), and the scientific success of the expedition contributed to Semon's growing reputation as a first-rate zoologist. The prestigious British journal *Nature*, for instance, lauded Semon's "brilliant investigations of Ceratodus and the Monotremes (1896, p. 135)." Similarly, a prominent British scientist later referred to Semon's Australian research in glowing terms: "Richard Semon is a professional zoologist and anthropologist of such high status for his original researches in the mere technical sense, that in these countries he could assuredly have been acclaimed as one of the Fellows of the Royal Society (Hartog, 1920, p. xxxi)." In fact, the development of Semon's career hardly could have been improved upon. He held an associate professorship at one of the most exciting centers for biological research in Germany; he remained on close terms with Haeckel, by then an internationally known figure in biology; and the success of his research made a large contribution to his own prominence. For all of these reasons, Semon's professional prospects seemed bright during the 1890s. He soon encountered some unexpected changes.

1897

Henrietta Semon turned 72 in 1897, and the year promised to be a good one for her. Almost 15 years had passed since the death of Simon Semon; Henrietta's slow adjustment to life without her husband was almost complete. Largely free from the senility that disfigured her final years, she was able to savor the success of her younger son's research and expedition during the 1890s. But Richard Semon's professional triumphs, however impressive, were not the only source of joy for Henrietta: Felix Semon's rise to prominence in England was even more remarkable. By 1897, Felix had consolidated his position as the leading laryngologist in Britain; the numerous honors that were conferred upon him testified to his status.[2] Felix's success, however, was not restricted to his professional pursuits. He had also established himself in the glitter and gold world inhabited by the élite of London society. Felix's boyish charm and infectious humor, in combination with his scientific prominence, rendered him an attractive figure to the upper-class of Victorian London. He became a regular guest at parties given by the Royal Family and served as both laryngologist and friend to the top names in London theater. Owing to his love of music, Felix established especially close relationships with some of Europe's major musical figures: Pianist Anton Rubenstein, violinist Joseph Joachim, and conductor Hans Richter were all frequent guests at Felix's parties (Semon, 1926, p. 174). Felix's ascent to some of the loftiest plateaus attainable in Victorian England reached a new peak in 1897. Henrietta Semon, enjoying an early summer visit in London, was at Felix's side on June 15th when he found a note from Lord Salisbury at his door: "It gives me great pleasure to inform you that in view of your remarkable professional eminence Her Majesty has been pleased to confer upon you the honour of knighthood." Felix first suspected that "the whole thing was a silly hoax (1926, p. 258)" before he appreciated the veracity of the communication. When he turned to Henrietta and informed her of the momentous distinction, she implored him not to "talk such nonsense (p. 258)." But after Felix convinced her that the honor was real, Henrietta Semon shared all of her son's excitement on that June afternoon in 1897. 1897 brought a different sort of happiness to her younger son in Jena—one that he paid for by relinquishing much that was dear to him.

Almost from the moment that he met her, Richard Semon sensed that Maria Krehl was a person blessed with special qualities. Most middle-class

---

2. The list of honors bestowed upon Felix includes the presidency or honorary presidency of almost every major European laryngological society.

FIGURE 4. Sir Felix Semon on his horse in London.

German women posed little fascination for Semon. Charming hostesses, dull conversationalists, and models of propriety, they each perfectly fulfilled the one desire that society had inculcated in them: "that I might one day be able to provide my husband with a proper domestic atmosphere (Lily Braun, cited in Craig, 1978, p. 208)." However, they lacked the spark of intellectual vitality that he immediately perceived in Maria. The woman who later produced noted translations of Darwin and Forel also combined a youthful attractiveness with her engaging personality. All this made Semon particularly sorry that Maria was married—to his friend and colleague Ludolph Krehl, a respected Professor of Pathology at Jena. Maria reciprocated Semon's feelings: The attractive, mustachioed Richard and his hypnotic tales of adventure in exotic countries posed an undeniable intrigue to the young Mrs. Krehl. Yet whatever mutual attractions they did feel, the two knew full well that strict contemporary morals would permit no indiscretions. Besides, Maria had several children and her marriage was a happy one; hence for good reasons they vowed to remain simply friends.

For a while they did. But logic and rationality play small roles in storybook romance, and the forces that drew Richard and Maria together proved more potent than their rational defenses. They initially attempted to conceal their emergent passion; little Jena, however, was hardly the place to keep such a secret, and word of the daring romance soon became known to their acquaintances. This was no flippant affair; it became "A profound attraction . . . which both believed they were not in a position to overcome (Lubarsch, 1920, p. xxviii)." Layers of physical, emotional, and intellectual resonance unfolded as their involvement intensified. They soon began to realize that the life of secret encounters and feigned formality at social gatherings would no longer suffice. Then came the move that stunned all of their friends and colleagues: Maria Krehl left her husband and children to live with Richard Semon.

Such behavior might hardly raise an eyebrow today; in stuffy Wilhelmian Germany it constituted the unthinkable atrocity, a horrifying violation of sacred middle-class morality: "For the married woman, infidelity was the unforgivable crime, to be punished by dispossession and déclassment (Craig, 1978, p. 209)." The pair knew that their action would be greeted with hostility, but the vehemence of the subsequent outcry exceeded their expectations. The acrimonious reproaches of their friends were accompanied by official censures from the University of Jena. Uschmann (1959), writing a history of the University some 60 years later, still referred to the episode as "a scandal (p. 125)." Such venomous responses plunged the pair into crisis: How could they continue to live amidst the poisoned atmosphere of judgment and condemnation? But the decision had been made the day that Maria left her family. When they finally agreed to leave Jena, they took a step that both knew was inevitable from the start. Semon's boyhood friend Otto Lubarsch recalled that both Richard and Maria were acutely aware of the likely consequences of their actions. Maria willingly left behind a secure future, a husband whom she respected, and children whom she cherished. Semon gave up treasured colleagues, a town he felt emotionally attached to—and his bright prospects for a future academic career. Just as Jena had no room for a moral pariah, neither did other universities. Lubarsch felt particularly indignant that his friend's decision rendered him an academic outcast: "It is itself deplorable that a man of such great abilities and such significant accomplishments did not again find a position in a University (p. xxxi)." He bitterly held that the University could not be excused for "leaving behind a man of Semon's significance (p. xxxi)."[3] Semon relinquished his academic life, Maria her family life; but, as Lubarsch remarked, "what they exchanged this for was simply worth more to them (p. xxxix)."[4]

The days of bold expeditions and active research had come to an unexpectedly premature end for Semon, and he would have to live with the consequences of this extraordinary decision for the remainder of his life. He had made controversial moves before—his conversion met with much criticism—and knew that he possessed at least some of the strength required to face a disapproving world. And, of course, he was not alone in this action.

Richard and Maria fled from Jena in the summer of 1897. They married in Munich, in 1899.

---

3. Lubarsch does not clearly state whether or not Semon seriously attempted to find another university position, and if so, how much opposition he encountered. Lubarsch is also rather fuzzy about the circumstances surrounding Semon's departure from the University of Jena. We do know, however, that Semon was not fired by the University—his letter of resignation is in the University Archives (Dr. H. Hiebsch, personal communication, October 1, 1980)—although Lubarsch indicates that there was pressure from the University for Semon to leave.

4. Richard and Maria were not the only ones whose lives were disrupted by the scandal. Ludolph Krehl, Maria's former husband, had been a Professor of Pathology at Jena throughout the 1890s. But he left Jena soon after the trauma of 1897, and lived a somewhat nomadic existence over the next few years: He went to Marburg in 1899, Griefswald in 1900, Strassburg in 1904, and Heidelberg in 1906, where he remained until 1931. Krehl was a highly regarded pathologist in his day—his classic *Pathologische Physiologie* went through 14 editions—and he was a perceptive critic of Freud's work (see Decker, 1977, pp.124–125). He apparently never remarried, and after his death in 1937 none of Krehl's obituaries (at least the several I have read) mentioned his disastrous marriage.

5

Battles Won and Lost

THE INITIAL STRUGGLES: 1904-1908

Germany was technically a unified country at the turn of the century, but the cultural divisions between its ancient states ran deep and wide. The broadest gulf traditionally separated North and South. The orderly Prussian proudly viewed himself as infinitely more pragmatic than his beerchugging Bavarian compatriot; the Bavarian was thankful to escape the excessive regimentation that rendered Prussians so unbearably stiff and obstinate. Tuchman (1966, p. 302) succinctly portrayed these long standing differences:

> Berlin meant Prussia, the natural enemy of Munich and Bavaria. The North German regarded the South German as easy-going and self-indulgent, a sentimentalist who tended to be deplorably democratic, even liberal. In his turn, the South German regarded the North German as an arrogant bully with bad manners and an insolent stare who was politically reactionary and aggressively preoccupied with business.

Richard Semon's past and present united these two opposing strains: The Prussian-bred youth had come to live in the heart of Bavarian decadence. We do not know why the pair fled to Munich. Although most of Richard's family resided in Berlin, Maria may have had relatives in the South. Regardless of what directed them there, they must have sought peace above all. Society's pariahs sometimes seek seclusion, and these two spurned the attractions of central Munich—there was a vital intellectual community in Schwabing, the most fabled and exciting sector of the city—and instead headed for the isolation of Munich's rural fringe. There they found not only solitude but beauty as well. The 1900 edition of the *Adressbuch von München* provides the surface facts:

> Semon, Dr. Richard. Professor, Privatgelehrter. Prinz Ludwigshöhe, Ludwigshöherstr. 6.

The Ludwigshöherstrasse is a lonely country road that winds along a steep embankment overlooking the lush Isar River Valley in the recesses of southern Munich. The church steeples of downtown were barely perceptible in the distance when Richard and Maria stood in their front yard; they could see expansive meadows, towering trees entangled with thick green vegetation, and an occasional country cottage. If they desired isolation, their choice was a wise one. Civilization had not yet encroached upon the Ludwigshöherstrasse and the area maintained a bucolic quality that provided an ideal setting in which the couple could recover after their tumultuous departure from Jena. Even today[1], the Ludwigshöherstrasse's rural environment is functionally isolated from urban bustle. Only a lone gas station and a strangely out of place chrome office building mar the tranquility that one feels looking out over the Isar from the fields that the Semons once inhabited.

The contrast between the hectic days of his departure from Jena and the slow pace of his country existence in Munich highlighted the distance that separated Semon's old life from his new one. The frenetic struggles of Jena had given way to a new sense of relaxed exploration in Munich. Work could again be fully attended to, and his relationship with Maria was able to grow naturally in the easy-going Munich environment, freed from the anxiety induced by disapproving friends and colleagues. Semon maintained only one firm link to his Jena life, and even this tie was somewhat painful. Ernst Haeckel had turned increasingly bitter in the years since Semon's departure; the aging oracle's isolation from the scientific community had accelerated during this time. But he remained on good terms with Semon, and spilled out his growing resentment to one of the few students whom he felt had not betrayed him:

> What I have experienced in the last few years in this area (not only the apostasy of the most important scientific convictions, but also the partly sincere, partly feigned disdain of my person and my life's work), and the disrespect of my 'dear students', who should be committed to the highest gratitude-this has now led me to the height of *Weltanshauung*, in which one follows the course of things *objectively* in *complete resignation* and gives up all subjective feelings and interests. If one sees what miserable fellows play the leading role in science and in life, and how uncritically the crowd applauds them—then 'the rest is silence'! (Haeckel to Semon, November 1902)

One suspects that Haeckel's gloom did not rekindle any fond memories of Jena for Semon. Munich was his reality after 1897, while Jena formed part of a hazy previous existence that he had permanently left behind.[2]

---

1. This observation was made at the time of my visit to the Ludwigshöherstrasse in July 1978. The house that the Semons once inhabited at Ludwigshöherstrasse 6 no longer exists; there is only an empty lot surrounded by several cottages and open fields.
2. Semon's official ties with the University of Jena remained severed for the rest of his life, so it is surprising to learn that he left part of his estate to a scientific research

The retreat to rural Munich initiated an intellectual, as well as personal, re-orientation for Semon. The scientific life of the *ausserordentlicher Professor* at an active research center such as Jena and the *Privatgelehrter* (private scholar) in his country home are necessarily worlds apart. Stripped of the sources required to continue serious biological research, Semon took on a personally novel role as theoretician and organizer of scientific knowledge. His new path led him to confront fundamental problems of biology and psychology that had been refractory to theoretical treatment. After laboring four years with these problems, he brought forth a book that he cherished above all of his other scientific contributions: *Die Mneme*. The ideas that he expressed here dominated the remainder of his intellectual life.

In *Die Mneme*, Semon attempted to explain heredity, memory, and organic development within a broadly conceived biological framework that emphasized the similarities between these phenomena. The book comprised an entirely new direction for him. A wide-ranging theoretical work, it sharply broke from his past empirical orientation. Semon's Ph. D. research at Jena, the work that he pursued at Naples in 1886, and the vast Australian project were all observational enterprises: Data dominated theory in each of these pursuits. But now he walked a thin line between science and speculation; the theoretical flights of *Die Mneme* led him into regions where the bond between data and theory was often uncomfortably tenuous.

It is not surprising that a sense of expectant tension accompanied his entry into such forbidding regions. Otto Lubarsch claimed that "He was very emotional about the fate of the book, and he was downright 'hungry' for encouragement (1920, p. xxxiii)." Semon sent copies of *Die Mneme* to a number of prominent scientists, and was particularly concerned about the reaction of one of them—August Weismann. Weismann was one of the most influential biologists of the period. Semon, however, had taken theoretical positions in *Die Mneme* that were directly contrary to Weismann's views (We will explore these issues in detail in Section II of the book). Consequently, he pessimistically anticipated Weismann's reaction to his work:

> They say it would be superhuman to expect an unprejudiced evaluation from Weismann. . . . Nevertheless, I have sent Weismann the book, because I have the greatest respect for him and his efforts, although I also believe that no one has damaged Darwinism so much as he has through exaggeration and schematization. I will naturally be beaten to death by his fanatical supporters,

---

foundation at the University (Lubarsch, 1920, p. xlii). This fact can be interpreted in a number of ways: (1) Semon never held the University responsible for his departure; (2) Semon's resentment softened over time; (3) Semon was extremely loyal to his former University, in spite of any bad feeling he might have harbored (this is Lubarsch's view). There is little evidence on which to base a choice between these hypotheses, but his action does suggest that Semon placed most of the responsibility for his exile upon himself.

and what remains of me then the Vitalists will gobble up raw under the stamp of war. (Semon to Forel, 1–31–05)

These times of anxious anticipation exposed Semon to an internal conflict that he found difficult to resolve. His erupting desire for recognition sharply contrasted with his view of himself as an objective observer of Nature who cared little for such trivial matters. Otto Lubarsch recalled the anguish that his friend experienced as he attempted to reconcile these two contradictory parts of his psyche. Semon could not emotionally detach himself from the fate of *Die Mneme*, nor could he relinquish his self-perception as an objective scientist. Semon expressed a painful awareness of his evolving conflict: He could not hide his pleasure when praise for his work was forthcoming, but confessed a "feeling of shame" (*Beschämung;* Semon to Forel, 12–27–04) that such matters of recognition were important to him.

Semon partially coped with these distressing events by releasing a part of himself that had remained dormant throughout the writing of *Die Mneme:* He decided to "live the nomadic life for awhile, with just a pair of suitcases and a box of books (Semon to Forel, undated; probably June 1905)." On this journey, however, there would be no research to carry out, no untamed bush to conquer, and no capricious aborigines to contend with; he and Maria confined themselves to the familiar territory of the European continent. They financed the trip by selling their house on the Ludwigshöherstrasse and included the Tirol, Italian Alps, French Riviera, Corsica, and Paris on a grand tour that started in the summer of 1905 and lasted over a year. The tensions induced by four years of concentrated work eased in Semon's changing environments; as he wrote from the Alps in October 1905, "I am using the time to diligently wear myself out walking (Semon to Forel, 10–9–05)." But no amount of travel could ease his anxiety over the fate of *Die Mneme:* Initial reactions to the book appeared during the course of his journey, and Semon awaited them in a state of fragile uncertainty.

One of the first to provide unqualified support was Haeckel: "I have used the idleness of these quiet weeks to study your 'Mneme' thoroughly and pensively! *Bravo! Bravissimo!* (Haeckel to Semon, 12–25–05)." The ever-cynical Haeckel offered assurance that Semon's broad coverage of wide ranging biological issues—just like his own disparaged work—would ultimately prove more valuable than the molecular experimentation that had monopolized the attention of their contemporaries: "Even if your work, rich in ideas, will have but a slow effect because of the little interest of our beloved biological colleagues for the great general questions, it will nonetheless be the more enduring in the future (12–25–05)." Haeckel's psychological support, however, was of limited value. He was too preoccupied with his own isolation to consistently bolster Semon's confidence, and he no longer carried the necessary clout in the biological world to effectively champion Semon's views. Semon needed a dependable psychological anchor in those precarious days following publication of *Die*

FIGURE 5. Richard Semon in his study in Munich, May, 1905. This photograph, which was sent to August Forel, contains a request from Semon for permission to correspond with Forel.

Mneme. The man who reached out to provide him with the confirmation that he required was a Swiss psychiatrist named August Forel. Darwin had Huxley and Copernicus had Rhaeticus; for Semon, it was Forel who tried to sway scientific opinion in his favor. Because of his incessant championing of Semon's work in professional circles, Forel came to play a major role in Semon's subsequent psychological existence. What manner of man was August Henri Forel and why was he so attracted to Semon's work?

Born near Morges, Switzerland in 1848, Forel studied medicine at both Munich and Zurich under eminent mentors such as Theodor Meynert, one of the most influential brain physiologists of the 19th-century and a teacher of Freud, and Bernard von Gudden, another distinguished brain physiologist. While working under Gudden at Munich, Forel became one of the first anatomists to achieve histological preparations of the brain. He also constructed precise anatomical maps of various cranial nerves, and his topographical studies of the hypothalamus were so revealing that his name was attached to one of its regions—the campus Foreli (Pilet, 1972). Although fascinated by the structure of the brain, Forel became increasingly interested in the pursuit of psychiatry, and decided to commit himself to this rapidly growing field by the late 1870s.

Neither anatomy nor psychiatry could compete with Forel's greatest scientific passion: the study of ants. He began collecting and classifying ants as a child, and had so thoroughly mastered his subject by the age of 27 that his book, *The Ants of Switzerland*, won the prestigious Thore Prize offered by the Paris Academy of Science in 1875; he went on to amass one of the world's largest ant collections. Forel utilized his knowledge of anatomy in his entomological studies, and eventually proposed a new taxonomy of ants based on their internal morphology. Forel's most important contributions to entomology, however, stemmed from his numerous insights concerning the psychology of ants. Sensory function, memory, communication, and social behavior were some of the topics that Forel probed in pioneering studies that brought him international recognition. These studies make absorbing reading even today (Forel, 1904; Forel, 1908).

In 1879, Forel accepted the post of psychiatric supervisor at the Burghölzi Asylum in Zurich. His efforts at reform turned this hospital into a model institution that received wide acclaim. It later achieved even greater recognition when Forel's student, Eugen Bleuler, and a promising young man named Carl Gustav Jung built upon the foundation established by Forel. Forel, however, was an irrepressible scientific eclectic, and his duties at Burghölzi comprised just one sector of his busy professional life. For instance, he became an early and ardent advocate of hypnotism as a therapeutic tool. Forel quickly achieved a marked facility as a practicing hypnotist—he recalled how "People began to regard me as a wizard (Forel, 1937, p. 167)"—and contributed to the professional advancement of hypnotism by co-founding the *Zeitschrift für Hynotismus und Suggestionstherapie* in 1892. Forel's major theoretical contribution to hypnosis, *Hypnotismus und Psychotherapie*, received widespread scientific kudos and went through 12 editions by 1923.[3] He continued his studies on ants, wrote an interesting monograph on human amnesia (Forel, 1885), and became an energetic advocate of psychiatry's role in legal matters.

His varied scientific concerns, however, commanded only part of Forel's seemingly inexhaustible reservoir of energy. A keenly sensitive and humane person, he could not be satisfied in the role of an insular, detached scientist: "the tide of human misery, strife, and misfortune was like a fierce and muddy torrent. To shut one's eyes to it, I felt, would have been cowardly and almost wicked (1937, p. 189)." Forel immersed himself in a variety of social causes. He became a staunch proponent of women's rights, worked on various projects that he believed would enhance human harmony, such as the implementation of the international language Esperanto, and helped to bring about major changes in the Swiss penal code. In his most idiosyncratic but also most heartfelt social pursuit, Forel vociferously advocated and practiced abstinence from alcohol, and waged numerous public campaigns against what he believed constituted one of mankind's fiercest enemies. Yet even the peripatetic Forel was constrained by human limitations of energy, and his intense involvement with each of his multiple pursuits brought him to the brink of collapse several times during the 1890s. After a particularly close brush with nervous breakdown in 1898, Forel grudgingly retired from his post at the Burghölzi to concentrate on the study of ants and pursue his various social causes at a more leisurely pace. It was in this condition—as an eminent, semiretired scientist and social advocate—that Forel received a copy of *Die Mneme* from Richard Semon in 1904.

Precisely why Forel was so immediately and profoundly taken by Semon's work is not entirely clear, but two candidate explanations can be offered. The first probable reason lies in Forel's approach to science. As a participant in numerous research areas, it is not surprising that Forel was impressed by Semon's bold attempt to incorporate phenomena from biology, anatomy, physiology and psychology under a single theoretical umbrella. Forel enthusiastically advocated the desirability of such an integrative approach at numerous points in his own writings. For instance, he expressed disdain for those who maintained that the study of brain anatomy had no place in psychology, and argued that multiple perspectives were required to understand the human mind: "Our mind must be studied simultaneously both directly from within and indirectly from without, through biology and the conditions of its origins (1904, p. 35)." Their unswervingly broad, integrative stances at a time of increasing specialization in science marked an important similarity between Semon and Forel.

There is, however, a second reason for Forel's powerful attraction to Semon's work, centering upon Forel's professional interest in memory. Forel had confronted problems of memory at various points in his work. He believed that

---

3. One of the earliest writers to enthusiastically praise Forel's treatment of hypnotism was a rising young neurologist from Vienna named Sigmund Freud (Freud, 1889).

memory is essential to the behavior of ants and other insects ("Many insects . . . possess memory. . . . Insects are not merely attracted directly by sensory stimuli, [1904, p. 18]."), and was in the midst of experiments concerning insects' memory (Forel, 1908, Chap. 11) during the period that he first became acquainted with Semon's work. However, Forel had no general theory of memory that he could use to help interpret his data; *Die Mneme* provided him with precisely such a theory. Consider also Forel's interest in human amnesia. As a practicing hypnotist and clinical observer of amnesic patients, Forel was acquainted with a phenomenon that had impressed other clinical psychiatrists: Seemingly lost memories can be recovered under appropriate psychological conditions of retrieval. Semon's theory of memory, as we shall later observe, was especially concerned with the important role played by retrieval conditions in memory function. Forel was careful to emphasize Semon's novel treatment of retrieval phenomena in many of his pro-Semon barrages (Forel, 1905; Forel, 1910), and further demonstrated his special fondness for Semon's theoretical emphasis on retrieval in his widely read monograph on hypnotism and psychotherapy (Forel, 1918). Forel here proposed to extend Semon's ideas by conceptualizing various pathological conditions as qualitatively specific disorders of retrieval, and created a special terminology for these disorders that relied upon Semon's ideas.[4]

Forel, then, was an eclectic thinker who endorsed the sort of integrative approach to science adopted by Semon, and also maintained a keen interest in phenomena of memory that Semon's theory might have helped him to better understand. Taken together, these points may provide some insight into Forel's enthusiastic advocacy of Semon's work.[5] Whatever its ultimate explanation, Forel's praise quickly became an important psychological crutch for Semon. *Die Mneme*

---

4. For example, Forel (1918, p. 7) argued that delusory states in which internal rather than external stimuli guide the stream of consciousness should be regarded as a special malfunction of the retrieval process or, as labeled by Semon, the *ecphoric* process, and called this malfunction *epecphory*. Similarly, he suggested that temporary amnesia without delusory content could be conceptualized as a different sort of retrieval pathology, and labeled this disorder anecphory. And Forel depicted dissociative phenomena such as those encountered in hypnosis as still another kind of retrieval disorder, in this case dubbed *parecphory*. Forel's conceptualization of these diverse phenomena as qualitatively different kinds of retrieval pathologies directly derived from his fascination with Semon's treatment of ecphoric processes.

5. The depth of Forel's respect for Semon's ideas can be gleaned from the following passage, in which an invalid Forel, close to his death in 1931, summarized the major influences on his life: "*This, in a few words, is my political and social testament.* Predatory, egoistic and hypocritical though human nature may be in itself by inheritance, yet it can be tamed from childhood upwards by *social education.* My perception of this I owe in the first place . . . to the study of the ants; then to the study of dead and living brains of men and animals; then to psychiatry, hypnotism, psychotherapy and medical psychology; further, to Darwin and Semon (1937, p. 332)."

received harsh criticism from most of the scientists who discussed it in print; we shall examine the content of the criticisms in subsequent chapters. Forel represented a welcome source of confirmation, and Semon poured out his gratitude often and effusively. Writing to Forel from the mountains in September 1905, Semon humbly acknowledged that "If the whole does ever capture the interest of biologists, before we are all dead and buried, I will have you to thank in all respects (9–29–05)." The same theme echoed through a letter written from the Tirol just two weeks later: "It is quite clear to me, that if I finally and in spite of everything do win through, I will have, to a very great degree, your valiant and untiring efforts to thank (10–9–05)." And again in December 1905, from Italy: "I thank you with all my heart for having acknowledged *Die Mneme*. If it were not for you, no one would give a straw for it, (12–29–05)."

These early letters cast the tone of their relationship for the next 15 years. Forel assumed the role of psychological provider and nourisher; Semon, the appreciative recipient of Forel's public praise, responded with unending thanks. But with Forel firmly entrenched in his corner, Semon answered the criticisms articulated by each of his successive opponents with confidence and sarcasm. The first objections were published by Detto (1905) in the *Natürwissenschaftliche Wochenschrift*, and Semon cynically depicted this critic's narrow approach to science in a letter written to Forel (10–15–05) from the Tirol:

> It is well enough put together but in the main is thoroughly objectionable. For this man, physiology and psychology are two areas separated from one another by two unbroken Chinese walls. Any attempt to do away with these walls evokes in this Man of Thought (as in most of his followers) not satisfaction, but horror. . . . Of course, it is also more comfortable to have one's little garden all pretty and fenced off, and not to have to worry about what lies on the other side of the wall.

Semon was similarly acerbic in a letter written just six days later as he brushed aside objections raised in a paper by the psychologist Jordan. "I find Jordan's article terribly weak," he commented, and mocked this critic's "highly self-satisfied discussion" and "pedantic enumerations." He assured Forel that these objections were the harmless rantings of an intellectual lightweight: "The man is simply not good, very inconsequent, and understands equally little about comparative and introspective psychology (10–21–05)!" A critique published by Meyer (1906) was likewise accorded but slight respect: "I have seen enough to judge that he puts forward no serious counter-argument and is an irksome opponent only inasmuch as he tends to circle round the subject in rather indeterminate fashion and is therefore less easy to pin down than someone whose arguments are more sharply formulated...the whole is so poor that I hope to deal with it in 3–4 sides (11–2–06)."

Semon's acid commentaries on the papers of Detto, Jordan, and Meyer were merely preliminary skirmishes that set the stage for a more serious encounter; his reaction to August Weismann's assault would provide a stringent

FIGURE 6. August Weismann at about the time of his controversy with Semon.

test of faith. Aware that Weismann was massing a major critique of his work, Semon psychologically prepared for it by attempting to convince himself—and Forel—that Weismann was a biased critic whose objections should not be taken too seriously:

> For the very reason that he enjoys the reputation of being a natural scientist of great quality and reliability, his role as arbitrator in the fundamental

questions of biology is a particularly dangerous one . . . you are right to draw the distinction between Weismann the conscientious and wide-ranging researcher in a specialized area and Weismann the scholastic and sophist. Truly the marriage between these two spirits is a psychological puzzle which can only be explained by saying that the scholastics absorbed in youth...destroyed all the seeds which an honest unprejudiced enquiry into an area of natural science allows to germinate . . . the human herd would soon enough have formed a flock of blind adherents and followers behind even such a strange bell-wether (10–9–05).

Buttressed by these defenses of his own creation, Semon remained unruffled when Weismann's lengthy attack finally appeared in print. Although not as condescending as in his treatment of other critics, he confidently informed Forel that supporters of Mneme had little to fear from Weismann's pen: "As far as facts are concerned, Weismann did not bring up anything that I did not know nor anything that in my opinion undercuts the foundation of my views or that shakes them in any essential point (8–5–06)." Whether or not Semon actually believed that Weismann's assault left his position undamaged is less important than the fact that his spirit remained high enough to withstand Weismann's polemics and rebut them in print. Sustained by Forel's continuing encouragement, he maintained the psychological strength to fight with confidence and resist with defiance.

As their European excursion drew to a close in the late fall of 1906, Richard and Maria were faced with the problem of deciding where to settle once they returned to Munich. Although the idyllic retreat on the Ludwigshöherstrasse had served them well when they required seclusion, the agony of Jena was by now almost a decade behind them, and they had lived in self-imposed isolation since 1897; the time for rustication was over. Instead of again seeking a quiet existence in the outskirts of Munich, the pair headed straight for its most dynamic intellectual and artistic sector: They elected to live in Schwabing. Located in the northcentral part of the city, Schwabing is to Munich as Greenwich Village is to New York and Soho is to London. Its reputation as a center for creative and unconventional intellects blossomed in the first decade of the 20th-century. Thomas and Heinrich Mann led a group of resident writers that included fellow Germans such as Bertolt Brecht, as well as promising foreigners like Rainer Maria Rilke. The Semons could also count as their neighbors members of the iconoclastic *Der blaue Reiter* (The Blue Rider) group of expressionist painters: Wassily Kandinsky, Paul Klee, and Franz Marc all walked the same Schwabing streets as Richard and Maria (see Obermeier, 1976).

The Semons rented a spacious second-floor apartment at Martiusstrasse 7 in the summer of 1907, and the locale of their new habitat was well chosen. The tranquil Martiusstrasse is located just a short block east of the Leopoldstrasse, the grand boulevard that runs south to the magisterial Arch of Victory and is at the center of Schwabing's energetic bustle. Munich's universities and libraries are also within walking distance and, equally important, Martiusstrasse is barely a stone's throw west of Munich's gorgeous and spacious park, the famous English Gardens. Dotted with lakes and patches of densely wooded trails, the Gardens provided a natural refuge for Semon when solitude was necessary.

Life in Schwabing promised to be good for the Semons, but the strains of moving intensified a problem that had been quietly building since 1905: Maria's health had become increasingly erratic. Semon initially attempted to deal with her occasional fits of nervousness through patience and understanding, later taking her to see numerous local physicians. None of these measures proved effective, and by the end of 1907 he looked to Forel for help:

> Today I come to you with a question and a request. It concerns my wife, whose health—since about two years ago—leaves something to be desired . . . she usually falls asleep quite easily but then awakens at midnight or in the very early morning as if she had been shaken awake and cannot fall asleep again. Then the next day she feels exhausted and depressed . . . I wondered whether *hypnotic* treatment might not be effective, and I wished to solicit your advice. If you agree, who should we go to in Munich? (12–31–07)

Forel responded to his friend's pleas with recommendations and words of encouragement, but in spite of Maria's willingness to be hypnotized—"she was trying hard to give in to the suggestions"—the treatment was unsuccessful. Fortunately, some medicine prescribed by the hypnotist yielded positive results, and Semon was relieved to tell Forel some months later that "she is back to sleeping without any drugs and her whole state has improved in the same way. I hope that she is now on the way to regaining her former cheerfulness and energy (3–23–08)." A trip to the Alps in May 1908 further revived the improving patient; by the fall Maria felt sufficiently energetic to proceed with her own work. The linguistically gifted woman agreed to translate Forel's *The Mental Life of Insects*, and she approached her task with renewed vibrancy.

In spite of his alarm over Maria's precarious condition, Semon's first year back in Munich after his European journey was a productive one. He had by then largely dispensed with his various responses to the critics, and completed work on a second edition of *Die Mneme*; sounding a familiar theme, he informed Forel that "the fact that the book has received attention sufficient for a second edition to be published is due *entirely* to your warm and unhesitating spokesmanship (3–23–8)." The road was now clear for a complete involvement with problems of human memory. As early as 1905, Semon had told Forel of his intention to write a purely psychological extension of Mneme and to immerse himself in relevant literature.[6] The work progressed well throughout 1907, and

---

6. Semon was very much aware of his status as a psychological outsider, and took it upon himself to become familiar with the work of psychologists: "It is moreover of great importance to me that my present work should bring me up to date with work done by professional psychologists in areas relating to Mneme. I cannot yet find very much, nevertheless it is indispensable to be conversant with it (Semon to Forel, 12–20–05)."

early in 1908 he predicted that it would be complete by summer. Semon's scientific spirits were high when he finally did finish the first draft in August 1908, and he wrote excitedly to Forel about his novel insights into the workings of the mind: "Entirely new connections have become clear to me, and I hope that this work will offer a significant simplification of our mental physiology and psychological observations (8–9–08)." The mixed reception of *Die Mneme*, however, served as a warning that his new book might not find a sympathetic audience, and Semon acknowledged to Forel that mainstream psychologists would likely be baffled by it. But he remained confident enough in himself to blame such failures of comprehension on the intellectual shortcomings of minds bound by tradition. While admitting to Forel that many of the questions about memory and the mind that he had posed were well outside the boundaries of contemporary psychological thinking, he offered no apologies for violating the accepted wisdom: "The 'psychological knowledge' which prohibits posing of such questions seems to me to be yet more preconceived 'herd' opinions (11–25–08)." For the intellectual isolate, assurance in the fundamental soundness of his position is crucial: It permits self-justification in the face of responses that provide evidence to the contrary. Bolstered by Forel's support, Semon internally maintained that assurance through 1908; but his grasp of it was far more tenuous than he yet had occasion to realize.

GERMANY, ENGLAND, AND THE THREAT OF WAR

The stability of the world around him was also much less secure than Semon could have imagined in 1908. Many of the emerging problems were traceable to developments in Germany's conduct of foreign affairs. Under the leadership of Kaiser Wilhelm II and high ranking government ministers such as Reich Chancellor Bernhard von Bülow and Naval Secretary Alfred von Tirpitz, the Second Reich's expansionist doctrine of *Weltpolitik* had given German foreign policy a "European reputation for dangerous irrationality (Craig, 1978, p. 303)." Most alarming was the sudden swelling of the German naval program. Under Tirpitz's command, Germany had mounted an impressive fleet that testified to its readiness for war. The continuing series of crises that plagued Europe in the first decade of the 20th-century—usually centering upon Germany—contributed to a growing atmosphere of trepidation throughout Europe. By 1908, "the course was set for disaster; after that date, international crisis became commonplace and all Europe became involved in a runaway arms race (Craig, p. 324)."

The principal target of the German arms build-up was clear: Great Britain. As early as 1897, Tirpitz had warned the Kaiser that "For Germany, the most dangerous enemy at the present time is England. . . . The military situation against England demands battleships in as great a number as possible (Craig, p. 309)." Although the Triple Entente, formed in 1907, partially eased British fears of Teutonic militarism, a growing anti-German sentiment enveloped the country as the prospect of war loomed ever larger.

The experience of Sir Felix Semon in London reflected the growth of Anglo-German tensions. As a German who had attained some of the most distinguished honors offered by British society—his Knighthood especially—Felix occupied a sensitive position. On the one hand, Felix represented a shining example of the immigrant who was able to rise to the top of his adopted country. Like his close friend Sir Ernst Cassel, a financier who had become one of England's richest men after leaving Germany, Felix came to epitomize the success attained by a small group of immigrant German Jews:

> These German Jews represented a pocket of talent and energy, distinctively German in all they did. They were soon absorbed into the dominant class of their own country—as opposed to the Eastern Ashkenazi, most of whom remained isolated in their Stepney ghettos, only a few miles distant from the Cassels and the Semons, but socially and financially a world away (Stevens, 1975, p. 50).

Many Englishmen openly expressed their affection and respect for Felix. For example, when he retired from active practice in 1909, the British medical world responded with a rare and passionate outburst of warmth: They organized a farewell banquet for him that was attended by over 250 of London's leading medical, social, and political figures. The *British Medical Journal*, not a periodical easily led to overstatement, reported the affair with some astonishment: "The retirement of Sir Felix Semon from active practice was made the occasion of a formal farewell ceremony such as has never to our knowledge been accorded to a member of the medical profession (1909, p. 1)."

But Felix's elevated position also carried some unpleasant consequences in a country that had become increasingly suspicious and fearful of all Germans. In 1901, the newly crowned King Edward VII appointed Felix as one of his Physicians Extraordinary.[7] Although this honor boosted Felix's prestige amongst upper-class London society, it also drew public attention to his special role as a German treating the King of England. Aware of his delicate position, Felix regretfully sacrificed his German citizenship and became a naturalized British citizen soon after his appointment as Physician Extraordinary. Still, Felix could not entirely escape from the effects of the British public's mounting fear of the German war threat, especially after King Edward's death in 1910, Edward's death "brought a reaction against all his circle, and the German Jews felt the

---

7. Felix's appointment as Physician Extraordinary constituted more than just a recognition of professional eminence. Felix was sufficiently liked and trusted by the King to be counted among his small "inner circle" of friends (Lee, 1927, p. 63). King Edward's biographer, Sir Sidney Lee, noted that Felix was "warmly welcomed at the court (1927, p. 62)," and recalled how Edward "constantly invited him to Windsor, Sandringham, and Balmoral, where he was in much demand as a witty raconteur, an expert bridge player, and a good shot—three qualifications that counted very highly with the King (p. 63)."

backlash (Stevens, 1975, p. 55)." With the threat of war ever-present, a painfully comic joke circulated among England's establishment Germans: "What's going to happen to us," one English German says to the other, "if we English go to war with us Germans (Stevens, p. 56)?"

There was little that these expatriate Germans could do to ease the tensions between their native and adopted countries; the policies of Tirpitz and the Kaiser took no heed of their plights. For Felix Semon, the stakes were particularly high: His brother, his family, and many of his friends remained in Germany. But Felix, like most other transplanted Germans, could do no more than quietly hope for a reconciliation between Europe's two greatest powers. That hope went decidedly unfulfilled.

THE HERMIT'S LAMENT: 1909-1914

"It hasn't been a very good winter for me," wrote a despondent Richard Semon in the spring of 1909 (Semon to Forel, 5–18–09). Semon's state of mind reflected the consequences of a scientific isolation that had begun to take its psychological toll. The initial sparks raised by *Die Mneme* gradually receded into the past, and Semon's dawning awareness that his cherished creation would not exert the influence that he had hoped for did more than just disappoint him; it also undermined his confidence in his latest efforts. Semon's evolving treatise on human memory progressed at a disappointingly slow pace during the winter, as he redrafted whole sections of the book that just months earlier seemed satisfactory and complete. Semon was acutely aware that a reception like that accorded *Die Mneme* might well await his new monograph, and when the exhausting revisions were finally completed he sent the manuscript to Forel and nervously awaited a response: "I am simply longing to know whether you will see it as a significant step forward on the road which the Mneme embarked upon (5–18–09)."

Forel delivered a predictable dose of glowing approval, and further informed the expectant Semon that he intended to again wage a public campaign on his behalf. Not surprisingly, Forel's accolades elicited a flurry of humble thanks from an appreciative Semon. However, unlike in earlier years, a noticeable tone of self-criticism had crept into Semon's acknowledgment of Forel's support: "I feel that you find the book somewhat too theoretical and obscurely written, which is moreover my wife's opinion too. I found it equally difficult and unavoidable to go through in a clear way all these subtleties (6–27–09)." As Semon awaited reviews of the book, his lingering doubts blossomed into blatant self-disparagement. In a remarkable passage that all too clearly warns of an approaching depression, Semon went beyond expressing gratitude for Forel's help and awarded him actual credit for the successful communication of ideas that he pictured himself as incapable of articulating: "I lack completely and cannot achieve the ability to express the most difficult and abstract questions in concrete form. . . . Who would bother at all about my indigestible tract on the

Mneme without your presentation of the essentials, imbued with a quite different life. I thank you for this a thousand times (12–5–09)." A denial of the value of one's most prized endeavor suggests approaching trouble in almost any human circumstance. It is doubly serious in the case of an intellectual isolate, who requires above all an unshakable faith in his own capability and acumen.

As the first months of 1910 unfolded, it became increasingly obvious to Semon that few besides Forel were going to seriously consider his treatise on memory. *Die Mneme* had at least garnered attention and put him at the center of an enlivening controversy; however negative its reception, at least people argued about it. Now Semon was simply ignored, and he wrote about it to Forel with unknowing and moribund irony: "If it were not for *you*, the thing would, at best, not be bothered about before I had been dead for twenty years (6–19–10)." The silence had immediate effects. Semon abandoned further work in the area of memory, and decided to mount a new series of arguments defending some of the biological theories put forward in *Die Mneme*. Semon believed that he was returning to trenches in which the action would be fast and furious, and braced himself for some bruising encounters on the way to an ultimate vindication of Mneme: "I think I am in a position to undermine absolutely and definitely the objections which have been raised against the Mneme (Semon to Forel, 4–3–10)."

But times had changed since 1904. The biological issues addressed by Semon had become problems for laboratory experiment, and new *data* were of interest to biologists, not the sharpening and reformulation of old arguments that Semon offered. His new series of articles defending *Die Mneme* brought him none of the combat that he hoped for and needed; the dreadful truth was that almost nobody cared about his latest crusade. Semon had now reached the most demonic impasse of his tenure as a private scholar: His work was ignored on all fronts. He sought refuge in Forel, and depicted his plight in words of quiet resignation: "I am heartily grateful to you that you refer to my work so often and so influentially. Without your help all my efforts would go unremarked. Even now the tendency is still to pass me over in deathly silence (5–28–11)." Incapable of mustering the freewheeling sarcasm of earlier years—there were no longer any clearly marked enemies to deflate—Semon could only surrender himself to a bleak present and passively envisage a brighter future: "One must just be patient and trust that truth will win through, if not today, then in a decade, or twenty years. If anything helps it is your firm support (5–28–11)."

It can be a jolting psychological reality when propitious visions of the future are only fractionally helpful in reducing the strains of the present, and Semon soon enough discovered this for himself. Sapped by his strenuous work in defense of *Die Mneme*, and burdened by his intellectual solitude, Richard Semon could no longer evade what he had been slowly heading toward since 1909: He endured a nervous breakdown in the summer of 1912. Recurrent insomnia and hyperexcitability combined to blot out his productive energies; he required complete rest and sought shelter with Maria in the mountain air of the Alps. Recovery was slow and difficult. On his best days, Semon could read in brief doses and engage in light correspondence; sometimes he slept through the night with only one or two minor interruptions. After three weeks in the mountains, Semon admitted to Forel that his rehabilitation had so far been "only moderately successful." He went on to retract his earlier acceptance of Forel's offer to regularly attend one of the large annual psychological conferences: "Given my deteriorating health, regular attendance at the annual meetings is not right for me (9–6–12)."

In the wake of his nervous breakdown, the caution and reticence that had characterized Semon's personality since 1909 accelerated in an alarming fashion. After withdrawing from the congress, Semon also reconsidered Forel's earlier request for him to lecture on the pathology of memory in Zurich. Semon had been working on a book exploring the 'pathology of Mneme' at irregular intervals since 1905, and he had several times expressed to Forel his willingness to publicly lecture on the subject. But now his decision was guided by self-doubt. Semon's letter of September 13, 1912 to Forel reveals the anguish of a man who has turned professionally gun-shy:

> If I take it upon myself to recommend certain innovations to an auditorium of professionals in a field in which I can with the best will in the world not be considered to have any authority, then these innovative suggestions must only be the fruit of thorough and conscientious study. A year ago I thought that I would be able to accept immediately . . . [however] it will need many years concentrated work before I can bring results or even suggestions before the public. I am a slow worker and accustomed to letting things ripen gradually. . . . Were I to change my methods, I would, as I am doing for once, produce impoverished work and thus harm my case. And that I don't want. It would make me most unhappy. Nor could you wish it. You would be sadly disappointed.

Semon never delivered that lecture. Shackled by incertitude, he carefully avoided terrain that posed intellectual threats.

With convalescence almost completed, Richard and Maria left the mountains in October 1912, and their arrival home brought an unexpected reversal of Semon's psychological fortunes. He was suddenly able to concentrate on work for sizeable chunks of time, regained some measure of confidence in his abilities and, as he triumphantly informed Forel, "even my insomnia is better and promises to disappear altogether (10–2–12)." Semon's reawakened energy brought with it a return of the buoyant critical spirit that he had lost over the last few years. For instance, he explained to Forel that his latest biological efforts were ignored largely because of the recent rise of Mendelism in biology. This approach to heredity, Semon realized, dramatically contrasted with his own. But instead of disparaging his personal failure to keep abreast of the new trends, the resurgent Semon taunted those who were too easily swayed by the latest scientific fashions: "It seems that every new discovery, and Mendelism is surely one of these, has a confusing effect on weak minds . . . so that they think that the floor is shaking, whereas it is merely their legs and heads (10–2–12)."

Those few lines leap out like a blazing comet of hope against the dull background of Semon's post-1909 psychological erosion, but it was a comet that faded as quickly as it appeared. His remission was unmercifully brief. Within three weeks he was back in the Alps searching again for an elusive inner tranquility: "I am not doing any work here and yet I still suffer from insomnia, three or four hours of good, deep sleep and then I wake up in the middle of the night and cannot get to sleep at all. Very burdensome (Semon to Forel, 10–19–12)." The internal unrest continued to plague Semon throughout 1913, as work on the pathology of Mneme chugged along in a sporadic fashion. On top of his own difficulties, some old ghosts returned to haunt: Maria succumbed to a variety of ailments during the year. Most serious was an attack of phlebitis that kept her hospitalized for over a month. An anxious Semon did little other than "take care of the very helpless invalid (Semon to Forel, 9–8–13)" for the duration of the illness. One of the few bits of bright news to arrive in an otherwise dark year was communicated by Haeckel just before Christmas. The last volume of research from Semon's Australian journey had been published in Jena, and sales of the large folio were surprisingly brisk. Semon expressed his 'joyful astonishment' at the welcome news, and profusely thanked Haeckel and others in Jena who had supervised publication of the research after his departure. The rekindled memory of his intrepid days as an adventurer seemed part of a different world to the now-sedentary Semon; as he remarked to Forel, "How far those old works lie behind me now (1–4–14)."

As 1913 drew to a close, the Semons once again changed their Munich address. They stayed within Schwabing, moving just a few blocks northwest to Hohenzollernstrasse 130. Their new residence was neither as ideally situated nor as picturesque as their old one on the Martiusstrasse. It is not entirely clear why they moved—their recent difficulties might have cast a pall on life at Martiusstrasse 7 or their finances might have been overtaxed[8]—but the effort of relocating proved stressful. Semon sent the enfeebled Maria to stay with relatives to guard against potential overexertion, and organized the time-consuming ordeal alone. They had completely settled in their new home by December, and after Semon returned from visiting a snowy Berlin at Christmas he looked forward to immersing himself in work. When he wrote to Forel just after

---

8. One of the most intriguing—and perplexing—question about Semon's post-Jena existence concerns his finances. Richard and Maria managed to buy a house, travel extensively, and meet their medical costs even though neither of them had a full-time job. It is unlikely that the income from Semon's books was substantial enough to cover these and other costs. Semon's parents both died in debt, and there is no evidence that Felix ever provided him with money. Since Maria willingly left her husband (and her children), it is difficult to believe that she was able to obtain any support from her former husband. The one remaining possible source of income is Maria's family. Unfortunately, I have no evidence to support or discredit the hypothesis that Maria's family provided the Semons with financial support during the years of their marriage.

the New Year in 1914, Semon expressed hope that both the internal and external barriers to his progress had been surmounted, and concluded by communicating a seemingly innocent wish: "I hope that I shall be spared further distractions." Although he was granted peace for awhile, the tranquility lasted only months. Like a thunderstorm about to shatter the calm of a summer's day, the black clouds of 1914 were swiftly approaching.

6

Prisoners in their Cells

CONSEQUENCES OF THE GREAT WAR

When war erupted in August 1914, few informed Germans were surprised. International crises involving the Fatherland had been common for almost a decade, relations with Britain were increasingly marked by mutual suspicion, and tax money endlessly flowed into Admiral von Tirpitz's burgeoning naval fleet. These and other developments contributed to a growing sense of internal tension during the pre-1914 decade, and an atmosphere of domestic uncertainty threatened to destroy the nationalistic spirit that had been established in 1871. The coming of war put a temporary curb on the rising tide of friction: Germans responded to the emerging conflict with unrestrained enthusiasm. The novelist Ernst Gläser, an elder German who had observed the decline in national purpose with some alarm, embraced the war in a spirit typical of many fellow countrymen: "At last life had regained an ideal significance. The great virtues of humanity . . . fidelity, patriotism, readiness to die for an ideal . . . were triumphing over the trading and shopkeeping spirit (cited in Craig, 1978, p. 340)." The noted historian Friedrich Meinecke offered a similar perspective: "The exaltation of spirit experienced during the August days of 1914 . . . is one of the most precious, unforgettable memories of the highest sort (Meinecke, 1950, p. 25)."

As most of his countrymen expressed elation at the prospect of achieving new glory, Richard Semon struggled to sort out his opposing feelings about the Fatherland's military venture. Although it had remained dormant for awhile, the conflict in Semon's personality between "Germanic-man" and "Universalman" suddenly came charging to the surface. The part of Semon that had witnessed the great unification parade in 1871 led him to hope for new national triumphs, but the man whose travels convinced him of the strong threads binding all humanity abhorred the prospect of international suicide. This psychological split in Semon's response to the coming of war was clearly displayed in his correspondence. Writing to Otto Lubarsch several months after the beginning of the conflict, Semon described the rush of patriotic fever that gripped him, and expressed frustration that he could not personally serve in the army (Lubarsch, 1920, p. xli). Too young for the Franco-Prussian war, Semon was now too old for the Great War. But his nationalistic visions of conquest were tempered by a growing awareness that German victory could be achieved only by paying a high price in human misery—a price that seemed increasingly terrible as the war continued. By mid-December 1914, Semon's revulsion in the face of mass suffering almost entirely overshadowed his patriotic zeal. What first seemed like a noble Germanic cause had turned into a colossal human folly, and when August Forel informed Semon of his pacifist plan for the establishment of a "United States of the Earth," he responded with unqualified assent: "I am in complete agreement with you, that the goal which you describe can and shall be attained, and that the leaders simply must begin to work towards it in spite of the backslide which we are now experiencing and which is shaking everything (12–20–14)."

Semon's disgust with the "backslide of humanity" grew sufficiently intense to infiltrate the one domain that he had hoped he could isolate from it: The pursuit of science. As the stark realities of the war became increasingly apparent, Semon regarded the detached contemplation of scientific intricacies as an inappropriate occupation; matters of purely abstract concern paled in comparison with the concrete brutality that encompassed Europe. Only the numbing effect of time, Semon realized, would permit him to work again with interest: "It is not easy for me to concentrate in these times on abstract questions of a general nature which can wait. However, the dulling power of habit is effective even in the face of the most awful events so that I am beginning to regain some of my interest in scientific problems as time goes by (Semon to Forel, 12–20–14)."

Semon's various responses to the onset of war were entirely private expressions. He had never been a politically active scientist, and did not use the deluge of 1914 as an occasion to publicly vent his opinions. His behavior was not typical of many other scientists. Accusations and counter-accusations were heatedly exchanged between scientists on opposing sides of the battle from the instant that war was declared. Many outspoken polemicists were eminent senior scientists, and two of them were aging members of the old guard who had figured prominently in Semon's life. An outraged Ernst Haeckel publicly decried the "egotistic spirit, the rottenness of character within (Haeckel, 1916, p. 148)" that characterized Germany's "treacherous, murderous English brother (p. 157)." Haeckel depicted the war in much the same manner that he presented scientific issues. One side was unambiguously right—his side—and the enemy was unambiguously wrong. Haeckel fulminated over England's "bloodguiltiness (p. 158)" in the war, and although he professed to regret that "England's egoistic envy and boundless megalomania have made us her bitterest enemy (p. 161)", he unswervingly blamed the entire calamity on "the deep rooted, brutal national egoism of the English (p. 156)." Haeckel believed that German military conquest was inevitable, and warned the English and their allies that the maligned German nation would justifiably negotiate a tough peace: "At all events, when the treaty of peace is concluded we must demand a considerable extension of the German Empire (p. 168)."

Haeckel's frenzied claims were expressed in various books and pamphlets, but are perhaps best known because of his endorsement of the notorious "Manifesto of the German University Professors and Men of Science (see Lutz, 1932, pp. 74–78)." This extraordinary document, addressed to "the Civilized world," belligerently affirmed Germany's innocence in the war, insisted that the widespread reports of excessive brutality by German soldiers were intentional fabrications of the enemy, and justified German expansion with the assertion that "Were it not for German militarism, German civilization would long since have been extirpated. . . . The German army and the German people are one (Lutz, 1932, p. 75)." Ninety-two prominent German intellectuals endorsed the inflammatory document, published during the first year of the war, and the list of signers contained some familiar names: Physicists Max Planck, Walter Nernst, and Wilhelm Röntgen, chemist Wilhelm Ostwald, psychologist Wilhelm Wundt, and mathematician Felix Klein were among those who publicly justified the German military venture.

In contrast with Haeckel's fury, August Forel endured the war with dignity and strength. As a resident of neutral Switzerland and long-time pacifist, Forel assumed an important role among non-aligned peacemakers. He published pacifist literature throughout the conflict, was a leading delegate at the International Peace Conference in 1915, and directly countered the inflammatory arguments of belligerents such as Haeckel.[1] Forel's efforts seem all the more remarkable when one considers that he suffered a stroke at the onset of the conflict, and was prey to glaucoma during subsequent years. He endured these handicaps with admirable aplomb, and also calmly weathered the storm of abuse that he received from the warring camps: "We neutral pacifists had gradually to accustom ourselves to the calumnious charges published in the Press of the two belligerent parties. Both were suffering from war psychosis. I was attacked by both camps in articles full of excited abuse (1937, p. 309–310)."[2] Although

---

1. Forel went as far as to write an open letter to Haeckel in response to indignant public statements of German innocence made by Haeckel just prior to the publication of the Manifesto. Forel noted the numerous previous occasions on which Haeckel had unambiguously advocated German military domination of Europe, and warned that such expansionism would be resisted to the end: "If these [Haeckel's] assertions have any reality, then all foreign countries, and even our little Switzerland, will be compelled to defend themselves against your schemes of hegemony to the last drop of their blood (Forel, 1937, pp. 303–304)." Haeckel never answered Forel's complaint.
2. Forel was deeply shaken by the horror of World War I, and culminated his personal search for peace by turning to the Baha'i religion shortly after the war's termination: "It is the true religion of the welfare of human society, it has neither priests nor dogma, and it binds together all the human beings who inhabit this little globe (Forel, 1937, p. 342)." He died in 1931.

Richard Semon did not participate in the political controversies that involved the great figures from his life, he formed strong opinions concerning the issues involved. Men such as Haeckel, he believed, furthered the cause of destruction by fueling the fires of international hatred. When he wrote to Forel at the close of 1914, Semon apologized for the appearance of the professors' "Manifesto" and lamented its consequences:

> I deeply regret the pitiful babble of some German professors such as Haeckel, Lasson, and Ostwald, not only because it is misleading but because it is positively harmful to their painfully struggling country. These people are then put forward by the enemy as the leading minds of the nation. One neglects to add that both Haeckel and Lasson are over 80, that Lasson was never a leading mind, and that for the last 10 years Ostwald has been no more than a pompous ass and a businessman. The world is divided by these people in an unbelievably childish manner. Senile dementia is the only excuse for it (12–28–14).

As the war moved into 1915, many outspoken leaders at home believed that Germany had attained an unsurpassable military advantage. The extremist Pan-German League, for instance, presented the Prime Minister with a document demanding radical extensions of the German Empire that was predicated on the assumption that Germany would "dictate the peace." German princes, smugly confident of victory, argued over who was entitled to what portions of enemy territory; as one prominent historian has noted, "The striking thing about the pretensions of these and other federal princes was their common assumption that Germany would, as a matter of course, acquire all of the areas for which they were competing (Craig, 1978, p. 359)." The growing expectation of imminent victory penetrated many spheres of German society, and a sense of this mounting confidence can be gleaned from Semon's correspondence with Otto Lubarsch. In a letter of January 26, 1915, Lubarsch painted a rosy picture of German military prospects and glowingly informed Semon that victory was near. Although Semon's part of the correspondence has not been preserved, the following passage from Lubarsch's letter suggests rather clearly that Semon shared the general optimism, but rejected the popular view that a victorious Germany should demand major territorial concession: "I am in full agreement with your last letter concerning our prospects for war and peace; from the beginning I thought that the naive opinion that we are entitled to the whole of Belgium and Poland, and the desirable parts of France, is quite foolish. Even if we are able to 'dictate the peace' . . . we would only be allowed what is absolutely necessary for our political security and economic development!"

Comforted by the conviction that peace would soon arrive, Semon was able to work enthusiastically for much of 1915. He had intended to immerse himself in his long-planned book on memory disorders, *Pathology of Mneme*, but as he penetrated more deeply into the subject he became increasingly involved with the fundamental problem of consciousness and the brain. He toyed with the prospect of completely devoting himself to the analysis of this ageless enigma, retreated several times to the less abstract domain of memory pathology, and finally conceded that the consciousness problem had to be confronted before he could do full justice to the *Pathology of Mneme*.[3]

The re-immersion in work also emphasized a depressing reality that even the horror of the war could not erase: Semon's scientific endeavors had passed into almost complete oblivion. Despair over his neglected work was not, of course, new to Semon, but one disturbing by-product of the war made it particularly hard to bear anew. Correspondence across national borders was exceedingly difficult during the conflict; the letters that did cross were closely monitored. Accordingly, Semon's contact with August Forel became distressingly infrequent. Stripped of the regular psychological nourishment that he had come to expect from Forel, and imbued with a dawning awareness that visions of an early peace were grossly inaccurate, Semon closed 1915 by reaching out to his Swiss ally with some familiar words:

> It has long been clear to me that nobody has understood my efforts nearly so well as you have, and that for a man such as you to be captured by my thoughts is an invaluable encouragement, especially when I see how utterly indifferently the specialists have treated my work. . . . When I am able to move onward in my work, and when this mass psychosis, this acute mania of the human species, finally ends, I look forward to the pleasure of visiting you again (12–22–15).

1916 brought little relief to Europe and new problems to Semon. Ever since the beginning of hostilities, Maria Semon had been feverishly working as an organizer of war relief efforts. Maria's fluctuating health had long been a concern to her husband, and she had collapsed under straining conditions in earlier years. Richard Semon nervously observed his wife's newly deteriorating condition and pleaded with Maria to cut back her long hours of volunteer labor; the determined woman ignored his admonitions and continued to work without respite. By the summer of 1916 she had reached the brink of nervous collapse. No longer able to resist Richard's entreaty to seek repose, she laid aside her work and accompanied him to a remote sanctuary in the Bavarian Alps. They remained in their mountain shelter from early August to late September; Semon played nurse to his recovering patient and watched with relief as Maria slowly regained her strength.

Perhaps the most numbing reality of 1916—for Semon and all Europeans—concerned the length of the war. The early predictions of a quick and decisive skirmish had proven hopelessly inaccurate. Europe was on its way to a fiasco of previously unimagined duration and few were prepared for its scope. Semon, who had expected the war to end well before 1916, expressed his bewilderment in a simple passage written to Forel: "It is now more than two years.

---

3. Semon never completed the ill-fated *Pathology of Mneme*, and to my knowledge no traces of it have been preserved. He did eventually complete the bulk of his essay on consciousness and the brain, and entrusted publication of the short book to Otto Lubarsch (Semon, 1920).

FIGURE 7. An aging Richard Semon.

When will we finally have peace once again (7–8–16)?" Although Semon could not answer that question, he became possessed by a growing conviction that Germany was on the brink of a massive defeat. The source of Semon's anxiety is not clear—most Germans in 1916 were still confident of eventual victory—but his nervous premonition of disaster altered his perception of the conflict. Before 1916, Semon's approach to the war was dominated by the concerns of "Universal man." He denounced the belligerent nationalistic propaganda of extremist professors, warned against excessive territorial demands in the event of German victory, and was upset by the suffering of all participants in the "mass psychosis"—not just Germans.

Toward the end of 1916 Semon began a retreat into fantasies of German glory. In a remarkable essay entitled "Das Land Goethes" (The Land of Goethe), Semon implored his countrymen to look to their heroic past as a source of inspiration for the current crisis.[4] The essay is replete with exotic images of intrepid German warriors from distant ages; it is characterized by the sort of bizarre romanticism so frequently encountered in the writings of Haeckel. Semon depicted the struggles of Thor, the ancient German God of Thunder, as he marched up the river Wimur into battle against the evil enemy. Although villains damned up the river and created torrential currents in an effort to crush Thor, the undaunted German hero simply donned a pair of iron gloves, enclosed himself with protective belts, and defiantly waved his magic wand at the onrushing river; he secured his triumph in spite of the obstacles placed in his way. Semon cast the contemporary dilemma of the German people in similar terms:

> Also today, the German people are striding through the rising Wimur, fighting against the highest currents. They have prepared themselves with strong belts, iron gloves, and magic wands, as did Thor during his time, and have thought and acted as this God of the farmers and warriors, who symbolized for the people in ancient times their peaceful work and their warring ability (cited in Lubarsch, 1920, p. xl).

One senses an eruption of Semon's youthful experiences behind this childlike allegory. His boyhood observation of patriotic fervor on the day that Germany was unified, the nationalistic pride that pervaded the Kaiser Wilhelm Gymnasium, and the reverence for German ideals that overshadowed his identification as a Jew all lie just below the surface of his mythical depiction of the Teutonic spirit.

By 1917 Semon was no longer alone in his vision of an emerging German apocalypse. The United States entered the war in April, plunging Germany into a torrent of political confusion that was exacerbated by the first major domestic strikes of the war. On July 6th, Reichstag deputy Matthias Erzberger delivered a speech in which he stunned many Germans by painting a gloomy picture "which for the first time gave the German people some idea of the true war situation (Balfour, 1975, p. 378)." Shortages of fuel, food, and clothing became increasingly commonplace as the year unfolded. The awareness of approaching defeat was particularly dolorous for those who had earlier believed that Ger-

---

4. It is unlikely that Semon ever published this essay. There is no record of it in the major German libraries or archives, and the sole description of it is found in Otto Lubarsch's (1920) biographical sketch of Semon.

man conquest was both morally appropriate and tactically inevitable. Ernst Haeckel, 83 years old and in failing health, watched in bewilderment as his visions of a new Europe under enlightened German rule were shattered. He wrote to Semon from Jena in May 1917, and waxed nostalgic as he contemplated the ongoing transformations in a world that he could no longer comprehend: "We talked a great deal of you and remembered with pleasure the *beautiful* 'good old times' which we had together here in the last 30 years. They are *gone!* There will come an entirely *new structure* out of the destroyed cultural world, and nobody can say *how* it will turn out. Unfortunately my mood is more and more pessimistic (5–2–17)."[5]

1917 also proved particularly trying for Semon, and he terminated an eight month drought of correspondence with Forel in bleak spirits: "It is a long time since I have written to you. Because in these times one cannot write so freely from the heart and mind, this constraint easily leads to total silence, the more so since I have had hardly anything positive to report (5–16–17)." He wrote again just a month later, and thanked Forel for sending along reprints of some recent articles. Semon also noted the evolution of his own essay on the relationship of brain to mind and, as in previous years, downplayed his efforts in comparison to Forel's: "Your essay on the human capacity for knowledge is wonderful. I hope that my present work will make a further contribution and entirely of the kind that you define (6–6–17)." He closed by informing Forel of his intention to take Maria to the mountains for some six weeks; work had again made her weary.

Richard and Maria quietly passed the summer in secluded hills near Salzburg. The mountains had become a necessary refuge for both of them during periods of excessive strain, and they easily fell under the soothing spell of the Alps once again. Semon used the time to ponder some of the unexpected personal tolls that the war had taken upon him. His wife had exhausted herself organizing relief efforts. He was largely isolated from his closest friend and sole scientific ally. He had watched his former mentor pathetically attempt to justify a military expansion of the German Empire. And his brother was on the opposite side of the battle.

FELIX AND THE WAR

Although Richard and Felix Semon saw little of each other during the years that Felix lived in England, the brothers did maintain a correspondence. But the coming of war put an end to their letters, as communication between English-

---

5. Haeckel died in 1919 when his health finally failed at the age of 85. He had been disillusioned with humankind for many years, and welcomed the end when it came. His readiness to die was expressed in a 1917 letter to Semon: "My children will report to you that my senile regression has been growing steadily since Easter as I prepare myself for the desired last journey (into the Bhuddist Nirvana) with resigned *serenity* (5–20–17)."

men and Germans became impossible.[6] Richard Semon, then, had no way of knowing how his brother fared during the war. He did not fare well.

Anti-German sentiment had swept through England like a tempestuous storm within days of the war's onset. Envenomed literature appeared daily in the newspapers, as "Racial hatred . . . went far beyond anything that the Government can have possibly desired or welcomed (Marwick, 1978, p. 50)." Like most other German residents of Britain, Felix Semon had to brace himself for a torrent of abuse from a citizenry prepared to hate all things German. Although his professional status and financial security partially shielded him from what H. G. Wells labeled the "shameful campaign against harmless Anglicised Germans (cited in Semon, 1926, p. 302)," Felix soon enough learned that even he was not immune to the atmosphere of suspicion that permeated the air around him. During the Autumn of 1914, a rumor that Semon was secretly a German spy circulated through his village. Felix's neighbors suspected that he had carefully concealed some concrete platforms under his lawns, and alleged that "I had secretly constructed them as emplacements for German giant howitzers (1926, p. 302)." Felix openly requested an inspection of his property by the police, and he was cleared of the ludicrous charge; the tone of his subsequent existence, however, had been established.

After the sinking of the Lusitania in May 1915, an outraged British public demanded disturbingly radical measures for dealing with naturalized Britons of German descent: The phrase "Intern them all" became a common admonition after the Lusitania incident. Felix felt caught in a delicate bind. He too abhorred the German war methods and genuinely wished to publicly rebuke them. He also knew, however, that in the wake of the Lusitania sinking any such efforts might well be interpreted as a thinly concealed ploy to protect his own interests. For a while he did nothing. But when a letter was published in *The Times* on May 12th that implored "distinguished Germans in our midst (1926, p. 306)" to speak out against German atrocities, suggesting that silence at such a critical moment could be interpreted as evidence of indecisive loyalty, Felix was forced to respond. He acted decisively. On May 15th Semon sent a letter to *The Times* in which he clearly restated his loyalty to Britain and unambiguously expressed his "detestation" of the "inhuman methods" of German warfare: "I beg to say that I emphatically abhor the barbarous methods, one and all, employed by Germany (1926, p. 308)."

The letter received wide notice in Britain, and was greeted throughout the country as an important statement by a leading figure of German descent. Although pleased with this response, Felix had not anticipated an official reply from the Fatherland—but German reaction was swift and ruthless. Felix was

---

6. In his *Autobiography*, Felix remembered with regret the end to his correspondence with Richard during the war years: "It had been a great deprivation to me to be unable to communicate with him (1926, p. 329)." It is interesting to note that this is one of the few pieces of evidence that the Semon brothers communicated with one another after Richard moved to Munich.

denounced as a traitor to the Fatherland and expelled from the Berlin and Vienna Laryngological Societies; he was later stripped of his German scientific honors. He endured these demeaning public calumnies in reasonable spirits, and could take comfort in the fact that other outspoken British scientists had been accorded similar treatment. Felix, however, soon received a more damaging blow. When he retired from professional life in 1909, Felix had carefully chosen Dr. George Finder, an eminent German laryngologist, as editorial successor of his beloved journal, *Semon's Internationales Centralblatt für Laryngologie*. But Finder, a patriotic Teuton, did not permit past favors to dampen his polemical proclivities and publicly blasted Felix's stance against the Fatherland. He backed up his indignant words with an action that wounded Felix in the core of his being: Finder removed Felix's name from the title of the journal that he created some 30 years earlier.

As Felix slowly recovered from the shock of this humiliating event, the British medical community rose to his defense.[7] But public expressions of sympathy did little to ease the tribulations of the offended Felix, and he continued to brood over the incident long after the initial shock waves had passed: "Of all the distressing experiences that fell to my lot during the war, this caused me most pain. The *Centralblatt* was my own offspring, and it was indeed bitter to be disowned by it, and betrayed by the man I had selected as my successor. *Amicus certus in re incerta cernitur* (1926, p. 310)."

As Felix bemoaned the iniquitous German responses to his letter of May 12th, he gradually became aware that his public stand against Germany had done little to ease British trepidation concerning his status as a German native. Semon's old friends from upper-class London society conspicuously avoided a man whose continued acquaintance could only cast doubt upon their own patriotic inclinations. And many fellow laryngologists found it all too easy to avoid an aging colleague once the initial sparks raised by Felix's controversial letter receded into the background. Sir Felix Semon was no longer welcome at gatherings of the London elite; the medical profession that once lionized him had no more honors to confer. Felix was caught unprepared for the rigors of his newly enforced existence as a recluse, and his memoirs reflect a dazed man attempting to sort out his confusion:

> The longer this unspeakable war lasts the more we feel our loneliness. A few
> of our local acquaintances still invite or call upon us, and we still exchange

---

7. The prestigious journal *Lancet*, for instance, noted the appropriation of Semon's German scientific honors as an unfortunate consequence of a passionately contested war, but held that Finder's action constituted a far graver transgression: "the action of Professor Finder . . . in removing the name of Semon from the famous scientific periodical which he founded is on a different plane. Semon's *Centralblatt* was the only international rhino-laryngological journal. It is simply an accident that it is published in Germany, and the deletion of the founder's name is an international offence (1915, pp. 404–405)."

cordial letters with some of our English and American friends; but the large majority of our English acquaintances . . . have become perfectly mute. One lives only for one's sad and painful thoughts. I endeavour to distract myself by working at these memoirs, by reading, and by walks with my darling wife; but what a sad decline of a once richly blessed life (1926, p. 313)!

Time passed and the permanence of his new status as an anchorite became clear, but Felix could not summon the strength to effectively battle the demons that haunted him. As 1915 drew to a close, he ruefully depicted his predicament in words tinged with self-pity:

My reflections on the last day of the most miserable year of my life are necessarily sad. Because I have had the courage of my opinions, I have been ostracised by my native country, because I was born a German I am boycotted by my adopted country. Outwardly the people are courteous enough and a few faithful friends do not desert us. But we live the life of hermits. Such are our prospects for the New Year (1926, p. 316)!

Felix's state of mind changed little over the remaining five years of his life. His diary entries reflect a bleak, uneventful existence made bearable only by the companionship of his wife. The conclusion of the war did not ease his isolation, and he also contracted a variety of serious illnesses. He weakened considerably in the winter of 1921. By late February Felix felt close to death, and he welcomed the prospect of relief from a life turned sour: "except my own family, I have nothing left that interests me, and if I knew that tomorrow morning I should not awake, I should go as quietly to bed as if a long life were in store for me (1926, p. 335)." He died a few days later with his family gathered around him.

MUNICH, 1918: JOURNEY'S END

Germany entered the final year of the Great War in a rapidly deteriorating state. Strikes in the major cities became increasingly frequent, and the necessities of life were in short supply. The German people had wearied of war, and sporadic outbursts of domestic violence warned the government that the winter of 1918 might be a chaotic one: "The January strikes convinced the leaders of the Majority Socialist party that, unless there was some tangible evidence of progress toward peace and political reform, there would be new violence and they might lose all control over the population (Craig, 1978, p. 392)." But power in Germany had fallen into the hands of one man—General Erich Ludendorff—and he rejected the pleas for peace while stubbornly maintaining that military victory was still possible.

Most Germans anxiously followed each new development with keen anticipation. Richard Semon, however, was largely numb to the outcome of events in the world around him—Maria's health had failed again. Semon originally believed that her latest illness could be simply ascribed to exhaustion; another sojourn in the mountains, he hoped, would prove sufficient for recovery. He soon enough discovered that the problem was more serious than he had initially imagined. Severe intestinal pain, combined with a persistent fever, sapped Maria's strength at an alarming rate. Semon confessed to Forel that neither he nor Maria's physician could specify the source of her illness; they could only continue to probe for its cause and pray for a quick reversal of her sinking fortunes.

By the end of the month a diagnosis of cancer had been confirmed. Semon strained to hold himself together. He decided not to let Maria know that she was dying, and drew upon waning energies to convincingly infuse her with hope. Otto Lubarsch recalled his friend's efforts during that difficult period: "Only a few weeks before her death he knew that he was going to lose her, and now he turned his whole mind to not only affectionately and devotedly caring for her, but above all concealing from her the seriousness of the illness (1920, p. xxix)." They passed hours together in quiet conversation, affirming that their tumultuous decision of 1897 had been justified by subsequent years; as Semon once confided to Lubarsch, "the exceedingly happy marriage that they had together for almost 19 years was proof to them that they were destined for each other, as they also lived for each other (p. xxix)."

She died shortly after Easter in 1918. Although Semon had tried to prepare himself for an event that he knew was inevitable, his desolation proved shattering. He tried to piece together his thoughts in a letter written to Forel just after Maria's passing:

> I thank you for your letter, and thank you too for your offer to come stay with you in Yvonne. Now, however, I must stay here. The first thing is my work, for me to come to myself once more. If only I were already at the point where I could concentrate on it. At the moment it is not possible at all, but I am convinced that it will only be possible again when the physical shock wears off. . . . It will not in any event give me any pleasure, but it at least gives me something to live for. Nobody can imagine the extent of the loneliness in which I am left. It is the consequence of a union of two individuals who over 20 years molded themselves ever closer and closer together.
>
> But I hope that when some time has gone by and this frightful war is over, I can come and spend some time with you. That will give me much pleasure. My wife, too, always looked upon you with such respect and gratitude, admired, yes loved you, and took such a heartfelt interest in you and in all your work (Semon to Forel, 4–13–18).

Semon remained a captive of his grief well into the summer. He had been able to work off depressions in the past, but he now found himself in unfamiliar emotional territory that permitted no easy escape. When Otto Lubarsch visited him in August, Semon was making his first tentative efforts to again find solace in science. Intellectual involvement came slowly, and he derived little satisfaction from his small progress; Semon admitted to Lubarsch that he feared he had lost much of his intellectual prowess. Semon also voiced his conviction that Germany had lost the war, and he forecast a catastrophic period for his country in the wake of defeat. In the face of such a barren landscape, Semon confided that he found comfort in the realization that he had nothing left to bind him to life and could leave it in peace when he desired. Lubarsch, shaken by the ominous tone of his friend's admission, did what he could to inject hope into Semon's panorama of melancholy: "I knew him so well that I realized that he would not be shaken by numerous replies, and sought only to convince him that his intellectual energies were still great enough to stop the intense state of turmoil (1920, p. xxxix)." Lubarsch's sermon had slight impact on his struggling comrade: Semon's perception survived the words of encouragement unscathed.

September 1st was August Forel's 70th birthday, and Semon wrote to convey his best wishes. The congratulations quickly turned into reflections, as Semon attempted to make peace with a life that was slipping through his fragile grasp:

> Since we celebrated your 60th birthday ten years have passed, but to me it seems as if only a few, although frightful years have gone by, years which have meant a shattering of our illusions about the cultural heights attained by Genus Humanum. On top of all this I was robbed a half year ago of the faithful partner who was the anchor of my personal life, and I have only very little left. Among the most valuable things, though, I include your friendship and the scientific camaraderie, the understanding, and the interest that you have accorded my scientific endeavors, which has so often been a support to me when my work found so little response, and provided an impetus for me to work on nevertheless. Your life work embraced an immeasurably wider area than mine, both scientifically and in a social sense, but even where it was far beyond my own circle of interest it always gave me the greatest stimulation and encouragement. I know that will be the case so long as we both shall live. . . . My present work is proceeding slowly. In parts it holds great difficulties for me, because at my age it is becoming difficult to find a firm foothold in strange areas unknown to me. When I begin to lose courage, often the thought that this work will also meet with your approval supports me (9–1–18).

Autumn 1918 brought nothing to ease Semon's despair. There had been a series of crushing German war losses in the summer—culminating with the calamitous "Black day of the German army" on August 8th—and by late September even top ranking figures conceded that defeat was imminent. Semon had long expected such an outcome and was not surprised by the accumulating military fiascos. He had not, however, foreseen the internal collapse of German society that materialized as the Fatherland's fate on the battlefield was sealed— and he had certainly not anticipated that Munich would be the center of social anarchy.

The Bavarian Revolution was spearheaded by the unlikely figure of Kurt Eisner, a Jewish journalist from Berlin who had been leading Socialist causes in

Munich since 1970.[8] Eisner was imprisoned for instigating anti-war strikes in early 1918, and obtained his release in mid-October. Once freed he promptly attempted to overthrow the government and the Bavarian monarchy. On November 3rd he implored a large crowd gathered at the Theresienweise, Munich's large open-air space that houses the Oktoberfest, to help establish a revolutionary Bavarian state and dissociate themselves from the government that had led them into a disastrous war. He gathered his forces at the Theresienweise on the afternoon of November 7th, led the revolutionaries on their way to a takeover of the city's major military outposts, and drafted a document declaring the triumph of the revolution in a crowded Munich beer hall at 11 o'clock that evening. The Munich Putsch had achieved an astonishingly rapid success, and declarations of the new revolutionary government were posted throughout the city by the morning of November 8th.[9]

Richard Semon read of the revolution in disbelief. The beloved German state whose establishment he witnessed as a child in Berlin had collapsed overnight just a mile from Semon's own home in the hands of an obscure intellectual rogue. His shock was intensified in the subsequent days and weeks. Taking their lead from the Eisner regime, revolutionary governments quickly appeared throughout a chaotic Germany. To exacerbate the widespread confusion, elation over the war's end on November 11th was severely tempered by the harsh Allied peace terms. Semon's faith in the heroic nature of the German people—a source of comfort even when all else in life was difficult—began to evaporate in the face of mounting hysteria.

As winter approached, Munich continued to be a center of political confusion. Elections were scheduled for January 1919, and numerous factions were competing for their share of power. During Christmas week, however, politics was of little concern to most residents: A wave of escapist dancing and drinking fever gripped a population that was fatigued by the consequences of war. The hedonistic mania also served to conceal a disturbing undercurrent of feeling that Munich was on the verge of massive violence against the revolutionary government. Reports of fighting in Berlin were widely circulated throughout the city during Christmas week, and the Eisner regime increasingly feared that it would not be able to keep the peace. The government took swift action. It authorized the formation of a *Bürgerwehr* (citizens militia) to help enforce the law and maintain an uneasy peace that threatened at any moment to erupt into

---

8. A detailed and absorbing account of this remarkable episode is chronicled by Mitchell (1965). The depiction of the events surrounding the Bavarian Revolution in the present chapter is based upon Mitchell's account, especially pp. 75–109, and pp. 198–211. See also Coper (1955) and Grunberger (1973).

9. Eisner's regime ended as suddenly and as dramatically as it began. During January and February 1919, Eisner "had been humiliated in the press, badgered in cabinet meetings, and vilified as a Jew and as a foreigner (Mitchell, 1965, p. 275)." About to resign on the morning of February 21st, he was assassinated in the street before he could do so.

bloodshed. Word of the *Bürgerwehr* was published throughout Munich early on December 27th, and the city buzzed with apprehension at the prospect of emerging chaos.

Richard Semon may have seen news of the *Bürgerwehr* posted while walking on the crisp morning of December 27th; perhaps he never saw it at all. But he chose that day to make a decision that had been brewing inside for months. He ached in solitude, worked without satisfaction, and felt like a stranger in a world that had come unhinged. With his judgment secure, Semon reached out to August Forel once more, searching this time for a different kind of understanding than he had sought in the past:

27–12–18   Hohenzollernstr. 130
                                                        München

Dearest friend!

The last letter that I shall write is addressed to you. I strongly suspect that it will not meet with your approval when you hear that I am voluntarily bidding life farewell. Nor would I have relinquished it and would have sought (as I have sought) the strength in work to support the terrible desolation into which I have been cast by the death of my incomparable life-partner. Work, however, has become impossible, for my brain, the Mneme above all, is ever-increasingly giving way. In many this makes itself apparent before the age of 80, in me it can be seen 20 years in advance. I have an hereditary disposition towards it. It was apparent in my mother in the same way when she was 60, at 70 it was already very noticeable, and when she died at 83 it was unquestionably senile dementia. As I have partaken of the apple of knowledge, I recognize the first signs and do not wish to disfigure my lifework by an end of diminished quality. Without work there is nothing in life for me. Nor do I have anyone to care for, and leave no gap behind me. And so, inasmuch as you understand me, pardon me.

You, respected friend, I have an exceptional amount to thank for: extraordinary intellectual stimulation, energetic advancement of my efforts and thoughts. I am leaving my last work, 'Consciousness and Brain Processes,' half-finished. Since, as I think, the fruitful kernel is clearly distinguishable in the six chapters so far completed, I have seen to it that it shall be published as the torso that it is. I regret that I shall now not hear your opinion of it.

And so, fare you well. May all go well for you and yours. My heart is filled with admiration and gratitude towards you.

                                       Your true,

                                       Richard Semon

Semon posted the letter before retiring to Maria's bedroom. He carefully spread a German flag across her bed and placed himself upon it. Staring at the ceiling, he pointed a gun at his heart. Outside, the citizens of Munich busily prepared for the turbulent weeks ahead.

FIGURE 8. August Forel at 70.

RICHARD SEMON: SOME FINAL PERSPECTIVES

During the nine months between Maria's death and his own suicide, Richard Semon maintained close contact with two people: Otto Lubarsch and August Forel. It is revealing to consider how these men viewed Semon's decision to take his own life. Both Lubarsch and Forel agreed upon the two major causes of

Semon's suicide—the death of his wife and the collapse of Germany—and they also rejected Semon's belief that he had been afflicted by an early senility. Consider first Forel's response to Semon's death:

> Shortly after the death of his beloved wife, and greatly depressed by Germany's defeat, my friend Richard Semon shot himself in Munich. He was born in 1859; he had no children; and quite without reason he imagined that he was growing senile. . . . Semon's death grieved me profoundly; in scientific matters I thought as he did. His depression had deceived him as to his condition (1937, p. 319).

Lubarsch echoed a similar theme. He recalled that Semon "no longer had any strength (1920, p. xxxviii)" after Maria's death, but struggled on as best he could. The physical and moral deterioration of his beloved Fatherland, however, proved more than Semon could bear: "With this [Germany's collapse] fell the last that tied him to life (1920, p. xl)." Lubarsch, like Forel, believed that Semon's mental faculties remained intact until the end: "On the whole, he demonstrated unswerving mental sharpness (*Geistesschärfe*) and strength of will (*Willensstärke*) in what he did up until his last moments (1920, p. xliii)."

It is difficult to say whether or not Semon's belief that he was growing senile actually contributed to his suicide, or had any basis in reality at all. Events that seem like signs of senility to a person in Semon's depressed state might be accepted as normal consequences of aging by an emotionally healthy individual. What does seem clear is that the cataclysmic events of Semon's final months left him extremely prone to contemplation of a self-destructive act such as suicide. And when we add to these events the numerous episodes of depression that he endured for a decade prior to 1918—periods of sustained melancholy that occasionally erupted into nervous breakdown or self-disparagement—then his eventual suicide is hardly cause for surprise. Semon had long been fighting the psychological demons within himself; the loss of his wife and collapse of his country in swift succession sapped him of the internal resolve necessary to continue that fight.

Although Semon's suicide is largely comprehensible when viewed in light of the circumstances prevailing at the time of his death, the demise of his brother Felix as a helpless recluse amidst the confusion of the Great War raises a disturbing question: Why could *neither* of the Semon brothers summon the necessary resolve to successfully combat their respective woes? Countless thousands of human beings faced personal nightmares during the apocalyptic years of the war that were at least as fiendish as those confronted by Richard and Felix. Many of these people managed to rouse internal defenses that were sufficiently powerful to enable them to withstand the misery and eventually rebuild their lives. But neither Richard nor Felix Semon emerged a survivor: One brother actively ended his life, the other passively looked forward to its termination. A speculative interpretation of this circumstance is that part of the reason for Richard and Felix's inability to overcome their difficulties might have derived from a common source—their family experiences. Unfortunately, there is little evidence that provides a basis for evaluating such a possibility. Felix Semon's memoirs suggest that he was acutely aware of the shortcomings of both his mother (1926, p. 17) and father (p. 15), but we do not know just how this awareness affected Felix's own behavior. More important, we do not know how Richard Semon reacted to, or was influenced by, the characteristics of his parents.

The extent to which Richard Semon's suicide can be linked with either Felix's downfall or the influence of his parents is something that can only be contemplated as a possibility. Like much else buried in the past, the psychological roots of Semon's demise cannot be unambiguously specified. Perhaps it is most appropriate to conclude by viewing Semon's suicide as the last in a series of difficult decisions that he was able to execute during periods of major crisis in his life. Like his decision to convert and his decision to sacrifice a professorship for a woman, this final verdict was reached after lengthy reflection and internal debate; as Lubarsch recalled, "He made his decision to leave the world with a peaceful clarity and determination, and prepared everything exactly, just as he prepared with care for his scientific investigations and travels (1920, pp. xlii–xliii)." His was not a decision born of momentary passion nor was it a thinly concealed plea for understanding. Semon maintained a Prussian love of order to the end. By choosing to die on a German flag in his wife's bedroom he indicated in a simple and direct manner the reasons why he took his own life.

PART *II*

THE ISSUES

7

Organic Memory, Lamarckian Heresy, and Semon's Mneme

*D*uring his years in Munich, Richard Semon's scientific efforts centered upon the analysis of memory. Semon attempted to build a conceptual framework that elucidated the role played by memory in diverse psychological and biological functions, and used the insights of both psychology and biology in this theoretical endeavor. His efforts resulted in two major books: *Die Mneme* (1904) and *Die mnemischen Empfindungen* (1909). We saw in the foregoing chapters that both of these monographs were given a largely negative reception by the scientific community. *Die Mneme* was a controversial work that received widespread criticism; *Die mnemischen Empfindungen* was almost entirely ignored. Semon's letters to Forel indicated that he had invested a great deal of emotion in his work, and experienced considerable difficulty attempting to cope with the resistance and neglect that his two major books encountered. We now begin our attempt to understand what Semon was saying in those books and why his ideas met with the reception that they did. The course that we follow in the next few chapters first leads us to examine a number of aspects of turn-of-the-century biology and psychology, and ultimately brings us to some rather broad questions concerning the role of psychological processes in the pursuit of science. This chapter is concerned with the biological issues that were addressed by Semon, and focuses upon two contexts that constitute the relevant background to his work: (1) the controversy over neo-Lamarckian theories of evolution and heredity, and (2) the little-known scientific underworld of theorists who attempted to explain hereditary phenomena in terms of memory. Semon's own neo-Lamarckian theory of memory and heredity, and its tumultuous reception, are examined in light of these contexts. We explore both of the relevant contexts in some detail. The goal of these explorations is to enrich our appreciation of Semon's work, and to provide some insight into two of the most fascinating chapters of 19th-century science.

NEO-LAMARCKISM AND
THE CHALLENGE OF WEISMANN

Edward Drinker Cope, Philadelphia's eminent paleontologist and naturalist, conveyed exciting news to the readers of the *Penn Monthly Magazine* in May 1872:

> In earlier days, when information was distributed slowly and books were few, it was long before any new truth or doctrine reached the majority of people, still less was adopted by the ruling classes. But the modern theory of evolution has been spread everywhere with unexampled rapidity, thanks to our means of printing and transportation. It has met with remarkably rapid acceptance by those best qualified to judge of its merits, viz., the zoologists and botanists. (Cope, 1887, p. 2)

Cope's message accurately reflected the outcome of one of history's most rapid scientific revolutions. When Thomas Huxley informed Darwin in 1868 that "You will have the rare happiness to see your ideas triumphant during your lifetime (cited in Himmelfarb, 1968, p. 307)," he overestimated the time required for evolutionary conquest; Darwin's victory came within a decade. Haeckel and Huxley led a polemical assault that produced numerous converts and left few scientists doubting that the evolution of species constituted an essential truth of nature.

The argument for evolution itself, however, comprised just one part of the Darwinian package. A second and crucial component of the *Origin* could be accepted or rejected independently of the evolutionary thesis—the idea of natural selection. Natural selection constituted in many respects the key to the *Origin's* success. Darwin ingeniously employed the idea to render comprehensible a vast array of phenomena that other, pre-Darwinian evolutionists, had failed to explain in a systematic or convincing manner. But in the wake of the *Origin*, various naturalists who wholeheartedly endorsed the evolutionary thesis expressed grave doubts about natural selection as an all-sufficient mechanism of evolution. Cope, one of the more prominent skeptics, posed questions that he believed presented serious difficulties for advocates of natural selection (Cope, 1904). Although Cope conceded that natural selection might adequately explain the differential preservation of the fittest variations, he argued that it could not satisfactorily elucidate their *origin*. Further, Cope argued, natural selection had little to say concerning the *cause* of variations. And Cope as well as others found it difficult to accept the idea that the seemingly haphazard process of natural selection preserving fortuitously advantageous congenital variations could account for the organized and complexly co-ordinated nature of adaptations exhibited by so many organisms. Herbert Spencer, an early English advocate of evolution, was particularly troubled by this problem. Although willing to concede natural selection a major role as an agent of evolution, he refused to believe that it could bring about nature's most intricate adaptations. After enu-

merating the various structural adaptations necessary for the execution of complex co-ordinated movements, he succinctly expressed his doubt that natural
selection acting upon fortuitous variations could offer an explanation of them:
"The chances against any adequate re-adjustments fortuitously arising must be
infinity to one (Spencer, 1887, p. 12)."

Those who agreed with Cope and Spencer began to cultivate theories that
relied heavily upon the use and disuse of organs, the direct influences of the
environment and internal organizing energies as primary causes of evolution—
in short, these theorists constructed models that closely paralleled the views
put forward by the great French naturalist Jean-Baptiste Lamarck a half-century earlier. The frequently cited problem of the length of the giraffe's neck
illustrates some of the basic differences between the Lamarckian and Darwinian approaches to evolution. According to the Lamarckian view, the length of
the neck can be accounted for by the adaptive *use* of the organ; the giraffe's
effort to reach higher and higher locations stretches the neck, and these structural changes are passed on to the progeny via heredity. In contrast, the basis of
the Darwinian position is that different giraffes are born with necks of differing
sizes. A long neck confers an advantage upon the giraffe in its struggle with
other animals for survival, so those giraffes possessing congenitally long necks
are preserved by natural selection. In the Darwinian account, a major emphasis
is placed on the organism's relationship to other organisms and consequent differential selection; in the Lamarckian view, greater importance is attached to
the organism's relationship to the environment and the hereditary significance
of functional adaptations made by the organism to that environment.

Herbert Spencer, perhaps the first of the middle 19th-century evolutionists to seriously advance Lamarckian views, emphasized the evolutionary importance of the environment as well as the critical role of use and disuse in his
Principles of Biology (1874). Other European naturalists independently cultivated Lamarckian notions. Theodore Eimer and Karl Semper in Germany
stressed the hereditary significance of environmental influences such as light,
temperature, and gravitation in their evolutionary systems; Swiss biologist Karl
Wilhelm von Nägeli, though minimizing the importance of the environment,
ascribed theoretical primacy to an internal organizing energy (*Vervoll-
kommungskraft*) as a director of evolutionary progress; in France, Felix LeDantec
highlighted the role of organismic "functional assimilations" and Alfred Giard
pointed to the importance of environmental influences as part of their evolutionary schemes. And although he endorsed natural selection with customary
vigor, Ernst Haeckel reserved an important place for Lamarckian ideas in his
evolutionary synthesis.[1]

But the new Lamarckian views found their real home in America; only

---

1. Contemporary overviews of these and other neo-Lamarckian evolutionary theories
   can be found in the monographs by Kellogg (1907) and DéLage and Goldsmith
   (1913).

there did a cohesive "school" of neo-Lamarckism flourish.[2] Cope and fellow paleontologist Alpheus Hyatt were the founders of the movement. They claimed to have developed their views independently of Lamarck—Cope (1904, p. 423) admitted in 1884 to "not having read Lamarck" just "several years ago"—and the term "neo-Lamarckism" was not coined until 1885 by entomologist Alpheus Packard. But members of the American school were not recalcitrant about aligning themselves with Lamarck, and "once they saw that Lamarck had anticipated them, they publicized him as a patron saint (Pfeifer, 1965, p. 162)." Cope, Hyatt, and Packard comprised the heart of the movement; they each enjoyed a great deal of prestige within the scientific community and wielded wide influence through their co-editorship, beginning in 1867, of the journal *American Naturalist*. Other prominent American neo-Lamarckians included geologist Joseph Le Conte, paleontologist William H. Dall, and Cope's student Henry Osborn, who eventually became one of the movement's leaders. All of these men downplayed the evolutionary significance of natural selection, but they did not entirely eliminate it; as Packard put it, the neo-Lamarckian "simply seeks to assign this principle to its proper position in the hierarchy of factors (Packard, 1901, p. 398)."

Although the various neo-Lamarckian advocates differed from each other on points of theoretical detail, there is one idea that they all accepted. This idea, which subsequently became the focus of an extended and often emotionally explosive controversy, constituted the cornerstone of the Lamarckian (or neo-Lamarckian) system: the inheritance of acquired characteristics. It does not make much sense to speak of use and disuse of organs, the influence of environment, or functional adaptations of organisms as primary factors in evolution if the structural modifications induced in an organism by these influences are not transmitted to the progeny via heredity. Thus, the validity of the Lamarckian conceptualization of evolution depended upon the strength of the evidence for the inheritance of acquired characteristics. It should be noted, however, that the inheritance of acquired characteristics was not a controversial issue for the early neo-Lamarckians or, indeed, for Lamarck himself. As Burkhardt (1977) has pointed out in his searching biography of Lamarck, the doctrine of acquired characteristics did not originate with Lamarck, and his contemporaries did not criticize his belief in it. The idea of inheritance of acquired characteristics was almost universally accepted in Lamarck's time, and for much of the 19th century. Darwin accepted the inheritance of acquired characteristics as an established fact, supplemented natural selection with Lamarckian notions of use and disuse in the first edition of the *Origin*, and relied increasingly upon these ideas in subsequent editions.

---

2. For a view of the American neo-Lamarackian school from one of its members, see the discussion in Packard's (1901, Chap. 20) biography of Lamarck. For a modern perspective on American neo-Lamarckism, the papers by Pfiefer (1965) and Stocking (1962) are informative.

The first systematic attack on the widely accepted theory did not appear until 1883.[3] This event is a crucial one for our purposes. August Weismann's energetic assault on the doctrine of acquired characters not only decisively shaped research and theorizing about this problem for the next half-century; it also cast the issues on which Richard Semon's scientific fate largely hinged, and revealed many of the tactics that Weismann later used in head-to-head battle with Semon. Weismann's attempt to discredit the notion that acquired characters could be transmitted through heredity made him a hero to many neo-Darwinians and an enemy to almost every neo-Lamarckian. Ironically, Weismann himself had provisionally accepted the doctrine of acquired characteristics during his early days of entomological research at Freiburg. He later regretfully admitted that "I was in this respect under the influence of Darwin for a long time (Weismann, 1889, p. 422)." Only in subsequent years—when encroaching blindness made it impossible for him to continue his cytological research—did Weismann turn to purely theoretical pursuits and confront the problem of acquired characters while developing this theory of heredity.

The core concept in Weismann's complex and often speculative theory is the one that led him to deny the Lamarckian doctrine: the continuity of the germ-plasm. Weismann sharply distinguished between the reproductive germ-cells, which are responsible for hereditary processes, and the somatic or body cells, which are not. The somatic cells die with the individual organism, but the germ-plasm passes on from generation to generation and achieves a functionally immortal status. Further, Weismann contended, the germ-plasm remains isolated from somatic influences.[4] This formulation did not permit evolutionary influence by the so-called Lamarckian factors of inheritance. In Weismann's view, the somatic changes arising from the organism's functional adaptations, or from use and disuse of organs, could not affect the isolated germ-plasm. Consequently, Weismann rejected the possibility that somatically acquired characters could be transmitted via the germ-plasm. Weismann's own evolutionary scheme largely depended upon the classical neo-Darwinian mixture of fortuitously occurring congenital variations and the *Allmacht* (omnipotence) of natural selection.

The manner of Weismann's assault on the Lamarckian doctrine was straightforward. He demanded evidence that unequivocally established the inheritance of acquired characteristics and contended that it did not exist. He stated his position unambiguously: "The inheritance of acquired characters has never been proved, either by means of direct observation or by experiment (1889, p.

---

3. Weismann was not the first to express doubts concerning the reality of acquired characters, but his was the most directed and certainly the most influential attack. Thomson (1926, pp. 162–163) points out that Immanuel Kant, James Pritchard, and Francis Galton had previously voiced doubts concerning inheritability of acquired characters; Weismann, however, gave the problem its real currency.
4. Weismann did specifically allow for some somatic influences on the germ, such as nutrition from the body, but downplayed their hereditary significance.

81).″ Further, argued Weismann, "no one has hitherto attempted to cast doubts upon the very existence of such a form of heredity (p. 80).″ As mentioned earlier, most naturalists prior to Weismann accepted the reality of acquired characters. Yet in spite of this widespread belief—or perhaps because of it—little systematic evidence supporting the theory could be adduced. William Bateson, an ardent opponent of neo-Lamarckism about to embark upon his famous controversy with Paul Kammerer,[5] reflected upon this circumstance from the vantage point of 1909: "Hitherto the transmission of many acquired characteristics had seemed to most naturalists so obvious as to not call for demonstration. Weismann's demand for facts in support of the main proposition revealed at once that none having real cogency could be produced (1910, p. 90).″

When pressed by Weismann, the evidence cited by neo-Lamarckians was frequently weak. Herbert Spencer, for example, argued that insanity is often acquired rather than congenital, and "no one questions the accepted belief that insanity is inheritable (1887, p. 28).″ Further, noted Spencer, "I find among physicians the belief that nervous disorders of a less severe kind are inheritable (p. 28).″ Such claims could not be expected to silence even a mild doubter. J. A. Thomson, reviewing the long and ragged course of the controversy over acquired characteristics in 1926, sarcastically depicted the quality of evidence cited by early neo-Lamarckians such as Spencer:

> Herbert Spencer twits those who are skeptical as to the transmission of acquired characters with assigning the most flimsy reasons for rejecting a conclusion they are averse to; but when Spencer cites the prevalence of short-sightedness among the 'notoriously studious' Germans, the inheritance of musical talent, and the inheritance of a liability to consumption, as evidence of the inheritance of modification we are reminded of the pot calling the kettle black (Thomson, 1926, p. 176).

A confirmed and capable skeptic such as Weismann found such "evidence" easy to discredit. At the time he launched his assault in 1883, only one source of positive experimental evidence could be cited by the neo-Lamarckians: the Brown-Séquard experiment. Weismann's response to the results of this experiment is of interest for two reasons. First, it illustrates tactics that he later used in his critique of Semon's theory; second, it brings into sharp focus the problem of precisely defining an "acquired character." The major result of Brown-Séquard's experiment was clear enough: When Brown-Séquard induced epilepsy in a parent generation of guinea pigs through a variety of neural lesions, some of the progeny manifested a marked tendency to epilepsy and other nervous disorders. Subsequent debate concerned the extent to which this result provided evidence for the inheritance of an acquired character. Weismann held that it did not. In addition to questioning the extent and reliability of the evi-

---

5. Arthur Koestler has written a concise and dramatic account of the Bateson-Kammerer controversy (Koestler, 1971); but Gould's (1972) criticisms should also be noted.

dence, Weismann made the following crucial objection: "The injury caused by the division of the nerve is not transmitted....The symptoms of the disease in the offspring are undoubtedly transmitted, but the cause of the disease in the offspring is the real question which requires solution (1889, p. 311)." Weismann postulated that an unknown "microbe" affected both the germ-cells and the somatic-cells, resulting in the transmission of epileptic symptoms. However, Weismann argued, such transmission did not constitute a "true" acquired character (i.e., one that resulted from an effect of a structural modification of the soma on the germ); rather, it represented a case in which the somatic and germ cells were separately affected by a foreign influence. In his later critique of experiments that claimed to demonstrate inheritance of acquired characteristics, Weismann used a similar logic to distinguish between "somatic" and "parallel" induction of an acquired character. A true acquired character could arise only when a morphological change in the soma induced by factors such as use and disuse *directly* influenced the germ-plasm. Cases in which it could be argued that an external influence affected both the soma and the germ in *parallel* did not qualify as "true" acquired characters.

Using such logic, Weismann was able to explain away many troublesome cases of apparently acquired modifications, especially those induced by variations in climate. For instance, Weismann examined the case of the butterfly *Polyamnatus Phloeas*, popularly known in Germany as the "Feuerfalter" (fire butterfly) because of its reddish-gold wings. He cited a good deal of evidence indicating that heat-induced changes in the color of the wings could be inherited. However, Weismann argued that such a phenomenon does not constitute valid evidence for inheritance of acquired characters, because the excessive heat could directly alter the germ-plasm as well as the soma. After subjecting several similar cases to such an analysis, Weismann forcibly stated his conclusion: "the supposition that climatic influences can produce modifications of the germ-plasm, has certainly nothing to do with the view that functional modifications of any particular organ can cause a change in the germ-plasm. I believe I have here furnished a proof that the former supposition is a correct one; the onus of proof of the latter lies with the neo-Lamarckians (1893, pp. 408–409)."

A second favorite tactic used by Weismann was to interpret apparent evidence of acquired characters in terms of congenital predispositions "released" by environmental influences. Weismann effectively disposed of a whole class of potential evidence by assuming that apparently acquired modifications in the parent are merely expressions of latent hereditary characters. Thus, transmission of such characters did not constitute evidence favoring Lamarckian inheritance:

> If we consider that each so-called predisposition (that is, the power of reacting upon a certain stimulus in a certain way, possessed by any organism or one of its parts) must be innate, and further that each acquired character is only the predisposed reaction of some part of an organism upon some external selection; then we must admit that only one of the causes which produce any acquired character can be transmitted, the one which was present before the

character itself appeared, viz., the predisposition; and we must further admit that the latter arises from the germ (1889, p. 171).

A third defense employed by Weismann, as well as by other neo-Darwinians, was to argue that data that seemed to favor the acquired characters position could be better accounted for by the theory of natural selection. Alfred Russell Wallace, co-founder with Darwin of the theory of natural selection and a staunch neo-Darwinian, put this logic to ingenious use. Consider, for example, Wallace's retort to the argument that the loss of eyes in various cave animals resulted from disuse of the organs and hence provided evidence of a somatically-induced acquired character. Wallace (1901) contended that natural selection could equally well account for the phenomenon. When the eyes become useless in total darkness, he argued, they might also become liable to accident or disease and therefore represent a danger to the animal; natural selection would then operate to eliminate those animals possessing the vulnerable organ. Such reasoning made it exceedingly difficult for neo-Lamarckians to find evidence in nature that unequivocally supported the hereditary transmission of use and disuse; as Wallace put it, "the very fact of *use*, in a wild state, implies *utility*, and utility is the constant subject for the action of natural selection (1901, p. 417)."

Weismann supplemented this formidable array of counter-arguments with a bias that betrayed his fundamentally unalterable opposition to the inheritance of acquired characteristics: "it is impossible to imagine any way in which the transmission of changes, produced by the direct action of external forces upon the somatic cells, can be brought about (1889, p. 80)." Confronted by these imposing defenses, many neo-Lamarckians in the 1880s and 1890s expressed exasperation as their attempts to establish the inheritance of somatically-induced characters met with stubborn resistance by Weismann and the neo-Darwinians. In the absence of well-controlled laboratory experiments, the debate had turned into one of imagination: If the neo-Darwinians could *conceive* of an explanatory alternative to inheritance of acquired characters, then they argued that the proposed evidence was inconclusive. The frustration experienced by those arguing the affirmative case for the inheritance of acquired characters is poignantly captured in the following passage from Cambridge biologist George John Romanes:

> how would Weismann himself propose that we should set about proof of such a fact, where the proof demanded by his assumption is, that the *abstract possibility* of natural selection having had anything to do with the matter must be excluded? Obviously this is impossible in the cases of inherited characters which are also *adaptive characters*. How then does it fare with the case of inherited characters which are also not adaptive? Merely that this case is met by another and sequent assumption, which constitutes an integral part of the neo-Darwinian creed—namely, that in nature there *can be no such characters* (1895, p. 55).

James Ward, a Cambridge psychologist, expressed similar sentiments. He ruefully depicted Weismann's pronouncement that the inheritance of acquired characters is inconceivable: "No process of transmission being conceivable, it is assumed that no such process is possible....We do not brush aside the facts of gravitation because we are utterly ignorant of the process which they involve (1913, p. 23)."

In spite of such objections, Weismann's assault proved successful.[6] He had exposed the lack of empirical foundation for a long accepted belief, and many scientists found his arguments convincing. By 1890, Oxford naturalist J. T. Cunningham could wistfully offer the following remark in his sympathetic preface to Eimer's (1890) neo-Lamarckian *Organic Evolution*: "When I saw that many of the ablest British biologists accepted Weismann's dogma that acquired characters are not inherited, it seemed to me that they were abandoning the richest vein of knowledge under a mistaken guide (p. vi)." But neo-Darwinians lauded Weismann's efforts and gave him credit for turning the problem of acquired characters into one that could be settled only by experiment. Bateson summarized the results of Weismann's attack in his 1909 paper: "Weismann's interpellation, though negative in purpose, has had a lasting and beneficial effect, for through his thorough demolition of the old loose and distracting notions of inherited experience, the ground has been cleared for the construction of a true knowledge of heredity based on experimental fact (p. 91)."

When Richard Semon entered the dispute over acquired characteristics with the publication of *Die Mneme* in 1904, he set foot in territory that had been shaped and molded by Weismann. A second and related issue that Semon confronted in that 1904 work was one that Weismann's efforts had also brought to the biological foreground: the nature of heredity itself. Amidst all the impassioned polemics of the acquired characters debates in the '80s and '90s, one point could be almost unanimously agreed upon: Scarcely anything was known about the actual mechanisms of heredity. In the absence of hard knowledge about hereditary processes these controversies settled little and, as noted earlier, often amounted to affairs of the imagination. Not that there was a dearth of theories concerning hereditary processes; far from it. The post-*Origin* era had witnessed the appearance of numerous speculative attempts to elucidate the process of heredity and relate it to the known facts of development, variation, and evolution. The strategy pursued by various naturalists is well-illustrated by

---

6. Revealing contemporary assessments of the effect of Weismann's attack on the acquired characters position are provided by Kellogg (1907), Thomson (1926), and Conklin (1915). Weismann's dogma has been accepted by nearly all biologists over the past century. However, it now looks as though the controversy over acquired characters is about to flare up again. Recent work reported by Gorczynski and Steele (1980) has provided experimental evidence that induced immunological tolerance to certain antigens can be inherited. Their work was the subject of a recent critique in *Nature* entitled "Lamarckist revival in immunology" (Taylor, 1980). Some of the arguments offered in opposition to a Lamarackian interpretation of their work are nearly identical to the ones put forward by Weismann 100 years ago.

Darwin's own provisional theory of "pangenesis" put foward in 1868: Invent a particle, endow it with suitable properties sufficient to account for the relevant phenomena, and name it. Darwin (1897) postulated the existence of tiny particles in each cell—he called them "gemmules"—that are dispersed throughout the body to the reproductive organs; each conveys representative information about its native cell. Darwin imagined that the gemmules manage to appropriately organize themselves upon reaching the reproductive organs. In order to account for developmental phenomena, Darwin further contended that "Gemmules are supposed to be thrown off by every unit, not only during the adult state, but during each stage of development of every organism (1897, p. 370)." The theory made many other like assumptions in order to satisfactorily account for the vast array of unsolved enigmas of heredity.

Similar approaches were advanced by many other biologists. Although they differed with respect to theoretical details, Spencer's "physiological units," Weismann's "biophors," Nägeli's "micellae," Haeckel's "plastidules," and Oskar Hertwig's "idioblasts," just like Darwin's "gemmules," all represented bold speculative attempts to make sense of baffling phenomena in terms of suitably endowed particles. The rediscovery of Mendel's work in 1900 and subsequent rise of experimental genetics ended much of the speculation; we shall have more to say about that later, in regard to Semon's theory.

Amidst the numerous particulate theories, another approach to the understanding of heredity quietly unfolded in the latter half of the 19th-century. Instead of (and sometimes in addition to) postulating microscopic particles to perform the feats of heredity, proponents of these theories attempted to unravel the mysteries of heredity by comparing them to other reproductive phenomena: the phenomena of memory. The conceptualization of heredity in terms of memory constituted a major component of Semon's *Mneme*; in many respects, Semon subjected this notion to its most searching analysis. His ideas can be best appreciated by viewing them against the theoretical background provided by his predecessors and contemporaries. And the story of this heterodox enterprise is itself an intriguing one: Although the various memory-heredity theories represent a largely lost page in the history of science, their obscurity belies a scientific netherworld that existed for over 50 years. Let us now turn our attention to it.[7]

HEREDITY AS MEMORY:
EXCAVATIONS OF A SCIENTIFIC ATLANTIS

The mnemonic conception of heredity was developed by a diverse collection of unlikely characters. Each approached the issue from a different angle, yet many

---

7. For one of the few modern acknowledgments of the memory-heredity theories, see Gould's (1977, pp. 96–100) brief discussion.

arrived at strikingly similar views of the problem. Proponents of the theory included an eminent Viennese physiologist, a quasimystical English novelist, Charles Darwin's eldest son, an author of a treatise on naval timber, and a physician-in-ordinary to the Queen of Scotland. Several already familiar names can be added to this unusual group, including the American neo-Lamarckians Cope and Hyatt as well as the ever-present Ernst Haeckel.[8] This heterogeneous collection of theorists demonstrated much imagination in their attempts to cast hereditary phenomena in terms of memory, as they seized upon even the most remote similarities between the two in building their position. Although the quality of their ideas ranged from ingeniously innovative to painfully strained, the basic proposition underlying the theory was straightforward: Memory is responsible for the preservation of an individual's experiences; perhaps it is also responsible for the preservation of hereditary characters.

The man who first systematically advanced this hypothesis was Ewald Hering, the Viennese physiologist whose work on sensory systems is still well known today. The central idea that motivated Hering's effort can be gleaned from the title of a lecture he delivered to the Vienna Academy of Sciences in 1870: "Memory as a universal function of organized matter" (*Das Gedächtnis als allgemeine Funktion der organisierten Materie*). Hering (1920, p. 68) objected to the usual conception of memory, noting that "The word 'memory' is often understood as though it meant nothing more than our faculty of intentionally reproducing ideas." Such a notion, argued Hering, is unnecessarily restrictive. Does not habit—although often involuntary and unconscious—also depend upon memory? For Hering, memory constituted the glue that gives meaning to personal existence, and unifies what otherwise would be a series of chaotic and discontinuous sensations:

> It seems then, that we owe to memory almost all that we either have or are; that our ideas and conceptions are its work, and that our every perception, thought, and movement is derived from this source. Memory collects the countless phenomena of our existence into a single whole; and as our bodies would be scattered into the dust of their component atoms if they were not held together by the attraction of matter, so our consciousness would be

---

8. There is one name that will not appear on the list of memory-heredity theorists—C. G. Jung—although many might expect to see it because of Jung's well known ideas concerning archetypes and the collective unconscious. But Jung had almost nothing to say about heredity (or Lamarckism), and viewed archetypes as part of the basic *structure* of the psyche rather than as inherited "racial memories." Modern Jungian scholars, such as Jacobi (1959), strenuously attempt to separate Jung's theory from Lamarckism: "It has been remarked in many quarters that from the standpoint of our present scientific knowledge acquired characters or memories cannot be inherited. Those who have raised this argument have assiduously overlooked the fact that Jung's archetypes are a structural condition of the psyche...and that this has nothing to do with the inheritance of definite images (p. 51)." Jacobi also specifically denied any connection between Jungian theory and Semon's Mneme (1959, p. 48).

> broken up into as many fragments as we had lived seconds but for the binding
> and unifying force of memory (1920, p. 75).

Given this broad view of memory as a process that unites an organism's present
with its past, it was a short step to suggest that this is the case not only within a
lifetime but also across generations. Memory, the fundamental property of organic matter, serves not only to bind together the temporally disparate elements
of *personal* existence, but can also serve as an *ancestral* link: It serves as a bridge
that preserves hereditary continuity across phylogenetic time.

   This fundamental notion was shared by many who advanced the memory-
heredity proposition. Although Hering is usually acknowledged as the father of
the idea, some of its rudiments are perceptible in work published prior to his
1870 lecture. Peter Willers Jessen argued in 1855 that memory represents a basic
property of nervous substance: "Memory is not just an abstract characteristic of
the mind, but a general property of the nerves (p. 478)." British physician Henry
Maudsley offered a similar notion in 1867: "There is memory in every nerve-
cell, and, indeed, in every organic element of the body (p. 209)." Although these
authors did not take the next step and explicitly link their conceptualizations of
organic memory to hereditary phenomena, others working independently of
Hering did. Thomas Laycock, a physician to the Queen of Scotland, extended
his idea of a universal, organic memory—which he labeled "synesia"—to various
features of heredity that we will soon examine. So did E. D. Cope, who conferred
the dubious title of "cryptopony" upon his idea of an organic memory, as well as
the versatile Cambridge parapsychologist F. W. H. Myers: "We cannot assert
that organic memory may not inhere in a single cell or neuron, or even in a
single living molecule. Neither can we assert that organic memory cannot be
prolonged backwards before birth (1903, p. 266)." French psychologist Théodule
Ribot made the point succinctly: "Heredity, indeed, is a specific memory: it is to
the species what memory is to the individual (1889, p. 52)."

   A more thorough exploration of similar ideas is found in the work of Henry
Orr. This American neo-Lamarckian received his Ph.D. at Jena in 1883, and
then returned to the United States, where he accepted a position as Professor
of Biology at Tulane University.[9] Orr's little known 1893 treatise, *A Theory of
Development and Heredity,* contains a detailed elaboration of ideas that closely
resemble those advanced by Hering. Orr, however, apparently worked in ignorance of Hering's efforts—at least he did not cite Hering in his book—and believed that his own theory represented a novel extension of the neo-Lamarckian
doctrine.

   The man who most energetically developed the notion of organic memory
independently of Hering was neither psychologist, biologist, physician, nor any
manner of scientist at all. He was a rambunctious English novelist who publicly

---

9. Orr studied at Jena during the same period that Semon did. Although there is no
   evidence that the two directly influenced each other, Semon is one of the very few
   who cited Orr's contribution.

accused Charles Darwin of begrudging his grandfather just recognition for his contributions to evolutionary theory, served as George Bernard Shaw's biological mentor, and unabashedly speculated about many scientific problems—the refreshing and infuriating Samuel Butler.[10] Butler attained literary fame chiefly through his saga of men and machines, *Erewhon*. His interest in evolutionary problems was sparked by the *Origin*, and he initially endorsed Darwinian theory with enthusiasm. But he soon began to doubt the explanatory usefulness of the construct of natural selection. By the late 1870s, he openly opposed Darwinian theory and engaged Darwin in acrimonious controversy concerning a variety of issues. Butler, like Cope and other neo-Lamarckians, focused upon Darwin's inability to convincingly explain the origin of variations by natural selection and went as far as to ridicule Darwin's theoretical reliance on chance variations.[11]

Butler attempted to succeed where he thought Darwin had failed by developing a notion of organic memory, similar in spirit to Hering's, that portrayed heredity as one aspect of the more general function of memory. Butler, indeed, catapulted memory into an exalted position in the organic world. He depicted it as the crucial feature that defined life itself: "Life is that property of matter whereby it can remember. Matter which can remember is living; matter which cannot remember is dead. *Life, then, is memory* (1910, pp. 299–300)." Butler's work was sometimes imaginative; more frequently, it was embarrassingly naive. His complete lack of scientific training freed him from the influence of the prevailing orthodoxy, but also led him to advance fantastic speculations that rendered him easy prey for abuse from more rigorous minds. Although Butler never claimed scientific authority, his avowed amateurism proved small comfort in the face of the scorn that he frequently encountered, and his writing about evolution became increasingly caustic over the years. Marcus Hartog, one of Butler's few scientific sympathizers, recalled the disillusioned novelist's dejection at the reception accorded his 1877 *magnum opus, Life and Habit:* "He was bitterly disappointed in the event, for the book, as a whole, was received by professional biologists as a gigantic joke—a joke, moreover, not in the best possible taste (1920, p. xii)." We shall hear a good deal more about Butler in subsequent pages, since he developed many of the individual comparisons between memory and heredity to which we now turn.

---

10. There is a wealth of biographical information on the enigmatic Butler; the books by Cannan (1915), Jones (1919), and Stillman (1932) are among the best. For a general perspective on Butler's involvement with evolutionary problems, see Hartog's introduction to Butler's *Unconscious Memory*. Butler's relationship to Darwin is described by Willey (1960), and the exchange of letters that comprised the Butler-Darwin controversy are published in Barlow's (1958) appendix to Darwin's autobiography.

11. Butler pulled no punches in criticizing Darwin's vacillating dependence on chance variations: "I submit that it is necessary to call attention to it here, inasmuch as it is impossible to believe that after years of reflection upon his subject, Mr. Darwin should have written as above, especially in such a place, if his mind were really clear about his own position (1910, p. 260)."

RELATIONSHIPS BETWEEN MEMORY AND HEREDITY

The phenomenon that formed the crucial bridge between memory and heredity for almost all of those who advanced the theory was a simple one: repetition. Observations of the effects of repetition on mnemonic processes provided a necessary link between conscious and unconscious memory in the life of an individual that rendered plausible the link to heredity. The basic argument was simple: In the individual, remembering can be transformed from a conscious and voluntary act into an unconscious, involuntary and automatic procedure with many repetitions of a task. The examples most frequently invoked were learning to walk, play the piano, or memorizing a poem. In all cases, the consciousness that initially characterizes performance of the task becomes unnecessary after many repetitions as memory takes on more and more of an automatic quality. Starting from such a position, all that one must do to explicitly link memory and heredity is to widen the *temporal* frame of analysis. The automatic quality that characterizes the appearance of hereditary characters in ontogeny can also be viewed as the unfolding of an unconscious memory, built up by countless repetitions across thousands of generations. This is the key element in most of the memory-heredity theories. Just as the expert pianist requires no intervention of consciousness to execute a well practiced passage, neither does the embryo require consciousness to direct the complex sequences of ontogeny, such a "performance" having been "practiced" countless times during the course of phylogeny. In both cases, however, memory underlies the observed phenomena; the consciousness required to execute the "habit" simply drops out in the course of automatization.

This shared quality of automaticity deeply impressed Hering, Butler, Cope, Ward, Hyatt, Orr, and others. Francis Darwin, who advanced his own version of the memory-heredity theory in a 1908 Presidential Address to the *British Association for the Advancement of Science*, clearly stated the case:

> My view is that the rhythm of ontogeny is actually and literally a habit. It undoubtedly has the feature which I have described as pre-eminently characteristic of habit, viz., an automatic quality which is seen in the performance of a series of actions. . . . This is the chief point on which I wish to insist—I mean that the resemblance between ontogeny and habit is not merely superficial, but deeply seated . . . memory has its place in the morphological as well as in the temporary reactions of living things (1909, p. 14).

The constructs of repetition and automatization received some of their most detailed applications to hereditary phenomena in Orr's theory. Orr invoked the usual examples of automatization following repetition to build his case, and argued that repetition effects extending across generations could account for behaviors, habits, and the unfolding of ontogenetical stages:

We have seen how the habits of growth and development were formed by long continued repetition of mechanical reactions, and how they perpetuate themselves in the hereditary impulse. In the same way, the more complex reactions of an animal, such as feeding, reproducing, and protecting the young, being repeated in each generation, tend by repetition to become as much a part of the hereditary impulse as the growth or development itself (1893, p. 240).

One point should be made clear at this juncture. If the notions of repetition and automaticity are to provide a legitimate link between phenomena of memory and heredity, then the inheritance of acquired characteristics must be assumed as fact. The performance of the pianist cannot become automatic unless he is able to retain the effects of his previous practice; similarly, the appearance of hereditary characters during the unfolding of ontogeny cannot become automatic unless the effects of "practice" by one generation are passed on to the next. British zoologist E. W. MacBride, a supporter of the memory-heredity hypothesis, concisely delineated the issue: "If these automatic actions were at first voluntary efforts they must have been so in previous generations, and the habitudinal memories acquired by one generation must have been handed on to the next. Is this possible (1928, pp. 8–9)?" Not surprisingly, MacBride answered his query in the affirmative; he and all others who advanced the memory-heredity hypothesis were devout Lamarckians with respect to the inheritance of acquired characteristics. In fact, some memory-heredity theorists used the notion of repetition as a tool in the fight to legitimize the theory of acquired characteristics. James Ward, who advanced his version of the memory-heredity hypothesis in 1913 amidst heated controversy over acquired characters, noted that numerous repetitions are required to convert a series of conscious memories into an automatized habit, and suggested that countless more would be needed to achieve the same effect over the course of phylogeny. Thus, he concluded, it is extremely difficult to observe acquired characters over just a few generations. Hering had laid the foundation for such an argument in 1870 when he suggested that the effects of practice penetrate "ever so faintly" to the germ and require numerous repetitions to influence the hereditary process. Cope invoked a similar argument: "It is evident that the kind of characters which have become such [inherited] are those which result from use in the fullest sense of the word; that is, by countless repetitions for immense periods of time (1889, p. 1059)."

The critical concepts of repetition and automatization were also used to explicate another shared feature of practiced habits and hereditary phenomena that seemed crucial to several theorists: their orderly procession. The deeply engrained habit runs off smoothly in the correct order, one component giving rise to the next; so too with the stages of ontogeny. As the expert pianist does not play an upcoming bar before the currently prescribed one, the embryo does not manifest hereditary characters in a random ontogenetical sequence. Alpheus

Hyatt pointed to the orderly remembering achieved by practice with mnemonic methods to illustrate his argument: "In mnemonics it is the machine-like regularity of the succession of cause and effect, of one word begetting the next, that surprises the student (1893, p. 73)." He further contended that the analogous process in ontogeny provided support for his theory of "mnemogenesis": "If characteristics were inherited irregularly there would be no parallel between the functions of memory and heredity, but the precision of the succession of hereditary characters in the development of the individual is precisely in accord with the theory of mnemogenesis (p. 73)." Samuel Butler also seized upon the orderly procession of habit and ontogeny and, with customary flair, made it one of the cornerstones of his theory. Just as "there is probably no living man who could repeat the words of 'God Save the Queen' backwards, without much hesitation and many mistakes (1910, p. 158)," Butler argued that "the offspring, whether in its embryonic condition, or in any stage of development till it has reached maturity, should adopt nearly the same order in going through all its various stages (p. 170)." Variation in the *length* of ontogenetical stages posed no problem for these theorists since, they argued, even the most frequently practiced habits vary in the precise duration taken for their execution. *Ordinal* invariance remains, constituting a key link between memory and heredity.

Another important characteristic of ontogeny that seemed to be gracefully accommodated by an analysis in terms of memory was the process of recapitulation. The bare existence of recapitulatory phenomena appeared to constitute prima facie evidence for the operation of memory in phylogeny; what better way to conceptualize the frequent re-appearance of ancient phyletic characters during the course of ontogeny. Cope stated the proposition bluntly: "the organic units of which the organism is comprised possess a memory which determines their destiny in the building of the embryo. This is indicated by the recapitulation of the phylogenetic history of its ancestors in embryonic growth (1889, p. 1065)." Butler posed the following question in a similar spirit: "Why should the embryo of any animal go through so many stages—embryological allusions to forefathers of a widely different type (1910, p. 25)?" The answer seemed obvious to him: Because the organism had traversed the same path many times in its past, and now did so out of habit. MacBride and Hyatt also viewed recapitulatory processes in a roughly identical manner. Haeckel, too, recognized the importance of memory for the biogenetic law in his endorsement and extension of Hering's position. He flatly stated that "Memory is a major determinant (*ein Hauptfactor*) of biogenetic processes (1876, p. 68)."

The phenomenon of recapitulation provided even more grist for the memory-heredity theorists' mill. The gradual *condensation* observed in the appearance of phyletic characters during ontogeny could be readily explicated by the automatization notion discussed earlier. As the stages of a habit become more tightly packed with repetition, the various components involved in the execution of the habit follow each other in increasingly rapid succession. According to the memory-heredity theory, the same idea could be applied to the observation that new phyletic characters appear at successively earlier stages of ontogeny in each new generation: The recapitulatory process becomes briefer because "practice" over the course of generations renders it more and more automatic. Henry Orr unambiguously articulated this idea:

> it is a familiar fact that repetition increases facility and rapidity of action, and thus we observe that frequent repetition of the processes of growth and development have rendered it possible for the brief life of an individual to encompass the development which the race has been untold ages in acquiring. We find the proofs abundant in nature that new characteristics of animals tend to appear earlier and earlier in each subsequent generation (1893, pp. 140–141).

Another feature of recapitulation that could be explained easily enough in terms of memory was the addition of new stages to the ontogenetic succession. Both Francis Darwin and James Ward argued that *recent* additions to a habit are initially labile and subject to fluctuation. Analogously, they argued, the stages added most recently to ontogeny are the most variable and susceptible to "forgetting" (Darwin, 1909, p. 14; Ward, 1913, pp. 140–141).

Butler and Cope took a different approach to the issue of recency in memory. They argued that we remember *best* what we have done most recently, and proceeded to apply this insight to heredity. Cope viewed "recency effects" as an explanation for the observation that organisms do not execute phylogenetically archaic sequences that may have been passed on in the germ: "That the entire record is not repeated in automatic and reflex acts, but only that part of it which was last acquired, may be regarded as due to the muscular and other systems concerned in it having performed it most recently (1889, p. 1069)." Butler addressed himself to another aspect of the recency issue. In one of the numerous portions of his work in which his fertile imagination seems out of control, Butler argued that recency biases in memory provide a key to understanding parent-child resemblances. Why, Butler asked, should the resemblance between child and parent be greater than between child and more distant ancestors? The explanation seemed clear: that the germ "should remember best what it has been doing the most recently (Butler, 1910, p. 168)." Child resembles parent for much the same (unknown) reason that we remember yesterday's activities better than those of last month; recency prevails in both cases. The facts of parent-child resemblance, Butler contended, supported his theory.

Butler also proposed that one of the more vexing hereditary phenomena— atavism—could be fruitfully conceptualized in terms of memory. The suppression of a specific hereditary character for several generations followed by its sudden reappearance posed a thorny problem for pre-Mendelian naturalists. Without the requisite concepts of dominant and recessive genes, these reversions constituted puzzling enigmas. Butler suggested that just as in everyday memory we sometimes "capriciously" remember long-forgotten ideas or events, in heredity long-suppressed characters might be "capriciously remembered

(1910, pp. 196–197)," Over a decade earlier, Adam Sedgwick argued a similar point at the conclusion of an article concerning sex and hereditary disease: "For atavism in disease appears to be but an instance of memory in reproduction . . . in the same way that memory never, as it were, dies out, but in some state always exists, so the previous existence of some peculiarity in organization may likewise be regarded as never absolutely lost in succeeding generations, except by extinction of race (1863, p. 197)." Alpheus Hyatt, too, ascribed the "sporadic" phenomena of atavism to "latent hereditary mnemism" in the germ cells (1893, p. 73). Not entirely satisfied with "capricious recall" as an explanation of atavism, E. W. MacBride suggested that atavistic phenomena could emerge only in the presence of some appropriate stimulus. For example, MacBride noted that the Olm, a blind cave newt, is able to develop a normally functioning eye if exposed to certain kinds of light when young, and contended that "the power to produce perfect eyes still persists as a suppressed memory, and it can be brought to surface when the proper stimulus is applied (1928, p. 13)"

The general theme of reversion formed the nucleus of Scottish physician Thomas Laycock's analysis of memory and heredity.[12] The starting point for Laycock's analysis of memory and heredity theory can be traced to his well developed ideas concerning processes of regression and dissolution in the nervous system—ideas that were later elaborated upon by his famous student, the eminent British neurologist John Hughlings Jackson. For Laycock, the critical observation concerned a particular feature often found in the amnesia that accompanies senility. Although senile people may be entirely incapable of forming new memories or retrieving information about recent events, they still seem able to reminisce, frequently and in much detail, about events of the distant past. Laycock argued that the form of this "reversion," which he believed resulted from defective nutrition of the brain, constituted a major fact of organic memory. Widening the scope of his analysis, Laycock contended that certain forms of cerebral pathology—those that produced "idiots" and "imbeciles"—provided evidence for the operation of exactly the same kind of processes extended over the course of phylogeny. Now, however, the defective brain nutrition expresses itself by a reversion to *ancestral* characters. Thus, much as the behavior of the senile person is controlled by memories of childhood, the behavior of the criminal or "idiot" is controlled by memories deposited in the "substrata of the race acquired during savage life in long-distant ages (1876, p. 179)." Largely based upon this point of correspondence, Laycock posited that the laws governing personal memory and hereditary memory are identical. He also suggested that any conditions favoring defective nutrition could result in

---

12. Although he is virtually unknown today, Laycock was an important 19th-century figure who influenced scientists from Darwin to Freud. An exceedingly productive man—he published over 300 scientific papers—Laycock reported a series of highly regarded studies concerning biological periodicity in the 1840s, and wrote a well known book exploring the origins of hysteria (see Sulloway, 1979, p. 156).

mnemonic reversions and, in the best spirit of preventive medicine, warned that parents who put too great a strain on cerebral nutrition by excessive indulgence in high culture might produce blemished offspring because of defective hereditary memory (pp. 178–179).

Laycock invoked the idea of mnemonic reversion to explain a variety of phenomena that he characterized as phylogenetically archaic. Others used somewhat different mnemonic concepts to elucidate an additional primitive hereditary phenomenon—instinct. The problem of instinct penetrated to the core of the disagreements between neo-Lamarckians and neo-Darwinians. The neo-Darwinian argument that natural selection of chance variations adequately accounted for even the most intricate instinctual phenomena seemed unreasonably strained to many neo-Lamarckians. The complexities of numerous instincts, they argued, exhibited too many interdependencies between components for natural selection to comfortably explain (see Morgan, 1896). Those who believed that heredity comprised just one form of memory suggested an alternative that was more palatable to them: Instinct can be viewed as hereditary habit. The similarity between habit and instinct seemed clear and striking; both represent automatized sequences that run-off without the intervention of consciousness. In addition, the *organized* quality of habit seemed to fit well with the complex interdependencies observed in instinct. Herbert Spencer, for instance, contended that "Instinct may be regarded as a kind of organized memory (1888, p. 445)." And just as the skilled pianist requires practice to execute smoothly automatic behavior, instinctual phenomena must also depend on prior practice. A baby bird, for instance, could not build a nest without the benefit of its' ancestors practice any more than a musician could perform a virtuoso concerto without having previously played the piano. The basic idea received early treatment by Patrick Matthew in his 1831 treatise on naval timber:

> These innate or continuous ideas or habits seem proportionally greater in the insect tribes . . . and forming an abiding memory, may resolve the enigma of instinct, and the foreknowledge which these tribes have of what is necessary to completing their round of life, reducing this to knowledge or impressions and habits acquired by a long experience (cited in Butler, 1879, p. 322).

Hering expressed a similar idea in his 1870 lecture, when he noted that the problem of instinct had been previously subjected to the "mysticism of natural philosophy." But, he argued, "if we regard instinct as the outcome of the memory or reproductive power of organised substance" then "instinct becomes at once intelligible (1920, p. 82)."

Samuel Butler advanced a similar thesis when he argued that memory is continuous between generations. Granted such a position, instinctual behavior presents no great mystery, since, "we would expect that it should be remembered by the offspring as something which he has done all his life (1910, p. 189)." Butler pointed to an additional similarity that he believed strengthened the contention that instinct is a variety of memory: both are context-sensitive.

Just as the expression of a personally acquired memory can be effected by re-establishing the context that accompanied the original experience, claimed Butler, manifestation of instinctual phenomena also partially depends upon contextual reinstatement. In the case of instincts, however, the conditions encountered by *previous generations* are reinstated: "when the offspring found itself in the presence of objects which had called up such and such ideas for a sufficient number of generations . . . the same ideas should also be called up in the minds of the off-spring (1910, p. 191)." Although Butler, Hering, and Ward believed that their portrayal of instinct as inherited memory provided a viable theoretical alternative to natural selection, they also encountered sticky problems that resisted simple explanations. How, for example, could the idea of inherited memory account for the complex instincts of neuter insects, since these organisms cannot pass on their acquired habits to the next generation? Butler spent an entire chapter wrestling with this objection, but could only salvage his hypothesis by valiantly introducing an unimpressive series of shaky assumptions (1910, Chap. 12).

Mechanisms of Organic Memory

We have now considered the body of evidence that the memory-heredity advocates used to build their positions. Phenomena such as repetition and practice, continuity of experience, automaticity, ordinal invariance, recency effects, recapitulation, condensation, atavism, pathological reversion, instincts, and contextual sensitivity all seemed to indicate that there was a genuine relationship between memory and heredity. But if heredity is a form of memory, what is the mechanism of such a "memory"? Opinion was sharply divided on this point. Some writers, such as Ribot, were content to characterize the similarities between memory and heredity as products of a more basic underlying process and go no further. Ribot depicted both memory and heredity as manifestations of one fundamental law, the conservation of energy: "In other words, nothing that has been can cease to be; hence, in the individual, habit; in the species, heredity (1889, p. 391)." Charles Patten, a British anatomist who wholeheartedly endorsed previous attempts to conceptualize heredity in terms of memory, made a similar point from a somewhat different perspective. Patten hypothesized that heredity could be understood as a manifestation of the operation of a basic "memory-rhythm" that serves as evolution's engine. This "memory-rhythm" drives cell division and underlies all organic events: "Truly, then, Memory must be the Font and Mainspring of Evolutionary forces (1926, p. 90)." Patten's rather hazy notion was never developed by others.

Italian biologist Eugenio Rignano argued much like Ribot and Patten that both memory and heredity are driven by more basic underlying forces. Rignano, however, presented a detailed exposition of the mechanics of a hypothetical system in which heredity is attributable to fundamental properties of organic matter. The theory, which Rignano labeled the "centroepigenetic" hypothesis, posited that the mnemonic quality of heredity is attributable to electrical properties shared by the nuclei of the germ cells and somatic cells. In both germ and soma, argued Rignano, cell nuclei are capable of storing a specific electrical current and discharging it under specifiable circumstances. According to Rignano, "This property confers on the specific potential elements or accumulators a true mnemonic nature (1926, pp. 81–82)." Thus stimuli encountered by the organism create similar electrical disturbances in the somatic cells and germ cells, and these perturbations later serve as the basis of both memory and heredity.

A slightly different approach to the mechanics of heredity and memory—a "vibration" theory in contrast to an electrical one—is found in the work of Hering and Haeckel. Hering noted the close interdependencies between nervous substance and bodily organs, and suggested that "events which happen to one are repeated in others, and a notification, however slight, of a vibration set up in one quarter is at once conveyed even to the farthest parts of the body (1920, p. 77)." These vibrations are the basis of memory and subsequently manifest themselves in the presence of similar vibrations. Although such vibrations must be often repeated in order to penetrate the germ, a sufficiently repeated vibration enables the germ of the embryo to respond "to the same or like stimuli in a like way to that in which the parent organism responded (pp. 78–79)." Haeckel extended Hering's theory by inventing suitably endowed modules ("plastidules") to transmit the necessary mnemonic vibrations. Haeckel contended that "Heredity is the memory of the Plastidule, variability is the power of comprehension (*Fassungskraft*) of the Plastidule (1876, p. 69)." He further speculated that in simple and nonvariable organic forms, the plastidule has "learned nothing and forgotten nothing"; in more complex and variable forms, the plastidule has "learned much and forgotten much (1876, p. 69)." Haeckel's opaque conjectures were ignored by later memory-heredity theorists.

The choice of mechanisms was not, however, limited to those suggested by Rignano, Hering, and Haeckel. Marcus Hartog, the British biologist who enthusiastically endorsed the mnemonic conception of heredity—especially Butler's development of it—offered yet another alternative in his introduction to Butler's *Unconscious Memory*. Hartog agreed with the general argument advanced by Hering, but he harbored "doubts as to the validity of Hering's invocation of molecular vibrations as the mechanism of memory." Instead, Hartog suggested that the mnemonic underpinning of heredity could be best understood as owing to "rhythmic chemical changes (1920, p. xxiv)." James Ward contended that neither vibrations, electrical potentials, or chemical alterations were viable mechanisms. Ward found the materialistic implications of such hypotheses distasteful: "Unhappily however—as it seems to me—most of those who uphold the mnemic theory of heredity seem to hanker unduly after a physical explanation of the *modus operandi*. Hering and Haeckel talked of peculiar vibrations: if they were writing today they would probably refer to wireless telegraphy (1913, p. 54)." Instead, Ward averred, *mind* should be granted its due role in both memory and heredity; theorists must go beyond mere physical explanations and incorporate "living experience or tradition" into their theories.

Mind had been granted a quite prominent role by one prior memory-heredity theorist—Samuel Butler. Not bound by the usual rules of scientific theorizing, Butler engaged in an astonishingly anthropomorphic mode of argument when considering the mnemonic processes underlying heredity: "immediately on impregnation, the germ's memory reverts to the last occasion on which it was in a like condition, and recognising the position, is at no loss what to do (1910, p. 150)." Butler's germ cells, then, are conscious creatures that recognize circumstances and make appropriate decisions based on their awareness of current contingencies. Proceeding in a similar spirit, Butler announced that he had uncovered a key reason why sexual reproduction is more common than asexual reproduction. His undoubtedly original theory is worth quoting at length:

> We should expect to find a predominance of sexual over asexual generation . . . inasmuch as two heads are better than one, and a *locus paenitentioe* is thus given to the embryo—an opportunity of correcting the experience of one parent by that of the other. And this is what the more intelligent embryos may be supposed to do; for there would seem little reason to doubt that there are clever embryos and stupid embryos, with better or worse memories, as the case may be, of how they dealt with their protoplasm before, and better or worse able to see how they can do better now (1910, pp. 172–173).

By imputing a "mind" to the germ as well as to the embryo, Butler believed that he had clarified a host of previously baffling phenomena. For Butler, the vision of evolution directed by mind presented an exciting alternative to the game of chance that he thought Darwin had offered. Memory was the feature of mind that he believed brought his theory into conformity with known facts and lent it a compelling cogency.

Patterns of Influence and Visions of the Future

At least three distinguishable groups can be identified among the memory-heredity proponents. First, there were those who noted a point or two of correspondence between memory and heredity, but did not proceed to cultivate a systematic theory. The ideas of Matthew (1831), Jessen (1855), Sedgwick (1863), Ribot (1889), and Hartog (1920) fall into this category. These men had no detectable influence on the development of ideas about memory and heredity; their brief encounters went largely unnoticed by the more systematic theorists. Second, it is possible to identify a group that will be labeled the *first generation theorists*, which included Hering (1920), Haeckel (1876), Laycock (1876), Butler (1879), Orr (1893), and the American neo-Lamarckians Cope (1889) and Hyatt (1893). Here we find the systematic development of various ideas about the relation between memory and heredity, and the application of them to specific problems in biology. Ewald Hering, because of his 1870 lecture must be acknowledged as the earliest of these systematic memory-heredity advocates, but most of the subsequent first generation theorists either specifically denied knowledge of his work (e.g., Butler), or simply failed to demonstrate awareness of it in their own efforts (Laycock, Orr, Cope, Hyatt). In fact, with the exception of Haeckel—who publicly acknowledged his debt to Hering—there was little cross influence among any of the first generation theorists (counting Cope and Hyatt as representative of one point of view). Although their ideas shared much in common, the available evidence suggests that they arose independently of each other.

The picture changes upon examination of the *second generation theorists,* including Francis Darwin (1909), Ward (1913), Rignano (1926), and MacBride (1928), who explicitly built upon the work of their predecessors. One can now discern the differential influence of first generation theorists. The work of Laycock, Haeckel, Orr, Cope, and Hyatt was entirely ignored by almost all later memory-heredity advocates. In contrast, Hering's work received serious attention from these men and clearly shaped the direction of their theorizing. Although met with much abuse, Samuel Butler's ideas were at least recognized and debated by later theorists. Within the group of second generation advocates, the British scientists MacBride, Darwin, and Ward demonstrated some awareness of each other's efforts, whereas the ideas of the Italian Rignano, initially articulated prior to 1910, exerted slight influence on his contemporaries. Richard Semon can also be counted among the second generation theorists, and his work was taken quite seriously by the others. I shall have more to say about Semon's place in the memory-heredity movement in succeeding pages.

Although one should exercise caution in labeling this loose collection of theorists a "movement," it is clear that a number of memory-heredity proponents held out bright prospects for the future of the theory. The mnemonic approach to heredity, many of them believed, provided a conceptual framework that conferred a new respectability on the idea of the inheritance of acquired characteristics. And, as Francis Darwin argued, it suggested an alternative to the dogma of Weismann: "If the mnemic theory is compared with Weismann's views, it is clear that it is strong precisely where these are weakest (1909, p. 20)." Still others painted a grander picture of the new vistas that might be attained by continued development of the memory-heredity hypothesis. Rignano envisaged "a magnificent synthesis of biology and psychology" in which memory would be conceptualized as "constituting the fundamental substratum and essence of all life (1926, p. 35)." An even more cosmic vision was articulated by S. J. Tomkeieff. He enthusiastically reviewed various of the mnemonic theories in 1923 and concluded that they "represent thus an harmonising movement in the trend of human thought" that formed a cohesive bridge between formerly disparate areas of science. Tomkeieff sounded what he thought would be the clarion call of the new synthesis: "I remember, therefore I exist (p. 172)."

The mnemonic theory never achieved such lofty status. For the most part, the vicissitudes of the theory were seriously debated only by the small band of renegades whose idiosyncratic views we have considered, and as we have seen, many theorists with substantially similar outlooks worked in ignorance of each others' efforts. Some of the reasons for the failure of the memory-heredity enterprise will become clearer when examining the reception accorded Semon's version of it, but one point should be attended to now. Almost without exception, those who advanced the mnemonic hypothesis regarded hereditary phenomena as the ones that required explanation. Heredity seemed deep and mysterious; memory did not. Most of the above-mentioned theorists tacitly assumed that the facts of memory are given by experience and need no deeper investigation.

An inquiry into the cognitive basis of this ill-founded assumption is beyond our scope. There were, however, critics who questioned the utility of the mnemonic theory precisely because it took so much for granted about the nature of memory. Biologist Arthur Dendy was one of them: "it may be questioned whether any great advantage is to be gained by comparing the phenomena of heredity with those of memory, which are themselves no less difficult to explain (Dendy, 1938, p. 217)." William Bateson advanced a similar criticism. He was perplexed by attempts to understand heredity in terms of what he believed was an even more difficult problem:

> To attempt any representation of heredity as a product of memory is, moreover, to substitute the more obscure for the less. Both are now inscrutable; but while we may not unreasonably aspire to analyse heredity into simpler components by ordinary methods of research, the case of memory is altogether different. Memory is a mystery as deep as any that even psychology can propound (1913, pp. 190–191).

It was with an eye toward explicating both the mysteries of heredity and memory that Richard Semon initiated work on *Die Mneme*.

THE MNEME

Otto Lubarsch provides one of the few glimpses into the genesis of *Die Mneme*:

> Semon conceived the first thoughts on "Mneme" in the winter of 1900/01, and wrote down the major ideas during January–February 1901 in a notebook entitled "Cell memory. An attempt to simplify the basic problems of biology." . . . The systematic working out of these thoughts did not go quickly for him; he completed the first part in the late summer 1903, which he let me see at the end of August when I visited him in Munich . . . the whole book was completed by the end of August 1904, and appeared on November 22 of the same year (Lubarsch, 1920, pp. xxxii–xxxiii).

The book that ultimately emerged from his four years' labor represented Semon's attempt to cast the major problems of biology in terms that conferred order upon previously chaotic terrain and brought unity to seemingly disparate processes. Conceived as a theoretical application of Monistic principles, *Die*

Mneme owed much of its inspiration to Ernst Haeckel. It constituted a grand, synthetic scheme that encompassed diverse biological phenomena in much the same style utilized by Haeckel in *Generelle Morphologie* and *Anthropogenie*. The unmistakable influence of his mentor on *Die Mneme* is nowhere more evident than in Semon's impassioned defense of the "historical method" in biology, a brief polemic that is strikingly reminiscent of Haeckel's admonition that biology is fundamentally an "historical science" that cannot solely rely on experimental endeavors.[13] The Haeckelian spirit of *Die Mneme* is also apparent in Semon's principal thesis, a unifying conception in the tradition of the biogenetic law that attempted to expand upon the views of first-generation memory-heredity theorists such as Haeckel, Hering, Butler, Orr, and Laycock. The construct of memory, Semon argued, can be extended to encompass more than is usually considered within the domain of "ordinary" remembering. Phenomena of habit, heredity, and even regeneration seemed to Semon indicative of a more fundamental underlying process. Hering had labeled it "organic memory," Laycock called it "synesia," and Cope invoked the term "cryptopony"; Semon dubbed the hidden generator of organic reproduction "Mneme."[14] For Semon, Mneme stretched the notion of memory to its widest conceptual limits. A broad theoretical construct, Mneme describes an organism's capacity to conserve the effects of stimulation and to interact with the environment on the basis of conserved experience. As Semon put it, it is Mneme "which in the organic world links the past and the present in a living bond (1921, p. 12)."

"Mneme" was just one of several terms that Semon created for his own scientific purposes. He believed that everyday language contains an excess of potentially misleading connotations that severely constrains its usefulness in scientific matters. Semon's new terms often preserved the bizarre quality so characteristic of Haeckel's terminological inventions, but only one of Semon's creations ever attained the popularity achieved by such Haeckelian gems as "ontogeny," "phylogeny," and "ecology." I refer to his notion of the engram.

---

13. Semon's harangue is worth quoting for its unmistakable echo of the spirit of similar lectures delivered by Haeckel:

   It has recently become the fashion among a certain group of biologists to deprecate the value of the historical method because of the indirect conclusions involved. It would be interesting to know how far these men of science would allow their scepticism to affect their reading of social history. Is the account of Erasmus and the Reformation to be rejected because it is not possible to set out an experimental repetition? Why should natural science be denied the valid use of the historical method? It is a comfort to know that the majority of men, learned and unlearned, will continue to devote thought and attention to mere historical, non-recurring phenomena (Semon. 1921, pp. 66–67).

14. "Mneme" is the Greek word for memory, or rememberance. It should be noted that an excellent English translation of *Die Mneme* is available, and I will cite from this volume unless otherwise stated.

Semon's stated conception of the engram generated much controversy; we will examine the various objections to it in subsequent pages. For now, it will be sufficient to present Semon's definition of the term: "the enduring though primarily latent modification in the irritable substance produced by a stimulus (1921, p. 12)." Semon labeled the *process* that gives rise to a new engram "engraphy." Another of Semon's terminological creations never attained the popularity accorded "engram," but in many ways represents the key to understanding Semon's approach to biology and psychology. This is the notion of ecphory: "the influences which awaken the mnemic trace or engram out of its latent state into one of manifested activity (p. 12)." Ecphory, then, is roughly equivalent to a modern term such as "retrieval"; it is Semon's way of talking about the *utilization* of information established by prior engraphic processes.

Semon initiated his analysis by recognizing previous attempts to characterize heredity with mnemonic concepts, and pointed to the lack of impact of these theories on mainstream scientific thought. Although he lauded Hering's pioneering efforts, and respectfully noted the work of Laycock and Orr, Semon had harsher words for Butler's theory, labeling it "rather a retrogression than an advance (1921, p. 10)." The problem with the post-Hering memory-heredity theories, contended Semon, concerned their failure to provide a theoretical framework that could convincingly explain why the apparent resemblances between memory and heredity are more than coincidental. This is the task that Semon set for himself in *Die Mneme*. Semon's approach to this problem differs from that of previous memory-heredity theorists whom we have encountered. Although just like Hering, Ribot, and others, Semon viewed memory-heredity resemblances as reflections of a more fundamental underlying process—in Semon's case, the operations of Mneme—he depicted this relationship by adopting a *stage-analysis*. Semon outlined four stages that he hypothesized as characteristic of all mnemic processes. Such a framework, Semon believed, constituted an important first step in the construction of a cohesive theoretical scheme.

The first mnemic stage, labeled by Semon the "primary state of indifference," refers to the state of the organism prior to any particular stimulation. In this state, the responses of the organism to a new stimulus are controlled by its general experiences and by the properties of the stimulus. Next comes the "engraphically acting stimulus" which, because of attributes such as intensity, duration, and so on, changes the "irritable substance" of the organism in such a way that a new engram is created. The new engram can be preserved in the somatic-cells of the brain and thus influence subsequent behavior of the organism within its lifetime. But the engraphic influence can, if repeated often enough, alter the germ-cells of the organism and thus affect the behavior of its progeny. The next two stages are the crucial ones, and provide the explicit theoretical link between memory and heredity. The "secondary state of indifference" signifies a period of *latency* in which the behavior of the organism is indistinguishable from its behavior in the "primary" state of indifference. There is, however, a critical difference. The organism now has the potential to respond to certain stimuli—those that gave rise to the new engram—in a manner that it could not prior to the engraphic act. This period of latency varies considerably, but it is characteristic both of memories that are acquired at one point in an organism's existence and manifested at a later one, and of hereditary characters acquired by one generation and manifested in succeeding ones. A latency period, then, comprises an essential feature of mnemic processes. What puts an end to this state of latency? Why are the newly established engrams not forever consigned to a dormant state? Here Semon appealed to the operation of ecphoric processes in memory and heredity as the chief characteristic of the fourth mnemic stage: "The organic substance reveals the working of a new law, in that it is now predisposed to the state of excitement by influences other than that of the original stimulus. . . . This principle is the *partial* recurrence of a definite energetic condition (1921, p. 39–40)."

In regard to inherited engrams, Semon believed that the notion of *partial* recurrence was crucial. The importance of the concept of partial recurrence can be illustrated by considering a simple question. If an organism responds to a particular stimulus configuration in the same way that its parents responded to the identical situation, is it permissible to infer the existence of an inherited engram that controls the behavior of the progeny? The answer is clearly negative. It is more parsimonious to assume that the two organisms simply respond to like stimuli in like manner, and that when all the requisite conditions are repeated, behavior of the parent and child organisms will be functionally identical. This criticism was directed at previous memory-heredity theorists, especially Butler: Why postulate the existence of an unnecessary variable such as memory when all the phenomena can be accounted for without it? One does not impute a memory to the tides simply because they behave in the same manner when all the requisite stimuli are repeated; why do so in the case of heredity? Butler had no satisfactory response to such a query. Semon met it head-on by contending that the distinguishing feature of mnemic phenomena lies in their capacity for reinstatement by just a *partial* repetition of the original circumstances. The tides will not behave on any one occasion exactly as they did on a previous one unless all of the critical circumstances are repeated. In contrast, only *part* of the circumstances that accompanied an engraphic process need be repeated at the time of ecphory for the complete reinstatement of a given engram. A true ecphoric influence, then, is a part that reinstates a whole.

The four-stage model of mnemic processes provided the anchor point for Semon's analysis of memory and heredity, and sets the stage for his treatment of individual memory-heredity correspondences. Semon did not, like many of those we have examined, enlist the "automatization" notion of repetition in constructing his theory. Though he assigned an important role to repetition, he approached the issue from a different perspective than his contemporaries. Whereas theorists such as Butler, Orr, Cope, and Francis Darwin viewed repetition as a means of strengthening and automatizing existing engrams, Semon argued that each repetition of a stimulus creates a separate engram. He believed that his conceptualization of hereditary engrams as separate "units" was in keeping with then-recent Mendelian conceptions of genetics that emphasized discrete characters as the material basis of heredity.

How, then, does repetition serve to increase the hereditary effect of acquired engrams if not by "strengthening" them over long periods of time? Semon confronted this problem by resorting to his conception of *homophony*. This idea was invoked by Semon to describe the manner by which information from different sources is combined. Semon conceptualized homophony as a "resonance" between engrams. When ecphoric conditions permit "homophonous interaction" between engrams, the net effect is that the engrams combine to form a more potent one.[15] With regard to the problem of repetition, the solution was simple: Although hereditary engrams are separate "units" in a Mendelian sense, repeated engrams gain added potency via the strengthening effects of homophony when they are elicited from their latent state at the time of ecphory. Thus, according to Semon, engrams are "distinct entities, and yet they display a joint homophonous activity (1921, p. 260)." Semon believed that his theory made close contact with contemporary research in genetics, and unequivocally expressed his enthusiasm about the apparent correspondence:

> NILSSON-EHLE BY HIS CROSS-BREEDING EXPERIMENTS HAS THUS ARRIVED AT EXACTLY THE SAME CONCLUSIONS IN RESPECT TO THE HEREDITARY FACTORS AS I HAVE REACHED BY AN ALTOGETHER DIFFERENT WAY IN RESPECT TO INDIVIDUALLY ACQUIRED ENGRAMS AND THE CO-EXISTENCE OF ISOLATED BUT QUALITATIVELY SIMILAR POTENTIALITIES, EACH OF WHICH ON ECPHORY CAN OF ITSELF PRODUCE THE CORRESPONDING REACTION, BUT THE HOMOPHONOUS COOPERATION OF WHICH BRINGS ABOUT UNDER CERTAIN CONDITIONS AN INCREASED EFFECT. (p. 262)

In the context of these ideas, it is not surprising that Semon's portrayal of unfolding hereditary characters during ontogeny did not rely on the notion of a smoothly executed habit invoked by others. Rather, Semon turned to his favorite conceptual tool for an explanation: ecphory via partial recurrence. Semon argued that the unfolding of hereditary characters in ontogeny is just like everyday memory because in both cases otherwise latent engrams are activated by appropriate ecphoric influences. In the "everyday" case, these influences are components of the original engraphic conditions. In the ontogenetic case, the situation is similar: The confluence of certain energetic factors at a given stage of ontogenesis serve as ecphoric cues that "release" the engrams required for the next stage of development. But in the ontogenetic case, "the necessary external ecphoric stimulus is an integral part of a previous engraphic stimulus

---

15. Semon distinguished between various types of homophony and applied the idea to numerous problems of memory. We will return to a more extended consideration of homophony in Chapter 9.

which, in the corresponding stages of development, has influenced the ancestors of the organisms in question (1921, p. 197)." Semon termed such a process
"phasogeneous ecphory," "which means that on reaching a certain phase of development a state of the irritable substance has been generated which acts
ecphorically on a certain engram (p. 56)." Variations in the precise energetic
conditions accompanying any given ontogenetic stage could be comfortably tol-
erated, since *partial* return is all that is required: "Slight deviations in the developmental phase will, in the greater number of cases, be practically of no consequence so far as the ecphoric action is concerned, seeing that for the ecphory
the partial return of the energetic condition is sufficient (p. 76)."

The notion of phasogeneous ecphory can be best understood by consideration of a simple example. Semon cited evidence indicating that lens development in the frog's eye is critically dependent upon the optical vesicle contacting
the epidermis. In his terminology, the optical vesicle acts as an ecphoric stimulus, liberating an engram-complex that contains the information necessary for
lens formation. Semon also noted research suggesting that other influences accompanying the developmental phase (besides the optical vesicle itself) could
initiate lens formation. Although such "irregularities" might present problems
for other theories, contended Semon, his theory could easily account for these
findings, because only a fraction of the excitations that normally accompany
lens formation need be present for ecphory to occur and for lens formation to
proceed in the usual manner. Semon firmly maintained that the normal unfolding of hereditary characters in the face of such irregularities could be understood *"only in the light of the theory of ecphory* (1921, p. 79)."

Like other memory-heredity theorists, Semon pointed to the *orderly* unfolding of hereditary characters as an important correspondence between mnemonic and hereditary phenomena. Semon argued that ontogeny is ordered because the engrams that underlie it are associated, resulting in a series of orderly
and regular ecphories: "The rational inference is that the morphogeneous engram-complexes are successively associated, and that the ecphory of the first in
a sequence effects the ecphory of the related series of engrams (p. 180)." It is
worth pointing out that Semon again framed his analysis in terms of ecphory
rather than habit.

Semon also considered a phenomenon that was not addressed by other
memory-heredity theorists. He labeled it "engram-dichotomy" and it is best
explained by example. In the memorization of a poem, we may encounter a
point at which either of two responses is possible. The illustrative example used
in the English edition of *Die Mneme* is the following extract from the Rubáiyat
of Omar Khayyam (1921, p. 221):

The Sultan's Turrent   in a Noose of Light
                      in a Shaft of Light

As we approach the word "Turrent" we are faced with what Semon called an
"engram-dichotomy": It is possible to retrieve the engrams representing either

of the alternative lines. Semon argued that similar dichotomies exist in ontogeny. For example, he noted research indicating that at certain points in the development of bee larvae, the potential exists for producing a worker or a queen. The ultimate form of the bee—worker or queen—can be influenced by feeding larvae "worker" food or "queen" food. In Semon's terms, the "worker engram" or the "queen engram" can be ecphorized by the appropriate stimuli. Thus, argued Semon, we find similar processes operative in both of the above cases: Either of two engrams may be activated at a particular juncture in the mnemic process. Moreover, in both cases the conditions of ecphory influence which of the two possible engrams is awakened; the resolution of the "engram-dichotomy" "depends entirely and without exception on the strength of *external influences* (p. 289)." Once again, Semon believed that he had elucidated a resemblance between mnemonic and hereditary phenomena that directly pointed to the underlying operation of Mneme.

Another subject that attracted several memory-heredity theorists also interested Semon: instincts. Rather than assigning theoretical importance to the notion of "hereditary habit," Semon ascribed a crucial role to ecphoric processes in the regulation of instinctual behavior. His argument here was straightforward: Inherited engrams underly instinctual phenomena, hence their manifestation is dependent upon the presence of appropriate ecphoric influences. For instance, the fact that young birds do not peck until they first see grain was regarded by Semon as a clear example of instinct operating via ecphory. The optical stimulus (the grain) serves as an ecphoric influence, and releases the hereditary engrams that control pecking behavior (1921, p. 70). Semon adduced similar sorts of evidence to support his contention that instincts are just one subset of mnemic phenomena.

The foregoing extracts from Semon's theory reveal both similarities and differences between his treatment of memory-heredity correspondences and the work of the theorists considered earlier. Like the other memory-heredity theorists, Semon's work is characterized by occasional flashes of ingenious insight mixed with clumsily strained comparisons that seem exceedingly unlikely to withstand closer scrutiny. But in fairness to Semon, we should acknowledge the countless experiments and observations that he analyzed in detail to build his case; the analytical difference between his treatment and those described earlier is large. *Die Mneme* did not bear the stamp of runaway speculation encountered in Butler's work. It was the product of an ordered and thorough Prussian mind, a performance that would have made the drill sergeants at the Kaiser Wilhelm Gymnasium proud to claim Semon as an exemplary product of their pedagogical methods.

But what applied to every other memory-heredity theorist applied to Semon as well: He had to believe in the inheritance of acquired characteristics for the system to work. It does not make much sense to speak of engraphic and ecphoric processes as critical determinants of hereditary phenomena unless the engrams underlying these processes are biologically transmitted from one generation to the next. Ironically, although Semon was often labeled as an enthusiastic neo-

Lamarckian, his sympathies were much closer to Darwin than to Lamarck. Semon openly ridiculed Lamarck's postulation of an internal organizing energy to explain evolutionary phenomena, chiding it as a "forlorn and barren explanation (1921, p. 289)." In contrast, he lauded Darwin's theory of natural selection as "one of the greatest triumphs of the human mind (p. 289)." Semon optimistically put forward the vision of Mneme and Natural Selection together offering a satisfactory account of evolution:

> Neither in the Mneme nor in Natural Selection is to be discovered an all-sufficient principle furnishing a universal key to the understanding of all organic phenomena. But in the Mneme there is to be found a conserving principle which is indispensable for organic development, in so far as it preserves the transformations which the external world unceasingly creates. Its conserving influence is, of course, restricted by that indirect factor of the external world, Natural Selection, for, in the long run, only fit transformations survive. (p. 291).

Regardless of his Darwinian sympathies, it was Semon's so-called Lamarckian stance concerning the inheritance of acquired characteristics that eventually determined his scientific fortunes. The bright future that he envisaged for Mneme was ultimately vitiated because of his necessarily ineradicable support of the doctrine of acquired characteristics.

THE RECEPTION OF *DIE MNEME*: SEEDS OF SCIENTIFIC ISOLATION

Scientific opinion emerged divided about *Die Mneme*, but it was a division of unequal numbers and ranks; Semon's few supporters wielded far less influence in the scientific community than did his many detractors. The pro-Semon forces were spearheaded by August Forel, who himself had enthusiastically endorsed Hering's views on organic memory (Forel, 1885). Forel initiated his defense in a lengthy article that opened the March/April 1905 issue of the *Archiv für Rassen- und GesellschaftsBiologie*. Forel depicted *Die Mneme* as the first systematic extension of Hering's work, and showered praise upon Semon's novel constructs while extolling his careful elaboration of them. After reviewing the book in detail, Forel delivered an unambiguous verdict on *Die Mneme*: "I believe not to be in error when I label this work as epoch-making (1905, p. 196)." He left no room for doubt concerning his opinion of Semon's book: "Semon's consistent elaboration of these ideas in morphology, biology, and psychology is illuminating; and the new perspectives which it gives are magnificent (1907, p. 137)."

Die Mneme received a positive reception from a variety of other scientists in the first years following its publication. Gustav Eichhorn, a physicist who endorsed the memory-heredity hypothesis, praised the "masterly form" (*meisterhafter Form*; 1909, p. 7) of Semon's exposition and pointed to the conception of Mneme as a basis for a new approach to biological problems. The psychologist Moritz Alsberg found much commendable in Semon's analysis, and like Eichhorn argued that the construct of Mneme represented the core concept in a new approach to biology (1906, p. 23). As might be expected, *Die Mneme* also found a friendly reception from those who systematically cultivated the memory-heredity hypothesis. Francis Darwin enthusiastically championed Semon's views in his 1908 Presidential Address to the British Association. This endorsement impressed Semon so much that he dedicated the English version of *Die Mneme* to Sir Francis. Eugenio Rignano also acknowledged Semon's valuable contribution to the memory-heredity hypothesis, and characterized his work as "the most perfect elaboration of all preceding mnemonic theories (1926, p. 110)." Perhaps the most spirited evaluation of Semon's contribution originated from the pen of a master of overstatement who remained loyal to his former student in evaluating *Die Mneme*: "The most important advance that evolution has made since Darwin and the most valuable amplification of his theory of selection is, in my opinion, the work of Richard Semon (Haeckel, 1910, p. 42)."

Haeckel's commendation, however, was of little value to Semon. Thirty years earlier, Haeckel's support would have substantially aided a daring theorist such as Semon. In the first decade of the 20th-century, the backing of this "harmless elder statesman," who had already offended a sizeable portion of the biological community, was more likely to damage than to help. The opinions of Semon's other supporters carried just as little weight; none of these men were recognized authorities on problems of evolution or heredity.[16] *Die Mneme*, then, had its supporters—but their influence paled in the face of the opposition.

The critics of *Die Mneme* can be roughly partitioned into three categories. First, there were those who accused Semon of re-casting ancient problems in new terms. Yves DéLage, one of the leading French evolutionary biologists, developed this theme in his review of *Die Mneme* for the prestigious *L'Année Biologique*. DéLage claimed that Forel's praise of the book "does not appear justified to us." He contended that the phenomena Semon believed to have explained still remained "obscure"; simply "grouping them under the rubric of mneme" did nothing to elucidate their underlying nature (1904, p. 9). The eminent French psychologist Théodule Ribot offered a similar criticism of Semon's work; he branded *Die Mneme* as a "metaphysical" work (1912, p. 267).

---

16. For instance, Gustav Eichhorn was a physicist who took a keen interest in the memory-heredity hypothesis and attempted to ground it in physics in his unabashedly speculative treatment of biological and psychological problems (Eichhorn, 1909). Even Ernst Haeckel—a formidable speculator in his own right—found Eichhorn's ideas excessively fanciful, and judged him rather harshly in a letter to Semon: "It was clear to me from the beginning that Eichhorn had bats in his belfry (12–25–05)." An endorsement from a scientist such as Eichhorn, then, could hardly be expected to have aided Semon's cause in the biological world.

Another prominent psychologist—the British neo-Lamarckian William McDougall—attacked Semon along the same lines as DéLage: "I, for one, cannot see that, inspite of the introduction of several new words, he has achieved any success (1911, p. 247)." One of the more vituperous criticisms of this sort came from the well-known German physiologist Max Verworn:

> With a series of new expressions the originator of the 'Mneme doctrine' deceives himself, as well as a number of his readers not endowed with the critical faculty, into supposing that he has achieved a serious analysis. Of such, however, there is not a trace. (1913, p. 47)

A second group of critics granted Semon more intellectual credit than Verworn did, but focused on his "mistaken" memory-heredity hypothesis in their critiques. The influential geneticist W. L. Johannsen—who coined the term "gene"—acknowledged Semon's "ingenious speculations," but accused him of establishing a "false analogy" between memory and heredity (1913, p. 423). A reviewer in the *Biologisches Centralblatt* argued that Semon had failed to establish identity of the processes underlying memory and heredity, and downplayed the significance of Semon's contribution by asserting that his major thesis "will always remain an analogy (Rosenthal, 1905, p. 368)." A similar point was advanced in a lengthy treatise by Walther Moede, who rejected the possibility that memory and heredity can both be traced to the same underlying process: "Eine spezielle Analyse zeigt bald die grossen Differenzen (1912, p. 381)." The most detailed critique of this variety was put forward by the brain physiologist Semi Meyer (1906) in a lengthy paper directly attacking *Die Mneme*. Meyer performed a detailed structural analysis of a variety of hereditary (i.e., instinctual) and learned movements (*ererbten und erlernten Bewegungen*), and concluded that the large differences between the two kinds of processes precluded the applicability of unifying conceptions such as Mneme (p. 629). A slightly different mode of attack is found in the paper published by Carl Detto (1905) in the widely read *Naturwissenschaftliche Wochenschrift*. Detto held that Semon's conception failed to theoretically unite mnemonic and hereditary phenomena because it crossed two different levels of analysis: The "mnemic laws" are physiological laws that have no direct bearing on psychological problems such as memory.

A closely related argument was advanced by a group that Semon himself had predicted would ravage his theory: the vitalists. Hans Driesch, perhaps the most influential among them, questioned Semon's application of the term "memory" to hereditary processes: Should we really believe that the organism "remembers" what happened to it in previous generations? Memory implied consciousness to Driesch, who warned that the term "may be applied to the phenomena of inheritance only in a very figurative meaning, if at all (1908, pp. 218–219)." Marcus Hartog, another avowed biological vitalist who championed Butler's theory precisely because it left sufficient room for "physical" factors in evolution, questioned the feasibility of Semon's "mechanistic" memory-heredity theory. Hartog expressed displeasure at Semon's disdainful references to the "backward path of vitalism," and forecast a dim future for Mneme: "Semon assuredly will never be able to complete his theory of 'Mneme' until . . . he forsakes the blind alley of mechanisticism and retraces his steps to reasonable vitalism (1920, p. xxxv)."

The list of critics in the two groups we have so far considered contains some impressive names. Any biologist or psychologist writing in 1904 would have become justly anxious to learn that the likes of DéLage, Ribot, Johannsen, Verworn, McDougall, and Driesch openly disputed the validity of his theory. The third group of critics, however, contained Semon's most feared opponents. These men opposed him on the issue around which the fate of *Die Mneme* most crucially hinged: the inheritance of acquired characteristics. Some critics, such as evolutionary biologist Arthur Dendy (1938, Ch. 14) and psychologist Victor Franz (1909), urged suspension of a final assessment of Semon's theory pending resolution of the acquired characters debate. Others were not so tolerant. William Bateson noted the dependence of the mnemic theory on the transmission of acquired characteristics, and subjected various cases adduced by Semon as evidence favoring acquired characters to a thorough analysis. He reached a negative conclusion on each one (1913, pp. 190–199). Bateson's criticisms were comfortably tucked away in a larger series of lectures; August Weismann's assault occupied biological center-stage. Weismann's 27-page critique of *Die Mneme* appeared as the lead paper in the 1906 volume of the *Archiv für Rassen- und Gesellschafts-Biologie*. The aging opponent of acquired characters wasted little time in coming to the point. He noted Forel's positive review of the book, and acknowledged the interest that Semon's theory had sparked. But, continued Weismann, "however brilliant are the explanations of this ingenious book (1906, p. 1)," Semon had advanced ideas in it that he had personally campaigned against for years and could not ignore now. The remaining 26 pages of the review display an experienced warrior at work in familiar territory; Weismann's numerous previous clashes over acquired characters prepared him well for his critique of *Die Mneme*. He interpreted much of the evidence cited by Semon as proof of somatically acquired characters in terms of parallel inductions. Other cases were tossed aside by recourse to natural selection, and still others were explained away in terms of atavism and the release of congenital predispositions. When these arguments failed to account for an apparent instance of acquired characters, Weismann resorted to adducing "logical evidence" (*logische Beweise*) that the transmission in question could not have occurred. The tactics were familiar ones, and the inevitably harsh conclusion came as no surprise: "I believe to have shown that all cases which Semon has cited as direct or 'indirect' evidence, for what is labeled by him inheritance of a somatogenic character, are not valid (1906, p. 21)." Further, averred Weismann, without the needed support of the discredited doctrine of acquired characteristics, the usefulness of the construct of "Mneme" was seriously undermined (p. 27). Weismann had nothing to say about the memory-heredity notion itself; his interest in *Die Mneme* stemmed solely from its intrusion into the forbidden territory of acquired characteristics.

Faced with the foregoing criticisms, Semon could have mounted a counterattack in any number of ways. For instance, he might have chosen to emphasize the explanatory strengths of the Mneme theory in areas where competing theories were weak, rather than embroil himself in direct controversy with his critics. Such a strategy had been pursued by Francis Darwin. Although Darwin realized that Weismann's attacks penetrated to the core of the mnemic theory ("It is clear that there must be war to the knife between the theory of Weismann and that of the somatists"), he respectfully declined to engage Weismann in a direct struggle: "I acknowledge also most fully that it requires a stronger man than myself to meet that trained and well-tried fighter (1909, pp. 18–19)." Instead, Darwin stressed the positive aspects of the mnemic theory. Semon chose the path of direct confrontation.

He did not devote equal time to answering each of the three groups of critics. Semon curtly responded to those who accused him of merely inventing some frivolous terminology in the third edition of *Die Mneme:*

> I reply that neither science nor philosophy has yet explained the 'real nature' of any phenomenon whatever. I claim, however, to have succeeded in discerning some phases of the engraphic action of stimuli in their orderly recurrence, and in reducing them to a minimum of fundamental law (1921, p. 275).

He expended somewhat more energy replying to those who objected to the validity of conceptualizing heredity in terms of memory. For instance, Semon (1907b) devoted an entire paper to rebutting in detail Meyer's arguments concerning the differences between learned and instinctual movements. The thrust of his counterattack was straightforward. He had argued that identical *laws* govern the two processes, not that the two processes are themselves structurally identical; Meyer had misinterpreted his position. Semon made a similar point when addressing critics of the memory-heredity hypothesis in the third edition of *Die Mneme:*

> That the cerebral process of memory is not identical with the process of growth in embryonic development, and that the latter is not identical with the unconscious movement of the plant—well, 'There needs no ghost . . . come from the grave to tell us this.' (1921, p. 279)

Semon continued by stressing the differences between a "process-identity" and a "principle-identity":

> A simple water-wheel attached to a lawn-sprinkler or garden-foundation is very much unlike a turbine of modern construction, and the processes of the two are by no means identical when compared in detail; yet the physicist will

tell us that the principle underlying both processes is *identical*, and not merely analogous. (p. 279)

Semon also had harsh words for critics such as Driesch who objected to his memory-heredity hypothesis because of the implications of consciousness inherent in the term "memory." Semon noted with some consternation that he had created his own terminology precisely in order to avoid such confusion. He wished to stress the physiological underpinnings of reproductive processes, and preferred use of the non-connotative term "Mneme" to the clearly connotative "memory." Still, Semon found "on the part of my critics a determination to involve me in the use of the word 'memory'." But, he concluded, "Such objections as those of Driesch ... fall to the ground as inapplicable to the subject actually in question (1921, p. 282)."

Semon's replies to the above criticisms, however, comprised just one small part of his counter offensive. In what ultimately proved to be a disastrous maneuver, he devoted most of his energies to arguing for the existence of the inheritance of acquired characteristics. Not that such a strategy lacked compelling logic. As we saw earlier, the applicability of the Mneme theory to hereditary phenomena squarely depends upon the existence of acquired characteristics. But Semon's campaign for the ill-fated doctrine was launched at the wrong time. By the first decade of the 20th-century, Weismann's crusade had turned mainstream biological thought against the acquired characters theory. Stanford biologist Vernon Kellogg gauged the situation in 1907:

> at present the weight of evidence inclines strongly against such an inheritance, chiefly because of Weismann's successfully destructive criticism of about all the evidence in behalf of it. . . . I cannot undertake to say whether more reputable biologists disbeleve in than believe in the existence of such inheritance, but it is obvious that the disbelievers have the present prestige of apparent victory: they call for convincing evidence of such inheritance, and it is not produced. (pp. 263–264)

In years subsequent to Kellogg's assessment, the issue seemed forever doomed to a series of emotionally-laden controversies that resulted in many aggravated accusations and few firm conclusions. Semon had hoped that his own labors would put an end to the debate; they did not.

His first major effort specifically directed at the problem of acquired characteristics opened the 1907 edition of the *Archiv für Rassen-und Gesellschafts-Biologie*. The lengthy paper reviewed in detail all existing evidence relevant to the problem at hand, but Semon established the central focus of the paper at the outset:

> If this important principle [inheritance of acquired characteristics] which deserves recognition has until now been continually denied, it is due to the unyielding opposition of a single researcher . . . who in the last 25 years has concentrated all of his energies on the exploration of problems of heredity

and in those areas has gained a leading influence in wide circles: August Weismann (1907a, p. 2).

Semon addressed each of Weismann's objections in detail, pointing to flaws in his opponent's argument or citing new evidence that he believed supported the acquired characters position. He ended the paper by restating his major purpose—to counter effectively all of Weismann's criticisms—and optimistically assessed the results of his endeavor: "This task has been served by the present essay, and it will, I hope, help to demolish the legend that the inheritance of acquired characteristics is not a proven fact (p. 45)." Semon relentlessly drove home the same conclusion in numerous journal articles, in his reply to the critics in the third edition of *Die Mneme,* and in a monograph exclusively devoted to the problem of acquired characters (Semon, 1912). He frequently corresponded with Paul Kammerer, whose notorious experiments on the midwife toad were cited by Semon as irrefutable evidence favoring the inheritance of acquired characteristics. Kammerer, too, leaned on Semon's authority: Semon is cited more frequently in Kammerer's (1924) book on acquired characteristics than any other scientist save August Weismann.[17]

In spite of Semon's rhetorical campaign, the scientific status of the acquired characteristics theory remained shrouded in doubt for the duration of his lifetime. The major consequence of his tireless efforts was that he became identified as a stubborn supporter of the doctrine. Franz (1909, p. 230) labeled Semon a "convinced supporter" of the acquired characters position; Bateson (1913, p. 203) referred readers to Semon's papers for an examination of the evidence "from the standpoint of a convinced believer"; and Dendy (1938, p. 203) characterized Semon as "one of the staunchest supporters of the doctrine of acquired characters." Yet for Semon the ultimate battle concerned Mneme. The issue of acquired characters was a subordinate, though necessary, component of his larger theory. His unflagging efforts to establish the existence of acquired characters stemmed from a deeper commitment to the furtherance of Mneme; the fact that his strategy failed should not obscure its larger purpose.

For Semon, Mneme eventually assumed the qualities of an *idée fixe.* Semon never abandoned the idea, and he concentrated nearly all of his scientific efforts on its vindication. Just as Johannes Kepler never relinquished a profound emotional attachment to the *idée fixe* in his life—the mystical notion of the "five perfect bodies" (Koestler, 1959, p. 254)—Semon remained under the spell of Mneme in all of his scientific activities. Kepler's attachment to his *idée fixee* functionally blinded him from fully appreciating the magnitude of his greatest achievement, the planetary laws of motion. Although Semon's most innovative ideas (concerning human memory) were somewhat more modest, his affective absorption in the vicissitudes of Mneme markedly attenuated his own appreciation of them. Like Kepler, he walked blindly in his own garden.

---

17. For the record, Weismann was cited 19 times by Kammerer, Semon 15 times. In comparison, Darwin received 13 citations and Lamarck just six.

There is one more point that deserves mention before concluding our treatment of the reception accorded *Die Mneme*. Semon's timing in advancing his mnemonic scheme of heredity was exquisitely poor not only because it led him into the quagmire of the acquired characters dispute. As mentioned earlier, many late 19th-century attempts to understand heredity were bold speculative ventures that also endeavored to account for a host of related phenomena. But there was an inflection point in the scientific approach to heredity that occurred around the year 1900; Semon advanced his theory on the wrong side of that inflection point. In 1900, Gregor Mendel's neglected breeding experiments were independently brought to the attention of scientists by biologists Hugh deVries, Carl Correns, and Eric von Tschermak-Seysenegg. The rediscovery of Mendel's work signaled the beginning of experimental genetics and a turn away from the expansive theorizing that characterized the late 19th-century approaches of Weismann, Haeckel, Nägeli, and Darwin himself. It was precisely during the years that Semon put together *Die Mneme* that the study of heredity became an experimental discipline concerned with the mechanics of hereditary transmission and the mathematics of Mendelian ratios. Dunn (1965, p. 33) described the gulf that separated the old and the new approaches to heredity:

> That period, say from 1900–1906, can now be seen as marking the chief break in the continuity of ideas about the transmission system of heredity. What happened prior to that time—except, of course, for the original publication of Mendel's pea experiments—had little connection with the later course of development of these ideas.

Although Semon did make several attempts to relate his theory to the Mendelian insights, *Die Mneme* spiritually belonged to the older synthetic approach best exemplified by Ernst Haeckel. Just as Haeckel's work seemed bloated and irrelevant to the concerns of the new experimental embryology, so too was Semon's approach hopelessly out of step with the Mendelian trends that eventually dominated the study of heredity. Thus it was partially owing to developments over which Semon had no control, and partially owing to his own efforts in defense of Mneme, that the seeds of scientific isolation were irrevocably sown.

Amidst all the furor over Semon's advocacy of the acquired characters doctrine, his mnemonic account of heredity, and the controversial notion of Mneme, the critics remained conspicuously silent concerning the view of memory itself developed by Semon in *Die Mneme*. Perhaps this seemed too prosaic in comparison with the more spectacular issues that attracted so much attention. There is one review of the book, however, that stands out in bold relief precisely because it penetrated the smokescreen created by Mneme and its attendant problems to identify the most innovative ideas offered by Semon. This passage from the review of *Die Mneme* published by Henry J. Watt in the 1905 *Archiv für die*

Gesamte Psychologie is doubly remarkable owing to its prescient characterization of Semon's approach to his own theory:

> The most valuable part of the book appears to be the concept of the ecphoric stimulus. . . . However, Semon in his attempt to find something common in the reproduction of the organism and in the reproduction in the sense of memory, has lost sight of his own objective (the discovery of the nature of the ecphoric stimulus) and has gone astray (1905, p. 130).

What of this "ecphoric stimulus"? Why does Watt label Semon's conception of it "the most valuable part of the book"? And why should we consider Semon's elaborate treatment of ecphoric processes to be an innovative contribution to the theory of memory? In order to achieve satisfactory answers to these questions we must cast the notion of ecphory in a broader historical context, and examine the contemporary status of memory theory in Semon's time. This investigation constitutes the chief task of the next chapter.

8

Retrieval: The Mnemonic Missing Link

*F*ranciscus de Oviedo, a 17th-century Jesuit, pondered many of Nature's deepest secrets. Amidst the formidable array of her many enigmas, one in particular seemed especially vexing—the process by which a dormant memory is brought into conscious awareness. To Oviedo, the phenomenon that he labeled "the excitation of species" constitutes "the very greatest mystery of all philosophy, never to be competently explained by human ingenuity." The puzzled scholar detailed his reasons for expressing pessimism that the problem of species-excitation could ever be solved:

> because we can neither discover the cause which, for example, in the recitation of an oration, excites the species in the order in which they are excited, nor the reason why often, when wishing to recollect a matter, we do not, whereas when not wishing to recollect it we sometimes do. Hence . . . Poncius says, that for the excitation of the species we must either recur at once to God, or to some sufficient cause, which, however, he does not specify (cited in Hamilton, 1859, p. 228).

Oviedo's problem is still with us. Although modern students of memory typically refrain from appeals to the Almighty when confronting it, most can empathize with the bewildered Jesuit's exasperation as he grappled with an exceedingly difficult issue. What Oviedo labeled "species-excitation" is, three centuries later, referred to as the problem of *retrieval*. Broadly stated, the retrieval problem concerns the psychological events that occur when one attempts to utilize, or bring into conscious awareness, previously acquired information. The vast amount of information contained in the human mind would not be very useful if specified bits of it could not be brought into conscious awareness under appropriate conditions. An efficient memory system must do more than just retain information: The system must have a way of rapidly and selectively retrieving stored information when the organism requires it. Both everyday experience and experimental investigations provide abundant evidence that rapid and selective retrieval of stored information is frequently—although not always—achieved by the human memory system. This remarkable ability, however, is not well understood. Contemporary psychologists are no doubt closer to solving the retrieval problem than Oviedo was in the 17th-century, but a great deal of further research and theorizing will be necessary before a satisfactory understanding can be attained.

Contemporary theorists typically view retrieval as one of the three basic processes that, taken together, comprise the information-processing system that we call human memory. The other two fundamental processes are *encoding* and *storage*. Encoding is the process by which incoming information is registered, perceived, and transformed into an appropriate format for representation in memory, whereas the storage process entails the conservation, over time, of the representations or traces of encoded information. This partitioning of components of the memory system is accepted by most modern theorists as a pretheoretical orienting framework within which a systematic analysis of memory can be pursued.

When the elucidation of encoding, storage, and retrieval processes is taken as a theoretical starting point, we are led to pose questions about memory that are consistent with such an orientation. Thus we might inquire into the nature of encoding operations, and ask whether different kinds of encoding have different mnemonic effects: How does visual encoding differ from verbal encoding? If the *semantic* features of incoming information are encoded, will more be remembered than if the *acoustic* features of that information are encoded? Can people be taught to develop more efficient encoding strategies? Questions are also directed at the process of storage: What is the storage capacity of memory? How is information represented in storage? Does stored information decay or otherwise change over time? And finally, this framework dictates that we ask questions about retrieval: What is the nature of the retrieval process? Under what spectrum of psychological conditions is retrieval successful, and when does it fail? Does the act of retrieval alter the subsequent state of the memory system, and if so, how? And so on. The systematic analysis of each of these processes—encoding, storage, and retrieval—occupies the attention of numerous researchers currently active in the area of human memory.

To the reader who is unfamiliar with current memory research, all of the above may seem terribly obvious. How else, he might ask, can it be? How could we ignore any one of the three component processes of memory enumerated above when it seems so clear that any complete account must take all three into consideration? But let us pause for a moment to consider ways of approaching the problem of retrieval. It is immediately apparent that an act of retrieval is necessary before we can make any inferences at all about encoding or storage. Information may have been adequately registered and conserved, but it will remain latent in the mind unless it is brought forth by some process of retrieval;

an act of retrieval is necessary before we can find out what has been encoded and stored. Conceptualized in this manner, the process of retrieval might merely be regarded as a "window" on the great storage bin of memory: Retrieval is a necessary tool for excavating the contents of memory, but holds little theoretical interest beyond its utilitarian value. It is also possible to imagine a similar, atheoretical approach to retrieval within a laboratory context. Suppose that one is interested in the effect of two different conditions of learning or encoding on memory. Before the effect of the manipulation can be assessed, memory must be somehow "tested." The test, of course, occurs at the time of retrieval. The test provides information about the contents of the memory store, permits assessment of the effects of the experimental manipulations, and is of no interest itself beyond these practical considerations. It is quite possible, therefore, to think of the retrieval phase of memory as equivalent to the "test" phase and to stop there.

If retrieval is regarded as either a "window" on the contents of memory, or merely as a means of "testing" memory, then the kinds of theoretical questions about retrieval that form such an essential part of present-day memory research will probably not be posed or pursued. To conceive of retrieval as a "window" or as a "test" is quite a different enterprise from approaching it as a process that requires systematic theoretical explication. But granted that it is *possible* to distinguish a theoretical from an atheoretical approach to retrieval, does such a distinction have any significance for our purposes? It has a crucial significance. One of the arguments put forward in this and the following two chapters is that Richard Semon offered a comprehensive theoretical analysis of retrieval phenomena at a time when the prevailing approach was largely atheoretical. Further, it is argued that this confluence of circumstances constituted one of the key factors contributing to the subsequent obscurity of Semon's work on memory. The reliance on ecphoric (retrieval) processes that characterized Semon's analysis of heredity applies equally well to his analysis of memory. Although the subsequent history of research on genetics did not justify the fruitfulness of an "ecphoric approach" to heredity, recent developments in memory research have demonstrated the crucial importance of the ecphoric phenomena that so intrigued Semon.

The task of the present chapter is threefold. First we survey the state of psychological research on memory in the years surrounding the publication of Semon's work. What were the major problems of interest to researchers of Semon's time? What can be said about the theoretical leanings of the field when Semon published his book on memory, *Die mnemischen Empfindungen*, in 1909? To anticipate one conclusion, we observe that these researchers demonstrated only passing interest in retrieval phenomena. Second, we explore the possible roots of this situation: Why did problems of retrieval occupy such a small role in the minds of most researchers? Third, we encounter some of the heretics who did demonstrate serious concern for various aspects of retrieval during Semon's time.

I have thus far referred to "retrieval phenomena" in a unitary fashion. To help make sense of the complex phenomena associated with the retrieval stage of memory, I will sharpen this conceptualization before beginning the historical survey. It is possible to distinguish between three classes of retrieval phenomena: the *processes, conditions,* and *functions* of retrieval. I use the phrase *processes of retrieval* to refer to the mechanisms by which retrieval is carried out; the phrase *conditions of retrieval* to refer to those factors in the internal and external environments of the rememberer that affect the success or failure of the retrieval process; and the phrase *functions of retrieval* to refer to the effects that the act of retrieval itself has upon the subsequent state of the memory system. Each of these aspects of retrieval is illustrated in the succeeding pages; it is useful to introduce them now in order to provide a working vocabulary for our explorations of the early years of memory research.

MEMORY RESEARCH IN THE ERA OF EBBINGHAUS AND MÜLLER: CRITICAL CONCERNS OF AN EMERGING SCIENCE

Experimental psychology traces many of its roots to the pioneering efforts of German scientists working in the middle and late 19th-century. Gustav Fechner, Hermann von Helmholtz, and Wilhelm Wundt are just a few of the giants whose efforts paved the way for scientific psychology. Although these men vigorously applied the scientific method to problems of sensation and perception, they initially refrained from treading upon the more forbidding turf of the so-called "higher mental processes": memory, thinking, problem-solving, and the like. The first systematic experimental excursion into these murky areas is found in Hermann Ebbinghaus's epoch-making study of memory, *Über das Gedächtnis* (1885). Ebbinghaus allegedly received the inspiration for applying experimental methods to mnemonic phenomena while browsing through a copy of Fechner's treatise on psychophysics in a second-hand Parisian bookstore one day in the late 1870s (Boring, 1929, p. 379). Fully cognizant that he had entered unexplored territory, Ebbinghaus cautiously carried out and repeated his experiments for several years, as a *Dozent* at Berlin, before thrusting them upon the scientific community in 1885.

To fully appreciate the magnitude of Ebbinghaus's achievement one must bear in mind that conventional psychological wisdom held that memory was "too complex" for experimental investigation. Ebbinghaus deferred to his critics in the introduction to his book by acknowledging the grave difficulties that the experimentalist encountered when approaching phenomena of memory; but he also attempted to silence them with a boldness appropriate to the pioneer of a new research area:

> If by any chance a way to a deeper penetration into this matter should present itself, surely, considering the significance of memory for all mental

phenomena, it should be our wish to enter that path at once. For at the very worst we should prefer to see resignation arise from the failure of earnest investigation rather than from persistent, helpless astonishment in the face of their difficulties (1885, p. 6).

The contents of Ebbinghaus's experiments are of interest to us not only because they represent the first comprehensive experimental treatment of memory, but more importantly, because his experiments had an almost immediate—and far-reaching—effect on the psychological study of memory. Ebbinghaus's methods and experimental interests powerfully influenced the direction and focus of the field in the years surrounding the publication of Semon's theory of memory.

At the center of Ebbinghaus's attempt to render mnemonic phenomena experimentally tractable was his novel tool of exploration: the nonsense syllable. Ebbinghaus reasoned that he could reduce the complexity of his problem by working with simple materials that would not be contaminated by a learner's prior experience with them. Hence he invented the now famous nonsense syllables—letter triads comprised of a consonant-vowel-consonant sequence—and personally set about committing to memory large numbers of such syllables. Ebbinghaus created the savings method (*Ersparnismethode*) in order to obtain easily quantifiable data. The procedure was simple: He would learn a string of nonsense syllables and note the time required for a perfect recitation. Then on some later occasion he would relearn the list, again note the time it took him to do so, and express the time *saved* in relearning as a percentage of the original learning time. In a similar manner, Ebbinghaus determined the amount of savings by ascertaining the difference between the *number* of repetitions required for successful learning and relearning.

Using this basic procedure, Ebbinghaus produced a number of important results. Perhaps the best known of his findings concerned the curve of forgetting. He found that most forgetting occurred during the first few hours of the retention interval and decreased thereafter. He contended that a logarithmic equation suitably described the observed forgetting curve, and thus produced one of the first mathematical characterizations of a mnemonic phenomenon. Another almost equally famous outcome was Ebbinghaus's systematic exploration of the relation between number of repetitions employed in original learning and the amount of subsequent savings; he found that savings steadily increased with large numbers of repetitions. Similarly, he investigated in detail the number of repetitions required to master lists of increasing length, and found that a negatively accelerated curve described the relation between repetition and list length. Ebbinghaus also presented data concerning the question of *massed* vs. *distributed* repetitions: Is repetition more beneficial to the learner when the repetitions are presented in immediate succession, or when they are distributed over time? Ebbinghaus argued that his data favored the latter alternative.

This brief consideration of Ebbinghaus's major findings does not do full justice to his experimental ingenuity or clarity of expression, but does serve to acquaint us with the source of many of the problems pursued in subsequent years by experimental psychologists concerned with human memory. Ebbinghaus's work also provides a clue concerning the neglect of retrieval phenomena in the period under consideration. Ebbinghaus's problems were, in terms of the three components outlined earlier, problems of *encoding* and *storage*.[1] Ebbinghaus ascribed major causal status to events occurring at the input stage of memory (the phenomena of repetition noted above) and focused theoretical attention on these events. But by producing quantifiable descriptions of various repetition effects and characterizing the retention capacity of memory storage with a mathematical forgetting curve, Ebbinghaus painted an empirical picture of memory that ignored retrieval factors. The effects of repetition and the temporal characteristics of storage can be revealed, of course, only through an act of retrieval; but Ebbinghaus neither experimentally investigated nor theoretically addressed either the conditions, functions, or processes of retrieval in his influential studies.

The tremendous impact that Ebbinghaus exerted on the experimental psychology of memory is all the more remarkable when we consider that the 1885 treatise represented his first and last contribution to the study of memory; Ebbinghaus moved on to other interests after 1885. But before more broadly characterizing the research interests of the field, we do well to mention the man who wielded an influence second only to Ebbinghaus: George Elias Müller. Commenting on Ebbinghaus's early retirement from memory research, E. G. Boring noted that "he was original and an originator, but, with the first task accomplished, he was content to let others, like Müller, work out the method to the end (1929, p. 381)." Müller made important theoretical as well as methodological contributions to the field, and unlike Ebbinghaus, he exerted additional influence through the numerous students that he trained for memory research in his laboratory at Göttingen.

Müller's first significant publication concerning memory (Müller & Schumann, 1894) made several noteworthy contributions. First, Müller and Schumann engineered useful technical improvements of Ebbinghaus's methods. Second, they empirically demonstrated the importance of grouping and organizational operations—that is, encoding processes—as determinants of retention. Third, the roots of Müller's most influential empirical contribution are found in the 1893 paper: the study of interference phenomena. Müller and Schumann noted that the learning of a second list did not proceed independently of learning on the first list. Items occupying the same serial position on the two lists were often confused. That is, instead of producing the appropriate item when tested for retention of the second list, Müller and Schumann's subjects often produced an item from the corresponding serial position on the first list. This observation was confirmed, extended, and studied in detail by Müller

---

1. I am using the term "encoding" here in a rather loose fashion that roughly corresponds to "registration."

and Pilzecker (1900). Using their newly developed *Treffermethode*,[2] Müller and Pilzecker discovered that the learning of a second list exerted a variety of powerful effects on memory for the first list, and labeled this general phenomenon "retroactive inhibition." Although the conceptualization of retroactive inhibition constituted the most influential contribution of this study, the paper contained several other noteworthy features, including their well known theory of the "perseveration" of the memory trace, and experiments using recall time to estimate the strength of associations.

The subsequent direction of memory research was closely tied to the methods, findings, and theoretical dispositions of Ebbinghaus and Müller. Let us now more generally characterize the principal interests of the developing field. We take as our temporal frame of reference the period beginning with the appearance of Ebbinghaus's experiments, leading up to the publication of Semon's monograph on memory in 1909, and extending several years beyond this date when the fate of Semon's theory in the psychological community was decided.

The study of memory was pursued during this period largely in two countries: America and Germany. Accordingly, our survey of the field's major research interests is principally based upon an examination of the prominent journals that published research and theory concerning memory in each of these countries: the *Archiv für die Gesamte Psychologie* and the *Zeitschrift für Psychologie* in Germany, and the *American Journal of Psychology, Psychological Bulletin,* and *Psychological Review* in the United States. I do not pretend to exhaustively consider the voluminous amount of research that appeared in these and other journals during the years surrounding Semon's work. Rather, the interests of the field are portrayed in terms of seven topics that I believe capture the major problems investigated by memory researchers of the late 19th- and early 20th-centuries: repetition effects, the curve of forgetting, stimulus attributes and presentation modality, individual differences, interference and inhibition, methods of learning, and recognition and affect.

The research published in the foregoing journals takes us into a world apart from the one we encountered in the preceding chapter. The names of Butler, Cope, Laycock, Orr, and other memory-heredity theorists found no place in the experimental psychology of memory. Conversely, the memory-heredity theorists took little notice of the rapidly growing number of experimental facts generated by the new psychological science; it remained for Semon to attempt to bridge these virtually nonoverlapping approaches to mnemonic phenomena.

---

2. The *Treffermethode*, or "method of hits," is similar to a paired-associate procedure. Müller and Pilzecker read nonsense syllables to their subjects in distinct rhythms; syllables were alternately stressed and not stressed. Müller and Pilzecker then tested subjects' memory for the series by providing them with a particular stressed syllable and asking for recall of the following non-stressed syllable. The number of "hits" attained in the test constituted Müller and Pilzecker's measure of memory performance.

However, the phenomenon that played such a critical role in the various memory-heredity theories also formed a central part of psychological investigations: repetition effects. Although there was a delay of almost ten years between the publication of Ebbinghaus's work and the first experimental follow-up, the study of repetition effects soon enough assumed a major position in the experimental hierarchy. Thus Smith (1896, p. 21) introduced his investigation of repetition effects in the *Psychological Review* with the following commentary: "Everybody knows that repetition plays an important part in the process of acquiring knowledge, but hitherto there has been no attempt experimentally to study this further beyond the experiments of Ebbinghaus." Smith focused upon the relation between number of repetitions and strength of memory in his experiments, and concluded that the first repetition of a stimulus is the most critical one. In that same volume of the *Psychological Review*, Mary Whiton Calkins (1896) published another important experimental study of repetition. Calkins evaluated the relative influence of four factors on the retention of experimentally-acquired associations: Frequency (repetition), primacy, recency, and vividness. In one of the earliest studies to use the paired-associate procedure, Calkins concluded—in defiance of her own expectations—that memory depends more on the frequency factor than any other: "This significance of frequency is rather surprising. For though everybody recognizes the importance of repetition in forming associations, we are yet more accustomed to 'account for' these by referring to recent or to impressive combinations. . . . The prominence of frequency is of course of grave importance (p. 49)."

Several other wide ranging investigations of repetition effects were published during the 1880s, including a particularly influential study by Jost (1897) that proposed that the effects of distributing repetitions could be expressed in the form of a general psychological law (known today as "Jost's Law"; see Murray, 1976). In the years subsequent to the publication of the foregoing studies, the problem of massed vs. distributed repetitions slowly became a major issue (Browning, Brown, & Washburn, 1913; Lipmann, 1904; Nagel, 1912; Perkins, 1914; Pyle, 1914; Starch, 1912), and investigations of topics such as the number of repetitions required for permanent retention (Knors, 1910), rate of repetition (McGamble, 1916), manner of repetition (Reuther, 1906; Strong, 1916), the relation between repetition and type of material memorized (Sleight, 1911), and the pedagogical significance of repetition (Meyer, 1904; Pyle, 1911) all received considerable attention from memory researchers.

All these investigations bore the unmistakable imprint of Hermann Ebbinghaus. This characterization also applies to a second major area of research activity—the time course of forgetting. Interest in this area developed rather quickly. Baldwin and Shaw (1895), Lewy (1895), Müller and Schumann (1894), and Wolfe (1886) all substantiated Ebbinghaus's major findings across a wide variety of conditions. Later investigators examined the shape of the forgetting curve for different materials (Dallenbach, 1913), as a function of degree of learning (Bean, 1912), and in recognition memory (Strong, 1913). All of these studies confirmed and extended the results reported by Ebbinghaus. Some dissident voices, however, did emerge. Radossawljewitsch (1907) examined the forgetting curve in both children and adults, and found less forgetting at short intervals than Ebbinghaus had reported. Finkenbinder (1913) argued that the shape of the forgetting curve depends upon the method of measuring memory. He found slower forgetting when employing paired-associates and the method of anticipation than had been found using the savings method, and suggested that his findings placed some constraints on the generality of Ebbinghaus's results. Luh (1922), in a later and more detailed study, reported data that he interpreted in a similar manner.

The third major area of research, concerned with the effect of stimulus attributes and presentation modality on memory, was less directly inspired by Ebbinghaus's work than either of the two areas that we have so far considered. For example, the first experimental study of memory to appear in the *Psychological Review*, originating from Hugo Münsterberg's Harvard laboratory (Münsterberg & Bigham, 1894), compared the memorability of stimuli presented in the visual and auditory modalities, and provided evidence of visual superiority. Kirkpatrick (1894) and Whitehead (1896) also reported evidence that materials presented in the visual modality are better retained than materials presented in the auditory modality. There was not, however, uniform agreement concerning the relative efficacy of visual and auditory presentation: Hawkins (1897) found evidence of auditory superiority in children, and Dana (1894) reported that a patient who had been rendered amnesic by gas poisoning retained more from an auditory presentation than from a visual presentation. A different approach to the visual-auditory problem was taken by Cohn (1897) and von Sybel (1909), who focused upon the joints effects (*Zusammenwirken*) of visual and auditory presentation; they found that joint presentation aided retention more than visual or auditory presentation alone.

Experimental attention was also directed at the mnemonic effects of other stimulus attributes. For example, von Kries and Schattelius (1908) examined memory for different colors, and Gordon (1903) as well as Ebert and Meumann (1904) explored memory for a whole range of stimuli differing in complexity, such as digits, nonsense syllables, words, sentences varying in grammatical structure, and poetry. This explosion of research generated an atmosphere of confidence among the new experimentalists, and their sense of accomplishment is well captured in Harvey Andrew Peterson's preface to his own work exploring the conditions that affect memory for complex materials:

> The question of the relative persistence of different kinds of materials has been worked out to a considerable extent. It is known that words in the form of connected passages are vastly better retained than an equal number of disconnected words or phrases; and that objects, actions, and pictures are better retained than their verbal equivalents (1909, p. 1).

The next major area of research is one that paid direct homage to the classical studies of Sir Francis Galton: individual differences in memory. Many of these experiments examined memory performance as a function of age (Binet & Henri, 1894; Hawkins, 1897; Jacobs, 1887; Lobsien, 1902; Pohlmann, 1906). The relationship between memory span and intelligence also received its initial investigation (Bolton, 1892), and sex differences in memory were the object of experimental attention (see Offner, 1913, Chap. 7). A number of theorists ascribed special importance to the difference in memory functioning between "fast" and "slow" learners. Meumann (1913, p. 169), for example, argued on the basis of recent research that "the rapid and the slow learner each represents a characteristic mental type." Further, he contended that such differences constituted a fundamental fact for the theory of memory: "These differences are exceedingly great; and they give rise to memory types, which are wholly different in their modes of operation (p. 169)."

A slightly different approach distinguished between "memory types" on the basis of characteristic sensory imagery used in recall (Cohn, 1897; Ogden, 1904; Segal, 1908; Frankfurter & Thiele, 1912). These analyses of individual differences in memory imagery, combined with studies directed at the nature of memory imagery itself (Hellwig, 1899; Martin, 1907; Talbot, 1896; Whipple, 1901), led Kuhlman to conclude in his 1907 review of the literature that the analysis of memory imagery and the "memory consciousness" had "come to the foreground of memory investigation (p. 285)."

The fifth major area of research derived fairly directly from Müller's early studies: the study of interference and inhibition. Not all of this work, however, owed its origins to Müller's studies; Bergstrom (1893, 1894) had independently performed and reported experiments that explored interference effects in the execution of an experimentally acquired habit. But the bulk of research concerning the effects of interfering activity on memory performance was inspired by Müller's findings, and almost all these studies were carried out by German investigators (Aall, 1908; Frings, 1914; Nagel, 1912; Poppelreuter, 1912; Ranschburg, 1902, 1905). Yet Müller's work on retroactive inhibition was well known to American psychologists, as can be verified by reading almost any American review of memory research published subsequent to Müller's studies. So much so that by 1915, J. Edgar DeCamp could offer the following introduction to his own experimental investigation of retroactive inhibition: "Since the rather exhaustive work of Müller and Pilzecker, investigating various aspects of memory, Retroactive Inhibition has held an unquestioned place among the principles of psychology (p. 1)."

The experimental psychology of memory had been transformed within 20 years from the one-man act of Hermann Ebbinghaus to a large cooperative venture that had successfully tackled numerous—and frequently complex— mnemonic phenomena. Robert Morris Ogden's 1904 address to the Western Philosophical Association glowingly exemplifies the enthusiasm of the early memory researchers: "Since the appearance of Ebbinghaus's work the number of investigations in this field has been so great, the problems attempted and solved been so manifold, it begins to seem worthwhile to pause a moment on the way and 'take stock' (p. 178)." After reviewing some of the most important discoveries of the young science, Ogden betrayed the applied orientation that had become increasingly popular in the field: "The most practical application of these results is to be found in the school room (p. 181)." The attention that many in the field turned toward the practical application of the new insights created another major area of research interest: the technique and economy of learning.

The concern with practical application of efficient learning methods can be at least indirectly traced to the work of Ebbinghaus and Müller. Both of these pioneers—Ebbinghaus with his data on massed vs. distributed repetitions and Müller with his work on rhythmic encoding—had demonstrated that some methods of study are more beneficial for memory than others. Subsequent researchers, most of them in Germany, mounted large scale investigations that contrasted various learning methods and evaluated their pedagogical significance. The most extensive and influential of the "economy of learning" studies was the mammoth investigation of Ebert and Meumann (1904), which provided a seemingly endless array of data concerning strategies and techniques of learning. Meumann became the leader of this field, and his findings exerted widespread pedagogical influence. Consider the following commentary on Meumann's work, offered by a leading British memory researcher: "Professor Meumann obtained results of so pronounced and definite a nature, and upon the truth of which so much of the practice of teaching and of education generally depends, that it becomes necessary to investigate with the greatest care the experiments upon which he bases his conclusions (Sleight, 1911, p. 389)." Several of Meumann's students made important contributions to the literature (Ephrussi, 1905; Steffens, 1900), and numerous investigators followed-up various aspects of Ebert and Meumann's groundbreaking study (Balaban, 1910; Knors, 1910; Nagel, 1912; Witasek, 1907). The widespread interest in strategies of learning also led to research that explored theoretical as well as practical aspects of the intentions, attitudes, and expectancies of the learner, both in Germany (Aall, 1913; Meyer, 1915) and the United States (Conrad & Arps, 1916; Kirkpatrick, 1914).

The final major area of research that we will touch upon concerns the analysis of recognition and affective factors in memory. To the contemporary student of memory, such a pairing seems misplaced: Recognition and affect occupy virtually non-overlapping spheres in modern memory research. This was not the case in the period of interest to us; in fact, the bulk of research on the process of recognition approached it as a special kind of feeling. Höffding (1891) labeled it the *Bekanntheitsqualität*, Claparède (1911) appealed to *moiité*, Katzaroff (1911) discussed the *sentiment de familier*, and Allin (1896) referred to the "strange feeling of familiarity." All reflected a common preoccupation of memory researchers with the sense of "knowing," "me-ness," and "familiarity" that accompanies the act of recognition. Many of the papers on recognition, including those cited above, attempted to lay bare the essential quality of the feelings that constituted an act of recognition (e.g., Meumann, 1911; Strong & Strong, 1916). Some of the descriptions of the feeling of familiarity reflected the almost literary nature of contemporary introspective analysis. For instance, consider Woods' (1915, p. 381) assessment of the ingredients of familiarity: "Our investigation has shown that the experience of familiarity is essentially a motile, flowing consciousness—the product of a peculiar sequence of clearness, durations and adjustments." The widespread concern with the feeling of familiarity, however, led some to question the fruitfulness of pursuing this elusive phenomenon in spite of its apparent importance:

> The feeling of familiarity . . . is the most fundamental factor in all forms of recognition. And it is because this feeling cannot be further analysed that recognition is called a primary mental quality. None of the attempts made to describe the feeling of familiarity have been especially enlightening (Feingold, 1915, p. 3).

Although several investigators did turn to the analysis of other, more tractable features of recognition (e.g., Myers, 1914), the problem of recognition gradually receded from the psychological foreground. Indeed, by 1935 Kurt Koffka could reminisce that "There was a time when recognition was a major problem in psychology (p. 593)."

Closely linked to the investigations of the feeling of familiarity was the more general concern with affective components of memory. Much of the early interest stemmed from French theorists concerned with the qualitative analysis of emotions that accompany recall (Mauxion, 1901; Pièron, 1902; Pillon, 1901), but the issue also received serious attention in both America (Titchener, 1895; Urban, 1901) and Germany (Peters, 1911). Analyses of the role of affect in memory were given a new direction by the publication of Freud's controversial theories. A number of researchers attempted to produce evidence of the differential retention of pleasant and unpleasant experiences (e.g., Baxter, Yamada, & Washburn, 1917; Henderson, 1911). This issue became the focus of a great deal of research in the 1920s and 1930s, but the frequently contradictory findings of the various studies did not provide a basis for drawing any firm conclusions about the controversial problem (see Rapaport, 1950).

WHERE IS RETRIEVAL?

We have now sketched in rough outline some of the interests and problems pursued by memory researchers in the several years preceding and following the appearance of Semon's work. The picture that emerges, however incomplete, depicts an energetic, thriving field characterized by a rapid expansion of theoretical problems and experimental methods. A principal aim of the foregoing discussion has been to draw attention to the fact that, in spite of the field's eclectic interests, research specifically directed at the conditions, functions, and processes of retrieval was exceedingly rare in Semon's time. Of course, it may be rightly questioned whether such a point can ever be completely established:

Most introductory statistics students know that it is impossible to prove the null hypothesis. And there were scattered studies that *did* specifically address problems of retrieval (e.g., Abbott, 1909; Hollingworth, 1913; Myers & Myers, 1916). Moreover, eminent figures such as William James (1890), Harald Höffding (1891), and Müller (1913) had offered some interesting commentary on various aspects of retrieval. But the experiments were isolated and the conjectures were not systematic; the sustained attention that characterized the seven major areas of research never developed in the case of retrieval phenomena.

This point may be corroborated by the testimony of those active in the field. Alexander Bain, for instance, noted the complete lack of attention paid to retrieval processes as early as 1887: "The subsequent rise or resuscitation of ideas consequent on association, is a fresh field of study (p. 179)." Bain probably would have been shocked to discover that Kurt Koffka arrived at a similar conclusion some 50 years later. Koffka (1935) conceptualized retrieval as an interaction between a "process" and a "trace," and noted initially that "The little that is known about this interaction will be discussed in the next chapter (p. 527)." When the time came to discuss the subject of interest, Koffka was forced to base his discussion on speculation rather than experiments, "because the empirical data are very scant (p. 597)." Indeed, there were virtually none. Similarly, when Koffka confronted a problem concerning retrieval conditions—the momentary inaccessibility of a memory trace that later can be retrieved—he again proceeded without the backing of experimental data: "unavailability of the trace at the moment, though it is of enormous significance, has as yet hardly been investigated (p. 525)." Ernst Meumann had confronted a similar problem some years earlier when noting the possible role played by non-associative conditions of retrieval and, like Koffka, could cite no evidence relevant to his concern: "the detailed investigation of these conditions of reproduction is one of the future problems of psychology (1913, p. 23)." The influential learning theorist Robert Sears summarized experimental psychology's neglect of retrieval problems in a 1936 paper: "In general the experimental psychology of memory has been most productive in studying the effects of various conditions of learning on recall; little or nothing has been done with the study of recall itself independent of the learning process (pp. 269–270)."

Another way in which to gauge the minority role ascribed to retrieval processes during our period of interest is to consult major reviews of memory published at the time. The contents of these reviews have been reported elsewhere (Schacter, Eich, & Tulving, 1978; see Appendix), and they depict the preoccupations of memory researchers in a consistent manner. Concern with the problems previously discussed—repetition effects, methods of learning, presentation modality, and so forth—was pervasive whereas concern with the conditions, functions, and processes of retrieval was minimal. Particularly revealing is the massive bibliography of memory and learning research published by John McGeoch in 1933. This sprawling catalogue contains references to some 1200 studies carried out in Germany, France, America, and Great Britain from the time of Ebbinghaus's work through 1930. Although there are scattered studies directed at various aspects of retrieval cited in the review, they pale in comparison to the proportion concerned with other problems. And the largest number of "retrieval studies" listed by McGeoch are grouped under the heading of "Relationships between different measures of retention (pp. 57–58)."

Thus we are brought back to the distinction made at the outset of the chapter between the retrieval stage of memory as a process that merits theoretical scrutiny, and as a "test phase" that poses measurement problems. The point is worth dwelling upon. One of the critical problems confronted by early researchers such as Ebbinghaus and Müller concerned the accurate measurement of memory; reliable methods of measurement are clearly a fundamental constituent of any young science. Ebbinghaus contributed the *Ersparnismethode*, Müller added the *Treffermethode*, and others in the field suggested a variety of new techniques for measuring retention (Ephrussi, 1905; McGamble, 1909; Wolfe, 1886). These and other methods of measuring retention substantially contributed to the vitality of the early memory research. But the emphasis on methodology had a negative consequence as well. With concern focused on the measurement problems encountered at retrieval, attention was largely diverted from the theoretical aspects of retrieval phenomena themselves: If one's concern with retrieval is primarily methodological, then one is led to ask questions pertaining to the reliability and validity of measurement.

The theoretical ramifications of such an orientation are not trivial. If retrieval is regarded merely as a neutral "test device," it is unlikely that the dynamic role of retrieval processes in the memory system will be explored. This point can be better appreciated by comparing the interpretations of similar experimental results offered by two theorists of radically different persuasions. The phenomenon addressed by the two theorists is straightforward: The expectation that a learner has about the way his memory will be tested exercises a marked influence on level of performance. First consider the views of Endel Tulving, a contemporary researcher who has devoted much theoretical energy to the elucidation of retrieval phenomena. Tulving's commentary pertains to an experiment reported by Tversky (1974) in which subjects who were instructed to expect a recognition test performed markedly better on the recognition test and markedly worse on a free recall test than subjects who had been instructed to study for the free recall test. Tulving uses Semon's term "ecphory" to designate retrieval in his analysis[3]:

> Subjects anticipating the recognition test may have performed, at input, a careful analysis of the details of each picture-word item, and the information stored as a consequence of this encoding operation permitted efficient selection of the previously seen item from a pair containing a similar alternative. The same information, however, may have been less compatible

---

3. Tulving is one of the few modern memory researchers (perhaps the only one) to have acknowledged Semon's ideas, and he has actively encouraged my own interest in Semon.

with the ecphoric information in the free recall task. Subjects anticipating the recall task, on the other hand, were encouraged to encode list items in relation to each other. Such an encoding activity is likely to result in the storage of a good deal of semantic information, and *to the extent that such semantic information matched that available in the free recall situation, recall was facilitated* (1976, p. 69; my italics).

For Tulving, encoding and retrieval processes are equal partners in generating the observed outcome. He seeks to understand the data in terms of the "matching" of information available to the subject at the time of retrieval with information previously encoded, and uses these data to support his thesis that memory is critically dependent upon the *interaction* between encoding and retrieval processes. Some 60 years earlier, Ernst Meumann addressed an almost identical experimental outcome, based upon free recall and paired-associate (rather than recognition) tests. Let us examine Meumann's approach to the data:

In these experiments, retention may be tested either by the method of free reproduction or by the method of paired-associates. Now it has been observed that when the learner undertakes his task with the intention of learning for the paired-associates test he can sometimes succeed in recalling all of the associates for which he is asked while he is wholly unable to recite the complete series. And conversely when it was his intention to learn the series for the recitation test, he may be unable to recall each syllable when he hears its predecessor in the series although his recitation of the series is fluent and free from error. *This phenomenon shows that a specific intention in the act of learning has a specific effect upon the result* (1913, p. 306; my italics).

The data described by Meumann are fundamentally the same as those addressed by Tulving—both sets demonstrate an interaction between study and test—but the interpretations are worlds apart. For Meumann, events occurring at the time of learning carry the full theoretical weight of interpretation. There is no hint of the importance ascribed to retrieval information by Tulving, and no concept of encoding-retrieval matching. Rather, the "method of testing" is important only to the extent that it reveals the "specific intentions" that derive from the act of learning; events occurring at the time of retrieval are ascribed no theoretical significance.

Thus far we have examined two factors that may have contributed to the general theoretical neglect of the conditions, functions, and processes of retrieval during the years of interest to us. First, the pioneering work of Ebbinghaus and Müller focused upon events occurring during the encoding and storage phases of memory, and these studies powerfully influenced the subsequent direction of the field. Second, I have suggested that the necessary concern with developing reliable methods of measuring memory relegated the problem of retrieval to a chiefly methodological status. These two circumstances may partially account for the scant attention paid to retrieval phenomena in the early years of memory research, but they do not entirely explain it. To more fully understand why problems of retrieval were neglected, we must view turn-of-the-century memory research in a broader intellectual context. Hermann Ebbinghaus did not initiate his experiments in an historical vacuum. The human mind pondered, analyzed, and glorified its ability to remember for some thousands of years before Ebbinghaus memorized his first nonsense syllable. It seems exceedingly unlikely that the conditions, functions, and processes of retrieval were neglected by theoreticians over all the millenia; they were not. But the 19th-century culmination of theoretical trends originating in the 4th-century B.C. may provide some insights into the subsequent fate of the retrieval problem. In a somewhat adventurous spirit of educated conjecture, we now briefly examine those trends and explore their possible relevance to the experimental psychology of memory in the late 19th- and early 20th-centuries.

ASSOCIATION AND THE PROBLEM OF RETRIEVAL

One of history's most heartfelt phenomenological descriptions of retrieval processes was articulated in the early years of the 5th-century A.D. Saint Augustine initiated his consideration of memory by acknowledging the vastness of the subject: "Great is the power of memory, a fearful thing, O my God, a deep and boundless manifoldness (Pusey trans., 1874, p. 196)." He proceeded to offer the following characterization of retrieval processes:

> I come to the fields and spacious palaces of memory . . . When I enter there, I require instantly what I will to be brought forth, and something instantly comes; others must be longer sought after, which are fetched, as it were out of some inner receptable; others rush out in troops, and while one thing is desired and required, they start forth, as who should say, 'Is it perchance I?' These I drive away with the hand of my heart from the face of my rememberance; until what I wish for be unveiled, and appear in sight, out of its secret place (cited in Yates, 1966, p. 46).

A somewhat different aspect of retrieval was later addressed by Saint Thomas Aquinas. Aquinas's commentary pertains to one of the few retrieval problems encountered by practitioners of the ancient art of mnemonics—a system largely devoted to the development of efficient encoding techniques (Yates, 1966)—namely, the importance of finding a starting point amidst the numerous "memory-loci" stored in the mind:

> It is necessary for reminiscence to take some starting-point, whence one begins to proceed to reminisce. For this reason, some men may be seen to reminisce from the places in which something was said or done, or thought, using the place as it were as the starting-point for reminiscence; because access to the place is like a starting-point for all those things which were raised in it (cited in Yates, p. 72).

A particularly interesting "pre-scientific" treatment of the *conditions* and *functions* of retrieval is found in Guglielmo Gratarolo's *The Castel of Memorie* (1562). Gratarolo was one of the most versatile scholars of the 16th-century; he published works concerning weather prediction, wine, travel, poisons, baths, and physiognomy. Thorndike (1941) claimed that "No one man in the sixteenth century did more to circulate and to perpetrate a varied selection of curious works, past and present, in the fields of medicine, natural science, and occult science than did Guglielmo Gratarolo (p. 600)." Gratarolo's treatise on memory, which first appeared in 1553 and went through several subsequent editions, contained both theoretical and practical sections. He detailed a number of points essential to good memory, and included some advice concerning retrieval conditions (more specifically, contextual reinstatement) amidst his various rules: "The fourth is, the remembrance of a place and time doe safely bringe the thinge to Memorie (p. 91)." Gratarolo also offered some dubious advice for keeping memory strong. He advised his readers to be sure to eat sufficient amounts of "temperate meate" such as "Hennes and Patriges," and also recommended a frequent "rubbying of the head with a combe (p. 46)." However, he did recognize an important *function* of retrieval in his practical prescriptions:

> An often callinge to mynde of things seene or hard, both strengthe and confirme the Memorie: for there is nothing that is so soone increased by diligence, or diminished by negligance, as Memorie it selfe is: because except it be thoroughlye [strengthened] with a continual meditation, it is soone corrupted by sluggishenes (p. 47).

Although Gratarolo, Augustine, and Aquinas deserve their due acknowledgment for discussing phenomena of retrieval, the temporal spotlight must be turned to a still earlier epoch. As with so many intellectual matters, the most decisive roots of our inquiry lie in the teachings of Aristotle. Aristotle directly addressed a variety of retrieval phenomena in his account of memory. For instance, he distinguished between two modes of retrieval, recollecting and remembering, and offered interesting commentary on memory search processes (Sorabji, 1972, p. 54–55). The most important of Aristotle's reflections concerning retrieval arose from his observation that ideas succeed each other during the act of recollection in a non-random fashion. Aristotle argued that idea A will lead to the recall of idea B if A has been previously associated to B by either similarity, contrast, or contiguity. These notions are usually regarded as the first statement of the laws of association. An important point to note, however, is that Aristotle applied these notions solely to memory (Sorabji, p. 42). It can be argued that they constituted Aristotle's answer to the problem of retrieval conditions: If during an attempt to remember one has a thought that has been associated to the sought-after memory in one of the above manners, then retrieval will be successful.

Aristotle's theory remained essentially undeveloped until the advent of

British associationism in the 17th-century. When Aristotle's ideas were incorporated into the philosophical systems of early associationists such as Hobbes and Locke, they were applied to a far wider range of phenomena than Aristotle had originally intended. The territory covered in the treatises of Hobbes and Locke ranged from psychology to political science; in the later writings of David Hume, epistemological concerns assumed a major importance. Even when the associationistic doctrine was applied solely to psychological phenomena in the important work of David Hartley (1749), the problem of memory constituted just one small piece of an expansive doctrine intended to account for all psychological phenomena by reducing them to a simple set of associative axioms. The same point may be applied to later psychological elaborations of the pure associationistic doctrine advanced by Thomas Brown (1820), James Mill (1829), John Stuart Mill (1843), and, in the most detailed associationistic attack on the mind, Alexander Bain (1855): Problems of memory were just one small subset of psychological phenomena that were subsumed under the laws of association. Perception, thought, judgment, belief, and the like were also explained in terms of associative laws.

An overriding question for the British associationists concerned which of the laws of association constituted the most *basic* one. Though Hume had accorded an equal place to contiguity, similarity, and contrast, most writers dispensed with contrast and focused upon the relative merits of contiguity and similarity. Thus Hartley argued that contiguity must be regarded as the most fundamental form of association and hence the sole true law of association; James Mill also favored contiguity, though allowing for secondary factors such as frequency and vividness; John Stuart Mill disputed his father's emphasis on contiguity, arguing that similarity should be ascribed prime importance in the associative process; and Alexander Bain contended that both similarity and contiguity deserved the status of basic laws.

Exactly what role did the problem of retrieval occupy in these debates? A curious one indeed. The most important point to keep in mind for the present purposes is that the British associationists drew no sharp distinctions between encoding and retrieval (cf., Anderson & Bower, 1973, p. 25). *Association* was the phenomenon of interest; whether the manifestations of association were considered at what we call the "encoding" phase of memory or the "retrieval" phase was a secondary issue. It was precisely in regard to this state of affairs that Sir William Hamilton criticized the British associationists in 1859. Hamilton drew a sharp distinction between component processes of memory that exactly parallels the distinction between encoding, storage, and retrieval that is used today; Hamilton terms his components acquisition, retention, and reproduction. Hamilton criticized previous theorists for ignoring these important distinctions: "The intimate connection of these three faculties, or elementary activities, is the cause, however, why they have not been distinguished in the analysis of philosophers (1859, p. 206)." Hamilton further criticized the associative account of memory as incomplete, arguing that it did not satisfactorily address the process of retrieval itself. But the Scottish philosopher's criticisms went largely unheeded.

Toward the end of the 19th-century, several conspicuous trends in the associationistic account of retrieval can be discerned. First, the debate concerning the relative importance of contiguity and similarity as fundamental laws of association, within which their role in influencing the outcome of retrieval was considered, continued in Britain (see Bain, 1887) and spread to Germany. For instance, Lehmann (1889) and Höffding (1893) engaged in a heated dispute, Lehmann arguing for the primacy of contiguity and Höffding favoring similarity. Others soon entered the arena, with Deffner (1898) favoring similarity and Ziehen (1899) hoisting the banner of contiguity. The controversy spread to France, where DuMont (1895) supported the similarity position and Goolot (1898) advanced the case for contiguity, and to the United States (Calkins, 1896). The debate also found its way into many of the prominent textbooks of the late 19th- and early 20th-centuries (e.g., Höffding, 1891; Judd, 1907; James, 1890; Stout, 1896; Wundt, 1907; Ziehen, 1899). The various intricacies of this controversy are beyond our scope, but there is one point about it that bears mention. An important function of these debates may have been to make the problem of retrieval conditions an uninteresting one. By casting the issue in terms of contiguity vs. similarity, the late 19th-century associationists excluded some of the most interesting features of retrieval conditions: the internal state of the rememberer, the environmental contexts within which stimuli for retrieval are embedded, and the role that variables such as attention and expectation play in influencing the outcome of the retrieval process. Associationism, then, "solved" the problem of retrieval conditions by reducing it to an issue of similarity vs. contiguity.

Similarly, it is not unreasonable to suggest that the associationists' "solution" to the problem of retrieval *processes* made this issue theoretically uninteresting: They simply assumed that association and retrieval are the same thing. Until now, we have spoken of association solely in reference to retrieval conditions; it is quite another matter to assume that association is the actual *mechanism* of the retrieval process. Yet Ebbinghaus (1908), for example, used the terms association and reproduction interchangeably: "We refer to this ability of expansion by the term *memory*, to the actual process of expansion by *reproduction* or *association* (p. 93)." Similarly, Ziehen was content to equate association and reproduction in his popular textbook: "It is just this process of reproduction that we designate as the association of ideas . . . 'assocation of ideas' is a brief term designating the *process* of the reproduction of ideas (1899, p. 198; see also, Wundt, 1907, p. 274; Pillsbury, 1911, p. 135)." Külpe (1895, p. 195) commented on the increasing tendency of psychologists to equate association with retrieval: "the word association is not always employed in the sense in which we have used it. It often signifies reproduction itself and not a condition of reproduction." It is possible to distinguish between association as a condition of retrieval and as the actual mechanism of the retrieval process; Semon forcibly made this distinction in 1909, and we will return to this point when considering his argument. But the fact that many psychologists failed to explicitly make this distinction reflects an important consequence of the theoretical dominance enjoyed by associationism: If association is assumed to be the mechanism of the retrieval process, there is no longer a problem that requires theoretical solution.

There are two additional features of the associative doctrine that may shed light on the relatively restricted treatment accorded retrieval phenomena in the theory. First, consider the variable that associationism traditionally ascribed prime causal importance in determining the outcome of the memory process: the strength of an association. Repetition, vividness, recency, and the like were all viewed as secondary variables contributing to the single dimension that critically influenced the outcome of recall. If an association between two elements was strong enough, then recall of one in the presence of the other was thought to be certain. Such a view de-emphasized the role of factors such as the retrieval context in affecting the outcome of memory performance. This failure of the philosophical and subsequent experimental associationists to achieve a thorough analysis of retrieval conditions was severely criticized by the later Gestalt psychologists. Wolfgang Köhler, for instance, protested the traditional reliance on the strength of associations at the expense of retrieval conditions: "psychological theory has gone much too far in assuming that, when strong associations have been formed, recall will happen spontaneously, and irrespective of what the present situation may be (1947, p. 313)."

Kurt Koffka sounded a similar theme and pointed to a specific instance of its manifestation. Reviewing the experiments that led to the formulation of Jost's Law around the turn of the century (see Koffka, 1935, p. 589, for details), Koffka critically noted the usual interpretation of the data: "The traditional explanation has been a one-factor explanation, in agreement with the traditional theory which knows only one variable: the strength of association (p. 589)." But, continued Koffka, "such a simple explanation overlooks the dynamics of the situation." Koffka contended that Jost's experimental outcomes crucially depended on specific retrieval conditions—previous writers had been content to speak of different methods of *testing* in reference to these data—and urged that the dynamics of the "communication between the present [retrieval] process and the trace" receive serious consideration in future accounts of Jost's data. But as long as the strength of association was regarded as the primary factor controlling recall, there was little reason to systematically explore the role of retrieval dynamics as a causal variable that crucially influences the ultimate success or failure of memory.

Finally, we should remember the principal goal of associative theory: the specification of laws that reduced all mental phenomena to associative processes. When the laws of association are taken as a starting point, the kinds of questions that will be pursued will reflect this orientation: Can phenomena of thought be explained on associative grounds? What are the primary factors in association and which are the secondary? What does associationism have to say about perceptual processes? One may also ask whether similarity or contiguity is a more fundamental form of association and condition of retrieval. By way of contrast, consider the approach later advanced by Semon. Semon's laws were not laws of association: They were laws of engraphy (encoding) and ecphory (retrieval). As we shall observe in the next chapter, when one begins with a law of retrieval, one pursues questions directly related to the conditions, functions, and processes of retrieval rather than questions pertaining to the vicissitudes of association.

It was in this intellectual atmosphere of associationism that the influential studies of Ebbinghaus and Müller were performed, and both of these giants worked firmly within the associative tradition. It should not be surprising, then, that neither Ebbinghaus nor Müller focused upon the conditions, functions, and processes of retrieval in their epoch-making experimental studies. Within the context of associative theory, what was there for them to focus upon? Association was assumed to be the mechanism of the retrieval *process; conditions* of retrieval were of interest only to the extent that the laws of association required specification of effective associative stimuli; and associative theory had nothing specific to say about the *functions* of retrieval. What did hold interest for associative theory were the variables that influence the strength of associations, and the investigation of these variables—such as repetition and interference—is precisely what Ebbinghaus and Müller pursued.

Whether or not we can say that the dominance of the associative doctrine "caused" the theoretical subjugation of retrieval phenomena in Semon's era is clearly open to debate. But associationism was widespread in both America and Germany during the formative years of memory research, and it provided the framework within which experimental problems were pursued. And as we have seen, in comparison with research concerning other features of memory, problems of retrieval were treated much as a theoretical Tom Thumb by mainstream researchers working within the associative tradition. The preceding conjectures, then, may not be entirely groundless. We can view them from a slightly different perspective as we now turn to the final section of the chapter.

VOICES IN THE WILDERNESS

Thus far in the chapter I have attempted to document a theoretical neglect of retrieval phenomena in Semon's era and examine several possible reasons for it. I now close the chapter by considering several heretics of Semon's time who did focus theoretical attention on retrieval phenomena. In the context of our previous observations, we will find that these iconoclasts shared two features. First, they were not working in the mainstream experimental field of memory that was dominated by the work of Ebbinghaus and Müller. Second, they were either sharp critics of the associative doctrine or they worked on problems that were unrelated to the principal theoretical concerns of associationism.

It seems appropriate—and somehow inevitable—to begin by mentioning a name that is difficult to exclude from any consideration of revolutionary psychological thinking: Sigmund Freud. Freud is of interest to us insofar as he took the strong position that failures of memory are at root failures of retrieval. Freud's proposed mechanism of retrieval failure was, of course, embedded in his theory of repression. When retrieval fails, contended Freud, it is because the threat of affectively unpleasant experiences contained in, or related to, the sought after memory generates a "protective" response by the unconscious—that is, a repression of the threatening memory. Freud's application of his theory to mnemonic phenomena is well illustrated in his 1901 *The Psychopathology of Everyday Life*. Here he subjected numerous cases of everyday forgetting to psychoanalytic scrutiny and concluded that each one could be best understood as a retrieval failure caused by the inhibitory effects of repression. Consider his conclusion regarding the forgetting of proper names: "The mechanism of names being forgotten...consists in the interference with the intended reproduction of the name by an alien train of thought which is not at the time conscious (1960, pp. 39–40)." He drew a similar conclusion with respect to the forgetting of 'impressions and knowledge': "*in every case the forgetting turned out to be based on a motive of unpleasure* (p. 136)." But Freud's primary interest centered on repression and not retrieval; retrieval was interesting to the extent that it represented a locus of repression. Even in his most ambitious attempt to construct a theory of memory (see Pribram & Gill, 1976), Freud did not expand his views on retrieval in a systematic fashion.

There was, however, a contemporary psychiatrist who took a much stronger interest in retrieval phenomena than Freud did. Although he is barely known to most modern experimental psychologists, Morton Prince (1916) elaborated revolutionary views concerning the importance of retrieval conditions that merit close attention even today. Prince, who advocated a *dissociationist* interpretation of subconscious phenomena (see Hilgard, 1977), specifically criticized the "older psychology" for ducking the problem of retrieval: "It did not concern itself with the process by which memory is effected (p. 7)." Prince specifically distinguished between registration, conservation, and reproduction as component stages of memory, and argued that it is more fruitful to approach memory as a *process* rather than as a "phase of consciousness" or "mental experience" (p. 2).

He then established the point that he believed represented the key to a deep understanding of memory: One cannot make statements about what is or is not conserved without first specifying the conditions of retrieval. For Prince, the most striking fact of memory was that an experience that is apparently forgotten—that is, one that cannot be recalled under a variety of retrieval conditions, no matter how great the effort expended—can later be recovered if the person is placed in an appropriate environment or psychological state. Prince drew on observations from hypnosis, psychopathological conditions, drug-induced states, and functional amnesias to support his contention that statements about the nonconservation of memories have no meaning without reference to specific retrieval conditions. Thus he made the following observations about hypnotic phenomena: "The memories which belong to one state cannot be recalled in another. Hence the fact that a memory cannot be recovered in one state is not proof that it is not conserved, nor is a failure to recover the memory of an episode in all states of hypnosis evidence of failure of conservation (p. 17)."

Prince must have known that standard psychological approaches to memory would have great difficulty assimilating or even understanding his views, as he steadfastly hammered away at the same point for nearly 100 pages. And well he should have: It simply makes no sense to attribute such overwhelming significance to retrieval conditions if the strength of associations is assumed to be the prime determinant of remembering and forgetting. Why should the same stimulus be an effective retrieval cue in one state and an ineffective one in another state? Clearly, the strength of the association between the cue and the desired memory should be the same no matter what the condition of retrieval. Prince's observations indicated that there is much more to understanding memory than simply studying variables that affect the strength of associations.[4]

Freud and Prince published their views on retrieval at about the same time that Semon did. Although the next heretic did not publish his ideas about retrieval until the mid-1920s, it is difficult to resist mentioning some of the sparkling ideas promulgated by Harry Levi Hollingworth. Hollingworth, a professor of psychology at Columbia University, published on such diverse topics as vocational psychology, thinking processes, functional neuroses, advertising, and hypnagogic imagery. Like Freud and Prince, he operated largely independently of the major concerns of mainstream memory research. Hollingworth was also an ascerbic critic of associationism, and claimed that "the association of ideas has been much overrated in the history of psychology (1926, p. 323)." After outlining several difficulties with the associationistic doctrine, he resorted to sarcasm: "With these puzzling entanglements psychology was enabled to enlarge its chapters to a formidable size. 'Laws of association' were writ large in every text. Lively debates were staged over similarity, contiguity, succession, and congruity (p. 323)." But, Hollingworth concluded, "If half of this energy had been directed toward discovering what ideas are, psychology might now be further on its way (p. 324)."

Hollingworth attempted to build a theoretical system applicable to all varieties of psychological phenomena based upon a single, fundamental operation:

---

4. It is important to keep in mind that both Freud and Prince made their observations of memory in *clinical* contexts. The phenomena that they encountered in these contexts—recovery of "lost" memories under appropriate psychological conditions, spontaneously shrinking retrograde amnesia, and so forth—clearly indicated that retrieval factors play an important role in memory function. However, as has been argued elsewhere (Schacter & Tulving, 1982), experimental psychologists concerned with the analysis of intact memory paid scant attention to these clinical phenomena. Had the experimentalists taken these clinical observations more seriously, their constricted approach to retrieval phenomena might have been considerably widened.

redintegration. Redintegration technically refers to the reinstatement of a whole via just one of its parts; the idea was not original to Hollingworth, and we shall have more to say about it when later considering Semon's redintegrative position. Hollingworth enthusiastically applied his redintegrative principle to almost every conceivable psychological phenomenon. More interesting for our purposes, however, is that Hollingworth's concern with redintegration led him to focus on retrieval phenomena in his analysis of memory.

Hollingworth defined his notion of memory in terms of retrieval conditions: "the memory of an object or an event is not a resurrection of it. Instead, it is some present event which, as a cue or instigating detail, functions redintegratively for the original context (1926, p. 259)." Hollingworth focused on the properties of such redintegrative cues, and he stressed that memory depends on their utilization: "it is important to realize that memory always involves the activity of cues (p. 261)." Hollingworth's acknowledgment of the critical role that retrieval cues play in memory led him to take an interesting position on what constitutes a "good memory." Most psychologists of Hollingworth's day would have answered that question in terms of the standard variables operative at the input stage of memory: "Good memory" may be attributed to numerous repetitions, recency of presentation, duration of the input stimulus, the meaningfulness of material memorized, and so on. Hollingworth advanced the unheard of proposition that "good memory" depends upon the conditions of retrieval: "Memory is efficient when the cues required are slight and when they are readily available or likely to occur (p. 262)." It is unfortunate that Hollingworth never further elaborated these ideas—they were conspicuously promising ones—but he remained under the spell of redintegration and its various applications to his eclectic interests.

Just as Freud, Prince, and Hollingworth were all outsiders to mainstream memory research, so was our final heretic: Otto Selz.[5] Selz's primary theoretical concern was the nature of thought processes; he expounded his views of thinking primarily in three books published between 1913 and 1922. Selz interests us because of his revolutionary approach to the problem of thinking. At a time when the dominant approaches focused on the *content* of thought, Selz explored the *processes* underlying thinking. He identified the utilization or actualization of knowledge (*die Wissensaktualisierung*) as a key problem for a theory of thinking—that is, he concerned himself with retrieval processes in the broadest sense of the term. Selz conceptualized the utilization of knowledge in a novel manner, as a process of "complex" or "pattern" completion (*Die Wissensaktualisierung als Komplexergänzung*; 1913, pp. 89–95). Selz viewed retrieval as a process of uniting fragmentary information in the environment with fragmentary information stored in memory, and, like Hollingworth, invoked the process of redintegration as a central mechanism in his theory. Selz also elabo-

---

5. There is little information available about Selz. For brief introductions to his life and work, see DeGroot (1965), Mandler and Mandler (1964), and Kintsch (1974).

rated upon the importance of what he labeled *Kontrollprozesse* (1922, p. 15), such as knowledge-based expectation (*schematische Antizipation*; 1922, p. 14), in his wide-ranging and often brilliant treatment of retrieval phenomena. Selz was a pointed critic of associationism, particularly Müller's development of it, and sought to replace it with a prescient cognitive orientation. Although Mandler and Mandler (1964, p. 223) were able to call Selz's work "the major turning point" in the psychological theory of thinking, his views found a small audience in his time. Selz occupied several minor academic positions and later tragically perished in a concentration camp during the 1940s.

The views of retrieval advanced by Semon's contemporaries Freud, Prince, and Selz, and later by Hollingworth, all contained elements of penetrating insight and bold conceptualization. But there were two important features that none of these theories jointly possessed. With the exception of Selz, the ideas developed by these theorists were rather fragmentary and were not woven into a larger system that attempted to systematically address the conditions, functions, and processes of retrieval. And none of these theorists specifically applied their notions of retrieval to mainstream memory literature; this is not surprising since their principal concerns lie elsewhere. These two features were found in later theories of memory put forward during the 1930s by Sir Frederic Bartlett (1932) and the Gestalt psychologists Wolfgang Köhler (1930) and Kurt Koffka (1935)[6], that stressed the crucial importance of retrieval operations in the memory system and offered blistering attacks on the associative account of memory. But they had already appeared in 1909, when an isolated *Privatgelehrter* from Munich emerged from passionate debate over the inheritance of acquired characteristics long enough to grant retrieval phenomena their due theoretical place in the memory system.

---

6. An intriguing but unanswered question concerns the extent to which Semon's work may have influenced the Gestaltists' theory of memory. Koffka's effusive praise of Semon's theory (1935, p. 598) indicates that the Gestaltists were aware of his ideas. And the Gestaltists' approach to memory was similar to Semon's insofar as it stressed the importance of conditions and processes of retrieval. It remains as an interesting historical task to attempt to specify the nature of Semon's influence on the Gestaltists.

9

Semon's Theory and the Modern Psychology of Memory

"We can add to our knowledge, but we cannot subtract from it." Arthur Koestler opened his classic historical narrative, *The Sleepwalkers* (1959, p. 19), with this simple message, and it initially seems like a mere truism. But Koestler's words are deceptively unambiguous. They apply in the nominal case—barring physical destruction or other forms of literal inaccessibility, we can never lose the epistemological advances that have preceded us—but they do not hold in the functional case. As several recently influential observers of science have convincingly argued, human knowledge does not grow by gradual, unrelenting accretion.[1] Science advances in fits and starts, some ideas forming part of a relatively permanent edifice, others achieving an initial popularity before being temporarily abandoned—that is, functionally subtracted from a communal knowledge base—only to return in some slightly altered form.

Many of the ideas included in the burgeoning psychological science of memory at the turn of the century were soon to endure this fate of functional subtraction: Mental events such as imagery and familiarity found no welcome in the behavioristic orientation that was about to engulf much of psychology. And the few instances of interest in retrieval phenomena displayed by psychologists such as Prince, Selz, and Hollingworth were not developed by behaviorists who disavowed such mentalistic constructs. Problems of retrieval, along with many other so-called mentalistic aspects of memory, became objects of theoretical concern only after behaviorism loosened its stranglehold over psychology in the late 1950s and early 1960s. As stimulus-response accounts of learning

---

1. The most well known advocates of this position are Kuhn (1962) and Polanyi (1958), and their ideas are examined in some detail in Chapter 10.

gave way to information-processing models that sought to elucidate the cognitive underpinnings of behavior, interest in the "mentalistic" phenomena scorned as unscientific by behaviorists again became legitimate objects of psychological inquiry.

It lies well beyond my scope to attempt to illuminate the myriad forces responsible for the cognitive revolution that has swept psychology during the past 25 years; others have done so in detail.[2] Similarly, I refrain from offering conjectures concerning the genesis of the theoretical attention that retrieval phenomena now receive from cognitive psychologists pursuing information-processing analyses of human memory. But the new concern for the conditions, functions, and processes of retrieval demonstrated by modern psychologists is used as an organizing device for outlining Semon's theory of human memory: The discussion focuses upon Semon's theoretical concern for retrieval phenomena, and his frequently prescient views are compared to modern psychological theories of memory. A more wide-ranging treatment of Semon's theory and its various anticipations of modern positions has been reported elsewhere (Schacter, Eich, & Tulving, 1978; see Appendix), and the interested reader is referred to this somewhat broader coverage. My strategy in the present chapter is to first outline in general form Semon's ideas on the conditions, functions, and processes of retrieval, and then to examine how he applied these ideas to several outstanding problems of memory theory. The chapter has two major purposes. The first is to convey to the reader some of the reasons why, as we saw in the introduction to the book, Kurt Koffka lauded Semon's "great achievement," Erwin Schrödinger called for a physiological model of his theory, and Bertrand Russell effusively praised Semon's analysis of memory. The second purpose of the chapter is to provide some of the necessary background for understanding why Semon's views concerning memory were ignored by his contemporaries.

Four important facets of my own approach to Semon's theory should be clarified before proceeding further. First, the issue at stake is not whether Semon should be granted "priority" for his ideas. Priority disputes are among the most fruitless exercises in science or history, and I have no interest in arbitrating one here. As Stephen Gould recently remarked, "Ideas are cheap. The use of ideas, the systematic reconstruction of a world in their light, is the stuff of intellectual revolutions (1979, p. 38)." Semon's insights concerning memory are interesting because they were woven into a cohesive and innovative theoretical system— not because a few isolated fragments anticipated recent developments. Second, it is all too easy in any historical endeavor to read meaning into isolated passages that is supplied only by the wisdom of hindsight and may sharply differ from the meaning intended by the author. Cohen (1980) has rightly pointed out that in many historical analyses, "stress is apt to be placed on aspects of the

---

2. For interesting discussions of the relation between the cognitive and behavioristic approaches to psychology in the context of history and philosophy of science, see Palermo (1971) and Weimer and Palermo (1973). A recent critique of the cognitive revolution can be found in Haugeland's (1978) paper.

science of the past that are in harmony with present science, or a deliberate attempt may be made to read today's scientific ideas into the concepts of the past (p. 195)." Precisely because his insights were woven into a larger conceptual framework, this problem has not proved especially severe in Semon's case: His ideas were not isolated shots in the dark, but emerged from a broader theoretical orientation. Yet it would be naive to deny that the present interpretation has not been guided by my own theoretical world-view and notions about what is important in the analysis of memory. I do not believe that one can reconstruct the past entirely independently of one's vision of the present. But one can be sensitive to the mixture of past and present that is perhaps a necessary component of historical analysis, and guard as stringently as possible against the intrusion of excessively idiosyncratic interpretations that recreate the past in the image of the present.

Third, we should keep in mind the distinction between *anticipations* and *foundations* of ideas when considering Semon's theory of memory. Sarup (1978) has argued that anticipations are "those antecedent ideas that have likeness to, but not developmental ties with, later modes of thought (p. 478)." In contrast, foundations "are the actual beginnings of later concepts and theories in the sense that the growth of thought is relatively continuous and the lines of influence are traceable (p. 478)." Sarup contends that the most appropriate interpretation of the historical significance of a set of ideas depends upon whether the ideas are anticipations or foundations of later developments. Semon's theory of memory had virtually no influence on the subsequent direction of memory research, and for this reason should be characterized as an anticipation, and not a foundation, of modern theory. One of the principal questions addressed in the next chapter concerns why Semon's anticipations never became foundations for later work.

Fourth, the temptation to portray Semon's ideas as uniformly original, incisive, and prescient must be resisted. It is as easy as it is misleading to depict a prophetical shining knight riding a theoretical white horse, who promulgates only visionary truth and tells no mundane lies. Semon's theory contains numerous gaps, flaws, and inconsistencies; we should harbor no illusions concerning the various deficiencies extant in his account, and they have been set forth elsewhere (Schacter et al., pp. 737–738). But this criticism applies at least as strongly to any other psychological theory of his time; indeed, Semon attempted to unify and explain more phenomena and problems than almost any other memory theorist of his day. We proceed, then, fully aware that Semon's account is by no means ideal or complete. These difficulties, however, are not unique to Semon's theory, and do not vitiate the importance of its often insightful and original contents.[3]

---

3. As was the case with *Die Mneme*, we are fortunate to possess a good English translation of *Die mnemischen Empfindungen—Mnemic Pyschology*, published in 1923. I shall cite from this volume unless otherwise indicated.

PRELIMINARIES: THE ENGRAM

Before examining Semon's views on retrieval, it is useful to say a few words about the one construct in his theory that many are at least casually familiar with: the engram. As we saw in Chapter 7, the idea of the engram played a crucial and somewhat controversial role in Semon's analysis of heredity. Although this notion aroused considerably less furor when applied solely to memory—many theorists prior to Semon had characterized the underpinnings of memory in terms of conceptually similar "traces"—there are several points concerning Semon's articulation of it that merit our attention. First let us consider his ideas concerning the neural representation of engrams. In accordance with his biological training, Semon strictly adhered to the view that engrams are physically represented by changes in the state of the brain; he expressly rejected the views of vitalistic writers such as Bergson (1911) and McDougall (1911), who believed that memories are preserved in some non-material, "psychical" field. Semon expressed caution, however, concerning unwarranted speculations about the precise form of biological storage: "To follow this into the molecular field seems to me . . . a hopeless undertaking at the present stage of our knowledge; and for my part I renounce the task (1923, p. 154)." But he did go on to debate whether engrams are neurologically represented in a *localized* or *distributed* manner, and rejected the then popular view of localization that posited a one-to-one relationship between cerebral cells and memory traces:

> We seem . . . to be placed in the dilemma of having either to reject altogether a localization theory which imagines that each single engram can be stored up in a single cell—or in a comparatively small complex of cerebral cells . . . or to admit that in the human organism a special interdependence exists between definite regions of the cerebral cortex and the ecphory or, as perhaps we ought to say, the possibility of the ecphory of distinct individually-acquired engrams. The latter admission, implies, however, the recognition of a certain localization, although it need not be the kind which makes each nerve-cell of the brain a repository for a specific engram (1921, p. 120).

One of the more interesting insights implied in the above passage is that statements concerning the localization of engrams must be distinguished from statements concerning the neural localization of the process of ecphory. Semon developed this point more explicitly after considering neuropathological evidence bearing on the problems of localization: "Either an actual localization of the *engrams* themselves takes place, or the 'localization of symptoms' is only a result of an interdependence between certain definite parts of the cerebral cortex and the possibility of the *ecphory* of specific groups of individually acquired engrams (1921, p. 128)." This distinction between "localization of storage" and "localization of retrieval" is interesting not only because it was a novel one that highlights Semon's theoretical sensitivity to ecphoric phenomena. It also reflects his caution regarding naive views of engram localization, a point to which we return when considering various historical misconstruals of Semon's position in Chapter 10.

It is also worth briefly considering some of Semon's *psychological* characterizations of engrams, since it is here that we first observe his break with the prevailing associative paradigm. One of the critical features of Semon's theory is his insistence that each experience or "simultaneous excitation complex" creates a *separate* engram. This seemingly innocuous idea sharply contrasted with the traditional associative view that new experiences are not individually represented, but are incorporated into existing webs of lowered-resistance pathways. Semon's distaste for the associative approach led him to formulate novel positions on a variety of problems, based on his "separate engram" theory, that we shortly consider.

Semon also viewed the psychological constitution of the engram in a way that radically differed from the ideas of most of his contemporaries. He based his characterization on an wholistic, Gestalt-like analysis of perception that emphasized the "primary unity" of perceptual experience and questioned the validity of atomistic associative accounts (see Schacter et al., pp. 727–729). Extending this notion to memory, Semon conceptualized engrams as unified complexes, comprised of "emergent components" that fuse to form a qualitatively unique whole. These ideas are similar to recent theories that portray the memory trace as a collection of features, attributes, or components (e.g., Bower, 1967; Flexser & Tulving, 1978; Underwood, 1969); they were further elaborated by Semon in a variety of interesting contexts. Semon's position that there is access to only *fragments* of these complexes at the time of retrieval is particularly relevant. Semon's attempt to cast the problem of fragmentation in his own multi-component terminology, which foreshadowed the recent systematic work of Jones (1976), highlights the intellectual distance that separated him from the traditional associative view:

> Out of all these different constituents mnemic reproduction gives us merely at best a fragment of the most important components, and these fragments we speak of as 'associative.' But a conception much more in accordance with our meaning leads us to regard such fragments not as associated, but as *integral components, as emergent points of a connected simultaneous complex of sensations* (1923, p. 164)."

In this passage we observe a theorist groping for a new language to characterize human memory, one that was not bound by the rigid confines of traditional associationism. The spirit of Semon's iconoclasm shared much with the later attempts of Selz, Bartlett, and the Gestaltists to free psychological thinking about memory from its antique associative straight-jacket. But Semon's attempt to overhaul associative concepts did not stop with his theory of storage; and we initiate our consideration of Semon's views on retrieval by examining one of his most incisive critiques of the associative doctrine.

CONDITIONS, FUNCTIONS, AND PROCESSES OF RETRIEVAL

As noted in the last chapter, memory researchers working within the associative tradition had little to say about retrieval *processes*, precisely because associationism provided such an obvious answer to the problem: Association was simply assumed to be the mechanism of the retrieval process. Semon, however, took the problem of retrieval processes much more seriously than his contemporaries, and believed he had uncovered a critical logical flaw in the associationistic account. Association, Semon argued, is a concept that may be legitimately used to *describe* the relationship between components of engram-complexes. Although he preferred to discuss these relations in his multicomponent language, Semon acknowledged that the concept of association could be loosely employed to indicate similar notions. But, he contended, when applied to retrieval processes, the construct of association was merely a convenient theoretical crutch that in no way *explained* the phenomenon of interest. He went on to propose that the terms *association* and *ecphory* must be clearly distinguished:

> the fact of the binding-together of engram-components, which alone deserves the name of *association*, should, logically, be sharply distinguished from this ecphoric process through which the fact itself is revealed. *Briefly, association is the result of an engraphy disclosed on the occasion of an ecphory.*
> This state of affairs does not seem to have been clearly apprehended up to now, and usually 'association' has been employed in two senses, first, quite correctly, as the complete union of engrams of mnemic sensations (latent or actual representations); secondly, also, as the process whereby this union becomes apparent. This inconsequent phraseology is the source of numerous misunderstandings and fruitless discussions (1923, p. 325).

By penetrating the deceivingly facile associative "explanation" of retrieval processes, Semon took the first critical step that innovative science always depends upon: He recognized the existence of a problem requiring theoretical scrutiny.

Semon's own conception of the retrieval process, freed from the intellectual shackles of associationism, was a synthesis of several different ideas: redintegration, component-overlap, and homophony. Semon, like his contemporaries Selz and Hollingworth, invoked the notion initially advanced by Sir William Hamilton in 1859 that retrieval occurs via a process of part-whole reinstatement. But Semon went beyond redintegration to articulate a view of the retrieval process that sounds much like modern theories in which *feature overlap* between retrieval cue and memory trace is granted a major role in the retrieval process (cf. Flexser & Tulving, 1978; Kintsch, 1974): "Resemblance, that is to say, partial coincidence between the components of an actual group of excitations and those of any previous engram-complex, causes ecphory of the latter through the former (1923, p. 326)." The critical conceptual basis of this idea is Semon's notion that both ecphoric stimuli and memory traces can be regarded as arrays of dissociable components or features; when a sufficient number of the components in the ecphoric stimulus and the engram-complex match each other, retrieval will be successful.

The idea that ecphoric stimuli and engram complexes are comprised of multiple components formed the basis of Semon's conceptualization of *homophony*. Homophony was briefly described in Chapter 7 as a resonance metaphor that Semon invoked to describe the way in which information from different sources is combined; we now consider the notion in greater detail. The following is a general characterization of homophony:

> At the ecphory of a combination of engrams...what is given is not a single indissoluble blend of mnemic excitations—'coalescence' some physiologists call it—but a unisonant chorus in which the single components of an apparently uniform combination of engrams, distinct indeed from each other as to their time of origin, may be individually discerned (1921, p. 165).

Semon held that homophony could occur between "original" and "mnemic" sensations or just between "mnemic" sensations. He also emphasized that the contributors to homophony run a "side-by-side" course and are superposed much in the manner of individual transparencies containing different information that are placed on top of each other: In the homophonous case, the superposed elements are components of ecphoric stimuli and engram-complexes. He went on to distinguish two sub-types of homophony. First, Semon described a "non-differentiating" homophony in which there is a combination of components, and "no opposition of one component to the others...but, on the contrary, the distinctions between the various homophonous components are suppressed (1923, p. 247)." Second, he outlined a "differentiating" homophony, which is "always the result of an antagonism between two components or two groups of components (1923, p. 248)." Whether a differentiating or non-differentiating homophony occurs, according to Semon, depends largely on the conditions of ecphory.

A concrete example may help to clarify these somewhat obtuse notions: Semon's analysis of generic vs. temporally specific memory imagery. Semon posited that the ecphory of generic images (e.g., a house) occurs when "all the engrams belonging to my view of the house are allowed to act homophonously (1923, p. 277)." However, with different retrieval demands, specific temporally dated images of the house may be ecphorized: "When I wish to ecphorize the images of this house I can do so by fixing my attention on a definite, temporally determined engram of the same (1923, p. 276)." Thus the information from the individual engrams is combined via homophony; and whether or not homophonous resonance occurs depends upon the intentions of the rememberer and the conditions of ecphory.

A notion such as homophony was crucial to a theorist of Semon's persuasion. If all engrams are represented as separate and unique constellations, then there must be some mechanism that permits interaction of these individual complexes. In Semon's theory, these interactions occurred at the time of retrieval through the process that he labeled homophony. Although the idea of homophony stands out as a unique contribution in its time—and again reflects Semon's idiosyncratic concern with retrieval phenomena—it does bear a strong resemblance to recent resonance metaphors of retrieval put forward by Lockhart, Craik, and Jacoby (1976), Moeser (1977), and Ratcliff (1978).

Semon's broad concern with the nature of ecphoric processes led him to address a variety of questions that were not considered by theorists whose conceptual schemata were driven by the doctrines of associationism, and we now consider one of his most unambiguously visionary interests. In Chapter 7, we witnessed Semon's concern for a phenomenon that he labeled "engram-dichotomy." Engram-dichotomy refers to the ecphoric choice-point that is encountered when it is possible to retrieve two different engram-complexes to an individual stimulus, such as in the recall of a poem in which a particular line (the ecphoric cue) is followed by different lines at various points in the poem. Although he initially utilized the phenomenon to illustrate the similar features shared by mnemonic and hereditary phenomena, Semon was sufficiently intrigued by the problem to further pursue its implications for the retrieval process. He was particularly interested in whether the two candidate engram-complexes could be ecphorized in *parallel* or only by a *serial* alternation between the two. Semon initially rejected the possibility of parallel processing—he believed that apparent cases of parallel ecphory could be attributed to rapidly alternating, serial retrieval—but he modified this position in a later discussion of the problem:

> It is not *altogether* impossible to produce side by side and simultaneously two manifestations of ecphorized verbal engrams and to let two series of such engrams run their course simultaneously side by side . . . side by sideness undoubtedly exists, if for a very short time, and therefore I have to abandon my first contention as to the impossibility of any simultaneous manifestation of two different chains of excitation ecphorized from verbal engrams (1923, p. 315).

Semon's interest in the problem of serial vs. parallel processing was virtually unique among his contemporaries; this issue was simply not a part of mainstream memory research at the time. But Semon's analysis clearly foreshadowed the explosion of psychological interest in parallel vs. serial retrieval that derived from Sternberg's (1969) pioneering experimental investigations. Semon's conceptual anticipation of this problem should not surprise us. When one begins with a wide-ranging interest in retrieval processes, the issue of parallel vs. serial processing is likely to emerge as a topic of theoretical concern.

Semon's fascination with retrieval processes was matched by an equally extensive concern with retrieval *conditions*: the influences in the environment of the rememberer that affect the outcome of the retrieval process. Semon's position on retrieval conditions followed directly from his redintegrative view of the retrieval process, and was succinctly described in his Law of Ecphory:

"The partial return of an energetic situation which has fixed itself engraphically acts in an ecphoric sense upon a simultaneous engram-complex (1923, p. 180)." For Semon, then, some *partial* reinstatement of the conditions of engraphy is a necessary antecedant of successful retrieval. As we saw when discussing his approach to hereditary phenomena, such an idea provided Semon with a key logical weapon for inferring the operation of a mnemonic factor in ontogeny. In regard to non-hereditary memory, Semon believed that the idea of partial re-currence made good *ecological* sense. He argued that organisms rarely encounter identical situations in their natural environments, thus it is highly adaptive for a retrieval system to operate efficiently when ecphoric conditions dictate that only fragmentary stimuli will be available to the organism.

One of the more interesting features of Semon's position is that it expressly allowed for the operation of *internal* stimuli as ecphoric cues. Semon had, in fact, specified that internally-generated stimuli—the emotional state of the or-ganism, transient sensations, fleeting thoughts, and so forth—are stored as com-ponents of an engram-complex. Not surprisingly, then, he argued that the par-tial recurrence of these same internal stimuli constituted sufficient conditions for successful retrieval: "ecphory can arise without any recurrence of an origi-nal stimulus through the mere partial return of the inner energetic situation which was present at the formation of the engram-complex (1923, p. 180)." With his emphasis on the mnemonic function of internal stimuli, Semon touched upon a subject that modern researchers are just beginning to confront. Ander-son and Bower (1973), for instance, specifically allowed for the representation of internal stimuli in their comprehensive model of human memory, and a num-ber of investigators have experimentally explored the role that internally gener-ated stimuli play in the mnemonic process (e.g., Donaldson & Bass, 1980; Dosher & Russo, 1976; Slamecka & Graf, 1978).

One of the most intriguing phenomena that has been uncovered in mod-ern research concerning internal stimuli and memory is known as *state-depen-dent retrieval.* Experiments on human state-dependence, most of which have been performed during the past 15 years, have demonstrated that memories stored when the organism is in a particular psychological state (e.g., sober or drunk) are later more often retrieved when that same state is re-established than when a different state is induced. Thus material studied under the influ-ence of alcohol (and numerous other influences) is better remembered in a subsequent state of intoxication than in a subsequent state of sobriety (see Eich, 1980, for review). Although state-dependent retrieval has just recently been systematically scrutinized by students of memory, Semon's concern for the rela-tion between ecphory and internal states led him to contemplate the phenom-enon well in advance of the first laboratory experiment: "in cases where the energetic condition has greatly changed . . . not even the recurrence of the origi-nal stimulus suffices for the ecphory of the corresponding engram. . . . Alcoholic intoxication may, under certain circumstances, create an energetic condition whose engrams are ecphorable in the next state of intoxication, but not in the intervening state of sobriety (1921, p. 144)." As in the case of the serial vs.

parallel processing issue, Semon's broad concern with problems of retrieval led him to address phenomena that were largely neglected by mainstream memory researchers.

Semon's conviction that memory cannot be properly understood without reference to retrieval conditions is also reflected in his frequent insistence that the conditions of ecphory are causal contributors to phenomena that others had been content to ascribe to the *encoding* and *storage* phases of memory. For instance, when considering the factors that contribute to the vividness of memory imagery, Semon acknowledged the traditional view that vividness depends upon "the effectiveness of the original engraphy (1923, p. 223)." But he also argued that homophonic processes occurring at the time of retrieval might also determine the vividness of memory imagery, and further contended that vividness depends upon "circumstances accompanying the ecphory, especially the output of attention (p. 224)." He concluded by stressing that "The engram of any form can be ecphorized either greatly magnified or greatly reduced, according to the nature of ecphoric influences, of homophonous original excitations, or co-operating associations (p. 234)." For Semon, then, the properties of the memory trace are not the sole determinants of the ultimate form of memory imagery; conditions and processes of retrieval are equal partners in shaping it.

Consider also Semon's position on what constitutes a "good" or "weak" memory. As noted in Chapter 8, Hollingworth's assertion that "good memory" depends upon the availability of retrieval cues radically differed from the usual psychological assumption that encoding and storage processes are responsible for strong or weak memories. Semon, too, disputed the traditional claim that "good memory" depends upon encoding and storage conditions: "We can easily convince ourselves that what we call in ourselves and in our fellow-beings good memory is only partially based on the facility and certainty with which stimuli act engraphically upon the organism (1923, p. 143)." Rather, Semon suggested, "good memory" also depends upon the availability of redintegrative cues that permit the "*ready* ecphory" of sought-after engrams.

In the foregoing passages, we observe Semon hammering home a point that few of his contemporaries, save visionaries such as Morton Prince, fully appreciated: It is difficult to make intelligible inferences about memory without specifying the conditions of retrieval. Whether we consider "good" and "weak" memories, vivid or fleeting memory imagery, memory for events experienced in states of intoxication, or the everyday episodes whose recall is dependent on partial reinstatement of engraphic conditions, we must do more than study how memory traces are established; we must also examine the various ecphoric influences that contribute to the probability and form of their manifestation. Although later writers such as Koffka (1935) and Köhler (1930), as well as less well known investigators such as Pan (1926) and Dulsky (1935), appreciated this point to varying degrees, it was not until the late 1960s that mainstream memory researchers began to systematically explore the myriad effects exerted by different retrieval conditions on memory performance. This research, owing largely to the seminal studies of Tulving and his colleagues (e.g., Tulving & Pearlstone, 1966; Tulving & Thomson, 1973), has experimentally established what theorists such as Semon and Prince had known a half-century earlier: Memory performance is exquisitely sensitive to specific conditions of retrieval.[4]

Semon's innovative attack on the processes and conditions of retrieval was complemented by an equally original concern for its *functions*: The effect that the act of retrieval itself has upon the subsequent state of the memory system. For Semon, ecphory was not a static test phase that merely served as a pristine window on the contents of the memory store; it was a dynamic process whose execution altered the state of the system. Semon contended that each act of ecphory establishes a new engram-complex comprised of the retrieved information and information in the present context: "each ecphory of an engram-complex produces not only a mnemic sensation . . . but through this creates a new engram which adheres to the new engram-stratum (1923, p. 178)." Semon applied this notion to all varieties of ecphory. He argued, for instance, that the products of both differentiating and non-differentiating homophony are fed back into the memory system as unique engram-complexes. It was through this endless recombination and recycling of engram-complexes, Semon believed, that man is able to achieve creative insights that transcend the simple sum of his originally separately stored engrams. Semon highlighted the mnemonic transformations effected by each act of ecphory throughout his exposition, and specifically suggested that experimental investigation of the process would prove fruitful:

> the mere return of a mnemic excitation suffices, as we have already many times explained, to create a new engram. . . . So far as I know, no experimental investigations have been made into this subject, for instance, by comparing an original with a mnemic excitation in regard to the creation of engrams and perfecting of mnemic reproduction. It would be an interesting task to formulate these comparative differences (1923, p. 272).

With the exception of several scattered studies, pursued in educational contexts (Abbott, 1909; Gates, 1917; Raffel, 1934), systematic theoretical concern with the phenomenon that so intrigued Semon did not emerge until recent years. But the numerous studies that have been reported in the past decade or so substantiate Semon's claim that the act of ecphory modifies the state of the memory system. Tulving (1967) and Izawa (1969), for instance, have pre-

---

4. For a sampling of recent studies that demonstrate the crucial significance of retrieval conditions in memory performance, see Barclay et al. (1974), Eich (1980), Fisher and Craik (1977), Light and Carter-Sobell (1970), Morris, Bransford, and Franks (1977), Smith, Glenberg, and Bjork (1978), and Thomson and Tulving (1970).

sented evidence clearly indicating that recall trials function as opportunities for storage; they have also examined some of the "comparative differences" between the mnemonic consequences of storage and retrieval that Semon called for in 1909. In a like spirit, Whitten and Bjork (1977) have examined how different *spacings* between retrievals affect later retention, and contrasted these effects with those obtained from different spacings of *study* trials. Whitten (1978) has also reported data exploring variations in the *depth* of retrieval upon later recall: Items that receive "deeper" or more extended retrieval attempts are more likely to be subsequently remembered than items that receive an initially "shallow" retrieval. A variety of other investigations of the functions of retrieval have also been reported (e.g., Bartlett, 1977; Darley & Murdock, 1971; Landauer & Bjork, 1978; Lockhart, 1975; Modigliani, 1976; Roediger, 1974; Rundus, 1973).

These and other recent studies of the functions of retrieval paint a picture of the retrieval process far removed from the sterile test phase of Semon's day; the modern view is much closer to Semon's portrayal of ecphory as a transforming process that serves multiple functions in the memory system. One interesting point to note, however, is that in almost all of the above-cited studies, facilitating effects of retrieval on later recall are attributed to some sort of "strengthening" process: The accessibility of an existing memory trace is increased via the strengthening effect of retrieval. Semon, in keeping with his "separate-engram" position, suggested that what emerges after retrieval is not a strengthened version of an existing memory trace, but rather a unique constellation of information that is newly represented in memory. Some modern research supportive of this view has been reported by Gardiner and Klee (1976; Klee & Gardiner, 1976) in their studies of memory for remembered events. These authors, much like Semon, posited that "Each act of remembering itself . . . constitutes a new event in episodic memory (Klee & Gardiner, p. 471)." They have also provided experimental evidence to substantiate this hypothesis. Semon, no doubt, would have applauded their efforts.

Semon's theoretical interest in the functions of retrieval did not stop with his concern for the engram-establishing capacity of ecphory. He also contended that every act of storage is partially comprised of, and affected by, a retrieval process. Semon argued that new input to the system acts as a redintegrative retrieval cue that elicits information from memory. This information is then stored as part of a new engram-complex: "nearly every complex of original sensations has grouped around it numerous mnemic sensations which are evoked by it and work engraphically in the grouping (1923, p. 168)." For Semon, then, there is a Janus-like duality in the way that the process of ecphory alters the state of memory. Retrieved information is not only recycled into the system, but new memory-traces are embellished by information supplied from the permanent memory store. Semon's memory-system is in a constant state of flux; the processes of engraphy and ecphory play multiple roles in shaping an ongoing transfiguration whose metamorphosis is never complete.

SEMON'S THEORY AND FOUR PROBLEMS OF MEMORY

Having now sketched some of Semon's most important ideas, we may observe how he made use of them in the analysis of four outstanding problems that have been confronted by numerous students of memory: input-output discrepancies, association by contiguity vs. association by similarity, repetition effects, and recognition memory.

One of the more intriguing as well as recalcitrant questions concerning memory is why the output from the system so frequently differs from the input. Remembering is only occasionally precisely accurate; it is often incomplete and distorted. Early researchers working within the methodological constraints imposed by Ebbinghaus paid scant attention to this problem: The nonsense syllable approach focused on literally reproductive features of memory and effectively dodged the problem of input-output variability. To the extent that the issue was broached at all, most theorists appealed to the role of unconscious processes in changing, distorting, and weakening the memory trace over time (e.g., Kennedy, 1898). A more enlightening approach to the problem was later cultivated by Sir Frederic Bartlett, who offered a biting critique of the Ebbinghausian approach and discarded the nonsense syllable methodology in favor of richer, more complex materials that provided an opportunity for systematic study of input-output discrepancies. Bartlett placed major theoretical emphasis on the role of "attitudes" constructed at the time of retrieval as causes of distorted remembering. Although he was neither the first to take such a position (see Crosland, 1921), nor the first to call for a broader approach to memory than Ebbinghaus's methodology permitted (see Müller-Freienfels, 1915), Bartlett's work constituted a significant advance over previous efforts. Modern accounts of input-output variability, increasingly influenced by Bartlett's position, have concerned themselves with the processes of generalization, abstraction, and construction occurring at both storage and retrieval (Bransford & Franks, 1971; Frederiksen, 1975; Hasher & Griffin, 1978; Loftus, Miller, & Burns, 1978).

As we might expect by now, Semon's approach to the problem ascribed a major role to ecphoric processes. First, Semon argued that distortion is introduced into the memory trace at the time of engraphy owing to the active role played by retrieval in the storage process. Mnemonic information is evoked by perceptual input, and stored with it as part of an engram-complex. Accordingly, the information that enters memory is not a faithful "snapshot" of experience:

> mnemonic sensations regularly accompany all parts of the original complex, whose image is thereby completed, embellished, or blurred, and often notably changed. Moreover, the engram retains these additions and, when next ecphorized, reproduces them. The new mnemonic sensation is consequently no true and exclusive image of the original sensation (1923, p. 231–232).

However different from a literal "snapshot" the memory trace might be, Semon also postulated, as we saw earlier, that only fragments of it become accessible to consciousness. But we have not yet considered his explanations of fragmentation. One of them is rather prosaic, whereas two others are more innovative and appeal to the operation of ecphoric factors. First, Semon contended that engram-complexes weaken over time; hence only the strongest components are later accessible for retrieval. This is a variant of decay theory, which has probably been promulgated in one form or another by most students of memory. Semon also argued that conditions of retrieval—specifically , the direction of attention—influence which fragments of the trace are brought into awareness: "The fixing of attention on specific points in the simultaneous complex acts as a dissolvent and dissociates these parts from the rest of the complex (1923, p. 165)." Finally, Semon also pointed to homophony as a cause of fragmentary remembering: Resonance between the ecphoric stimulus and certain components of the retrieved engram-complex accentuate some fragments at the expense of others. In his reliance on decay as a cause of input-output discrepancies, Semon did not differ from his contemporaries; but in his appeal to retrieval factors, Semon was clearly ahead of then-current theorizing.

The second problem that we consider is that old standby of associationism: contiguity vs. similarity. Although this issue was at the center of many controversies among associationistic theorists, for Semon it was merely one of many problems whose solution he hoped to derive from his laws of engraphy and ecphory. But it is not Semon's answer to the problem—he favored the view that all association is by contiguity—so much as the route traversed in coming to that conclusion that is important. The most popular argument advanced by those who attempted to supplant similarity with contiguity was that association by similarity can be reduced to association by contiguity because similar things are likely to have co-occurred in space and time. If we associate dogs with cats, the argument runs, it is not because they are similar, but because they are likely to be experienced in spatial and temporal proximity.

Semon approached the matter from an entirely different perspective; he accounted for association by similarity via an appeal to the conditions, functions, and processes of ecphory. Semon began by analyzing what happens when stimulus X evokes a semantically, visually or otherwise similar memory trace Y, and invoked his redintegrative principle of partial return. Owing to shared components between stimulus X and trace Y, Y is retrieved in the presence of X, just like in any other ecphory dependent upon partial return. This *ecphoric* process, however, must be distinguished from the consequent *association*. It is only after the initial retrieval that the two events are contiguously associated and, due to the engram establishing function of ecphory, are stored as a unique engram-complex. Hence Semon argued that association by similarity is produced by "an ecphory based on the partial recurrence of certain components of an excitation-complex. When departing, it leaves behind a new engram-complex in which the two images are associated (1923, p. 189)." He went on to hypothesize that previous confusion centering upon the contiguity vs. similarity problem partially stemmed from "a confusion of two concepts: association and ecphory (p. 189)." Semon, attuned to distinctions between ecphory and association that others overlooked, was able to point the way toward an altered conception of an ancient problem.

In our discussion of Semon's memory-heredity theory, we briefly glimpsed his approach to the third problem that we shall consider: repetition effects. The fact that memory performance improved with successive repetitions of a stimulus is one of the most well known facts of psychology; the problem of repetition has been with us for countless years and is unlikely to make any sudden exits from the focus of psychological attention. There are at least two ways in which the mechanism of repetition effects can be conceptualized. First is the *strengthening* view: Repetition exerts its beneficial effects on memory by strengthening the mnemonic representation of the repeated item. Ebbinghaus clearly stated this position in his 1885 treatise: "as the number of repetitions increases, the series are engraved more and more deeply and indelibly (1885, p. 53)." This notion was the overwhelming—indeed, the virtually unanimous—theoretical favorite in Semon's era. So much so that it would be more accurate to label it a *doctrine* rather than a *theory*. In spite of the numerous empirical investigations of various repetition effects that were noted in Chapter 8, the validity of the strengthening view was not questioned.

There is, however, at least one other way to theoretically characterize repetition effects; I refer to this as the *multiple trace* view. This theory states that rather than strengthening an existing memory trace, each repetition of a stimulus creates a separate, unique representation. This idea was not considered by researchers of Semon's era, but the multiple trace view has recently been put forward by several prominent theorists (Bernbach, 1969; Bower, 1967; Hintzman & Block, 1971), and has received empirical support from a number of experimental investigations over the past decade. The evidence in favor of the multiple trace hypothesis is quite compelling. Recent critical reviews contrasting multiple trace and strength theories have concluded that the bulk of the experimental evidence supports the multiple trace theory (Hintzman, 1976; Howell, 1973).

It is against this background that we can appreciate the novelty of Semon's approach to repetition effects, which we first glimpsed in Chapter 7: "Every repetition of a stimulus and, consequently, of an original excitation deposits a new engram (1923, p. 254)." Semon, then, extended his "separate engram" notions of memory to include repetition effects, and articulated an hypothesis that unambiguously anticipated the current multiple trace views. However, whereas most modern multiple trace theorists postulate some sort of read-out of the number of stored traces as the vehicle of repetition effects, Semon had something quite different in mind. As we earlier saw in his analysis of ontogeny, Semon accounted for repetition effects in terms of homophonic processes: Although multiple traces are stored, output from the system can be in the form of separate traces or some strengthened amalgam of traces, depending upon ecphoric conditions and consequent homophony. Semon was intentionally explicit in juxtaposing his theory with the strength theory, remarking that "if the formation of an engram through excitation were a question of mere facilitation of channels, the repetition of an excitation would, at best, only enlarge the engram, but could not create a new, distinct, isolatedly ecphorable engram (1923, p. 255)." The distaste for "strengthening" views of memory that runs like a red thread throughout Semon's exposition is nowhere more clearly stated than in the following passage:

> REPETITION OF A STIMULUS DOES NOT STRENGTHEN AN ALREADY EXISTING ENGRAM, BUT GENERATES A NEW ENGRAM, AND THE MNEMIC EXCITATIONS RESULTING FROM ANY SUBSEQUENT ECPHORY ARE IN HOMOPHONY (1921, p. 169).

These words leave little room for doubt concerning Semon's position on the problem of repetition effects.

The final problem that we consider is, ironically, interesting to us precisely because it held so little special appeal for Semon: recognition memory. Semon conceptualized recognition as the product of a comparison between information in the environment and information stored in memory; he relied heavily on the notion of differentiating homophony in developing this theory, which we shall not consider in further detail here.[5] There is, however, one idiosyncratic feature of Semon's approach to the problem of recognition that merits attention: He refused to enshrine the phenomenon in the mysterious, almost mystical garb that was characteristic of theorists who conceptualized recognition in terms of unanalyzable sensations and affects. Rather than debating the subtleties of these various phenomenological distinctions, Semon simply characterized recognition as a sub-type of ecphory; that is, as one mode of bringing stored information to bear upon a current situation. Consistent with this view, Semon hypothesized that each act of recognition, just like any other ecphory, functions to establish a new engram-complex. Perceived in this context, it is not surprising that when he confronted the dispute over whether recognition is primarily an affect or a sensation, Semon expressed scant concern: "The question whether

---

5. It is worth noting that Semon distinguished between two kinds of recognition. He conceptualized simple recognition of a previous event as "the manifestation of differentiating homophony between an original and mnemic sensation (1923, p. 83)." This form of recognition does not entail conscious awareness of the difference between the original and newly perceived stimuli. However, in recognition accompanied by the "sensation of difference," the differentiating homophony gives rise to a "differential of sensation"—a discrepancy between the original and new stimuli that is large enough to be consciously perceived by the rememberer. Semon did not specify the conditions under which these two kinds of recognition occur.

it is more correct to describe recognition as sensation or feeling . . . has for us little interest (1923, p. 287)." Similarly, he attempted to discredit the notion articulated by various theorists that recognition deserves special status as a psychological process owing to feelings of "pleasure" and "relief" that accompany successful recognition: "Such a feeling of pleasurable relief is accompanied by every ecphory which implicates a fixing of attention, and is specially characteristic of such an ecphory; so that the attempt at localization of such a recognized sensation is only a special case of the kind of ecphory in question (1923, p. 288)." Although not in theoretical step with the times, Semon's attempt to minimize the special status of recognition by portraying it as a sub-type of ecphory fits well with recent ideas advanced by theorists who have stressed the continuity between recognition and recall (Lockhart, Craik & Jacoby, 1976; Tulving & Watkins, 1973). It also demonstrates again how Semon's broad concern with retrieval processes led him to perceive a problem of memory in a fundamentally different way than his contemporaries.

I stated at the outset of the chapter that Semon should not be treated as a theoretical shining knight, one who sees only the truth and discards all that is misleading in the often ambiguous signals sent by Mother Nature. Semon's exposition is sometimes awkward as well as disconcertingly obscure, and he was blind to the theoretical importance of a number of important phenomena, such as interference effects, the role played by attentional processes in selecting input for storage, and coding operations that actively direct the flow of information through the memory system.

Semon's occasional stumblings and oversights may also provide one clue concerning a question that can only be speculatively answered: What enabled Semon to view memory from such a different standpoint than the one adopted by most of his contemporaries? Semon's theoretical blind spots partially resulted from his unfamiliarity with much of the psychological territory that he explored; his conceptual framework derived from anatomy and biology, not from psychology. But his same nonpsychological background may also have freed him from many of the conceptual constraints imposed by an intellectual upbringing within the confines of psychological associationism. And in attempting to render his system applicable to hereditary phenomena as well as to psychological phenomena, Semon confronted numerous problems that required explication in terms that mainstream psychology did not include in its theoretical vocabulary. Semon drew on his biological past to solve such problems and then applied these originally non-psychological constructs to the analysis of memory. Unfortunately, there is almost no available information concerning the genesis of Semon's ideas—his correspondence provides few useful clues and his diary, to the best of my knowledge, has not been preserved—so I must remain disconcertingly vague about the origins of Semon's approach to the problem of memory.

Whatever the source of his ideas, there can be little doubt that Semon's analysis of memory was full of possibilities; it contained myriad innovative features that pointed the way toward some exciting and then unexplored theoretical vistas. These sentiments were shared by the English writer Vernon Lee[6], who lamented that Semon expended so much intellectual effort on the "hopeless" Lamarckian thesis, but expressed optimism concerning the fate of his psychological theory of memory:

> The psychological part of his work remains, however highly elaborated, a fragment—a fragment, however, whose shape and substance are so suggestive that I cannot but think that a part of Semon's importance may consist in what will be added by others to the work he left unfinished (1923, p. 27).

Vernon Lee's hopes were never fulfilled. With the rare exceptions of praise from intellectual giants such as Koffka, Schrödinger, and Russell, Semon's work on memory lay dormant for over a half-century, and did not serve as the foundation for future research that Vernon Lee believed it would. It is difficult to answer the question of whether progress in the analysis of memory would have been accelerated had Semon's ideas been recognized in their time. However, the neglect of Semon's work raises an equally enticing (and considerably more tractable) question: Why did his theory fail to find a sympathetic audience amongst his psychological contemporaries? We explore some possible answers to this query in the next chapter, and the path that we tread in doing so leads to a broader perspective on the nature of the scientific enterprise than has yet been developed in the course of the book.

---

6. Vernon Lee is one of the intriguing characters in the Semon story whose precise role in the drama is not entirely clear. To begin with, Vernon Lee is a pseudonym used by the British authoress Violet Paget. Born in France in 1856 of English parentage, Paget became a popular essayist, travel writer, and novelist who wrote more than 30 books. She lived in both London and Italy, and died in 1935. Paget's relationship to Semon can only be speculatively inferred. In her preface to *Mnemic Psychology*, Paget twice referred to Semon as her "friend"—once as "my late and very deeply lamented friend (p. 14)," and once when bemoaning Semon's involvement in the acquired characters dispute: "I cannot but regret the time which my friend bestowed upon this subject (p. 26)." As one can discern by reading the preface, Paget was extremely sympathetic to Semon's ideas, and almost certainly was responsible for having *Die mnemischen Empfindungen* translated into English (she was a sufficiently close acquaintance of the book's translator, Bella Duffy, to dedicate her own *Proteus* (1925) to this woman: "To my dear friend Bella Duffy with thanks for a lifetime of intelligent talk"). However, neither the name Violet Paget nor Vernon Lee is mentioned in any of Semon's correspondence that I have read. What could have linked Semon and Violet Paget? My own speculation is that Semon's brother Felix may have played the role of intermediary. It seems possible that Paget and Felix frequented some of the same London artistic circles (Felix was very much at home in the London elite of the late 19th-century), and that Felix introduced her to his brother on one of Richard's visits to London. This is admittedly an unsubstantiated conjecture, but the ways in which an English essayist could come to know a reclusive German *Privatgelehrte*r are not exceedingly numerous.

10

Revolutionaries, Cranks, and the Research Community: Perspectives on Unrecognized Scientific Contributions

*F*orgetting can be a social as well as a personal malady. Just as an individual is sometimes unable to retrieve facts and experiences that were at one time familiar to him, history is replete with once well-known names and events that are inaccessible to the collective modern consciousness. The history of science is no exception. Although the name of Tobias Meyer is likely to elicit few appreciative nods from modern scientists, this 17th-century astronomer was considered one of the foremost geniuses of the day by his contemporaries (Forbes, 1970). Most of us would likely omit Thomas Peel Dunhill from a list of those who have made fundamental discoveries in medical science; yet this "forgotten pioneer of thyroid surgery" (Vellar, 1974) devised ingenious techniques that many later surgeons have built upon. And although few contemporary psychologists are aware that Karl Bühler published well-known studies of language and cognition over 50 years ago, Weimer (1974a) has lamented Bühler's exclusion from the history of psychology and reminded us of the importance of his work.

History also contains numerous instances in which a scientist's work is initially ignored, and then at some later time hailed as a significant contribution. Whereas the efforts of men such as Meyer, Dunhill, and Bühler are "forgotten" over time, temporarily unrecognized contributions are "recovered": Little-known to contemporary researchers, they are only recognized by subsequent scientific generations. The phenomenon of temporarily unrecognized contributions raises important questions for theories of scientific development and change. In this chapter, we approach some of these questions in the context of attempting to understand the neglect of Richard Semon's theory of memory. The discussion draws upon a number of different perspectives. First, the problem of neglected scientific contributions is placed in a general framework suggested by the psychological theory of signal detection. I then examine the historical record and utilize recent ideas from the history, philosophy, and sociology of science in order to evaluate the various possible factors underlying Semon's virtually nonexistent status among memory researchers. Next, the range of the discussion is broadened to include other cases of initially overlooked contributions from the history of science: How similar are the profiles of these unrecognized scientists to the picture that has been sketched of Semon? Finally, I conclude by discussing the implications of the various cases and ideas that have been considered, and by briefly noting the relevance of the problems discussed in the chapter to some contemporary concerns.

THEORY EVALUATION AS SIGNAL-DETECTION: AN HEURISTIC ANALOGY

Although it has thus far escaped systematic scrutiny, the problem of the unrecognized scientist has exerted at least a passing fascination for many observers of the scientific enterprise. The specter of the misunderstood revolutionary whose theory is later vindicated by the selfsame scientific establishment that initially slighted it possesses undeniable elements of high drama. Not surprisingly, there is a discernible tendency among those who have pondered the fate of such scientists to portray their often tragic fates in a romantic fashion. These writers frequently depict the plight of neglected scientists in a manner that "curries our moral indignation (Brannigan, 1979, p. 453)." The earnest seeker of truth is typically pictured in an heroic struggle against an authoritarian, self-assured scientific orthodoxy that clings to its outmoded dogma in the face of the new vistas championed by the heretic whom it conveniently ignores. Consider the despairing commentary offered by R. H. Murray (1925, p. 316) after reviewing numerous cases of 19th-century scientists whose work was initially either neglected or resisted by the reigning authorities:

> Is there any punishment equal to that which in the name of Science and with the august authority of Science, has been inflicted upon Jenner and Simpson, Lyell and Helmholtz, Joule and Darwin, Pasteur and Lister, in some cases by ignoring their epoch-making ideas, and in other cases by fighting them to the death? Did any set of men so torture the body as scientists tortured the minds of these discoverers by bitterly criticising them?

Murray concluded his indignant reproach on a note of bewilderment:

how are we to account for SO MANY cases of neglect? A case here and a case there we might understand, but we encounter many cases. What are we to conclude? All the names we have given are those of men admittedly to-day in the foremost position. They are not the names of second-rate and third-rate observers.

Murray's analysis depicts a repressive group of dogmatic conservatives struggling to protect the traditional bastions of science from potential intrusions by forces of change. One is indeed tempted to concur with some of the opinions offered by authors such as Murray when one studies the numerous cases of neglected scientists, but it quickly becomes apparent that one cannot understand the phenomenon without viewing it in a wider context. The problem that Murray and others have lamented concerns one subset of outcomes that potentially characterizes a scientific theory or fact: It is initially treated as irrelevant to the current body of scientific thought and later shown to be both relevant and important. But what of other potential outcomes? What about scientists whose work was ignored—and rightly so—because of methodological inadequacies or theoretical naiveté? And what about scientists who have advanced new and important ideas that *were* recognized as such by their contemporaries?

Let me pause to put forward an analogy that will help to develop the point. Imagine that the task of scientists in evaluating the multitude of theories and data that they encounter is similar to the task of a person attempting to perceptually extract some specified information from an array of irrelevant background noise. The problem for this person is one of *signal detection*: He must decide whether any given input contains relevant information or irrelevant noise. The standard theory of signal detection recognizes four possible outcomes for a person in this situation. He may say "yes" when the relevant signal is present (a *hit*), "yes" when the signal is not present (a *false alarm*), "no" when the signal is not present (a *correct rejection*), or "no" when the signal is present (a *miss*). Thus there are two kinds of mistake that an observer in this situation can make—a false alarm or a miss—and the type of error that he most frequently commits depends upon the *decision criterion* that he adopts in the task. If the person adopts a liberal criterion, he is likely to say "yes" often and hence achieve many hits, but will also commit an excess of false alarms. If he adopts a conservative criterion, he is more likely to say "no," and maximize correct rejections, but at the same time accumulate a larger number of misses. Accordingly, it makes little sense to talk about the hit rate independently of the false alarms; similarly, intelligible inferences about the misses cannot be made without reference to the correct rejections.

Let us now apply this mode of analysis to scientists. The job of the scientific community is to extract a useful signal (data or theory that furthers our understanding of Nature) from a potentially distracting mass of background noise (unreliable data or ill-founded theories). Much like the observer in a signal detection experiment, scientists seek to maximize their hits and minimize their misses; the success of the enterprise clearly depends on a high ratio of hits to misses. But scientists are also confronted with a criterion problem not unlike the one confronted by the signal detecting observer. If a liberal criterion is adopted, hits will be increased at the expense of an accompanying rise in false alarms—that is, acceptance of a novel theory or datum that eventually leads to nothing more than a time consuming trip down the garden path. However, if a more conservative criterion is adopted, less time will be wasted chasing down theoretical pies-in-the-sky—correct rejections will be increased—but the probability of neglecting a potentially useful contribution also increases.

In regard to unrecognized scientific contributions, the critical point to bear in mind is that we cannot offer a complete analysis of these cases—the misses in a signal detection matrix—without reference to the correct rejections. This is precisely what the emotion-laden analyses of writers such as Murray fail to take into account. If the scientific community concerned itself solely with the maximization of hits, then cases of neglect would be exceedingly rare. But chaos would also ensue, because the number of false alarms would quickly become prohibitively high. A judgmental criterion must be set that achieves an appropriate balance between hits and correct rejections; we must risk bypassing some of the hits so that we attain a sufficient number of correct rejections. Hence cases of *mistaken* neglect necessarily accompany cases of *appropriate* neglect, and the former phenomenon cannot be properly grasped without reference to the latter. This point becomes doubly significant in our historical analyses of Semon and other neglected scientists, when I suggest that consideration of the "correct rejections" not only places the "misses" in a more comprehensible context, but also presents key insights into the possible causes of mistaken neglect. We pursue this issue after exploring the reception accorded Semon's psychological theory of memory, and it is to this task that we now turn our attention.

NULL EFFECT:
SEMON'S INFLUENCE ON MEMORY RESEARCH

When *Die mnemischen Empfindungen* appeared before the psychological community in 1909, Semon anticipated a battle. He had just emerged from the various heated controversies over *Die Mneme*—his rebuttals to Weismann, Meyer, and Driesch were written as he prepared his new monograph—and Semon expected new protests and experimental refutations to await his treatment of human memory: "I will surely be taken to task by the professional psychologists (Semon to Forel, 5–24–08)." But the conflict never took shape. As we observed in our earlier consideration of Semon's correspondence, *Die mnemischen Empfindungen* fell to the ground with a quiet thud. The reception accorded this new treatise was quite different from the response to *Die Mneme*: In place of the angry protests advanced by Weismann and other scientific chieftains there was only a disturbing silence punctuated by occasional murmurs of praise and criticism.

Initial reviews of the book ranged from inappreciatively disinterested to genuinely admiring. Erich Becher, a well-known psychological vitalist, gave the book a lukewarm reception in the 1910 volume of the *Archiv für die Gesamte Psychologie*. Becher paid lip service to Semon's ingenuity in several places, but largely confined himself to a description of the book's contents and the enunciation of minor criticisms. The *American Journal of Psychology* (unsigned review, 1909) briefly noted the appearance of *Die mnemischen Empfindungen*, but merely listed several of the topics addressed by Semon; there is no evidence that the reviewer appreciated any of his conceptual innovations. In the *Révue Philosophique*, Kostyleff brushed off the book as "toujours superficielle (1911, p. 752)." He assured his audience that "far from engaging French readers to decode the incomplete formulas of its author (p. 753)," the book could be conveniently ignored. On a more positive note, Franz (1909) informed psychologists in the *Zeitschrift für Psychologie* that Semon's ideas were "extraordinarily original and valuable (p. 228)." He praised Semon for offering "wholly new conceptions (p. 230)" (*ganzlich neue Auffassungen*) of memory, and applauded his effort to portray the subject from "an entirely new perspective (p. 231)." Although Franz also registered some doubts and criticisms, his brief review portrayed *Die mnemischen Empfindungen* in a generally positive light.

There was one feature of the reception accorded *Die Mneme* that did carry over to *Die mnemischen Empfindungen*: the presence of August Forel. Just as he championed *Die Mneme*, Forel greeted Semon's newest creation with unrestrained enthusiasm in a lengthy, 34-page article (Forel, 1910). There is good reason to expect that such an endorsement would have significantly advanced Semon's cause. Although, as noted in Chapter 7, Forel lacked authority concerning evolutionary problems, this was not the case in regard to psychology. Forel's professional eminence largely stemmed from his multifaceted investigations of numerous psychological problems; he had even published a monograph on human memory and amnesia in 1885. But Forel's laudatory review did little to excite psychological interest in Semon's work, and the probable reason for this is painfully obvious: He published it in the *Archiv für Rassen-und Gesellschafts-Biologie*. When the fate of *Die Mneme* was at stake, this journal was an entirely appropriate vehicle for Forel's efforts; specialists in evolutionary and hereditary biology regularly read and published in the *Archiv*. The *Archiv*, however, simply was not a psychological journal, much less a forum for exchange of views concerning human memory. Neither Ebbinghaus, Müller, Meumann nor any of the other major memory researchers published in the *Archiv*, and it is extremely unlikely that more than a few scattered students of human memory regularly consulted this biological journal. This time there were no critics such as Weismann or DéLage to question the validity of Forel's unmitigated praise; there is in fact scant evidence to suggest that any memory researchers ever read the review.[1]

---

1. The only citation by a psychologist to Forel's article that I have uncovered is found in Baird's (1911) review paper.

In spite of the endorsements by Forel and Franz, the influence of *Die mnemischen Empfindungen* on mainstream memory research was virtually undetectable. Most contemporary citations to Semon's work were brief and reflected little appreciation of his major concepts and theories. For instance, Woods (1915) noted Semon's contribution when she reviewed various theories of recognition memory, but mistakenly classified him along with Höffding as an advocate of the "fusion" position—a view that he had expressly and emphatically rejected. Even when accuracy was preserved in citations to Semon's work, there is a notable lack of critical discussion or debate concerning his theories; they are simply noted and passed over. My own efforts have turned up but one article in which any of Semon's positions were put to experimental test: Wohlgemuth's 1915 paper on successive vs. simultaneous association. Wohlgemuth, who labeled *Die mnemischen Empfindungen* "a decidedly suggestive and clever book (1915, p. 449)," was particularly intrigued by Semon's account of successive association, and constructed an experimental test of his views. Wohlgemuth claimed that his experiments strongly supported Semon's theory, but inspection of his data leaves the contemporary student of memory sceptical. More to the point, the fact that Wohlgemuth's effort was probably the sole experimental investigation directly aimed at testing Semon's theory of memory highlights just how extensively the theory was ignored.

It is ironic that the feature of Semon's memory theory that has historically attracted the most attention is perhaps the least innovative and most uninteresting component of it: the engram. The idea that memories are physiologically represented in the form of "traces" has an extensive history; its roots stem from the ancient Greeks and numerous thinkers have articulated similar notions since that time.[2] In Semon's theory, the concept of the engram is only interesting or controversial to the extent that it is tied to hereditary phenomena. Even here, it is the general idea that a memory trace underlies hereditary phenomena—not Semon's specific conceptualization of an engram—that is unique and problematic. Semon simply articulated a common assumption of his era and attached a label to it that was consistent with the rest of his nomenclature. Yet a variety of critics found Semon's concept of the engram a convenient target for abuse. Semon's reply to such criticism is worth noting precisely because it demonstrates that he was not committed to any particular physiological interpretation of the engram:

> I should be as able as anyone else to turn out some sort of schematic representation on the model of the diagram of Mendelian determinants in which engrams would be naively represented, schematized as tiny particles and conveniently packed together. This would meet the views of those readers whose thirst for causality requires such schematic representation, and who cannot resign themselves to leaving such questions open for the time being.

---

2. For an informative history of the numerous "trace" theories of memory, see Gomulicki's (1953) scholarly account.

> My own conception of inductive science is a different one, and I attribute
> more value to an honest note of interrogation than to constructions which
> are only representable through an effort of imagination. (1923, p. 329)

In spite of the fact that it represented an innocuous and conventional part of
Semon's theory, the notion of the engram garnered undue attention; by 1934
Campion and Smith (p. 105) could object that "It is held by many that Semon's
'engrams' have no neurological significance." Campion and Smith were right;
they do not.

More modern citations to Semon also reflect an inappropriate focus on the
engram. Although these vary in degrees of inaccuracy, not all of them criticize
Semon's idea. Particularly interesting is the following passage from a popular
treatise on memory by Halacy (1970, p. 182):

> When the French physiologist [sic] Richard Semon in 1904 advanced his
> theory of the memory 'engram', he suggested that it was chemical. For most
> of the intervening time the engram has generally been considered an electrical
> pathway rather than a chemical state. However, in recent years there have
> been increasing reminders that the brain is not an electrical or electronic
> computer but a chemical computer.

It would be exciting if Semon had in fact anticipated recent chemical theories
of the memory trace—but he did not. Semon did no more than argue that the
formation of engrams must entail a changed state of the brain; he nowhere
debated the relative merits of the chemical and electrical views.[3]

One of the most intriguing inaccuracies found in modern citations to
Semon's engram "theory" is the notion that Semon believed each engram to be
separately represented in a single cell or small group of cells. As we saw in
Chapter 9, Semon disavowed any such ideas; he in fact leaned more toward a
distributed than localized view of storage. Why, then, should anyone think otherwise? I believe that one reason for such misattribution is found in an article
published some 30 years after Semon's death: Karl Lashley's famous paper, "in
search of the engram" (Lashley, 1960). In that paper, Lashley reported data
from numerous experiments that failed to find evidence supporting the view
that engrams could be localized in single cells or small neuronal populations.
Consider the following passages that closely link Semon's ideas to Lashley's investigation:

> Semon (1904) places the engrammes in the Nissl bodies of the nerve cells;
> his idea was, however, challenged by Lashley, who tried in vain by ablation

---

3. A similar misattribution was made by Ungar (1970, p. 167) in his book *Molecular
   Mechanisms in Memory and Learning*: "Interpretations implying chemical storage
   of acquired information in the brain can be traced as far as Ribot (1882), W. James
   (1890), and were expressed somewhat more definitely by Semon (1904). He coined
   the term 'engram'."

experiments to find the specific site of memory in the brain. (Katchalsky & Neumann, 1972, p. 175)

searchers for the 'engram' (Semon, 1923; Lashley, 1950), or neural locus of learnt information, have conjectured that particular experiences or knowledge are stored in a unique locale in the central nervous system (Marshall & Fryer, 1978, p. 14).

The assumptions that implicitly underlie such statements seem clear: (1) Lashley suggested that localized engrams could be found; (2) he never found them; (3) Semon coined the term "engram"; (4) Lashley showed that Semon was wrong. Yet Lashley did not cite Semon in his classic paper, and he never explicitly "challenged" Semon's ideas—it would have been strange if he had, since Semon nowhere articulated the sort of localization view that Lashley's experiments discredited.

In spite of its checkered historical legacy and relatively insignificant role in his theory, the word "engram" is essentially all that has survived from Semon's analysis of memory. Even so, it is likely that most of those who use the term are entirely unaware of its inventor's identity. Let us briefly examine the extent to which modern memory researchers are aware of his work. One simple way in which to do this is through an inspection of the *Science Citation Index*. I have counted the citations to Semon's work since the inception of the *Index* in 1961 through the end of 1978, when the Schacter, Eich, and Tulving article that explored Semon's work was published. This citation census revealed, somewhat surprisingly, that Semon had been cited 67 times in the *Index* during the period of interest. A closer analysis of these citations indicated that 53 of the citations referred to Semon's anatomical and zoological work of the 1880s and 1890s. In contrast, there were only 14 citations to *Die Mneme*—and none to *Die mnemischen Empfindungen.* Upon examining the sources of the *Mneme* citations, I found that in almost every case Semon was cited for his stance on the inheritance of acquired characteristics, or for having coined the term "engram." Semon was credited with concern for retrieval processes in only one of these papers, and this citation is exceedingly brief (Weiner, 1966). Thus in the voluminous scientific literature included in the *Science Citation Index* from 1961 through 1978, there is no evidence that anyone has been significantly influenced by Semon's work on human memory. Examination of recent textbooks about memory tells a similar story: There are no references to Semon, although prominent historical figures such as Bartlett, Ebbinghaus, James, and Müller are regularly cited.[4]

There are at least two critical questions that can be asked about Semon's status: (1) Why do we know so little about Semon's theory today, and (2) Why was Semon's theory of memory ignored by his contemporaries? Clearly, there

---

4. The textbooks consulted were those by Baddeley (1976), Crowder (1976), Murdock (1974), and Spear (1978).

will be a great deal of overlap between the answers to these questions; we cannot answer the first without also considering the second. Several conjectures concerning the possible cause of Semon's virtual non-existence to modern students of memory have been advanced elsewhere (Schacter et al., 1978), but the present discussion focuses on the second question: Why was Semon's theory passed over in silence by his contemporaries?

We can sharpen the focus of this question by first considering one possible contribution to the neglect of Semon's theory: his failure to present original experimental evidence in support of his views. Semon frequently cited the contemporary experimental literature, and attempted to employ his theory in the analysis of outstanding empirical problems; he explicitly commented that "The results of experimental psychology must be reckoned with (1923, p. 57)." Yet Semon offered no original evidence other than his own introspections in support of his theory. Introspective analysis remained a partially acceptable tool of psychological inquiry in 1909. Mainstream memory researchers, however, tended to spurn introspective evidence in favor of more reliable and quantifiable experimental observations. Semon's introspective evidence, although occasionally buttressed by citations to experimental observations in the literature, must have seemed flimsy and unconvincing to his contemporaries. Still, this analysis is only partially informative. It may tell us why Semon's views were not *accepted* in their time, but it does not tell us why they were not recognized and subjected to experimental scrutiny. This is the crucial problem in Semon's case: Why was such a theory, more comprehensive than most of its competitors and full of intriguing postulates that we now know pointed to critical features of human memory, virtually never put to experimental test by psychologists of the time?

Historical, Philosophical, and Sociological Perspectives

We now seek guidance from the modern history, philosophy, and sociology of science in framing our questions concerning the possible causes of the neglect of Semon's work. It is useful to first consider two ideas concerning the fundamental attributes of a scientific theory that stem from a pair of widely differing philosophies of science, the tradition of logical positivism and the system of Karl Popper. In the logical positivist account, the key feature that demarcates a scientifically meaningful statement is its *verifiability*. If a statement about the world cannot be empirically verified, then it lacks the most basic attribute of a scientific theory. According to the logical positivists, a theory or idea may be original, elaborate, and internally consistent, but not scientific: It must also be possible to verify the theory or idea by empirical measurements. The notion that verifiability constitutes a necessary feature of a scientific theory was turned on its head in the revolutionary philosophy of Karl Popper.[5] Popper, who broke

---

5. See Popper's *The Logic of Scientific Discovery* (1959) and *Conjectures and Refutations* (1963) for a thorough exposition of his views.

sharply with the positivist tradition in numerous ways, replaced the idea of veri-fiability with notions of *testability* and *falsifiability* as criterial features of a sci-entific theory. According to Popper, a statement about the world is scientific insofar as it is testable, and it is legitimately testable only to the extent that it is falsifiable.

Let us apply these ideas to the problem of the neglect of Semon's theory: Were his ideas ignored because they violated criteria of scientific validity—that is, they were neither verifiable nor falsifiable? Clearly, if the internal structure of Semon's theory were so flawed as to preclude either verification or falsifica-tion of it, then we should not be surprised that it received scant attention from scientists of the day. A bit of reflection upon the subsequent fate of the ideas promulgated in Semon's theory suggests that this is not the case. Consider three of the most striking propositions advanced by Semon: his multiple-trace theory of repetition, his contention that each act of ecphory establishes a new engram, and his insistence that memory performance is critically dependent upon the internal and external conditions of ecphory. As we saw in the previous chapter, all three of these ideas have been experimentally tested in recent years. Each has obtained a large degree of verification, and all three have been pitted against alternatives that rendered them potentially falsifiable. These ideas were stated quite unambiguously by Semon, and were potentially falsifiable or verifiable by anyone who cared to test them; but nobody did. Accordingly, it seems advisable to look elsewhere for the key to understanding the neglect of Semon's work, because possible flaws such as a lack of verifiability or falsifiability seem to have limited relevance to this case.

A more enlightening perspective on the problem is found in a classic mono-graph that has almost single-handedly initiated sweeping changes in the recent history, philosophy, and sociology of science—Thomas Kuhn's (1962) *The Struc-ture of Scientific Revolutions*. Kuhn's multidimensional essay attacked numer-ous standard conceptions of scientific practice and scientific change. His em-phasis on the discrete, sudden nature of scientific revolutions, his sharp distinction between "normal" and "revolutionary" science, and his acknowledg-ment of the role that psychological factors play in the evolution of science all challenged traditional approaches to the scientific enterprise. Kuhn's work has exerted an astonishingly wide influence, and has been both praised and criti-cized; I can only point the reader to some of the voluminous literature that has been concerned with various aspects of the Kuhnian thesis.[6]

I focus on one critical concept introduced by Kuhn, itself the subject of much controversy: his well known idea of the "paradigm." In broad outline, the Kuhnian paradigm refers to a set of shared assumptions about the nature of the world and the proper methods of investigation possessed by the members of any scientific community. One must tread rather cautiously when presenting

---

6. The most useful entry point into the debate over Kuhn's views is the volume edited by Lakatos and Musgrave (1970). For an informative sample of Kuhn's thoughts on a variety of historical and scientific issues, see Kuhn (1977).

Kuhn's original conception of the paradigm since, as his critics frequently point out, Kuhn initially used the term in myriad fashions; Masterman (1970) has documented 21 different senses of "paradigm" employed by Kuhn. Kuhn himself has noted these inconsistencies—he regretted that paradigms "can be too nearly all things to all people (1977, p. 293)"—and has suggested that the potentially misleading term "paradigm" be replaced by the phrase "disciplinary matrix": "'disciplinary' because it is the common possession of the practitioners of a professional discipline and 'matrix' because it is composed of ordered elements of various sorts (p. 297)."

These terminological problems are less important for our purposes than the principal idea that underlies the foregoing expressions: The endeavors of a scientific community are structured and directed by shared assumptions that specify relevant phenomena and problems. Recent writers pursuing a "neo-Kuhnian" orientation have explicitly followed up Kuhn's contention that these shared assumptions can be traced to basic cognitive and social-psychological features of scientists themselves. Thus Mulkay (1972) invoked "cognitive norms," Weingart (1974) offered the notion of "cognitive orientation complexes," and McDonagh (1974) appealed to "attitudes" as psychological bases of the Kuhnian paradigm or disciplinary matrix. Each of these conceptualizations emphasizes that scientists' ability to assimilate new ideas and contributions is constrained by their expectations, preconceptions, and notions about what constitutes an important scientific problem. Thus, sciences at all stages of development—not just mature or so-called "paradigmatic" sciences—are guided by commonly held assumptions that direct research and delineate relevant problem areas. As Kuhn himself has noted, "Whatever paradigms may be, they are possessed by any scientific community, including schools of the so-called pre-paradigm period. My failure to see that point clearly has helped make a paradigm seem a quasi-mystical entity or property which, like charisma, transforms those infected by it (1977, p. 295)."

How, then, do these ideas apply to Semon's case? In the Kuhnian perspective that has been sketched, it is possible—in fact likely—that a theory or datum will be ignored by the scientific community when it is not assimilable by the prevailing "disciplinary matrix," "cognitive norms," or "cognitive orientation complexes." One need not posit a lack of verifiability or falsifiability in order to render the neglect intelligible; it becomes comprehensible once the functional significance of something like a "disciplinary matrix" or "paradigm" is recognized as an organizing and structuring component of the scientific enterprise. With regard to Semon, the Kuhnian perspective suggests two critical questions: How relevant were Semon's ideas to the shared concerns of memory researchers in 1909? What kind of sense would Semon's theory make to a mainstream memory researcher of the time? The answer to these questions emerges from a concatenation of the major themes developed in Chapters 8 and 9: Retrieval phenomena were of prime theoretical concern to Semon and of minor theoretical concern to his contemporaries. Why, then, *should* anyone have taken note of Semon's ideas? Semon focused theoretical attention on areas that did not exist as major problems in the eyes of mainstream researchers dominated by the traditional associationistic framework; phenomena that Semon construed as theoretically crucial were largely viewed by his contemporaries as measurement problems. In the Kuhnian terminology, his ideas were simply not assimilable by the prevailing associationistic paradigm.[7]

We may also ask how well Semon's theory addressed problems that *did* form part of the shared concerns of memory researchers. Recall the seven principal problem areas that were delineated in Chapter 8: repetition effects, the curve of forgetting, stimulus attributes, interference effects, individual differences, methods of learning, and finally, recognition and affective phenomena. It is apparent that Semon's theory, however wide ranging it was, had virtually nothing to say about these problems, with the exception of repetition effects; we shall shortly return to this interesting exception. But by and large, Semon's theory violated the disciplinary matrix. There was an extensive mismatch between the problems perceived as relevant by Semon and those construed as relevant by mainstream researchers; the intellectual distance separating Semon from his contemporaries was sizeable. Toulmin (1961, p. 57) concisely summarized such a state of affairs in science: "Men who accept different ideals and paradigms have really no common theoretical terms in which to discuss their problems: events which are 'phenomena' in one man's eyes will be passed over by the other as 'perfectly natural.'"

Relevant insights are also provided by considering the fate of the "retrieval heretics" that we encountered earlier: How were the views of retrieval put forward by Freud, Prince, and Selz, who promulgated their theories at about the same time as Semon, treated by memory researchers? As the Kuhnian perspective would lead us to expect, they were almost entirely ignored.[8] The later views of retrieval advanced by Bartlett, Hollingworth, Köhler, and Koffka all endured a similar fate; they were not incorporated into the ongoing stream of memory research.

Although the foregoing account provides some insights into the causes of

---

7. There is one potentially serious problem with the application of Kuhnian analysis to neglected scientific contributions that should be noted: It is difficult to define a "paradigm" or "disciplinary matrix" independently of the reception accorded a given theory or experiment. Unless suitable criteria can be devised for characterizing "paradigms," we run a clear risk of entrapment by circular reasoning: Scientific contributions are neglected when they violate the prevailing paradigm, and the prevailing paradigm is inferred to be what a neglected scientific contribution departs from. Although I have tried to avoid such reasoning in this chapter, this is clearly a problem that requires extensive consideration in future work.

8. Freud, of course, was well known to his contemporaries. But Freud's influence on experimental memory research was slight. The one serious attempt by memory researchers to evaluate Freud's theory can be found in the symposium on repression published in the *British Journal of Psychology*, 1914, 7, 139–165.

the neglect of Semon's work by his contemporaries, it does not tell the complete story. It was noted above that Semon's theory made contact with at least one problem of vital interest to the field: repetition effects. Semon's bold multiple-trace theory of repetition directly opposed the widely accepted strengthening view. Why was there no attempt to experimentally refute his challenge to the orthodoxy? Semon's position was stated as emphatically and unambiguously as possible; the problem of repetition was a highly visible and shared concern; yet Semon's challenge went unanswered. It is extremely unlikely that if eminent researchers such as Meumann or Müller had advanced such a view, only silence would have ensued; one suspects that a major controversy would have been sparked. This circumstance suggests a second possible factor in Semon's obscurity: his social isolation.

In addition to the revolution inspired by Kuhn, a second important ingredient in altering the way that we think about the scientific enterprise stems from the work of sociologists who have analyzed the role played by social processes in science. These analyses, owing largely to the seminal studies of Robert Merton, provide a useful framework for approaching Semon's isolation. The explosion in sociology of science research during the past 15 years has produced a wealth of informative data; only the most relevant insights can be noted here.

A variety of studies have established that the scientific community is a highly stratified and organized social system in which prestige affiliations, scientific reputation, and competition for recognition play a critical role. An important recent task has been the identification of socially defined *research* or *problem* networks:

> Research networks are the social units responsible for scientific innovation in the sense that their members encourage or discourage certain lines of work, in the sense that the initial response to research findings is made by a particular network, and in the sense that approved results are taken up and disseminated by the network (Mulkay, 1972, pp. 35–36).

Just as in other social systems, there is little chance that an outsider who is isolated from one of these highly structured social networks can successfully compete for the recognition regularly conferred upon insiders. As Hagstrom (1965, p. 49) concluded in his classic study, "in general, isolation means that the scientist will receive less recognition for his work and that he will lack information necessary for its completion." A similar notion was advanced by Merton (1973) in his study of the effects of a scientist's social standing within the research community on the reception of his ideas. Merton argued that the amount of recognition accorded a scientist's work depends upon his perceived status by

---

9. Many of the important studies that have lent support to these conclusions can be found in the monographs by Barnes (1972), Cole and Cole (1973), Hagstrom (1965), Merton (1973), Price (1963), and Whitely (1974).

other researchers, and labeled this phenomenon the "Matthew effect": "a scientific contribution will have greater visibility in the community of scientists when it is introduced by a scientist of high rank than when it is introduced by one who has not yet made his mark (1973, p. 447)."

The applicability of the foregoing ideas to Semon's case is straightforward. Working alone in Munich, Semon operated in almost total isolation from the research networks that comprised the psychological community. He did not attend psychological conferences, did not publish in psychological journals, and had no graduate students to work on his theory and increase its visibility to the psychological world. Moreover, Semon had no training in psychology or a past track record of psychological investigations to boost his authority; he also had no personal communication with psychologists other than Forel. It is important here to recall the large differences in the reception of *Die Mneme* by biologists and *Die mnemischen Empfindungen* by psychologists. However severely it was criticized, *Die Mneme* was seriously and extensively debated by biologists. This is not surprising in light of Semon's growing zoological reputation in the 1890s and his close association with the important biologists at Jena prior to 1897. But he had no such credentials in psychology.

These considerations acquire added significance when we recall that at the time Semon advanced his theory, mainstream psychology was sharply partitioned into various rival "schools"—small problem networks located in different universities that typically attempted to advance the views of one dominant professor. In German speaking countries alone, one can identify Külpe's school at Würzburg, the Leipzig contingent headed by Wundt, Müller's circle at Göttingen, the early Gestaltists headed by Max Wertheimer at Berlin, Franz Brentano's Austrian school of Act Psychology, and Meumann and his followers at Zurich.[10] Ben-David and Collins (1966, p. 459), in a paper that traced the origins of psychology in Germany, have argued that these social groups constituted an "autonomous network for the regular transmission of the new ideas." Semon belonged to none of these social units, and hence could not benefit from the prestige and legitimacy conferred by membership in one of the prominent schools.

Another contribution to Semon's status as a psychological outsider stems from his involvement in the neo-Lamarckian and memory-heredity issues that comprised much of *Die Mneme.* As discussed earlier, Semon's tireless crusade in favor of the acquired characters position closely tied his name to the "wrong" view on that troublesome topic. More relevant to the present concerns is the fact that Semon never slashed the umbilical cord to Mneme. By doggedly pursuing his defense of Mneme in the dangerous territory of the acquired characters dispute instead of explicating his aparadigmatic theories of memory to relevant researchers, Semon could only have heightened his status as an outsider

---

10. For a history of psychology that deals extensively with these "schools," see Sahakian (1975).

to the psychological community. Ben-David and Collins noted the fate of self-styled eclectics who, like Semon, pursued non-psychological interests and lacked official ties to the psychological community: "These men did not consider themselves psychologists, nor were they so identified by their contemporaries. Generally they remained isolated from any specific discipline until historians of the science . . . offered them a posthumous home (1966, p. 454)."

One final point concerning Semon's status as an outsider merits brief consideration: his terminological inventions. We earlier saw that Semon created his own scientific terms in order to avoid the misleading connotations inherent in the everyday language typically used to describe memory. Unfortunately, his invocation of admittedly bizarre terms such as "engraphy," "ecphory," and the "acoluthic phase" may have created a barrier to the uninitiated reader. More important, these strange expressions clearly identified Semon as a theoretical outsider; his jargon bore no discernible resemblance to the customary terminology employed in the mainstream psychological journals. Thus in his quest for precision of expression, Semon may have unwittingly heightened his status as an outsider and, ironically, contributed to the isolation of his own work.

THE SCIENTIFIC CRANK AND CORRECT REJECTIONS

The preceding analyses of the neglect of Semon's work have been restricted to just one cell of the signal detection matrix that was invoked earlier: We have examined some of the reasons why Semon's theory was "missed" by the scientific community. In keeping with my earlier assertion that the significance of the misses cannot be properly understood without reference to the correct rejections, we now enlarge our perspective and consider Semon's case in relation to one important subset of correct rejections—the scientific crank. The crank has assumed numerous historical guises, and various attempts to define this intriguing figure have been made. Gardner (1957, p. 8), for instance, offered the following portrayal of the crank in his popular study of scientific aberrations: "If a man persists in advancing views that are contradicted by all available evidence, and which offer no reasonable grounds for serious consideration, he will be rightfully dubbed a crank by his colleagues." Joravsky (1970, p. 39) has defined the crank by way of contrast with the scientist: "The word 'crank' is a pejorative, but it cannot be avoided, for cranks are quite different from scientists. . . . The essential difference is the crank's individualistic self-assurance versus the scientist's collectivistic self-doubt."

Crank contributions to science highlight the problem of signal detection that the scientific community must solve. A criterion must be set that excludes extremist contributions that are likely to have little value, so the crank is usually ignored in spite of the possibility that he may be right. In almost all cases the behavior of the scientific orthodoxy is ultimately justified; the crank's bold assertions about the possibility of perpetual motion or the earth's flatness are correctly rejected. The problem of the crank has been a persistent one in the history of science, and recent times have witnessed the domination of Soviet genetics by a small group of men, under the leadership of T. D. Lysenko, who may be legitimately described as cranks (Joravsky, 1970). It is precisely because the scientific community has historically had to guard against such crank intrusions that non-crank scientists who in certain respects resemble these pariahs will also be ignored.

Consider two of the most conspicuous features typically found in the crank. Gardner (1957, p. 8) has highlighted the crank's frequent social isolation from the mainstream scientific community: "First and most important of these traits is that cranks work in almost total isolation from their colleagues." The crank engages in little fruitful interaction with mainstream scientists, rarely publishes in reputable journals, and most often works without prestigious institutional affiliations. In connection with this social isolation, the crank also exhibits a second significant trait: His methods and theories violate the shared disciplinary matrix of mainstream science. The crank pursues theories that propose bizarre, idiosyncratic solutions to scientific problems that maintain a barely recognizable relationship to the form of the solutions proposed by those working within professional research networks. The crank contributes to this aparadigmatic stature by inventing "a complex jargon, in many cases making use of terms and phrases he himself has coined (Gardner, 1957, p. 1)." Noting the frequent incommensurability between crank contributions and "paradigm-sharing" sciences, Dolby (1975, p. 174) has depicted the almost inexorable fate of the crank theory: "If we totally fail to understand it, we can only ignore it." In addition to constructing unconventional approaches to scientific problems, the defiant crank also delights in attacking many of the assumptions most cherished by those who share the contemporary disciplinary matrix:

> This . . . defiance can be seen in a tendency to assert the diametrical opposite of well-established beliefs. Mathematicians prove the angle cannot be trisected. So the crank trisects it. A perpetual motion machine cannot be built. He builds one. There are many eccentric theories in which the 'pull' of gravity is replaced by a 'push'. Germs do not cause disease, some modern cranks insist. Disease causes germs (Gardner, 1957, p. 13).

We have in fact already encountered one man who exemplified well the picture of the crank thus sketched—Samuel Butler. Butler's unstructured method of inquiry, selective disregard for available biological evidence, contempt for the reigning authorities, and shockingly idiosyncratic theories, in combination with his complete social isolation from establishment biologists, branded him as a classical crank. Butler's theories were received by the scientific community with a poisonous silence that the heretical outsider did not anticipate: "He waited patiently for objections to his Memory theory of heredity . . . just as later on he waited for six years for criticism of [other] theories; but in neither case was any serious criticism forthcoming (Harris, 1916, p. 132)." Butler, of course, does not stand alone in the correct rejection cell of the scientific signal detection matrix. Countless numbers of cranks from various historical eras have met with similar silence; Ignatius Donnelly's treatise on Atlantis, John Symmes' theory of the hollow earth, Alfred William Lawson's self-constructed cosmological school of Lawsonology, and George McCready Price's Protestant fundamentalist "refutations" of organic evolution are just a few of the crank theories that have passed quietly without recognition from the scientific community.

The relevance of the preceding discussion to Semon's neglect should be clear by now. The two factors that I previously argued contributed most heavily to the "miss" of Semon's theory—his intellectual violation of the disciplinary matrix and his social isolation from the scientific community—are also the two factors that identify that important component of correct rejection, the crank. Precisely how such a relationship should be interpreted poses a problem. One might argue that Semon was ignored because scientists viewed him as a crank, or that both Semon and genuine cranks were ignored for the same reasons; it is difficult to tease apart these two interpretations. More important for our purposes is the acknowledgment that "missed" theorists such as Semon and "correctly rejected" crank theorists share critical features in common—namely, their intellectual and social distance from what Dolby (1975) has labeled the "paradigm-sharing" scientific community.

With this guiding thought in mind, we now move on to consider other cases of "missed" contributions in the history of science. Semon's case plays a dual role in the discussion: The reception of his theory leads us to analyze other instances of ignored theories, and our examination of these cases provides us with a more refined appreciation of Semon's fate. We examine a spectrum of scientific contributions whose due recognition was delayed in terms of the features that characterized Semon's case. The chapter concludes with some final perspectives on the difficulty of distinguishing revolutionaries from cranks, and two dramatic contemporary manifestations of this problem are considered.

THE MARCH OF THE INVISIBLE MEN: PROFILES IN SCIENTIFIC NEGLECT

A valid scientific theory can be "missed" in more than one way, and this detection error can be potentially attributed to more than one source. *Active* resistance to an ultimately acceptable new idea constitutes one major means of temporarily relegating a contribution to the miss cell in a signal detection matrix. Active resistance to novel contributions is as old as science itself; tales of the initial protests encountered by Copernicus, Galileo, and Newton are familiar to most of us. In these cases, the sources of resistance were twofold: Intra-scientific rejections were accompanied by protests from extra-scientific sources, most notably the church. But even as extra-scientific social and religious institutions loosened their control over scientific theorizing, intra-scientific resistances continued unabated. Pasteur's experimental refutation of spontaneous generation, Ignaz Semmelweis' theory that puerperal fever is caused by germs, William

Jenner's advocacy of small-pox vaccination, Max Planck's initial enunciation of the quantum hypothesis, Alfred Wegener's theory of continental drift, and Einstein's theory of relativity were all actively resisted for varying periods of time within the scientific community.[11] William Harvey, who endured sufficient abuse from scientists after advancing his theory of the circulation of the blood to make him a charter member of the above club, articulated a fear that many of science's greatest names have felt:

> what remains to be said about the quantity and source of the blood which thus passes, is of so novel and unheard-of character, that I not only fear injury to myself from the envy of a few, but I tremble lest I should have mankind at large for my enemies so much doth want and custom, that becomes as another nature, and doctrine once sown and that hath struck deep root, and respect for antiquity influence all men (cited in Stern, 1941, p. 185).

Active resistance, then, is one way in which scientists can "miss" a contribution that is later recognized. But in keeping with the silent reception accorded Semon's theory of memory, we focus upon passively ignored contributions in the present discussion; active resistance, though relevant to our concern, will only be noted here.[12]

My primary interest in this discussion of neglected scientific contributions is to gauge their degree of resemblance to the picture that has been painted of Semon's neglect. The discussion draws upon available historical scholarship, and is not in any sense intended to be a definitive evaluation of the numerous variables operative in each case. The information concerning many of these cases is rather fragmentary, and my conclusions are necessarily tentative ones. A major purpose of the discussion will be served if bringing together these disparate stories leads to more detailed scrutinies of each individual case in future work.

Let us begin by examining perhaps the most famous instance of a neglected scientific contribution: Gregor Mendel's experiments on heredity. Mendel's case is a particularly useful one to start with because a good deal of historical scholarship has been devoted to it. The facts of the case are fairly well known. Mendel carried out a series of experiments in which he crossed different strains of peas in his monastary garden at Brünn during the years 1857–1865. A careful observer, Mender noted the characteristics of the 19,959 crosses that appeared in his first and second hybrid generations, and claimed to have observed consis-

---

11. An informative discussion that includes several of these cases has been provided by Barber (1961).
12. An interesting problem is raised by the juxtaposition of cases of active and passive scientific resistance: Under what conditions are these different forms of resistance elicited? Although beyond the scope of the present discussion, elucidation of the conditions that encourage active and passive resistance to deviant contributions poses an interesting challenge for future research.

tent numerical ratios relating the different types of offspring to each other. Mendel read a paper that reported his data to the *Naturforschender Verein* at Brünn in 1865, and the paper was published in the society's proceedings. Instead of rousing scientific interest with his data, Mendel's presentation and subsequent publication received little attention from the scientific community. With the exception of a few scattered citations to his paper, Mendel's work lay dormant for 35 years; when it was rediscovered in 1900, his data served as a cornerstone for the new science of genetics.

A variety of hypotheses have been put forward to explain the neglect of Mendel's experiments. Clearly, lack of experimental evidence was not a crucial factor in this case; in fact, it has been suggested that Mendel's emphasis on data at the expense of theory contributed to his obscurity (Zirkle, 1965, p. 124). The suggestion that the neglect of Mendel owes to the presentation of his paper before an "unknown" society and its publication in an "obscure" journal has also been discredited. The proceedings of the *Naturforschender Verein* were distributed to some 120 libraries, and as William Bateson noted, they were exchanged with "most of the Academies of Europe, including both the Royal and Linnean Societies (cited in Glass, 1953, p. 148)." The fact that Mendel's paper was cited in some reputable contemporary textbooks also suggests that mere inaccessibility did not itself cause naturalists to overlook his paper. Similarly, the notion that biologists were not interested in heredity when Mendel published his paper is difficult to maintain in light of the evidence (Zirkle, 1965, p. 123).

Why, then, was Mendel's work ignored? The two factors that emerge most clearly from scholarly analyses of this case turn out to be similar to those we discussed earlier with regard to Semon. First, Mendel's approach to heredity was a significant departure from previous attempts. The relationships that Mendel uncovered did not fit with existing interpretive schemes of hereditary phenomena; in Kuhnian terminology, they could not be assimilated by the disciplinary matrix. It was this mismatch between Mendel's approach to heredity and the ideas of his contemporaries that led Glass (1953), Wilkie (1962), and Zirkle (1965) to independently conclude that "the failure to comprehend, and not inaccessibility of his work, was the reason for the neglect of Mendel's discovery (Glass, 1953, p. 153)." Similarly, Gasking (1959) has pointed to the intellectual distance that separated Mendel from his contemporaries: "One is forced to conclude that Mendel was ignored because his whole way of looking at the phenomena of inheritance was foreign to the scientific thought of his time (p. 60)."

Perhaps the most dramatic demonstration of this incommensurability was Karl Nägeli's failure to understand the significance of Mendel's experiments in his correspondence with Mendel. One of the leading contemporary authorities on heredity, Nägeli not only had access to Mendel's data, but also had the advantage of Mendel's personal commentary concerning its significance. Nägeli, however, never understood the importance of Mendel's results and could only advise the disillusioned monk to carry out some pedestrian breeding experiments that Nägeli himself had initiated. Further information on this point is provided by considering the circumstances under which Hugo DeVries, Carl Correns, and Erich von Tschermak independently rediscovered—and appreciated—Mendel's work in 1900. Biological conceptions of heredity had markedly changed between 1865 and 1900; the intellectual context within which the rediscoverers encountered Mendel's work sharply differed from that of 1865. Gasking has noted the effects of this change: "What chiefly prevented the earlier workers from observing the regularity [in Mendel's data] was their theoretical outlook: all the men who later rediscovered the laws had abandoned the old assumptions about 'specific essences' and so were ready to observe individual characters and their mode of transmission (1959, p. 83; see also Wilke, 1962)."

The intellectual gulf between Mendel and his contemporaries is not, however, the sole relevant feature of this case; we must also consider Mendel's social isolation. Working alone in the Brünn monastary, without academic qualifications or affiliations, and possessing no professional track record, Mendel could not command the necessary authority as a biologist to force others to seriously consider his experiments. The combination of this reputational poverty with an idiosyncratic approach to his subject had all the earmarks of the crank: "the high degree of elaboration of the theory, which now seems one of its principal merits, must have made it appear the work of an eccentric unacquainted with the complexities of the problem (Wilkie, 1962, p. 5)." There may be, of course, other ways in which to account for the neglect of Mendel's work (see Brannigan, 1979), but it seems reasonable to suggest that intellectual and social distance from the paradigm-sharing scientific community played some role in it.

The intellectual distance and social isolation from fellow scientists that characterized both Mendel and Semon is also conspicuously present in the case of John James Waterston. Although not nearly as well known today as Mendel, the story behind Waterston's kinetic theory of gases is a classic one of widespread neglect followed by dramatic rediscovery. Waterston formulated his theory while working for the East India Company at Bombay in the 1840s. He sent a paper describing his new theory to the Royal Society in 1845, and soon received news of its rejection. Both referees who read the paper recommended that it should not be published, and one of them repudiated it with an arrogance that is especially ironic in hindsight: "the paper is nonsense, unfit even for reading before the Society (cited in Rayleigh, 1964, p. 559)." A brief abstract of the paper appeared in the 1846 *Proceedings of the Royal Society*, but it remained virtually unknown until Lord Rayleigh discovered it in the Royal Society archives and communicated its content to an incredulous scientific world in 1892. The value of Waterston's paper can be gleaned from Haldane's (1928, p. 65) remorseful commentary on its neglect: "It is probable that in the long and honourable history of the Royal Society no mistake more disastrous in its actual consequences for the progress of science and the reputation of British science than the rejection of Waterston's papers was ever made."

What did Waterston say in that 1845 paper and why was he ignored? Waterston's paper presented a mathematical theory that viewed gases as molecules that move at high velocities and continually collide with each other at various angles. This *kinetic* theory directly opposed the widely accepted *caloric* theory, which postulated that an hypothetical element (caloric) permeated gases and possessed properties that accounted for their behavior. The caloric theory had been worked out to a large degree of mathematical precision, and contemporary theorists were not interested in radical kinetic alternatives. Waterston's ideas not only conflicted with those of his contemporaries; they called into question the most basic assumptions of the caloric theory.[13] Thus, a "paradigmatic violation" once again turns up in our profile of a neglected scientist; but once again it is not sufficient to account for the case at hand.

The caloric theory that Waterston attempted to overthrow in 1845 was eventually replaced by kinetic conceptions similar to his own. The critical period began just 10 years after Waterston published his paper, when eminent scientists such as James Clerk Maxwell, Rudolf Clausius, and Karl Krönig formulated kinetic theories that closely resembled Waterston's unknown attempt. The acceptance of these theories partially depended upon related conceptual advances that rendered the kinetic theory more comprehensible, but also partially depended upon their authors' established reputations. Brush (1961, pp. 203–204) noted the confluence of circumstances that eased reception of Krönig's 1856 paper: "Its favorable reception was due primarily to the fact that the mechanical theory of heat had been experimentally established, and also to the fact that Krönig was important enough for other scientists to pay attention to him." Waterston, an unknown amateur stationed in India who lacked scientific credentials, could not command the serious attention that mainstream scientists could. Lord Rayleigh realized that both Waterston's low social status and intellectual nonconformity were critical factors that contributed to the neglect of the theory, and criticized the Royal Society for "missing" Waterston's contributions: "By refusing to publish work by authors without established reputations, or theories which contravert accepted doctrines, a scientific society shirks one of its most important functions (cited in Brush, 1961, p. 210)."

For Waterston, scientific recognition was not forthcoming within his lifetime. His several published attempts to call attention to his theories had no productive effects, and he was ultimately haunted by the specter of the crank: "As his views were at variance with those which had been accepted by all the younger physicists of the time, and the rejection by the Royal Society of some of his papers was known, he had probably been set down as an old Anglo-Indian 'crank' (Haldane, 1928, p. 43)." There were probably other factors that contributed to the neglect of Waterston's theory—his paper contained several technical flaws—but the resemblances to Mendel and Semon are striking.

Another example of neglect that possesses features in common with the foregoing cases derives from 19th-century chemistry. Like Waterston's theory, the substantive issues in this case concerned the properties of gases. Amedeo

---

13. Excellent analyses of the relation between Waterston's ideas and those of his contemporaries are provided in Brush's (1957, 1961) incisive papers.

Avogadro's hypothesis that equal volumes of gases contain the same number of molecules was initially advanced in a paper that appeared in the 1811 volume of the French *Journal de Physique*. Avogadro offered his hypothesis as a reconciliation of two contemporary trends in chemistry: Dalton's atomic theory and Gay-Lussac's law of combining volumes. He also showed that molecular weights could be directly determined once his major thesis was accepted; this alone was a major contribution. But these attractive features of his hypothesis did not engage the attention of scientists: "Avogadro's proposals were essentially sound, yet in the years between 1811 and 1858 they were almost completely ignored by the vast majority of chemists (Nash, 1957, p. 292)."

Why were Avogadro's "essentially sound" proposals neglected? We can begin by noting several problematic features of Avogadro's paper: It was not a particularly clear presentation, Avogadro demonstrated only a limited application of his hypothesis, and there was a dearth of evidence for several of his fundamental assumptions. Such considerations, however, apply to numerous scientific documents; they do not convincingly explain the neglect of a paper that later proved to be a milestone of chemistry. But there are also two familiar circumstances that shed more light on Avogadro's case: his intellectual and social distance from his contemporaries.

Consider first Avogadro's intellectual nonconformity. At a time when most chemists spurned the use of mathematics, Avogadro offered a complex mathematical treatment of his subject; as Coley (1964, p. 198) argued, Avogadro's mathematical venture beyond the bounds of experiment "did not recommend itself to the vast majority of chemists." Avogadro's contribution was relevant to the concerns of *physical* chemistry; but in the 50 years following the appearance of his paper most attention was paid to *organic* chemistry (Crosland, 1970, p. 347). And as Mauskopf (1969) has pointed out, a number of conceptual distinctions that are necessary to appreciate and utilize Avogadro's hypothesis were not sufficiently clear to most chemists in 1811. When these conceptual clarifications were finally made, and scientific attention focused upon physical chemistry, Cannizzaro's rediscovery and explication of Avogadro's hypothesis in 1858 struck the world of chemistry like a lightning bolt: "neglect of the hypothesis, coupled with adherence to the atomic hypothesis led, by 1860, to a state of extreme confusion in chemistry. On the reassertion of Avogadro's hypothesis by Cannizzaro this confusion was dispelled, almost as if by magic (Meldrum, 1904, p. 113)."

Avogadro's intellectual uniqueness was complemented by a deadly social isolation from mainstream science. Avogadro held the chair of mathematical physics at the University of Turin in Italy. Italy was then at the outskirts of the scientific world, and the reticent Avogadro did nothing to alleviate his alien status:

> His modesty was one of the factors contributing to his comparative obscurity, particularly outside of Italy. Unlike his great contemporaries Gay-Lussac and Davy, he worked in isolation. Only toward the end of his life do we find

letters exchanged with leading men of science in other countries (Crosland, 1970, p. 344).

It is difficult to know just how much Avogadro's isolation from other scientists contributed to the neglect of his work, but his status as an outsider constitutes a clear similarity between his case and those of Semon, Mendel, and Waterston.

Our explorations of neglected scientific contributions have so far been confined to the 19th-century. As a final illustration of the joint presence of intellectual and social isolation in a neglected scientist, we examine a thoroughly documented case from the 20th-century: The indifference that Torsten Hagerstrand's spatial diffusion theory received from researchers in human geography. This case has been analyzed in detail by Duncan (1974), who used citation counts, personal testimonies, and data on research networks of geographers in an attempt to explicate the initial obscurity and subsequent popularity of Hagerstrand's theory. The facts of the case seem clear. Hagerstrand, a geographer at Lund University in Sweden, published highly original papers in the 1940s and 1950s that attempted to account for social change through analysis of the spatial diffusion of innovations and ideas. Hagerstrand is today recognized as a founder of the "new geography," and his pioneering experimental papers and books are now given widespread credit for their multifaceted contributions.

Why, then, was Hagerstrand steadfastly ignored by scientific geographers until the period beginning around 1967? Let us consider the conclusions that Duncan drew from his data. Casting his analysis in a Kuhnian framework, Duncan has provided empirical evidence supporting the view that the major factor responsible for the neglect of Hagerstrand's work was the "aparadigmatic" status of his theory. Hagerstrand championed his epoch-making ideas at a time when few were intellectually prepared to listen: "Those researchers exposed to the new ideas, but dominated by orthodox geography, ignored Hagerstrand's work (p. 129)." Indeed, there were few compelling reasons to attempt to incorporate Hagerstrand's ideas into the prevailing paradigm: "The new work would have been of minor relevance to their preoccupations (p. 128)." Duncan argued on the basis of his data that Hagerstrand's theories were assimilated only after a major paradigm-shift in geography: "Hagerstrand's diffusion ideas generally went unrecognized until paradigm change was widespread (p. 128)."

Hagerstrand's aparadigmatic status, however, does not fully account for his neglect. As Duncan has shown, the acceptance of Hagerstrand's ideas by the "new geographers"—scientists who shared his theoretical visions—was also delayed. Duncan argued that this circumstance derived from Hagerstrand's low social status among geographers: "Hagerstrand's reputation remained low among those new geographers not personally linked to him, until his new ranking became obvious . . . their neglect of Hagerstrand seems to show the operation of a 'Matthew effect' on a researcher of low visibility and prestige (pp. 131–132)."

We have thus far encountered neglected scientists who, in spite of wide variations in the specific circumstances that accompanied their obscurity, display profiles that share two important features in common with Semon's case:

intellectual and social distance from the mainstream researchers in their respective fields. It would be convenient if all neglected scientists shared these two features, but they do not. The next group of invisible scientists conspicuously manifests only one of these characteristics: social distance from mainstream researchers. Social isolation may contribute to neglect in a number of ways. For instance, the social isolate may publish in remote locations that constrain the physical accessibility of his work to other scientists. Consider the case of George Green (see H. G. Green, 1946). Green had a scientific career as brief as it was unorthodox. He worked with his father as a miller in Nottingham before attending Cambridge at age 40 in 1833, and died just eight years later. Green published a paper that contained fundamental contributions to the theory of electromagnetic attractions in 1828 that exerted no detectable influence on other scientists by the time of his death. Green's paper was brought to the attention of the scientific world by William Thomson in 1845, and was shortly thereafter granted its due recognition. But there is in fact little evidence to suggest that any important scientists were aware of the paper's existence prior to Thomson's discovery: It was published as a monograph by a small house in Nottingham and was distributed to a few scattered subscribers.

Cases such as Green's, then, are of limited interest: When a social isolate privately publishes an epoch-making theory, it is not surprising if the theory fails to influence the field. It is only interesting or informative if the isolate publishes a contribution that is physically accessible to some mainstream scientists. Such a condition was at least partially satisfied by P. H. Maille's theory of storms. Maille submitted a manuscript to the French *Académie des Sciences* at the end of 1834 in which he attempted to explain meteorological disturbances with a quantitative treatment of the properties exhibited by a rising column of moist air. This theory, when announced but a year later in less elaborated form by the well known American, James Pollard Espy, gained wide recognition. But Maille, "a completely unknown amateur from the little town of St. Florentin (Middleton, 1965, p. 320)," failed to impress the stodgy *Académie*. Although it has been contended that Maille "understood the phenomena of rising air much more clearly than Espy (Middleton, p. 324)," his paper was rejected by the referees and only appeared years later in private circulation.

A somewhat more dramatic instance of a neglected social isolate is found in the case of Mikhail Semenovich Tswett. Tswett is known today for his invention of chromatography, a method for separating components of complex mixtures that has played a major role in the progress of modern organic chemistry. Although the method was sound when Tswett first announced it in 1906, chromatography found few sympathizers among organic chemists; they ignored it for 25 years before two German scientists redemonstrated its usefulness in 1931. Once recognized, the impact of Tswett's method was enormous; as chemist Paul Karrer remarked in 1947, "No other discovery has exerted such a great influence and widened the field of investigation of the organic chemist as much as Tswett's chromatographic analysis (cited in Meinhard, 1949, p. 387)."

The reasons for the neglect of Tswett's method are not entirely clear, but the specter of the unwelcome outsider looms large. Tswett was a Russian botanist who held a minor post at a Polytechnical Institute in Warsaw when he invented chromatography. Although he published his original paper and his book on chromatography in Russian, Tswett published other papers on the technique in German and in French, and actually demonstrated the new method before a meeting of the *Deutsche Botanische Gesellschaft* in 1907 (Zechmeister, 1946, p. 109). Tswett, who lacked professional credentials in chemistry, is alleged to have encountered a great deal of professional snobbery at the hands of chemists: "for a lowly botanist to assault thus the whole chemical profession was unthinkable (Meinhard, 1949, p. 387)." Additionally, the simplicity of the method—later considered one of its principal virtues—may have contributed to the perception of him as an outsider unacquainted with the complexities of chemical analysis; it is not surprising that "Tswett's work aroused a 'tacit distrust' in many a colleague (Sakodynsky, 1970, p. 13)." The extent of Tswett's social isolation from other scientists can be gleaned from the following extract of a letter written by his wife to the Russian government in an attempt to enhance Tswett's chances of obtaining a better academic position: "If positions at the departments are not to be obtained on a competitive basis, which gives priority to scientific standards alone, but just by selection, which, alas, more often depends upon connections, then my husband, who has none, will have only a very slim chance of penetrating the exclusive University community (cited in Sakodynsky, 1970, p. 14)." In spite of his wife's plea, Tswett died in isolation some 13 years before his method revolutionized organic chemistry.

The final case of a social pariah whose work eventually triumphed is set in 19th-century Germany, and involves a man who, at different points in his life, was a practicing doctor and a patient in a mental hospital—Robert Mayer. Mayer received his medical degree at about the same time that he set out on an expedition to Java in 1840. During the journey, he made observations concerning the transfer of heat into work that led him to put forward one of the most influential ideas in 19th-century physics: the conservation of energy. After returning to his native Heilbronn and setting up a private practice, Mayer attempted a formal exposition of his ideas. His initial, technically flawed effort was rejected by Poggendorf's *Annalen der Physik und Chemie*. But the persistent Mayer revised his paper, calculated a mechanical equivalent of heat, and published his paper in Liebig's *Annalen der Chemie und Pharmacie* in 1842.

This is where the story of Mayer's neglect begins. In spite of his attempts to call attention to his ideas in various articles, Mayer's theory received virtually no recognition in the 20 years following its initial publication. This scientific indifference is all the more striking when we consider that the notion of conservation of energy was a popular one in the 1840s and 1850s: It was advanced by James P. Joule in 1843, Hermann von Helmholtz in 1847, and by L. A. Colding in 1851—all without reference to Mayer. Similarly, Karl Holtzmann computed a mechanical equivalent of heat in 1845 without citing Mayer's paper (Turner, 1974, p. 239; see also Kuhn, 1977, pp. 66–104). While these men received credit for helping to shape the first law of thermodynamics, Mayer seethed in isolation. He endured a nervous breakdown in 1850, and by 1858 had receded so far from scientific consciousness that Liebig could tell a Munich audience that "unfortunately Mayer had died in an insane asylum." Although Liebig was wrong, "Mayer's 'death' was officially recorded in Poggendorf's *Handwörterbuch* (Lindsay, 1973, p. 11)."

The reasons for Mayer's status as a scientific dead man are reminiscent of Tswett's case. Turner (1974, p. 240) has offered the following conclusions: "His [unorthodox] style, his status as an outsider to the scientific community, and his lack of institutional affiliation were all factors that limited Mayer's access to influential journals and publishers and hampered the acceptance of his ideas." Others have likewise contended that many viewed Mayer merely as a "lucky amateur" at a time when German science was becoming rapidly professionalized (Blüh, 1952, p. 215). Mayer's status as a dilettante led Gardner (1957, p. 10) to include his theory as a case of "important contributions made by persons of a crank variety." It should not be surprising, then, that although scientists may have been intellectually prepared to accept the idea of conservation of energy, they were probably not socially prepared to embrace Mayer's version of that hypothesis. Fortunately for Mayer, he eventually received recognition for his ideas after 1860, when Clausius, Helmholtz, and John Tyndall all championed Mayer's rights to priority; his star had risen so far within the next 10 years that he received the Royal Society's prestigious Copley Medal in 1871.

The cases of Mayer, Green, Maille, and Tswett mirror Semon's circumstances insofar as all of these neglected scientists were socially distant from the centers of power and prestige in their respective epochs. In the final cases that we consider, a wide intellectual gulf separated the ignored scientists from their contemporaries. Following our consideration of Robert Mayer, it seems appropriate to begin with the neglect of an idea frequently mentioned in connection with the conservation of energy: the second law of thermodynamics. The basis of the idea that all natural processes are irreversible was initially articulated by the French scientist Sadi Carnot, in an 1824 book concerned with the engineering of steam engines.[14] Although Carnot's ideas were eventually seized upon by Clausius and William Thomson in 1850–1851 as a critical basis for the second law, they held little interest for Carnot's contemporaries: "Possibly the most astonishing fact about Sadi Carnot's work is that it was received in complete silence by the world of French science. It was perhaps the most original production of a period when French physics sparkled with mathematical genius, yet it was ignored (Mendoza, 1959, p. 389)."

Various hypotheses have been advanced to account for this neglect—including the difficulty of Carnot's style and his failure to reach practical conclusions for steam engineers—but the most conspicuous of these hypotheses concerns the sheer novelty of Carnot's conceptions. As Barnett (1958) has argued in his detailed study of Carnot's work, there were few previous ideas that even

---

14. Carnot has been credited with unambiguous priority for this idea by Koening (1959, p. 61).

remotely resembled his formulation of the second law. Further, Barnett contended, "the Second Law, unlike the First, appeared foreign and unnatural (p. 334)." And in addition to Carnot's 'radically new' (Challey, 1971, p. 80) ideas, his scientific style markedly differed from that of his contemporaries: "Carnot developed his theorems in a synthetic, geometric manner that, although clear and logically rigorous, was in sharp contrast with the mathematical analysis dominant in the scientific community (Challey, p. 82)."

A similar picture of intellectual uniqueness emerges in the case of the mathematician Evariste Galois. Galois's tale contains all the classic elements of unrecognized genius meeting a tragic fate. Although Galois had completed the papers containing his pioneering formulations of what modern mathematicians know as group theory while still in his teens, Galois's superiors humiliated the insurgent youngster by refusing him admission to a Polytechnique. Apparently driven to despair by this and other intellectual rejections, and depressed by the suicide of his father, Galois embraced the revolutionary fervor sweeping France and perished in a duel in 1832 at the age of 20 (see Birkoff, 1937; Sarton, 1937).

The fate of Galois's papers on group theory was equally confused. One of his articles was lost, and others were rejected by referees not prepared to understand Galois's innovations: "In all the history of science there is no completer example of the triumph of crass stupidity over untamable genius than is afforded by the too brief life of Evariste Galois (Bell, 1937, p. 406)." Galois's papers were finally rediscovered and published some 14 years after his death, and complete assimilation by mathematicians occurred only after 1870. The reasons for this long neglect are strikingly similar to those encountered in Carnot's case:

> Galois's terse style, combined with the great originality of his thought and the modernity of his conceptions, contributed as much as the delay in publication to the length of time that passed before Galois's work was understood, recognized at its true worth, and fully developed. Indeed, very few mathematicians were ready to assimilate such a revolutionary work directly (Taton, 1972, p. 264).

The recognition of Galois's work awaited the evolution of a shared intellectual awareness—a paradigm or disciplinary matrix in the Kuhnian terminology—that permitted comprehension of his novel concepts within a wider context. Similar considerations may be equally applicable to the case of William Charles Wells' theory of natural selection. Wells, an American physician, read a paper before the Royal Society of London in 1813 in which he specifically applied the idea of natural selection to the origin of species.[15] Although Darwin among others later acknowledged that Wells was perhaps the first to systematically use natural selection to explain the origin of species, Wells' theory was ignored by his contemporaries. This neglect is especially intriguing because Wells enjoyed an excellent reputation for various other contributions to phys-

---

15. A partial reprint of Wells' paper is provided in Zirkle's (1941) article.

ics, medicine, and biology; his celebrated theory of dew brought him wide scientific recognition.

The most informative analysis of the failure to recognize Wells' theory is found in a paper by Shryock (1946). Shryock rejected a number of potential explanations for the neglect of Wells' theory: Wells' presentation was not obscure, he was known to other scientists, he did not arouse personal antagonisms, and there were no detectable cultural or social forces actively repressing his work. Shryock concluded that two plausible explanations remain. First, Wells apparently did not appreciate the far-reaching significance of his own ideas, and advanced them with caution. Second, Wells' theory was presented to an intellectually unprepared scientific world: "Wells was 'ahead of his time' in the sense that in his day there was as yet no wide-spread interest in biological evolution. There is no question that the world was 'ready' for Darwin as it was not for Wells (p. 202)." Much as the dense styles of Carnot and Galois made their iconoclastic ideas all the more difficult to assimilate, Wells' personal reticence probably attenuated whatever potential impact his novel theory might have had.

We conclude our survey with another 20th-century case of neglect: Michael Polanyi's theory of the adsorption of gases. The details of the theory, originally published in 1916, are described in an account of the case written by Polanyi himself (1969, pp. 87–96). After being initially discredited and then forgotten, Polanyi's theory gained gradual recognition during the 1950s, and by the time he wrote his 1963 account, the theory had gained wide acceptance. The circumstances underlying this cycle of rejection, neglect, and ultimate recognition should be by now familiar ones. Polanyi's 1916 theory violated accepted assumptions about the nature of electrical forces, and the evidence that he presented to support it had little impact on scientists committed to a contrary view of nature: "My verification could make no impression on minds convinced that it was bound to be otherwise...my evidence was rejected unexamined, though it was valid (1969, p. 92)." The most interesting feature of Polanyi's paper is his commentary on the implications of the long neglect suffered by his ultimately vindicated theory:

> Could this miscarriage of scientific justice have been avoided? I do not think so. There must be at all times a predominantly accepted scientific view of the nature of things, in the light of which research is jointly conducted by members of the community of scientists. A strong presumption that any such evidence which contradicts this view is invalid must prevail. Such evidence has to be disregarded, even if it cannot be accounted for, in the hope that it will eventually turn out to be false or irrelevant (p. 92).

For Polanyi, then, the silence encountered by his theory was an unavoidable consequence of the directive functions of the prevailing paradigm or disciplinary matrix. This is a point that we find ourselves in agreement with as the thematic threads that have been developed in the course of the chapter are now woven together.

THE REVOLUTIONARY AND THE CRANK:
SOME FINAL PERSPECTIVES

As noted earlier in this chapter, the present discussion of neglected theories is a preliminary one. Each of the cases covered deserves more detailed historical scrutiny and elaborate theoretical interpretation. Additionally, there are various cases of neglect in which the possible causative agents have not yet received attention: Why did one of Joseph Fourier's most important contributions to physics lie unnoticed in the archives of the French *Académie* for thirteen years? How can we account for the temporary neglect of Jean Henri Fabre's work in entomology? Why were Oliver Heaviside's pioneering contributions to the engineering of long distance telephone cables ignored for 20 years? And what factors are responsible for the delayed recognition of theories advanced by the 19th-century American physicists Joseph Henry and J. Willard Gibbs?[16]

The profiles that will emerge from consideration of such cases may or may not agree with the pictures that have been painted in the preceding discussion. But in this admittedly limited sphere of observation, the resemblance between the features characterizing the neglect of Semon's theory and the circumstances found in other cases is unmistakable. Although we have ranged across many fields of scientific endeavor, either the intellectual uniqueness or the social isolation that we encountered in Semon's case have been present in every other instance, whereas qualities such as a technically flawed presentation, an impenetrable scientific style, or a failure to present original experimental evidence have inconsistently appeared.[17] What do these observations tell us about Semon's case and, more generally, about the problem of the unrecognized scientist?

---

16. For Fourier, see the monograph by Herival (1975). Fabre's life and work are discussed rather informally in A. Fabre's (1921) biography. Little has been written about Heaviside, but a brief biographical sketch was published by Berg (1936, pp. 173–192). Henry's life and work are described in a scholarly biography by Coulson (1950), and a similarly informative biography of Gibbs is available (Rukeyser, 1942).

17. The force of these conclusions is limited not only by the small number of cases considered in the chapter. My concern has been with the misses and correct rejections in the signal detection matrix, and I have not examined the other two cells—the hits and the false alarms. According to the ideas put forward in this chapter, neither the hits (contributions that are incorporated into mainstream science) nor the false alarms (contributions that are initially accepted but later found to be seriously flawed) should originate from scientists who possess the characteristics associated with the subset of missed and correctly rejected theorists whom we have considered—intellectual or social distance from the mainstream scientific community. At least one potential counterexample quickly comes to mind—Albert Einstein—and no doubt others can be found. Discussion of such cases and the issues raised by them will hopefully be found in future analyses of the scientific community's reception of new ideas.

I have argued throughout this chapter that the significance of the missed theories cannot be properly understood without reference to the correct rejections, and it is to this point that I now return. It was noted earlier that both Semon and the classical crank were characterized by an intellectual and social distance from the mainstream scientific community; we can now see that many other scientists whose work was denied recognition possessed either or both of these traits. These shared features, coupled with the fact that the scientists we have considered were accorded treatment usually reserved for the crank, suggest that both the unappreciated revolutionaries and the cranks were subject to similar kinds of judgments by the scientific community.

Some insight into the quality of those judgments may be obtained by noting a case of neglect that we have not yet considered: Dmitri Mendeleev's periodic law. This case may be appropriately labeled one of "mini-neglect," since Mendeleev's ideas were accepted within a dozen years after his initial announcement of a new method of classifying the elements in 1869. But until various predictions of new elements made by Mendeleev's scheme were spectacularly fulfilled, the scientific world treated his ideas with distrust (see Venable, 1896, Ch. 4). The lack of any apparent logic behind the orderly relationship of dissimilar elements that Mendeleev claimed to have discovered put scientists on guard against a conceptualization that smelled of crank qualities. This sentiment was clearly expressed in criticisms of the periodic law advanced by the French chemist Berthelot. Berthelot accused those who constructed the periodic table of insuring success through utilization of a 'trick' (Venable, p. 112), and warned against the dire consequences that would accompany naive acceptance of such a questionable scheme: "such is the seduction exercised by these dreams, that it is necessary to guard against seeing in them the fundamental laws of our science and the basis of its facts, under pain of falling again into a mystic enthusiasm parallel to that of the alchemist (Venable, p. 113)."

Mendeleev was not a crank, and acceptance of his periodic law did not result in the intellectual backslide that Berthelot suspected it would. But Berthelot's commentary highlights the difficulty of distinguishing the signals from the noise—of finding the legitimate revolutionaries and weeding out the cranks—and exemplifies the uneasy suspicion that frequently greets unorthodox contributions to science. It also brings us back to the problem of criterion-setting addressed earlier: We say "yes" to radical contributions, or to those from authors on the fringes of the scientific community, at the risk of inundation by the "mystic enthusiasm" that Berthelot feared. This trade-off between hits and false alarms—what Kuhn (1977, pp. 225–239) has labeled the "essential tension" between tradition and innovation in science—does not, of course, apply only to eccentrics and geniuses. Revolutionaries and cranks occupy the extreme tail of a plausibility distribution. As we move further out to one extreme of this distribution, the probability that we find a revolutionary contribution increases, but so does the probability of encountering a crank. Even in the mid-ranges of the distribution, which include "paradigm-sharing" specialists at work in a given area, there are ranges of plausibility that must be considered as scientists attempt to make sense of the overwhelmingly large number of facts, theories, and methods that come their way. Polanyi has captured the essence of the predicament that our various musings in this chapter have been concerned with:

> Journals are bombarded with contributions offering fundamental discoveries in physics, chemistry, biology or medicine, most of which are nonsensical. Science cannot survive unless it can keep out such contributions and safeguard the basic soundness of its publications. This may lead to neglect or even suppression of valuable contributions, but I think this risk is unavoidable. If it turned out that the scientific discipline was keeping out a large number of important ideas, a relaxation of its severity might become necessary. But if this would lead to the intrusion of a great many bogus contributions, the situation could indeed become desperate. The pursuit of science can go on only so long as scientific judgements of plausibility are not too often badly mistaken (1969, p. 79).

Polanyi solves the problem of signal detection by advocating adoption of a conservative criterion: He is willing to risk some misses so that the necessary number of correct rejections are achieved. It is precisely because the stability of the scientific community would be threatened if all contributions were taken seriously that scientists have traditionally feared the emergence of an excessively liberal plausibility criterion. In the context of such thoughts, the similarity of the treatment accorded a Semon, a Mendel, and a Samuel Butler becomes intelligible. These men occupied the fringes of a plausibility distribution in which the criterion for potential acceptance has typically—and not without good reason—been set closer to the middle than to the extreme. In the case of a Butler, a George McCready Price, or the endless array of "nonsensical" papers that Polanyi laments, we see the system operating efficiently; in the case of a Semon, a Waterston, or a Tswett, the vulnerabilities of the scientific signal detection machinery are evident.

The most pressing problem raised by these observations is quite relevant to contemporary concerns: How can we accurately distinguish between legitimate scientific revolutionaries and misguided cranks? I need only cite two developments of recent years in order to demonstrate just how vexing this problem still is: the Velikovsky affair and the field of experimental parapsychology. Velikovsky is a psychoanalyst who has advanced various radical astronomical theories during the past 30 years that have been variously ignored, abused, and, until quite recently, rarely subjected to dispassionate criticism by mainstream scientists. Velikovsky possesses the two traits that characterize both cranks and neglected pioneers: His theories violate all known astronomical paradigms and he is a distant outsider to the astronomical community (see DeGrazia, 1966; Ransom, 1976). Dolby (1975) has portrayed the lengthy Velikovsky affair as an example of the difficulties encountered when attempting to separate "revolutionary" and "cranky" science, and has proposed various criteria to segregate the two. Whether or not Dolby's interesting solutions to the problem are adequate is less important than the fact that he has shown how the treatment of

Velikovsky illustrates the dearth of extant criteria for clearly isolating desirable revolutionaries from undesirable cranks.

The fate of experimental parapsychology exemplifies a similar theme. Once again, the dual marks of revolutionary and crank are present. The data and theories of parapsychology violate the world view of most established sciences, and a large percentage of parapsychologists work in social isolation from mainstream scientists. The treatment of experimental parapsychology by the scientific orthodoxy highlights the difficulty of the revolutionary-crank discrimination. The initial findings of J. B. Rhine and his colleagues were, with few exceptions, either severely criticized or steadfastly ignored by mainstream scientists, and parapsychology in general was frowned upon as a quasi-mystical enterprise. In the late 1960s, scientific opposition to the serious pursuit of experimental parapsychology softened to the extent that the Parapsychological Association was accepted into the American Association for the Advancement of Science—an endorsement that at least tacitly suggested that there might be something genuinely "revolutionary" about parapsychology. In recent years, however, a backlash against parapsychology has been swelling among scientists who fear that the AAAS affiliation may confer undue prestige upon what they believe is a fundamentally "cranky" enterprise. This negative sentiment is clearly apparent in several documents recently published by the eminent physicist John Wheeler (one of them entitled "Drive the pseudos out of the workshop of science") in which he recommends that the Parapsychological Association be stripped of its AAAS affiliation. These papers, published as part of a thematically similar article by Martin Gardner (1979) entitled "Quantum theory and quack theory," disavow any meaningful relationship between parapsychological "pseudoscience" and "real" science. Thus, as the signal detection criterion changes, so too does the status of parapsychologists: The outcasts of the '40s and the '50s, and potential revolutionaries of the '60s and '70s, may become the probable cranks of the '80s.

In closing this chapter, I should reiterate that the problem of neglected scientists does not apply solely to revolutionaries and cranks: They are simply extreme cases that demarcate the issue in a dramatic fashion. The perspectives developed in this chapter suggest, much as Polanyi argued in regard to his adsorption theory, that delayed recognition is an integral, perhaps necessary component of the scientific enterprise. As long as science is characterized by a discriminative tension between misses and correct rejections, as long as Kuhnian "paradigms," "cognitive orientation complexes," or "disciplinary matrices" serve to shape scientific perception of relevant phenomena and hence constrain appreciation of new contributions, and as long as the social dynamics of a scientific community influence its treatment of substantive contributions, we can expect that some proportion of initially ignored or resisted ideas will later be hailed as important advances.[18] Science operates within constraints imposed

---

18. Cole (1970) claims to have shown that delayed recognition is now a relatively rare phenomenon. There are, however, two problems with this study that undermine

not only by the complexity of the phenomena under investigation, but also by the complex cognitive and social structure of the investigators themselves.[19] These are conditions of scientific existence that were well-known to the likes of Amedeo Avogadro, Robert Mayer, Torsten Hagerstrand, and, of course, Richard Semon. We began this chapter seeking to elucidate some of the reasons why Semon's theory of memory, which seems so insightful and promising in hindsight, fell on deaf contemporary ears; in the course of pursuing that task, we have seen how the neglect of Semon's theory fits into a much larger panorama of science.

---

the force of Cole's conclusions. First, Cole defined "delayed recognition" contributions as papers that receive "few or no citations" in the first year after publication, but do receive a "substantial number" of citations five years after publication. Such a temporal window hardly seems wide enough to capture the phenomenon of interest. Second, Cole has acknowledged that delayed recognition will apply to "discoveries that are truly ahead of their time (p. 304)." It is precisely these cases that constitute the bulk of our sample, and should be of major concern to those interested in the phenomenon of delayed recognition.

19. Various philosophers of science have wondered if "progress" is in fact still possible once psychological factors such as those articulated by Kuhn are permitted entry into the business of theory evaluation and justification. Scheffler (1967), for instance, has bemoaned the scientific irrationality implied by the Kuhnian position: "Instead of reality's providing a constraint on scientific belief, reality is now to be seen as a projection of such belief, itself an outcome of non-rational influences (p. 74)." The epistemological problems raised by Scheffler and others are intricate ones that space does not permit me to confront. The interested reader is referred to Laudan's (1977) monograph for a stimulating attempt to preserve the notion of epistemological progress within a framework that shares much with Kuhn's ideas.

11

The Psychology
of the Isolated Scientist

*I*n the preceding chapter, we approached the cases of Semon and other neglected scientists by exploring their work and placing its neglect in a broad
conceptual framework. We attempted to gain some insight into why their
ideas were temporarily ignored by the scientific community, and also tried to
arrive at some general formulations concerning the factors that underlie the
recognition of ideas in science. We have not yet, however, systematically considered one of the most absorbing components of these cases: The personal
struggle that accompanies the rejection and long neglect of a scientific contribution. The names of Mayer, Tswett, Waterston, and others are not just curiosities retrieved from the backwater of history; they are the names of human beings whose intellectual and social isolation left them with deep psychological
scars. Our explorations of Semon's correspondence in Part I of the book provided some insights into the sorts of difficulties faced by a scientist working in
isolation. In the present chapter, I attempt to make sense of the psychological
plights of Semon and other isolated scientists in the context of more general
ideas about the importance of recognition and emotion in the pursuit of science.

The bulk of the chapter is comprised of two major sections. The first part
attempts to place the isolated scientist in a larger psychological perspective by
examining the fundamental importance of emotion, commitment, and the need
to be recognized in the functioning of the "normal," non-isolated scientist. This
background provides a useful starting point for the examination of selected case
studies of isolated scientists in the second section. The section begins with a
review of the major features of Semon's isolation, which is then used to organize
the discussion of the psychology of other isolated scientists. The range of emotions expressed by the men that we encounter—anger, despair, arrogance, and
frustration are among the most frequent—provides both similarities to and differences from Semon's case.

ISOLATION, RECOGNITION, AND INTELLECTUAL PASSIONS

One of the keys to understanding the psychology of Semon and other isolated scientists is furnished by recent analyses of the profound need for personal recognition demonstrated by scientists. The need for recognition is not, of course, a newly discovered human desire. Thomas Sprat, writing a history of the Royal Society in 1673, observed that "This desire of Glory, and to be counted Authors, prevails on all (cited in Hagstrom, 1965, p. 16)." Recent research, however, has cast the phenomenon in a systematic theoretical framework. Much of this research derives from Robert Merton's pioneering analyses, and a good place to begin is with a work firmly entrenched in the Mertonian tradition, Hagstrom's *The Scientific Community* (1965). Hagstrom conducted a wide ranging investigation of the social structure of the scientific community by collecting interview data from various groups of scientists. Among other topics, he examined scientists' motives for research, expectations of reward, and social relations with other scientists. Hagstrom's data suggested that the quest for recognition constitutes a central component of the scientific enterprise. Likening science to social gift-giving systems, Hagstrom hypothesized that scientists give one sort of a gift (publications) in return for another (recognition): "The organization of science consists of an exchange of social recognition for information (1965, p. 13)." Hagstrom distinguished between two kinds of recognition. First, *institutional* recognition is conferred by citations to a scientist's work, or by collective honors such as special medals or prizes. Second, *elementary* recognition is attained through interpersonal contacts at society meetings or informal visits with other scientists. Hagstrom contended that both forms of recognition are strenuously competed for by scientists and are integral to the achievement of a satisfactory career.

Similar perspectives have emerged from sociological research reported by Glaser (1964). Based on an empirical study of scientists working in a high prestige research organization, Glaser concluded that "Recognition is the prime mover (along with reward) of a professional career (1964, p. 3)." Glaser closely examined the importance of achieving recognition at successive *stages* of a scientist's career. His findings were entirely similar at all career stages: The scientists' sense of having achieved an adequate amount of recognition mediated their evaluations of the progress their careers had made. As Glaser observed, "those who feel that they have been recognized adequately are more likely to feel a good measure of resolution of their concern at each career stage (1964, p. 48)."[1]

---

1. There is one caution that should be observed when interpreting the results of Glaser's research. Since it seems probable that high recognition scientists are also high *productivity* scientists, and low recognition scientists are low productivity scientists, recognition and productivity may be confounded in Glaser's study. Stated in slightly different terms, the probable positive correlation between recognition and productivity makes it difficult to assign causal priority to one or the other as a mediator of career assessment.

Granted that studies such as those reported by Hagstrom and Glaser have established the importance of social recognition for professional scientists—with certain qualifications that I shall return to shortly—a simple question suggests itself: Why should the notion that scientists desire recognition require any empirical confirmation at all? All of us seek recognition of our efforts; why should scientists be any different? These questions can best be addressed by inquiring into scientists' own reactions to their desires for recognition: Do scientists view their quests for recognition as perfectly natural components of the research enterprise?

The answer is no, and the reasons underlying it are important. An example may help to clarify the issue: Charles Darwin's response upon learning that Alfred Wallace had independently formulated a theory of natural selection and evolution nearly identical to his own.[2] Darwin had been working on his theory for nearly 20 years before he received the shocking communication from Wallace in 1858. He wrote to his friend and mentor Charles Lyell on June 18, shortly after receiving the news, and lamented that he had ignored Lyell's earlier warning against procrastination: "Your words have come true with a vengeance—that I should be forestalled. . . . So all my originality, whatever it may amount to, will be smashed (Darwin, 1908, p. 185)." Just a week later, on June 25, Darwin was tormented less by his potential loss of glory than by the thought that he would be acting ignominiously if he quickly published and received recognition: "I would far rather burn my whole book, than that he [Wallace] or any other man should think that I had behaved in a paltry spirit (1908, p. 186)." By June 29, Darwin was berating himself for his concern with recognition: "It is miserable in me to care at all about priority (1908, p. 186)." Two weeks later, Darwin expressed both astonishment and disappointment that he had experienced a desire for recognition at all: "I always thought it very possible that I might be forestalled, but I fancied that I had a grand enough soul not to care; but I found myself mistaken and punished (1908, p. 186).

Darwin is not alone in his conflict between a desire for recognition and a conviction that he should renounce it. In Chapter 5 we observed a similar conflict taking shape in Richard Semon: He acknowledged strong needs for social recognition of his work yet felt ashamed of himself for experiencing them. A more recent example of a nearly identical problem can be clearly observed in one of the biologists who participated in the study of the adult life cycle conducted by Levinson (1978). This man could not deny a powerful need for recognition: "I simply can't get away from the thing that really does trouble me, which is an intense desire for kudos. Now that means being recognized (1978, p. 272)." But such needs could not be easily accepted by this scientist: "Why do you want kudos anyway? What difference does it make? It doesn't. It seems to me that there must be something missing from one's inner man if you need to

---

2. A more extensive analysis of this episode can be found in Merton's *Sociology of Science* (1973), pp. 305–308.

be supported by having adulatory comments of the external world in whatever form they come (p. 272)."

Examples such as these suggest that desires for recognition are not easily or naturally accepted by practicing scientists; I suspect that many of the scientists reading these pages could point to similar experiences of their own. This conflict between a powerful desire to be recognized and a similarly strong need to deny the importance of recognition has been analyzed by various sociologists of science. Merton (1973), who first called attention to the phenomenon in his treatment of priority disputes, conceptualized it as a consequence of the opposition between two conflicting norms of scientific behavior. The norm emphasizing originality in science leads scientists to desire that their contributions receive recognition, whereas the norm that stresses humility impels them to deny that recognition is important. Hagstrom has taken a somewhat different approach to the phenomenon, suggesting that conflicts concerning recognition arise from the gift-giving nature of the scientific enterprise. On the one hand, Hagstrom argued, "as in all gift-giving, the expectation of return gifts (of recognition) cannot be publicly acknowledged as the motive for the gift (1965, p. 13)." But, he continued, such behavior should not blind us to the underlying expectations; the scientist, like any ritual giver of gifts, fully expects that his efforts will be rewarded in return.

Whatever the validity of these two views, the crucial point for our purposes is that psychological conflicts aroused by needs to be recognized demonstrate just how deep and explosive the desire for kudos can be among scientists. How, then, does the powerful need for recognition in science bear upon our understanding of isolated scientists? One of the striking similarities that binds together most of the isolates whom we encounter here is that they felt deprived of due recognition for their scientific efforts. In light of the prestige structure of science and the importance of group and institutional affiliations, it is not surprising that scientists working without these supports experienced less recognition than their socially well-entrenched peers. By appreciating how passionate the desire for recognition can be among scientists, we may be better able to understand some of the emotional eruptions of scientists who felt robbed of their just glory.

The work of Merton, Glaser, Hagstrom, and other sociologists of science suggests that the quest for recognition is perhaps the most basic—or at least the most evident—source of psychological motivation for practicing scientists. According to this view, the attainment of recognition is an end in itself that scientists will work strenuously to achieve. It is not clear, however, that this position provides an adequate understanding of the psychology of the scientist. Is the desire for recognition the dominant source of motivation and sustenance for scientists, or might there be something else that also emotionally binds them to the reception accorded their work? I believe that there is something else involved in the psychology of the scientist beyond mere thirsting for recognition, and further believe that we must grasp the essence of this "something else" before we can properly comprehend the psychology of the isolated scientist.

Michael Polanyi has lucidly described this critical component of the scientific psyche in an essay exploring what he calls "intellectual passions." Polanyi portrays the pursuit of science as a highly charged dialogue between the discoverer and the natural world. He views the exploration of Nature as a consuming pursuit that involves the scientist's most profound emotions as he moves closer to formulating a personal view of his chosen terrain. When a scientist articulates a particular theory, then, he presents the world with a vision to which he has committed himself with intense personal passion. According to Polanyi, such passions demand a sympathetic audience: "In order to be satisfied, our intellectual passions must find response. This universal intent creates a tension: we suffer when a vision of reality to which we have committed ourselves is contemptuously ignored by others (1958, p. 150)." For Polanyi, recognition is a necessary catalyst for fueling the flames heated by more basic emotions: "intellectual passions perpetuate themselves by their fulfillment (1958, p. 173)." In Polanyi's view, intellectual passions behave much as romantic passions; intellectual passions that find no response, just like the unrequited love of a spurned suitor, may become disfigured by consequent eruptions of bitterness and rage.

Polanyi's vision of science as a passionate pursuit has been articulated by others, but nowhere more eloquently than by sociologist Max Weber: "Without this strange intoxication, ridiculed by every outsider; without this passion . . . you have *no* calling for science, and you should do something else (Weber, 1946, p. 135)." Although the theme of science as passionate pursuit may seem excessively romantic to some, the ideas promulgated by writers such as Polanyi and Weber have been substantiated by empirical studies. Consider first Eiduson's (1962) inquiry into the psychological features of 40 research scientists from mixed backgrounds and different areas of specialization. Eiduson's study, which was largely based upon questionnaire techniques and psychological tests, uncovered a good deal more diversity than uniformity in the personality traits of her participants: Scientists exhibited a wide and variable range of psychological characteristics, and could not be adequately described by one or two well chosen diagnostic labels. There was, however, one common feature that stood out in bold relief against the general background of diversity: emotional investment in work. Almost all of Eiduson's sample showed a profound affective attachment to their work, and channeled their strongest emotions into the pursuit of science. Eiduson conveys a sense of the intensity that these scientists brought to their work:

> The phrase 'emotional investment' may not suggest the intense nature of intellectual experiences. These activities are described by such adjectives as 'thrilling', 'intimate', 'completely possessing', and the long hours, the dedication, the slavish devotion are only the external manifestations of the almost inexpressible affective content (1962, p. 89).

Similar perspectives emerge from an investigation conducted by Mitroff (1974) of 42 eminent geoscientists who participated in the Apollo 11 moon project. Mitroff based much of his study on structured interviews with the lunar scientists that ranged over a variety of issues. He found scant support in his data for the traditional "storybook" image of scientists: The participants in his study were not emotionally detached men in white coats who dispassionately studied the world around them. Rather, much like in the Eiduson study, Mitroff's scientists were affectively attached to their work. And, most interestingly, many of these men viewed emotional commitment as a necessary and healthy feature of science. Let us directly examine some brief extracts from interviews that Mitroff claims are representative of the entire sample (1974, p. 65):

> We must be emotionally committed to the things we do energetically. No one is able to do anything with liberal energy if there is no emotion connected with it.

> The idea of the dispassionate, disinterested observer just isn't so. The more you work on a subject the deeper the commitment becomes.

> The uninvolved, unemotional scientist is just as much a fiction as the mad scientist who will destroy the world for knowledge. Most of the scientists I know have theories and are looking for data to support them; they're not sorting impersonally through the data looking for a theory to fit the data. . . . Without commitment, one wouldn't have the energy, the drive to press forward, sometimes against extremely difficult odds.

These testimonies provide some concrete insights into the nature of the intellectual passions that Polanyi and Weber described: Such passions help to drive the scientist onward in his work, and affectively bind him to the eventual reception of it by the scientific community. They may also provide us with a wider perspective on the crucial role of social recognition in the psychology of the scientist. Rather than merely constituting an end in itself, the desire for recognition may also be seen as the fulfillment of a more fundamental intellectual passion—a personal view of the world that a scientist has emotionally committed himself to—that comprises a basic part of the scientist's psychological constitution. Consider, for example, Semon's emotional attachment to his work. Although his correspondence leaves little doubt that Semon craved recognition of his ideas, it seems equally clear that he was not primarily motivated by a lust for glory, but rather by a passionate conviction that he had solved one of Nature's more refractory mysteries. Semon's intellectual passions, much in the manner Polanyi described, required response; when they were met with disapproval and neglect, he felt both anger and despair. Many other isolated scientists have shared similar fates. Thoroughly committed to the dissemination of their ideas, they suffered when the products of their intellectual passions met with contempt—or still worse—were passed over in silence.

THE ANCHORITE GALLERY:
STRUGGLES OF THE ISOLATED SCIENTIST

The term "isolated scientist" has so far been used in a rather loose fashion, but I will now give a more precise indication of what is referred to when the term is invoked. First consider the notion of "isolation." Must a scientist work as a literal hermit, operating in a secluded subterranean laboratory without human contact before he can be labeled an "isolate"? Some of the cases that will be considered do fit such a description—certainly Semon came close to it—but not all of those who will be included as "isolated scientists" lived the life of the anchorite. Although physical seclusion from other scientists may be a *sufficient* condition for consideration as an isolate, it is not a *necessary* one. I have found it useful to employ two principal criteria in the selection of isolated scientists. First, the scientist fails to participate in the activities of the larger scientific community over an extended period of time. He does not regularly report his work to established societies, is not a member of such societies, and engages in scant interaction with mainstream scientists in his field. Second, the scientist continues to work on problems that lie at the fringes of the field's concern or steadfastly advocates solutions to problems that most others in his field have long abandoned. The first criterion might be labeled one of *social* isolation, the second, one of *intellectual* isolation. These two criteria, although obviously rather general, have been jointly satisfied by most of the scientists labeled as "isolates" in the following pages; the exceptions who violate one or the other of these criteria are noted when they appear.

Before initiating our case studies of isolated scientists, let us recall some of the major features of Semon's response io isolation that emerged in the correspondence presented in Chapters 5 and 6. First there was his dependence on August Forel. As it became apparent over the years that acceptance by the scientific community would not be forthcoming, Semon grew ever more dependent on the confirmation that his friend provided. Semon's ceaseless thanks for Forel's support and profuse praise of Forel's own work are dramatic barometers of just how addicted Semon became to the psychological sustenance provided by his nourishing ally. A second feature of Semon's response to isolation—most evident in the period just following publication of *Die Mneme*—concerns his acerbic retorts to the attacks of his critics. Semon repeatedly lashed out against those who opposed him in early correspondence with Forel; his mockery served to lessen the perceived threat of his enemies' critiques and to buttress the strength of his own convictions. A third feature of Semon's struggle with isolation, although not as prominent as the first two, emerged only after 1909: the replacement of his hopes for scientific triumph in the present with visions of vindication in the distant future. Semon began to perceive himself as a scientist whose conquest would have to await the coming of a future generation better equipped to appreciate his contributions than the narrow-minded contemporaries who ignored him. When he confided to Forel in 1911 that victory might be attained only in the distant future, and that faith was required to trust that the "truth will win through," he attempted to provide justification of his efforts in spite of the largely negative response to his work. The fourth major feature of Semon's behavior as an isolate was also the most disheartening one: his increasing reticence and resignation in the face of continuing neglect. Semon's nervous breakdown, bouts with depression, and rapidly vanishing confidence in his own abilities had become prominent components of his psychological existence following the failure of *Die mnemischen Empfindungen* in 1909.

Although the foregoing features do not fully characterize Semon's psychological reactions while in isolation, they perhaps reflect some of the most consistent and striking patterns observed during the years that followed publication of *Die Mneme*. These four features of Semon's isolation—dependence upon a nourishing figure, anger with his critics, faith in the future, and despondent resignation—serve to structure the present discussion. Each of the features is used to explore one principal case study of an isolated scientist as well as several less detailed examples. After consideration of the various case studies, several general issues raised by them are discussed. As in the preceding chapter, the present treatment should be regarded as a preliminary one. My major purpose is to provide a rough sketch of a landscape that has not yet received serious attention, and to raise some basic questions concerning the quality and shape of that landscape. Answers to questions, and more systematic analyses of this terrain, are the province of future explorers.

The Nourisher and the Isolate

Few people can meet the demands of scientific work entirely on their own. The effort that is required to sustain years of frequently frustrating and inconclusive research requires encouragement; the conviction that one's stated views are valid requires confirmation. For mainstream scientists working in a university or research organization, encouragement and confirmation can be obtained from a variety of sources: Colleagues who share their working environment, fellow members of professional societies, scientists who are plugged into common research networks, or students and assistants are all potentially powerful sources of support. Isolated scientists confront a bleaker situation. Both socially and intellectually estranged from the support systems that other scientists utilize, these people must generate alternative strategies for meeting psychological needs that are no less urgent to them than to other scientists.

Perhaps the most conspicuous feature of Semon's isolation was his psychological dependence on August Forel. In the context of the foregoing remarks, it may not be surprising to learn that dependence upon a nourishing figure is a feature found in many cases of isolated scientists. The nourishing figure may take many forms, but is most frequently a well known scientist who becomes entranced by the isolate's iconoclastic vision of reality. One of the most crucial functions that such a figure can serve is to offer assurances that the isolate's daring theoretical flights meet with his own authoritative approval. Since the isolate frequently doubts the validity of his own efforts, such approval can become a profound source of relief and comfort. Consider the case of Charles Darwin.[3] Darwin formulated his theory of natural selection in the solitude of his country cottage in Down. He felt that he was standing on shaky intellectual ground as he neared completion of the *Origin*, and required someone to dispel his uncertainty about the validity of his theory. When he received an enthusiastic letter of endorsement from the eminent Thomas Huxley, who later became one of Darwin's staunchest supporters, he responded with the joy of a man freed from the anxieties of incertitude:

> Your letter has been forwarded to me from Down. Like a good Catholic who has received extreme unction, I can now sing 'nunc dimittis'. I should have been more than contented with one quarter of what you said. Exactly fifteen months ago, when I put pen to paper for this volume, I had awful misgivings; and thought perhaps I had deluded myself, like so many others have done, and I then fixed in my mind three judges, on whose decision I determined mentally to abide. The judges were Lyell, Hooker, and yourself. It was this which made me so extremely anxious for your verdict. I am now contented, and can sing my 'nunc dimittis' (Darwin to Huxley, 11–25–1859; cited in Darwin, 1908, p. 214).

Fortunately for Darwin, the forceful support of men such as Huxley, Lyell, Hooker, and Haeckel brought him almost immediate triumph; secure in victory, he was spared the further psychological rigors of carrying his banner alone.

For a second giant of 19th-century biology, however, there was no such exalted ending, and part of the reason for this can be traced to a frustrating and unproductive relationship with a potential nourishing figure. We examined the circumstances surrounding Gregor Mendel's neglect in Chapter 10; let us now look a bit more closely at his relationship with Karl Wilhelm von Nägeli. Nägeli was one of the world's leading authorities on heredity when Mendel wrote to inform him of his breeding experiments on New Year's Eve, 1866. Mendel, working in nearly total seclusion, humbly approached Nägeli and pleaded for support: "I address myself to you in the confident hope that you will not refuse me your esteemed participation when, in any instance, I need advice (cited in Iltis, 1932, p. 190)." Nägeli's reply was a mixture of criticism, condescension, and failure to perceive the value of Mendel's work. Mendel, however, was apparently excited that the mighty Nägeli had bothered to reply at all; he wrote

---

3. Darwin is one of the scientists whose inclusion as an isolate merits some commentary. Although he was undeniably a *physical* isolate, it can be debated whether or not he was a *psychological* isolate: Darwin was well known to other naturalists, and the problem of evolution had been addressed by various of his contemporaries. The important point for our purposes, however, is that the *Origin* was worked out in intellectual isolation.

back and profusely thanked Nägeli for his interest. But if Mendel believed that he had found a dependable supporter in the scientific community, his hopes were soon dashed. Nägeli's replies to his letters became increasingly infrequent, and he showed continually less interest in Mendel's breeding experiments. Although the hopeful Mendel attempted to accommodate himself to Nägeli's interests, it finally became clear that the self-absorbed professor was not the dependable source of encouragement that Mendel required. By 1873 Mendel had abandoned his experiments on heredity: "he was tired of endeavouring to make his way along this path beset with thorns (Iltis, 1932, p. 273)." It is difficult to know whether Nägeli's failure to understand and support Mendel caused the frustrated monk to give up his work. There can be little doubt, however, that Nägeli's encouragement would have enhanced Mendel's desire to continue his research.

The cases of Darwin and Mendel illustrate two extreme outcomes of an isolate-nourisher relationship. Darwin received confirmation, encouragement, and polemical aid on his way to scientific conquest; Mendel received none of these critical supports on his way to obscurity. The principal case study in this section—Sigmund Freud—encompasses both triumph and tragedy. Whether or not Freud should be considered an isolate is itself a problematic issue. Clearly, in the years following World War I, when the roots of psychoanalysis had taken firm hold in many psychological and lay circles, Freud was anything but an isolate; he was the internationally recognized leader of a movement that grew larger and more powerful each year. But these times of glory were far removed from the days in the 1890s and early 1900s when Freud and a small group of disciples formulated the doctrines that later achieved such astonishing popularity. Although a number of contemporary historians have argued that the extent of Freud's isolation during this period has been grossly inflated by his own later writings and reminiscences,[4] the plain fact is that Freud expressed an acute sense of isolation numerous times during the early years of psychoanalysis. Consider the following extracts from letters to his friend Wilhelm Fliess. Freud complained to Fliess of his growing isolation as early as 1890: "Although quite satisfied, even happy if you like, I nevertheless feel very isolated (Freud, 1960, p. 227)." Some six years later, isolation has become an accepted feature of Freud's psychological existence: "I feel isolated, but I take this for granted (1960, p. 232)," And by 1902, Freud's complaints were colored with self-pity: "I came to the conclusion that I could easily spend the greater part of my life waiting for

---

4. Both Decker (1977) and Sulloway (1979) have persuasively argued that the extent of abuse, isolation, and neglect endured by Freud has been greatly exaggerated as part of a developing mythology of Freud and psychoanalysis. It has further been suggested by both these historians that Freud's sense of isolation was not merited by the reception accorded his work—it was not nearly as bad as Freud made it out to be. This may well be so, but it is not of major concern here: Freud *felt* isolated, regardless of what he "should have" felt.

recognition and that in the meantime none of my fellow men would lift a finger on my behalf (1960, p. 244)."

How did Freud cope with his acute sense of isolation during the formation of psychoanalysis? A large part of that story centers upon his relationships with the various men whom he depended upon for encouragement and support during the era of isolation, and we examine his interaction with one of these nourishing figures: Wilhelm Fliess.

Fliess, a nose and throat specialist from Berlin, was a bold thinker who articulated a variety of iconoclastic theories concerning biological periodicity, sexuality, and other topics of interest to Freud. He attempted to link the length of the menstrual cycle, fluctuations in sexual desire, and the mucous membrane of the nose through a series of mathematical formulae that he believed held the key to understanding organic life.[5] Freud, fresh from a recent and venomous break with his former mentor Joseph Breuer, first met Fliess while lecturing at Vienna in 1887. He was immediately captivated by Fliess's radiant personality and gift for daring scientific theorizing, and concluded his first letter to Fliess on a note of unabashed admiration: "I have hopes of continuing the intercourse with you . . . you have left a deep impression on me which could easily tempt me to say outright in what category of men I would place you (cited in Brome, 1967, p. 2)." The two began to correspond regularly, and arranged increasingly frequent meetings—their famous "Congresses"—at which they discussed scientific issues of mutual interest.

The evolving relationship performed multiple functions for Freud. Fliess and Freud were deeply involved with many similar scientific issues—most importantly, the role of sexuality in human development—and Fliess's innovative approach to these issues attracted and influenced Freud (as well as many other contemporary physicians and scientists). This intellectual component of the Freud-Fliess relationship has been thoroughly described by Sulloway (1979, pp. 171–237). However, there is a second component of their interaction—a *psychological* component—that is more relevant to our concerns. Numerous psychological accounts of this engrossing relationship have been put forward; each has emphasized one or another of its numerous facets. Some have cast Fliess as a temporary transference or father figure for Freud (e.g., Jones, 1961, p. 196; Kris, 1954, pp. 43–45), whereas others have viewed the friendship as a consequence of the neurosis that Freud suffered throughout much of the 1890s (e.g., Ellenberger, 1970, pp. 444–450). These interpretations may well be valid ones, but I believe that a key element in the Freud–Fliess relationship centers upon Freud's self-perception as an isolated scientist.

---

5. The most informative analysis of Fliess's ideas and their impact on Freud's thinking is found in Sulloway's (1979) book. Sulloway shows rather clearly that Fliess's ideas were not simply the "fanciful crackpottery" that much subsequent Freud scholarship made them out to be. Fliess's theories were taken seriously by many of his contemporaries and influenced numerous other scientists besides Freud.

Freud required a receptive forum for his emerging theories of psycho-analysis, and Fliess—a man whom Freud intellectually respected—provided such a forum. In return, Freud responded with unending gratitude and profuse praise for Fliess's own work. Freud was acutely aware that he required an atten-tive ear from his colleague; as he wrote to Fliess on January 30, 1899, "I need you as my audience (Freud, 1954, p. 275)." By providing the steady encourage-ment that Freud craved, Fliess injected confidence and self-assurance into an uncertain scientist. Freud's own words are the most revealing: "when I talked to you, and saw that you thought something of me, I actually started thinking some-thing of myself (1954, p. 60)."

The importance of Fliess's confirmation can also be gauged from Freud's flowery, almost romantic expressions of thanks to his friend. He waxed poetic in a July, 1894 letter: "Your praise is nectar and ambrosia to me (Brome, 1967, p. 7)." His letter of January 3, 1899 sounds more like the musings of a distant lover than a genius on the eve of scientific revolution: "I live gloomily or in darkness until you come, and then I pour out all my grumbles to you, kindle my flicker-ing light at your steady flame, and feel well again; and after your departure I have eyes to see again, and what I look upon is good (1954, p. 272)." Satisfied by a visit from Fliess in mid-January, Freud expressed his gratitude some three weeks later: "You have no idea how much your last visit raised my spirits. I am still living on it (1954, p. 274)." He also confessed a sense of wonderment upon hearing of Fliess's discoveries concerning biological periodicity: "Yesterday the glad news reached me that the enigmas of the world and of life were beginning to yield an answer, news of a successful result of thought such as no dream could excel (Brome, 1967, p. 5)."

An appreciation of Freud's intellectual respect for Fliess is the key to un-derstanding these testimonies. Although various biographers of Freud, most notably Ernest Jones, have offered apologies for Freud's "subordination" to a man who was "intellectually his inferior (Jones, 1961, p. 182)," I believe that it was precisely because of Fliess's authentic intellectual stature—not in spite of his "quackery"—that Freud valued his praise so highly. Just as Semon's admira-tion of Forel, Darwin's respect for Huxley, and Mendel's veneration of Nägeli rendered these men especially desirable supportive figures, Freud's genuine esteem for his friend's widely recognized intellectual abilities (see Sulloway, 1979, pp. 136–170) heightened Fliess's value as a nourisher.

Unfortunately, disagreements did not form an acceptable part of Freud's relationship with Fliess—at least not disagreements that cast aspersions on the utility of Freud's most treasured ideas. When Fliess cynically depicted the psy-choanalyst as a "thought-reader" and intimated that his own periodicity theo-ries subsumed Freud's work on sexuality, the friendship collapsed like a house of cards.[6] For Freud, the function of a supporter was to confirm, soothe, and

---

6. There are various hypotheses that attempt to pinpoint the causes of this break. For differing points of view, see Ellenberger (1970, pp. 444–450), Jones (1961, pp. 198–203), and Sulloway (1979, pp. 216–217).

praise—not to attack. Fliess remained useful and necessary so long as he served these crucial functions; when 'he began to question the importance of Freud's work he simply ceased to be a dependable nurturing figure.

The association and break with Fliess can be better understood by considering Freud's subsequent relationships with men who also served as nourishing figures for him, such as Alfred Adler and C. G. Jung. Freud cast these men—who, like Fliess, impressed him with their scientific acumen—in nurturing roles. He expected them to loyally advance the psychoanalytic movement and his sexual theories against what Freud perceived as a hostile scientific world; as he once wrote to Ludwig Binswanger, "what unites us against the world is our conviction of the importance of libido (Binswanger, 1957, p. 29)." Freud was emotionally committed to psychoanalysis, and he expected all followers to share his intellectual passions. Jung recalled one of Freud's pleas for unquestioned support:

> I can still recall vividly how Freud said to me, 'My dear Jung, promise me never to abandon the sexual theory. That is the most essential thing of all. You see, we must make a dogma of it, an unshakable bulwark.' He said that to me with great emotion, in the tone of a father saying, 'And promise me this one thing, my dear son: that you will go to church every Sunday (Jung, 1961, p. 150).

So long as men such as Adler and Jung faithfully cradled Freud by confirming his passionate conviction that sexuality represented the key to unlocking the mysteries of the mind, they were showered with the same sort of affection that Freud heaped upon Fliess. But when Adler and Jung, both independent thinkers at heart, wearied of supporting Freudian dogma and voiced grave doubts concerning the importance of sexuality—or in Freud's terms, when the traitors announced their "defection" from the cause (Freud, 1963, p. 91)—they were quickly, spitefully, and entirely ejected from Freud's life. Freud's own words are powerful testimony to the rage of a man who felt betrayed by his closest allies in time of war. After his break with Adler, he informed his friend Oskar Pfister of a plan for retaliation: "I am in the process of carrying out the revenge of the offended goddess of the libido (cited in Brome, 1967, p. 61)." Similarly acrid recriminations followed his break with Jung: "So we are finally rid of them," Freud commented to the still-faithful Karl Abraham, "the brutal, sanctimonious Jung and his disciples (cited in Brome, 1967, p. 140)."

As noted earlier, Freud's relationships and subsequent breaks with his various supporters have been objects of fascination to many, and attempts to analyze these interpersonal fiascos in terms of Freud's personality are plentiful.[7]

---

7. Erich Fromm (1959), for instance, devoted an entire chapter to Freud's dependence on men. Fromm viewed the acrimonious ending that characterized so many of Freud's friendships with other scientists as evidence of his difficulty accommodating strong needs to be nurtured: "Freud's dependency on the mother figure was not restricted to his wife and his mother. It was transferred to men, older ones like Breuer, con-

Our concerns, however, lie less with the vicissitudes of Freud's character than with the implications of his experiences for the understanding of isolated scientists. There are two principal lessons to be learned from Freud's case. The first concerns the crucial emotional significance of a nourishing figure for an isolated scientist. I do not believe that Freud's emotional dependence on men such as Wilhelm Fliess reflects some critical flaw in his personality. During the early years of psychoanalysis, Freud faced a potentially terrifying situation: He confronted the scientific world with intellectual passions that he believed were foreign to many of his contemporaries. In an attempt to ease his anxieties, Freud sought shelter in the support of one who could enthusiastically confirm the validity of these passions. It is perhaps not excessively dramatic to say that the nourisher rescues the isolate from the prospect of working silently in an intellectual vacuum. Given the important task that they perform, it is not surprising that men like Freud become so emotionally dependent on the support of their closest scientific allies.

A second point that emerges from Freud's experiences concerns the narrow range of behaviors that an isolate may permit a nurturing figure. When Fliess, Adler, and Jung voiced fundamental doubts about the validity of Freud's most treasured theories, they entered forbidden territory and effectively abdicated their supportive roles. Whether or not Freud's subsequent attacks on these men is a property of other isolate-nourisher relationships marked by similar transgressions is a matter to be explored in future work. In light of the intense affective dynamics that seem so central to the psychology of this relationship, it would not be surprising to find that Freud's recriminations are typical of other isolates who have felt betrayed by those who once offered them confirmation. As we see in the next section of this chapter, intellectual passions are capable of violent explosion in a variety of circumstances.

The Wrath of the Isolate

One need only inspect the case histories of a few isolated scientists in order to encounter one of their most striking features: a deep sense of resentment concerning lack of recognition of or stern opposition to their work. These emotions, to be sure, may be expressed by non-isolated scientists faced with neglect or rejection; given the importance of social recognition and central role of emotional commitment in science, one would not expect to find otherwise. But isolation adds an extra element of pathos to the already difficult situation of the neglected or resisted scientist. The isolate, unlike the socially mainstream scientist, cannot seek comfort in prestigious institutional affiliations, membership

---

temporaries like Fliess, and pupils like Jung. But Freud had a fierce pride in his independence and a violent aversion to being the protégé. This pride made him repress the awareness of dependency and negate it completely by breaking off the friendship when the friend failed in the complete fulfillment of the motherly role (1959, p. 38)."

in respected professional societies, or the informal recognition conferred by colleagues working on similar problems; he can only stew in solitude and lash out at those whom he believes are responsible for his predicament.

One index of the strength of the isolate's umbrage is its tenacious persistence over time: This persistence is well illustrated by the case of Rober Mayer, which we became acquainted with in Chapter 10. Mayer, whose pioneering ideas concerning the conservation of energy were ignored by mainstream scientists for some 20 years, eventually did receive due recognition for them. Owing primarily to the energetic advocacy of British physicist John Tyndall, who became something of a nourishing figure for Mayer, his priority was recognized and Mayer received virtually unanimous international acclaim. But the wealth of honors and awards that came his way in old-age did little to assuage Mayer's long festering wrath. He continued to express indignation concerning the neglect he had endured in earlier years and, in a venomous public controversy, accused Hermann von Helmholtz—one of the scientists who had championed Mayer's rights to priority—of casting veiled aspersions on his character (see Lindsay, 1973). Mayer's sullen anger is well-captured in the following letter, written after he had achieved worldwide recognition: "I can't deny that my opponents applied against me every possible means, among them the most effective one as you will know, that I have been declared insane, and, of course, incurably insane. All the greater is my pleasure in the final and complete victory of my cause (Blüh, 1952, p. 213)." Mayer's rage found expression throughout his remaining years; as one of his biographers commented, "it all seemed so unnecessary as the somewhat childish resentment of a bitter old man (Lindsay, 1973, p. 16)."

Similar features are found in the case of Max Meyer. A German born psychologist who emigrated to America in the early years of the 20th century, Meyer is all but unknown to contemporary psychologists.[8] He was a student of the eminent Carl Stumpf at Berlin, and carried out research on auditory processes at the University of Missouri. Meyer became socially estranged from American psychologists soon after his arrival in the United States; he was a regimented German professor who had trouble adjusting to the informal style of American life, and alienated his colleagues by engaging in fierce scientific controversies. Meyer's isolation became complete when a scandal erupted in the Missouri state legislature over a questionnaire prepared by one of his students that included items concerning sexual behavior; he was forced to leave the University of Missouri in 1932 and take up residence as an academic exile in Miami.[9] He spent his remaining years there, growing increasingly out of touch with new developments in auditory theory and nursing a long-felt animosity toward those who had rejected his work. In 1950, at the age of 77, Meyer published a small

---

8. The only scholarly treatment of Meyer's life and work that I am acquainted with is found in Esper's (1966, 1967) papers.

9. The student who prepared that questionnaire was O. H. Mowrer, later to become one of the most prominent learning theorists of his day and President of the American Psychological Association. See Esper (1967) for an account of this fiasco.

book entitled *How We Hear*, and introduced it with reminiscences that one might expect from a man whose intellectual passions had been abused for over a half-century:

> In 1896 I conceived a mathematical analysis of the compound sound waves brought to the ear which discarded all sinusoidal vibrations within the cochlea. I published it. A German physiology professor reviewing it called the idea 'childish'. That did not discourage me. In 1898 I published the mechanical counterpart to the same mathematical analysis. Reviewers of acoustical literature did not read my publications with enough care to avoid reading into them their own notions instead of mine and either left my ideas totally unmentioned or mentioned them so distortedly that I could not recognize as my own the ideas presented as mine (1950, p. 1).

The persisting dudgeon of isolates such as Mayer and Meyer provides a clue to the depth of resentment that may be experienced by an isolated scientist, and other like examples could be cited. Ivan Michurin, the crank Soviet geneticist who played a key role in the rise of Lysenkoism, was a typically embittered isolate on the eve of his rise to power (see Joravsky, 1970, pp. 42–50); Immanuel Velikovsky, who has probably endured more abuse than any crank or revolutionary of recent times, has publicly vented his resentment on various occasions (see Ransom, 1976, p. 222; Velikovsky, 1968, p. 2); and we earlier encountered the fulminations of Ernst Haeckel as the aging oracle's isolation from the biological community deepened in his later years.

All of these instances may help to prepare us for the eruptions of Ignaz Semmelweis, whose story comprises the major case study of this section. William J. Sinclair, Semmelweis's most authoritative English biographer, contended that "in the whole history of medicine there is only one Semmelweis in the magnitude of his services to Mankind, and in the depth of his sufferings from contemporary jealous stupidity and ingratitude (1909, p. 2)." Sinclair's rather dramatic claim may not be entirely exaggerated; Semmelweis's contributions were enormous and his suffering was severe.[10]

Semmelweis was born in Budapest in 1818. He earned a medical degree in Vienna and started work in 1846 at an obstetrical clinic in the Vienna General Hospital under the tutelage of an eminent physician, Johann Klein. One of the most severe problems encountered by doctors at this clinic concerned the high incidence of death due to puerperal fever: The combined mortality rate for mothers and infants exceeded 13% when Semmelweis arrived there. Much to the bewilderment of the resident physicians, a second Viennese obstetrical clinic

---

10. The importance of Semmelweis' work, coupled with his extensive suffering, have made him one of the most romanticized figures in the history of science. See, for instance, Rich's *The Doctor Who Saved Babies* (1961) and Slaughter's *Immortal Magyar* (1950).

reported a far lower mortality rate attributable to puerperal fever (just over 2%). There was only one major difference between the two clinics—Semmelweis' clinic taught medical students whereas the second clinic trained midwives—and no one prior to Semmelweis could link this difference to the puzzling gap in the number of puerperal fever mortalities at the two clinics.

Semmelweis proposed an elegantly simple solution to the problem. He suggested that an infection carried by the hands of young doctors who performed autopsies prior to delivering babies (a cadaveric contamination) caused puerperal fever. He immediately instituted strict disinfectant washing procedures for all physicians seeing patients in labor, and obtained some dramatic results: Mortalities caused by puerperal fever dropped to almost 2% within a month. But news of Semmelweis' novel prophylaxis was not enthusiastically greeted by the medical world of Vienna. Committing the first of several crucial mistakes that contributed to his own undoing, Semmelweis refused to officially report his methods or results to the Viennese medical community. The reasons for this tactical blunder are not clear, but Semmelweis' findings were finally reported in print only through the efforts of a colleague. To further complicate matters, Semmelweis' data provided evidence against the theory of puerperal fever held by his supervisor Johann Klein. Threatened by the implication that Semmelweis' work disproved his theory and discredited his clinical procedures, Klein refused to reappoint Semmelweis to his position in the clinic.

When he was later appointed to a position that contained unpalatable restrictions, Semmelweis committed his second crucial mistake: He fled from Vienna in 1850 without informing a soul of his actions. He returned to Budapest, found a position in a local hospital, and continued his research on puerperal fever in nearly total isolation from the larger scientific community. Although his disinfectant methods consistently reduced the incidence of puerperal fever, Semmelweis was not able to persuade the medical establishment that his ideas and methods were sound.

The turning point of the story was in 1861. After perfecting his treatment and developing his theory for over a decade, Semmelweis finally presented his work to the medical world in a lengthy book written in German. A ponderous, over-detailed work that was written in a harshly polemical style, Semmelweis' bold claims alienated many physicians; the book received negative reviews in a number of prominent medical journals. But instead of attempting to present his results in a more convincing manner, Semmelweis publicly vented his frustrations in a series of open letters that attacked the critics of his work. The following accusations, aimed at one of his staunchest critics, sound more like the proceedings of a criminal trial than of a scientific controversy: "In this massacre you, Herr Professor, have participated. The homicide must cease, and with the object of bringing this homicide to an end, I shall keep watch, and every man who dares to spread dangerous errors regarding puerperal fever will find in me an active opponent. For me there is no other means for checking the murder than to unsparingly unmask my opponents (cited in Sinclair, 1909, p.

247)."[11] Semmelweis prosecuted his other enemies in a similar fashion, and the verdict was always the same: Physicians who resisted his theory and methods were guilty of murder in the first degree. He accused one detractor of sending "ignoramuses" and "murderers" all over Europe because he failed to teach his students Semmelweis' methods (Sinclair, pp. 248–249). The festering wrath of an isolate whose most profound intellectual passions had been rejected by the established authorities is nowhere more evident than in the following passage:

> Your teaching, Herr Hofrath, is based on the dead bodies of lying-in women slaughtered through ignorance. . . . If, however, Herr Hofrath, without having discussed my Doctrine as an opponent, you go on to write...in support of the doctrine of epidemic puerperal fever, to teach your students the doctrine of epidemic puerperal fever, I denounce you before God and the world as a murderer, and the History of Puerperal Fever will not do you an injustice when, for the service of having been the first to oppose my life-saving *Lehre* it perpetuates your name as a medical Nero (cited in Sinclair, pp. 250–251).

The last of Semmelweis' open letters jointly addressed all professors of obstetrics. Full of the same vitriolic accusations that characterized the others, it was prefaced by a declaration that must have seemed like the megalomania of a fanatic to those to whom it was addressed: "In May 1862, it is fifteen years since I discovered the only eternally true cause of puerperal fever, no single case of puerperal fever excepted (cited in Sinclair, p. 256)." These letters served only to deepen Semmelweis' isolation; they made it easy for his opponents to characterize him as a "despised Hungarian 'crank' (Sinclair, p. 268)." Semmelweis' psychological state further deteriorated when his letters elicited no positive responses, he was committed to a mental institution in 1865, and died there just two weeks later. By 1880, the work of Pasteur and Lister had provided a firm scientific basis for Semmelweis' disinfectant methods, and they were soon implemented in hospitals everywhere.

Semmelweis' case is clearly an extreme one; it presents a certain type of personality interacting with a set of unusually trying circumstances. But it is difficult to avoid the conclusion that bitterness abounds like apples in autumn in cases of isolated scientists. The isolate may be a misunderstood revolutionary like Semmelweis, a crank such as Michurin, or an aging outcast like Haeckel, Mayer, or Meyer; one need not search long before the inevitable expressions of cynicism and wrath are encountered. Although none of these and other similar cases can be entirely understood without penetrating the dynamics of the individual personalities involved, Polanyi's notion of intellectual passions may pro-

---

11. A good deal of Semmelweis' anger stemmed not only from the rejection of his ideas, but also from his genuine humanitarian concern for the people whose lives, he believed, were needlessly lost because of the stupidity of his enemies.

vide some insight into the widespread incidence of negative affect expressed by isolated scientists. These men found scant sympathetic response to ideas that they had nurtured on their own for extended periods of time—ideas that frequently constituted the central emotional events of their lives—and with little to fall back on when their work was opposed, they lashed out at the enemies of their cherished creations. The intensity and persistence of these emotions may be somewhat unexpected to those nurtured on the storybook image of the detached scientist, but such outbursts are not surprising in light of the studies by Eiduson, Glaser, Hagstrom, Mitroff, and others. As Polanyi observed, intellectual passions require response; the plight of the isolated scientist is a reminder of the emotional consequences that may follow when the desired affirmation is not forthcoming.

The Comfort of History's Judgment

The cases discussed in the preceding section indicate that the psychological strains of isolation can be severe. One way to ease these strains may be to seek shelter in a nourishing figure, but this strategy is not always effective in countering the strains of intellectual solitude. The isolate may still doubt the value of his own work, question his scientific abilities, or contemplate withdrawing from science altogether; a powerful incentive is needed to combat the self-doubt that the isolate is likely to encounter.

One way in which an isolate can find potent psychological sustenance in the face of continuing disapproval is to place his predicament in a larger historical context. Aware that numerous scientists of the past have been denied recognition for work that later generations applauded, the isolate can portray himself as the unfortunate victim of the same unjust circumstances that afflicted previous iconoclasts. Once convinced that his difficulties can be attributed to the ignorance of his contemporaries—just like in the cases of Copernicus, Galileo, or William Harvey—the isolate can sustain his motivation by taking refuge in the belief that his efforts will be celebrated by future generations of scientists. There is perhaps no clearer example of this strategy at work than in the following extract from a letter written by Freud to C. G. Jung during the period of their close friendship. Jung had despondently informed Freud of some biting attacks on psychoanalysis that he had attempted to rebut. Freud responded by reminding Jung that history's verdict would likely prove the critics wrong:

> And yet don't worry, everything will turn out all right. You will live to see it, even if I don't. We aren't the first who have had to wait for the world to understand their language. . . . Every time we are laughed at anew I am more than ever convinced that we are in the possession of something great. In the obituary that you are to write for me one day, don't forget to bear witness that all the opposition has not once succeeded in diverting me from my purpose (Freud, 1960, p. 254).

Freud's faith in the wisdom of later generations was ultimately justified: Psychoanalysis did achieve a large following in years subsequent to the foregoing remarks. Gregor Mendel was a similarly accurate prophet. Although official science ignored him and Nägeli failed to understand his experiments, Mendel stubbornly maintained that scientists would someday appreciate the importance of his work. As his biographer argued, "he was inwardly convinced that his own discoveries would be of great importance for future research. Talking the matter over with Niessl, he said as much, in the prophetic words: 'My time will come' (Iltis, 1932, p. 282)."

Not all isolates have been as accurate in their forecasts of temporally distant triumph. Consider, for instance, the case of George McCready Price, a religious fundamentalist and geologist whose theoretical opposition to the theory of human evolution was briefly noted in Chapter 10. Price was widely regarded by orthodox geologists as a hopeless crank, and he expressed an acute awareness of his lowly status in the eyes of his scientific contemporaries. In an article entitled "Cranks and Prophets," Price argued that many scientists who were called cranks by their peers were later regarded as prophets by subsequent generations. Price, who firmly believed that he, too, would someday enter the ranks of the prophets, cast his own plight as yet another chapter in the long struggle against scientific orthodoxy: "The history of science is replete with instances where the proponents of new ideas, in spite of using the utmost deference for the scientific powers sitting in the chairs of the great societies or of the big universities, have humbly presented their evidence only to be rebuffed without consideration, or browbeaten and ridiculed by those clothed with a little brief authority (1930, p. 45)." Price's protest, however, did not secure him scientific immortality: His theories remain as obscure and untenable today as they were when he articulated them.

The predictions of self-salvation made by the Soviet biologist Michurin turned out to be as inaccurate as those made by Price. On the eve of his temporary glorification by the Lysenkoist movement, the isolated and ignored Michurin ridiculed the stupidity of the "forces of the enemy camp" and ruefully predicted that his work would eventually garner due recognition, "as a foundation that we are bequeathing to natural scientists of future centuries and millennia (cited in Joravsky, 1970, p. 56)." Although Lysenko and his followers enshrined Michurin's theories for a number of years before the movement collapsed, non-Soviet biologists have continued to view Michurin as little more than a cantankerous professional gardener.

These variably accurate forecasts of vindication—Freud and Mendel eventually triumphed whereas Price and Michurin retained their crank status—set the stage for our principal case in this section, a man whose historical status is still in doubt: Wilhelm Reich. Reich's story must surely rank as one of the most bizarre intellectual odysseys of the 20th-century. Trained as a psychoanalyst under the tutelage of men such as Freud and Wilhelm Stekel, Reich was a committed member of the psychoanalytic movement in the 1920s. After his own idiosyncratic theories had developed, he separated from the Freudians and left his native Austria in the 1930s to establish an institute for research and therapy in Oslo. In 1939, Reich emigrated to New York with the hope of finding a wider audience for his work.

The crucial event in Reich's scientific life occurred while he was in Oslo: the discovery of the orgone. The orgone, according to Reich, is the fundamental energy that underlies all organic life. Reich's system of therapy attempted to release the inhibited orgone energy of his patients, and focused in particular on the improvement of sexual functioning.[12] But Reich was no ordinary therapist. He established an institute in the backwoods of Maine entitled "Organon," where he worked in isolation with a few devoted disciples. Reich constructed his controversial "orgone accumulators" at Organon (box-like machines that were supposed to infuse the patient with orgone energy as he sat inside one of them) and used these devices to "cure" problems ranging from impotence to cancer. Reich's unorthodox methods first drew criticism from the American Psychiatric Association, and the federal government later investigated his work. He was tried by the government in 1956 on charges of fraud and quackery, and was imprisoned in 1957. Reich died in prison seven months later.[13]

Reich's responses to isolation share several features in common with other cases that we have considered. For instance, he established a correspondence with Einstein, and believed that he had found a suitable nourishing figure in the aging physicist; when Einstein eventually lost interest in his work, Reich responded with anger.[14] Although he publicly disclaimed interest in attaining recognition from mainstream scientists, Reich's wife recalls how he desperately clung to the few paltry stars of official recognition that were granted to him (I. O. Reich, 1969, p. 70).

The most striking feature of Reich's isolation centers upon the incessant comparisons that he drew between his own persecution and the fate of other misunderstood pioneers. Reich viewed himself as more than a mere psycho-

---

12. The best introduction to Reich's theories and therapies is his well-known *The Function of the Orgasm* (1973). But his most widely acclaimed work predated his "discovery" of the orgone: *The Mass Psychology of Fascism* (1970). The book was stimulated by the Nazis rise to power in the 1930s, and is regarded by many as an insightful and innovative treatment of a difficult subject.

13. Various accounts of this lurid affair have been published. An historical account can be found in Boadella (1973), and a description of the evolving tragedy from the standpoint of a participant in it can be found in the monograph published by Reich's wife (I. O. Reich, 1969).

14. Reich's bitter personal disillusionment in the face of Einstein's silence was recalled by his wife: "Reich's personal reaction to Einstein's sudden silence was one of bafflement, which gradually turned to deep disappointment. Reich's dream of becoming a member of a community of scientists, which he had spoken of again and again...was not going to come true (1969, p. 59)."

therapist: He believed that he had made fundamental biological discoveries that earned him a place in the first rank of scientists. Ilse Olendorff Reich contended that her husband's self-perception as a victim of inexorable historical circumstance eventually formed a central component of his personality: "How did Reich see himself?...He felt that his discoveries put him in a class with Galileo or Giordano Bruno, and he took his very real persecutions as the inevitable fate of every great discoverer (1969, p. xxi)." Reich apparently felt that it was not a breach of modesty to place himself in the loftiest echelons of misunderstood genius, and did so with passionate conviction:

> It is an old story . . . Giordano Bruno, who fought for scientific knowledge and against astrological superstition, was condemned to death by the Inquisition. It is the same psychic pestilence which delivered Galileo to the Inquisition, let Copernicus die in misery, made Leeuwenhoek a recluse, drove Nietzsche into insanity, Pasteur and Freud into exile. It is the indecent, vile attitude of contemporaries of all times. This has to be said clearly once and for all. One cannot give in to such manifestations of the pestilence (cited in Gardner, 1950, p. 454).

Similar statements abound in Reich's writings. In his well-known *The Function of the Orgasm*, he likened himself to Peer Gynt, the Ibsen character who is mocked by society for his strange ways but ultimately emerges victorious: "I read and understood Peer Gynt. . . . I was ostensibly like Peer Gynt (1973, p. 39)." In his frenzied outburst of indignation, *Listen, Little Man*, Reich again compared himself to Galileo, triumphantly proclaimed that history would vindicate his ideas, and concluded by effectively placing himself beyond any criticisms that might be advanced by his contemporaries: "Whatever you have done to me or will do to me in the future, whether you glorify me as a genius or put me in a mental institution, whether you adore me as your savior or hang me as a spy, sooner or later necessity will force you to comprehend that *I have discovered the laws of the living* (1971, pp. 125–126)."

Reich's fulminations may appear self-delusory, but it seems clear that they performed important psychological functions for him. If Reich had accepted the judgment of his scientific peers, he would have been forced to conclude that the intellectual passions he had nurtured for years were worthless. This was an unacceptable alternative for Reich, who had built a complete life structure at his Organon retreat that was based upon his intellectual passions. He retaliated against the scientists who mocked his work by attempting to bury their criticisms in an historical grave. Because Galileo and others had been vindicated by the judgment of history, Reich felt that his own fate would necessarily be the same. The logic is muddled, but the psychology is clear. The current status of Reich's work is also fuzzy. Although his orgone theories are still largely regarded as scientifically barren fantasies, a growing number of psychologists and psychiatrists have acknowledged Reich's prescient anticipations of, and contributions to, several currently popular therapeutic methods; sexual therapy and body awareness techniques are two of the more conspicuous ones."[15] Although Reich will surely never attain the elevated scientific status that he predicted he would, neither have his rather brazen forecasts proved entirely misguided.

Surrender of the Scientist: The Resigned Isolate

In the cases that we have so far considered, the difficulties of isolation have been met with active responses. By seeking a nourishing figure, lashing out at the scientific establishment, or boldly predicting exculpation by history, isolates are able to resist the potentially crushing impact of extended resistance or neglect and continue with their work. But not all isolates are able to muster the necessary resolve to push onward when prospects of victory remain bleak over lengthy periods of time. These scientists may retreat to other activities such as teaching, withdraw from science altogether, or become prey to episodes of depression and anxiety.

Consider, for example, the final years of Mikhail Tswett, the neglected founder of chromatography whose case was discussed in Chapter 10. Although Tswett fought vigorously for acceptance of his method in the first years following its publication in 1903, he eventually tired of working alone in an isolated Warsaw technical institute. By 1914, Tswett had become so exasperated by his failure to achieve recognition from mainstream scientists that he abandoned research and confined his activities to teaching. In an attempt to alleviate her husband's scientific isolation, Elena Tswett urged government ministers to offer him a position appropriate to his abilities:

> Time is not wholly unimportant for my husband. If he is to be saved from hard conditions and onerous work, which are virtually ruining him, for he has a poor health, it must be done at once . . . All his energy is consumed in teaching, which brings no moral satisfaction. Scientific ideas are a dead weight, for there is nobody who cares enough to inherit and take an interest in them. All his personal research is cut down to a minimum. And the best years are being wasted (cited in Sakodynsky, 1970, pp. 14–15).

As noted in Chapter 10, Tswett's salvation was not forthcoming. After fleeing German invaders during World War I, Tswett spent his last year living alone in

---

15. Reich's growing influence on some sectors of contemporary psychological and psychiatric thought and therapy can be gleaned from the collection of neo-Reichian papers recently published in the volume edited by Boadella (1976). As the editor commented, "increasingly now Reich is taken seriously in many quarters where previously he would have been attacked or ignored (1976, p. vii)." The British psychiatrist R. D. Laing made a similar point: "Even his later work on what he called bio-physics cannot be so glibly confined to cranksville as it was ten years ago (cited in Boadella, 1973, p. 8)."

a small room of a colleague's house, where he succumbed to heart disease in June, 1919.

The final years of John James Waterston, neglected author of the kinetic theory of gases, paralleled Tswett's experience in a number of ways. Waterston first advanced his theory while stationed in India, and after his initial papers were ignored he returned to Britain with the hope of cultivating a more sympathetic audience. But Waterston's papers received no more attention after he arrived in Britain than they had when he was stationed in India: He was still working on his own, without any institutional affiliations. Waterston apparently became extremely sensitive about the neglect of his scientific efforts. He refused to inform his family that his papers had been rejected by the Royal Society, although, as his nephew recalled, "any mention of the Royal Society led to very strong and contemptuous language, which we thought a little eccentric (cited in Haldane, 1928, p. xlii)." He also remained entirely aloof from other scientists; his strong sense of pride and consequent refusal to ask for support may have prevented him from seeking a much-needed nourishing figure. Branded as a crank by many of his contemporaries, Waterston sullenly withdrew from science in 1868, at the age of 57. His biographer contended that the frustrations of isolation and neglect had dulled Waterston's enthusiasm for science: "he was weary, as one gets weary of struggling with a telephone when there is no response from the other end (Haldane, 1928, p. lxiii)." Waterston quietly lived the rest of his life in seclusion in Edinburgh, and perished under bizarre circumstances: He went for a walk on the morning of June 18, 1883, and was never seen or heard from again.[16]

There are any number of reasons why Waterston and Tswett abandoned their research, but one strong possibility is that neither of these men established a relationship with a nourishing figure who could bolster their confidence in difficult times. The same can be said of Gregor Mendel, and similar notions may be applicable to Ludwig Boltzmann, whose story constitutes the final case study of the chapter. Boltzmann is one of those scientists whose inclusion as an isolate requires some explanation. For the bulk of his career, this 19th-century physicist was anything but an isolate: Professor of physics in Vienna, respected for his statistical analyses of mechanics, and the author of the second law of thermodynamics, Boltzmann enjoyed an international reputation as a first-class scientist for much of his career. But his fortunes underwent a drastic change in the closing years of the 19th-century. An ardent champion of the atomic theory of matter—which enjoyed widespread scientific acceptance for most of the 19th century—Boltzmann was confronted by a revolt against atomism that had swept the field of theoretical physics by the late 1890s. The revolt, spearheaded by the phenomenological school of Ernst Mach and the energetic

---

16. It is thought that Waterston drowned, and suicide has been suspected, but no traces of the body were ever found. See Haldane (1928) for an account of Waterston's final days.

school of Wilhelm Ostwald, left Boltzmann as the virtually sole defender of atomism; it is in this context that we approach him as an isolate.[17]

Boltzmann looked on in horror as increasing numbers of young physicists abandoned the atomic theory and enthusiastically adopted the positions developed by Mach and Ostwald. He felt that his lifetime's work had been cavalierly swept aside by a barbarous horde of youthful insurgents, and voiced a painful awareness of his new status as an isolated scientist:

> I seem to myself like a veteran on the field of science; nay, I might even say that I alone am left of those who embraced the old doctrines heart and soul; at least I am the only one who is still sturdily battling for them. . . . I appear before you, therefore, as a reactionary and belated thinker, as a zealous champion of the old classical doctrines as opposed to the new (Boltzmann, 1901, p. 233).

Although Boltzmann vowed to defend his beloved atomistic doctrines to the end, he was fighting a battle in which his individual efforts were no match for the strength of the opposition; as he himself acknowledged, "I am conscious of being only an individual struggling weakly against the stream of time (cited in Brush, 1964, p. 216)." The supporters of Mach and Ostwald, whose youthful zeal bordered on outright fanaticism (see Feuer, 1974, pp. 335–341), brought a type of vicious polemics to the debate that disgusted the sensitive Boltzmann. For Boltzmann, science was a profound spiritual pursuit that provided a sanctuary from the irrationality of everyday life. He drew his inspiration from Schiller and Beethoven, and expected similarly lofty ideals from other scientists.[18] The aggressive tactics of the anti-atomists, in Boltzmann's view, debased the nobility of science.

In spite of his dedication to the cause of atomism, Boltzmann eventually tired of the struggle. He experienced increasingly frequent episodes of depression while at Leipzig from 1900 to 1902 and, during a particularly severe attack, unsuccessfully attempted suicide. At about the same time, Boltzmann published an article reviewing his battle against the anti-atomists in which he all too clearly linked his own mortality with the scientific struggle that emotionally consumed him: "These are, indeed, interesting questions. One regrets almost that one

---

17. For discussion of the theoretical issues at stake in the debate over atomism, see Boltzmann (1901, 1974) and Feuer (1974).
18. Boltzmann's profound sense of communion with the great German Romantics is best captured in his own words: "My thanks for the loftiest spiritual elevation must go to the works of Goethe. . . . But with Schiller the case is otherwise. It is through Schiller that I have come into being. Without him there might have been a man with a beard and nose of the same shape, but I should not have existed. If anyone else has had on me an influence of the same order of magnitude, it is surely Beethoven. But is it not significant that he, in his greatest work, leaves the last word to Schiller (Boltzmann, 1974, p. 3)."

must pass away before their decision. O arrogant mortal! Thy destiny is to exult in the contemplation of the surging conflict (1901, p. 256)." His sense of isolation deepened over the next few years, and Boltzmann finally could no longer summon the strength to continue. He took his own life on September 6, 1906. The irony surrounding Boltzmann's isolation and suicide is that the atomic view emerged victorious just a few years after his death: The classic work of physicists such as Ernst Rutherford and Niels Bohr convincingly refuted the views of the theorists whom Boltzmann had opposed.

Boltzmann's suicide, of course, cannot be simply ascribed to his intellectual isolation; a complete understanding of its causes would require careful study of his entire life. But it seems reasonable to hypothesize that the two were linked; indeed, Boltzmann's biographer shared this opinion (Broda, 1955, pp. 35–37). To the extent that his isolation did contribute to his suicide, Boltzmann's case raises an important question: What critical psychological ingredients are required to sustain an isolate through extended periods of frustration and disappointment? It is simple enough to observe that some isolates give up and others do not, but it is more difficult to understand these differences. I earlier suggested that Boltzmann's predicament resembled the situations faced by Mendel, Tswett, and Waterston, who also ended their scientific lives with passive resignation, insofar as none of these men could depend upon a reliable nourishing figure to provide support and motivation. It is tempting to suggest that the absence of such a figure played an important role in their ultimate retirements from the scientific arena, and I suspect that there is some validity to this hypothesis. But it must also be acknowledged that none of these men exhibited the potent psychological defenses that were displayed by other isolates; part of the reason for their passive declines is no doubt lodged deep in the recesses of their individual personalities. Clearly, it would be presumptuous to offer any final verdicts based upon just a few examples. Whatever their ultimate explanation, cases such as Boltzmann's are important because they impel us to confront questions that penetrate to the roots of the isolate's dilemma.

THE PSYCHOLOGY OF THE ISOLATED SCIENTIST: SOME FINAL PERSPECTIVES

The territory that we have surveyed in this chapter can be safely described as a psychologically rich one: Isolated scientists are characterized by a diverse spectrum of emotional qualities that pose an immediate fascination for the student of human behavior. But as noted earlier in the chapter, the present discussion is no more than a beginning descriptive attempt to understand the psychology of the isolated scientist, and many key questions remain to be asked and to be answered. Perhaps the most important of these questions concerns the ancient problem of the interaction between personality and situational demands: How do scientists with different psychological constitutions respond to the rigors of isolation? Are there particular kinds of scientists who are more likely than others to take the path of the isolate? A second outstanding problem concerns the four psychological features of isolates considered in the present chapter: Are there important features found in other isolates that should be appended to these four? Do particular constellations of features occur more frequently than others? Such questions may well merit attention in future analyses of this little traveled terrain.

Although fully cognizant of the preliminary nature of the present discussion, I conclude the chapter by extracting three major points from it. First, I would like to argue that the responses of isolated scientists should not be dismissed as the behavioral curiosities of a lunatic fringe. Rather, I believe that isolates should be viewed as crucial sources of insight into the psychology of mainstream scientists. Many critical facets of normal human psychology are most clearly observed under extreme or stressful circumstances; phenomena that are weakly apparent in the normal case emerge with blazing intensity in the extreme case. The powerful emotions expressed by so many isolates provide fully blown-up pictures of intellectual passions that are less dramatically expressed in the everyday pursuits of normal, non-isolated scientists. These passions, described in the studies of Eiduson and Mitroff that we considered earlier, rarely achieve the searing intensity observed in isolates like Semmelweis or Reich. But the absence of spectacular expression should not blind us to their existence. The trauma of the isolate provides an index of just how deep the wellsprings of scientists' passions can run; if these emotional tragedies can teach us anything, they can teach us to be more aware of the role played by affective factors in the pursuit of normal science. Scientists receive a technical training that does a marvelous job of preparing them for confronting an astonishing variety of intellectual situations. But scientists are not taught how to cope with the emotional exigencies of a psychologically demanding profession. It seems reasonable to suggest that more attention should be devoted to studying this salient component of scientific existence; advances in understanding may ultimately help to provide scientists with better training in the psychological requirements of their profession than is currently available.[19]

A second point that emerges from our survey of isolated scientists concerns the problem of discriminating scientists from cranks. Several writers have contended that cranks can be distinguished from scientists on the basis of certain psychological characteristics that cranks uniquely possess: Cranks work in isolation, depend upon small groups of disciples to support and confirm their work, express anger and paranoia over their persecution by establishment scientists, and offer bold predictions that history will vindicate their views (e.g., Gardner, 1950; Gruneberger, 1964). The cases reviewed in this chapter, however, suggest that such psychological features do not accurately distinguish cranks

---

19. One of the few serious attempts to address this problem is found in two papers published by Kubie (1953, 1954). More recently, Mahoney (1976) has addressed this issue, but it is clear that much work needs to be done.

from scientists. Our gallery of isolates included both scientists and cranks, and their responses to isolation were not obviously dissimilar. Scientists and cranks both depend upon nourishing figures, lash out at their opponents, express bitterness about their predicaments, and forecast triumph in the future. The judgment of history may indeed separate the geniuses from the crackpots, but it seems unlikely that contemporaries can do so purely on the basis of a psychological profile. Rather, the psychological plights of isolation seem to be shared by those labeled as cranks or scientists.

A third lesson that can be extracted from this chapter's survey brings us back to our point of departure: What do these cases tell us about Richard Semon's isolation? Having set out to explore the psychology of isolated scientists on the basis of the principal features of Semon's case, it would not be terribly informative to conclude that the discussion demonstrates how well Semon's experience typifies some sort of isolation syndrome; the circularity entailed in such an argument is clear. But the various cases reviewed can be legitimately used as contextual aids to help gauge the degree to which Semon's responses to his dilemma were more or less extreme than those of other isolates. When compared with Darwin's humble thanks to Huxley or Freud's profound emotional dependence on Wilhlem Fliess, Semon's reliance on Forel does not seem so excessive or pathetic. Viewed in the context of Semmelweis' anger, Semon's cynical remarks about his critics seem like the harmless name-calling of a child at play. Similarly, his resentment appears comparatively mild in light of the long-stewing bitterness of a Robert Mayer or Max Meyer. And Semon's prediction that the truth of his argument would be perceived by future scientists looks like the cautious hope of a modest man when placed next to the bold proclamations of a Wilhelm Reich. In short, Semon does not emerge as any more dependent, indignant, or arrogant than other isolates; in fact, he seems considerably less venomous and insolent than most. The case is otherwise regarding his nervous breakdown, bouts with depression, and periodic retreats from work. These signs of resignation do not seem less serious than the indicants of withdrawal observed in Tswett, Waterston, or Boltzmann. For Semon as for the other isolates, they were ominous warnings of further hardship. The quality of Semon's isolation seems closest to Boltzmann's: Both men enjoyed success early in their careers, then championed unpopular causes over extended periods of time and experienced severe depressions when their voices went unheeded. Boltzmann's demise ended in self-destruction; Semon, too, followed that path.

Epilogue:
Past, Present, and
Future in Psychology

*I*n spite of their diverse contents, I believe that one dominant theme can be found winding its way through the preceding pages. Much of this book has been concerned with the resurrection of forgotten figures, episodes, and movements from the history of psychology and other sciences. The story of Richard Semon with its attendant characters, Semon's various theoretical endeavors, the renegade band of memory-heredity theorists, turn-of-the-century experimental psychology of memory, and many of the neglected and isolated scientists whom we encountered can all be regarded as forgotten fragments of the past summoned out of their historical cocoons. My involvement with these missing pages of the past has led me to rather generally consider the role played by history in the pursuit of science, and I by briefly discussing the relation of past to present in my own field—which I broadly define as modern experimental psychology. What role does history play in contemporary experimental psychology and what role might it play?

Consideration of the level of historical awareness displayed by most modern experimental psychologists does not, unfortunately lead one to conclude that the insights of the past have been thoroughly digested by contemporary practitioners. The relevant past in psychology seems to be defined in terms of a decade or two: Events occurring prior to the onset of the latest research trend are too often regarded as ancient history, and ancient history is dead history—it does not inform or affect the direction of the present in a productive manner. To the extent that the topic is broached at all, history of psychology is frequently viewed as a harmless pursuit for aging scholars who have nothing better to do with their time. Although there has been a modest flaring of interest during the past year or two in psychology's past that can largely be attributed to the celebrations in 1979 of the 100th anniversary of experimental psychology, history of psychology is still a province left almost entirely to the historians: Its relevance to the concerns of the present is rarely acknowledged in a discipline that seems all too anxious to embrace the newest research fashions.[1] Jacoby (1975) has labeled such a condition *social amnesia*, and noted some of its unfavorable consequences:

> Problems and ideas once examined fall out of sight and out of mind only to resurface later as novel and new. . . . The sign of the times is thought that has succumbed to fashion; it scorns the past as antiquated while touting the present as best.

> Today's banalities apparently gain in profundity if one states that the wisdom of the past, for all its virtues, belongs to the past. The arrogance of those who come later preens itself with the notion that the past is dead and gone. (p. 1).

Jacoby's words may be harsh ones, but I believe that they point to a problem of pressing contemporary relevance in almost all areas of scientific psychology. Let us examine this problem in the context of a simple question: Why need we bother ourselves at all with the events of psychology's past? There are several answers to this query that probably occur to many readers: It is desirable to be in touch with the past so that we do not repeat mistakes that have already been made by others, so that we do not reinvent the wheel anew in each succeeding generation, and so that we can benefit from the different approaches to a contemporary problem that may have been taken by an illustrious predecessor. These are all important reasons for encouraging a more active historical awareness on the part of psychologists than now exists: Our own history may have more to teach us than we are presently extracting from it.

There may be, however, an even more compelling reason for seriously integrating the study of psychology's past with the research concerns of the present—a reason that penetrates to one of the most troublesome areas surrounding contemporary psychology. The past several years have witnessed lively discussion concerning the status of psychology as a science: Is psychology an

---

1. It would be both unfair and inaccurate to apply this statement to all modern experimental psychologists, and some outstanding examples in which "ancient history" is actively related to contemporary concerns are worth noting. Anderson and Bower (1973) provided an exemplary discussion that integrates the centuries-old tradition of associationism with their modern development of it; Mandler and Mandler (1964) gave us a fine collection of readings that presented past students of the thinking process as relevant sources of contemporary insight; Weimer's (1974a, b) incisive work clearly links our understanding of the past to the pursuit of present concerns; Crovitz's (1970) delightful book places the work of Sir Francis Galton in a relevant modern context; and Hilgard (1977) has fused the insights of late 19th-century disassociationism with modern perspectives on cognitive function. More such integrative efforts would be warmly welcomed.

"immature" science (e. g., Ravetz, 1973, pp. 364–402), a "preparadigmatic" science (e. g., Palermo, 1971; Warren, 1971), or any manner of science at all? Although the debate of these contentious issues lies beyond my scope, there is one point that clearly emerges from discussion of them, as well as from a study of the history of psychology: Psychology cannot yet be characterized as a *cumulative* science. Research fashions change at an alarmingly rapid rate in almost every domain of psychological inquiry, and as each succeeding movement proclaims its own importance the deeds of their predecessors are too often discarded like so much excess intellectual baggage. A changing panorama of research trends, of course, is not necessarily undesirable; it may well be a sign of scientific vitality. But this change must be tempered by an awareness of, and respect for, what has come before. Without such historical awareness, each new research movement ironically assures that its own fate will be identical to that of its predecessors—it will be passed over in the next wave of enthusiasm for a new approach.

This unfortunate cycle is particularly difficult to alter because most new research movements are possessed by a conviction that they have uncovered a crucial theory or method that will stand the test of time by virtue of its revolutionary importance. Consider two examples that were encountered earlier in the book: early 20th-century experimental psychology of memory and the memory-heredity movement. Recall the glowing commentaries in Chapter 8 made by contemporary researchers about the rapid progress of the new experimentalists and the plethora of problems that had been solved by the young science. These researchers thought that they were bequeathing a foundation of hard facts to future psychologists. Surely none of them would have believed that their work would be functionally lost to later generations of memory researchers. Similarly, spirited adherents of the memory-heredity movement such as Tomkeieff and Rignano wholeheartedly believed that they had at last evolved the conceptual machinery necessary to effect a meaningful integration of psychology and biology—but their insights were never assimilated by future generations. It would be easy to point to other similar examples from the past; perhaps the most striking is the recent theoretical demise of behaviorism, once the unchallenged ruler of North American experimental psychology. As one surveys the various emerging forces in contemporary experimental psychology— the movement toward "ecological validity" and the application of artificial intelligence models to psychological problems are two of the most energetic—one must wonder whether their convictions about the nature of psychological reality will be shared by future generations. Proponents of ecological validity, artificial intelligence, and other contemporary movements may well believe, of course, that theirs is the approach that can alone provide the key to understanding the mind—but so did the early memory researchers, the memory-heredity theorists, and giants of behaviorism such as Hull, Watson, Tolman, and Skinner.

Most scientific movements share this conviction of their own special significance. But, as Feuer (1974) has eloquently shown, they must also learn that their efforts are part of a broader historical fabric: "Each revolutionary generation moreover is destined to find out that its revolution was an illusion, that its standpoint was only partial and remained circumscribed by a reality that is perhaps transgenerational (p. 361)." The crucial test for psychology, then, is not whether any individual movement or generation can singly conjure the magic formula that provides a uniquely valid approach to its chosen terrain; as Feuer argues, no scientific generation may be capable of accomplishing that. Rather, the challenge is to build upon the insights of those who have gone before—to infuse the present with the wisdom of the past. If we cavalierly dismiss the efforts of our predecessors as hopelessly out of step with the latest research trends, then we forfeit the opportunity to build a science that is truly transgenerational. A profound respect for the ideas of the past is necessary to insure the historical integrity of *contemporary* thought. Without such respect, the efforts of the present, however imaginative or extensive, stand but a slight chance of historical survival; without it, psychology is unlikely to become a cumulative science in the future.

Richard Semon's Theory of Memory

DANIEL L. SCHACTER
JAMES ERIC EICH
ENDEL TULVING
University of Toronto

In the first decade of the 20th century, Richard Semon put forward a theory of memory that anticipated numerous recent developments in memory research. The theory is discussed both in its historical context and with reference to modern ideas. Semon's theoretical concern for retrieval phenomena is particularly noteworthy. Several reasons are suggested why the theory is virtually unknown today.

*C*urrent research in the area of human memory owes many of its present orienting attitudes and research techniques to pioneering psychologists of the late 19th and early 20th centuries. Among the most well known and important of these early investigators are Hermann Ebbinghaus, who performed the first systematic laboratory studies of human memory; William James, whose distinction between primary and secondary memory is still today the target of much research and theorizing; G. E. Müller, who performed important early research on grouping and interference; and Sir Frederic Bartlett, whose reconstructive approach to memory has become influential in recent years. It is likely that most modern students of memory are familiar with the writings of the above psychologists, and have probably been influenced, to varying

---

This paper was written while Daniel Schacter and Endel Tulving were visitors at the Department of Experimental Psychology, University of Oxford. The work was supported by a National Science Foundation Predoctoral Fellowship to D. L. Schacter, University of Toronto Predoctoral Fellowship to J. E. Eich, and by the National Research Council of Canada, Grant No. A8632 to E. Tulving. We thank Margaret Boden, Douglas Hintzman, Gregory Jones, and George Mandler for helpful comments on the manuscript. Requests for reprints should be sent to Daniel L. Schacter, Department of Psychology, University of Toronto, Toronto, Canada, M5S 1A1.

degrees, by their research and theories. It is much less likely that these same students of memory are familiar with the work of Richard Wolfgang Semon, a German scientist who wrote two books on the subject of human memory in the first decade of the 20th century. In fact, Semon's work has been almost completely ignored by mainstream psychologists concerned with processes of memory and learning; later in this paper we will explore some of the reasons why Semon's work has been bypassed. Yet prominent anatomist J. Z. Young (1965, p. 288) commented that " . . . many modern ideas on the subject [of memory] go back to Richard Semon . . . ;" Gestalt psychologist Kurt Koffka (1935, p. 598), though refraining from discussing Semon's theory in detail, noted that " . . . this omission is not due to a lack of appreciation of Semon's great achievement;" Nobel Prize winning physicist Erwin Schrödinger (1964, p. 44) regretted that a physiological model of Semon's theory of memory had not yet been developed " . . . important though it would be for the advancement of our knowledge" and Bertrand Russell who, in a chapter in *The Analysis of Mind*, introduced Semon's work to English readers, flatly stated that, "The best writer on mnemic phenomena known to me is Richard Semon . . . " (1921, p. 83).

What in Semon's work elicited the accolades of the distinguished scientist-philosophers mentioned above? It is the purpose of the present paper to explore in some detail Richard Semon's analysis of human memory, place this analysis in its historical context, and elucidate some of the reasons why Semon's work is virtually unknown to present-day students of human memory. It is our thesis that Semon's analysis anticipated many current research problems and approaches to the study of memory in a most striking fashion, and that his work contains potentially valuable suggestions and implications for contemporary researchers.

THE BACKGROUND

Richard Semon was born in Berlin on August 22, 1859. His father Simon was a stockbroker; his older brother Felix became a prominent laryngologist in England, received a knighthood in 1897, and was appointed physician to King Edward VII in 1901. Semon was awarded his Dr. Phil. for zoological work at Jena in 1883, and earned his Dr. Med. in 1886. During this period, Semon studied with some of the most prominent scientists of the day, including the noted biologist Ernst Haeckel; Haeckel's emphasis on the theoretical unification of diverse biological phenomena had a particularly strong influence on Semon. After receiving an associate professorship at Jena in 1891, Semon led a successful biological expedition to Australia from 1891–1893 (Semon, 1899). He left Jena in 1897 for personal reasons, and established himself as a private scholar in Munich.

It was during this period that Semon published his two books on memory: *Die Mneme* (1904) (translated into English as *The Mneme* in 1921) and *Die mnemischen Empfindungen* (1909) (translated as *Mnemic Psychology* in 1923).[1] *Mnemic Psychology* is devoted completely to the analysis of human memory. However, in *The Mneme*, Semon examined not only the phemomena of human memory but also advanced and attempted to support the thesis that the mechanisms of memory and heredity are identical. As we shall argue later, advocacy of this thesis, that also led Semon to support the highly controversial Lamarckian doctrine of the inheritance of acquired characteristics, proved to be a key scientific error. At Easter 1918, Semon's wife succumbed to a long illness. Severely disturbed by this loss, shattered by the collapse of his native Germany in World War I, and deeply disturbed about the lack of recognition of his work, Richard Semon ended his own life on December 27, 1918.

Before we move on to a consideration of Semon's work and its historical context, it will be useful to clarify two points. First is the problem of terminology. Semon believed strongly that everyday terms commonly used to talk about memory had too many undesirable connotations to be of precise scientific value. Accordingly, he invented his own terms to correspond more exactly to his intended meanings. One of Semon's terminological creations, the word "engram" [defined by Semon as " . . . the enduring though primarily latent modification in the irritable substance produced by a stimulus . . . " (1921, p. 12)] has persisted in present-day usage, and is probably most closely associated with the famous paper of Lashley (1960). Another of Semon's creations, the term "ecphory" [defined by Semon as " . . . the influences which awaken the mnemic trace or engram out of its latent state into one of manifested activity . . . " (1921, p. 12)] has been used quite infrequently. Since "engram" is roughly equivalent to the phrase "memory trace" and "ecphory" is roughly equivalent to "retrieval" or "recall," we will use these terms interchangeably throughout this paper.[2] We will, of course, define all new terms as they arise.

Second, when we speak of the "historical context" of Semon's theories, we refer specifically to the period from 1885–1935. Consideration of memory research during this period will enable us to describe the theoretical concerns of the field in both the years preceding and following publication of Semon's work. We chose the year 1885 to initiate our historical consideration because this was the year in which Ebbinghaus published the first experimental studies of memory; we terminate our historical survey in 1935 because in subsequent years interest in the general problem of memory gave way to the more restricted concerns of the verbal learning tradition before surfacing again in the early 1960s.

---

1. We will cite the English versions of these two books throughout this paper. Although we will quote most extensively from *Mnemic Psychology*, the reader should bear in mind the most of Semon's major ideas concerning human memory date to 1904.
2. It is possible to distinguish between ecphory and retrieval, as noted in Tulving (1976). We will not concern ourselves with the distinction in the present paper.

PRELIMINARY OVERVIEW OF THE THEORY

Semon's theory of memory was based upon two fundamental postulates, which the author termed the "Law of Engraphy" and the "Law of Ecphory." The first law was Semon's characterization of memory storage: "All simultaneous excitations . . . within our organisms form a connected simultaneous complex of excitations which, as such, acts engraphically, that is to say leaves behind it a connected and, to that extent, unified engram-complex" (1923, pp. 159–160). There are several points contained in this law that subsequently emerge as critical features of Semon's theory. First there is Semon's emphasis on the unitary, wholistic nature of engram complexes that he later applies to the analysis of various mnemonic phenomena. Second there is the notion that each event, or corresponding "simultaneous excitation-complex" leaves behind a separate engram-complex; this idea is elaborated upon and utilized in Semon's analyses of repetition effects and recognition. The law of engraphy also sets the stage for Semon's law of ecphory, which represents his view of memory retrieval: "The partial return of an energetic situation which has fixed itself engraphically acts in an ecphoric sense upon a simultaneous engram-complex" (1923, p. 180). Thus Semon's view of retrieval is redintegrative. Only *part* of the total situation at the time of storage need be present at the time of recall in order for retrieval of the original event in its entirety to occur. This view of retrieval (one of the very few such views that had been explicitly formulated in Semon's time) was further developed and utilized by Semon in analyses of problems such as association by contiguity vs. association by similarity and the temporal organization of memory, and led Semon to formulate novel positions concerning matters such as the active role of ecphory in establishing new engram-complexes and the role that ecphory plays in the storage of new engram-complexes. Also, by allowing for the representation of internal or "energetic" stimuli in engram-complexes, Semon was able to offer surprisingly modern statements concerning phenomena such as state-dependent retrieval. We will explore these points in greater detail shortly.

A third notion that is part of the kernel of Semon's theory (although it was not granted the status of a "law" by Semon) is the concept of homophony. Homophony may be most simply viewed as a resonance metaphor; Semon used it to describe the mechanism by which information from different sources is combined, defining it as " . . . the concordant action of closely allied mnemic and original excitations, a consonance which I have found it convenient to call *Homophony*" (1921, p. 13). Homophony can exist between two "original sensations," between "original and mnemic sensations," or between two "mnemic sensations." This resonance principle was invoked by Semon in constructing what we might want to call "retrieval explanations" of repetition effects and problems of recognition; he also applied it to various problems of perception that will not concern us here. The major point that we wish to extract from this highly condensed overview of Semon's position, and which we will document more fully later in the paper, is that the analysis of retrieval was one of Semon's principal theoretical concerns. More specifically, we will argue that Semon's focus upon the *conditions, functions,* and *processes* of retrieval[3] was one of the few systematic attempts to elucidate the role of retrieval in memory during the period under consideration, that his ideas about retrieval anticipated much modern research, and that his emphasis on retrieval phenomena at a time when few were interested in this problem may well have contributed to his subsequent obscurity.

MEMORY RESEARCH BETWEEN 1885 AND 1935: A BRIEF REVIEW

In this section we sample the memory literature between 1885 and 1935 in order to convey a general idea of the problems and theoretical issues that concerned memory researchers of the time. We will consider in somewhat more detail research that examined specific problems of interest to Semon in the next section of the paper.

One useful indicator of research concerns in a given period of time is a listing of the topics considered in major review papers of the area. Accordingly, we have examined the topics covered in major reviews of memory published in the *American Journal of Psychology, Psychological Bulletin,* and *Psychological Review* during the late 19th and early 20th centuries. First we will examine papers published before and during the time that Semon wrote his two books; then we will examine papers published after this time and up until 1935.

The first major review of theory and research on memory was Burnham's (1888–1889) classic four-part article. The first two parts covered theories of memory from the Greeks into the 19th century. Some of the important, recurring issues during this period of time were whether memory is physical, psychical, or "of the soul;" the relative importance of different kinds of association; the role of habit in memory; and so on. More recent topics of interest, discussed by Burnham in the latter two parts of his paper, include the physiological basis of association, the effects of retention interval on forgetting, the usefulness of memory span as an indicator of educability in normal and retarded children, and the nature of "memory illusions." Of course, Ebbinghaus' pioneering work had just been published. This initiated serious experimental interest in the study of memory and brought the study of repetition effects and the quantification of forgetting curves to the fore of the field. Interest in problems of retrieval, however, was negligible in the years covered by Burnham's review. With the exception of Sir William Hamilton (1859), who explicitly divided memory into three

---

3. The phrase *processes of retrieval* refers to the mechanisms by which retrieval is carried out; the phrase *conditions of retrieval* refers to those properties of the cognitive environment of the rememberer which affect the retrieval process; and the phrase *functions of retrieval* refers to the effects that the act of retrieval has upon the subsequent state of the memory system.

stages of acquisition, retention, and reproduction, and offered an early redintegrative theory of retrieval, and some passages from William James (1890), these
early writers had little direct interest in either the functions, conditions, or processes of retrieval.

Kennedy's (1898) review reflects the emerging concerns of the young experimental science of memory. After discussing methods and materials used in
memory research, Kennedy outlined the problems of interest to contemporary
researchers: measurement of the depth of "initial impressions," the role of attention and repetition, the qualitative change in the memory "image" over time,
individual differences in memory ability, and the nature of the to-be-remem-
bered material were all major issues of the day; and the initial investigation of
grouping and organization had just been reported by Müller and Schumann
(1894). In Kuhlmann's (1908) review (which appeared just after *The Mneme*
and just before *Mnemic Psychology*) we observe continued concern with many
of the topics reviewed by Kennedy, and observe heightened interest in problems that had been barely touched at the time of Kennedy's review. For instance, the problem of massed vs. distributed practice, first attacked by
Ebbinghaus, was now a major research concern; the introspective analysis of
the "memory consciousness," concerning the form and content of memory imagery and individual differences in this imagery, had " . . . come to the foreground of memory investigation" (p. 285); and the analysis of recognition was
becoming a full-fledged experimental problem. But again there was a remarkable absence of attention paid to problems of retrieval. In the years before and
during which Semon published his two volumes on human memory it is extremely difficult to find any theory or research that raises questions specifically
directed at the conditions, functions, or processes of retrieval. Association was
assumed to be the mechanism of the retrieval *process*, an assumption that Semon
criticized elegantly, and that we will examine shortly; there was interest in retrieval *conditions* only insofar as the laws of association required some specification of effective associative stimuli; and the possible mnemonic *functions* of
the act of retrieval itself were simply not considered by theorists of the time.
(For a more detailed account of memory research during this period, see the
paper by Murray, 1976).

We now move ahead to the 1920s and consider the lengthy review paper
by Robinson (1924). Robinson's paper was divided into five major sections. The
first section, on "memorizing," considers many of the topics previously mentioned, as well as the role of intention in learning and studies of associative
inhibition, for example, the Ranschburg effect. The second section, concerned
with retention, reviews several topics that had not previously been given much
attention. Studies of retroactive interference, which originated in the classical
work of Müller and Pilzecker (1900), are now well under way; the problem of
affective tone and retention, owing largely to Freudian influences, has become
a major research topic; and the problem of reminiscence, first addressed in
Ballard's (1913) monograph, has been given experimental attention. We also
find reference to studies comparing the effect of recalls vs. extra study presen-

tations on retention; that is, studies exploring the *functions* of retrieval. The third section of Robinson's review, entitled "Recall," indicates just how sparse research in this area was. A few studies that examined various aspects of legal testimony are cited, and one study (Laird, Remmers, & Peterson, 1923) that was concerned with retrieval *conditions* is mentioned; but the problem of recall is still clearly of minor experimental and theoretical interest at the time of Robinson's review. The remaining sections of his review cover qualitative studies of memory, and memory in the "insane and defective."

The final reviews we will consider were published by McGeoch (1928, 1930). The topics reviewed in these papers, as well as many of the studies we have already made reference to, are brought together in McGeoch's (1933) massive, 1200-item bibliography of learning and memory research. These reviews reflect heightened interest in serial postion effects and problems of transfer; a new concern with the establishment of general laws of learning; and continued interest in traditional problems such as quantification of the curve of retention, the most economical methods of practice, the role of sensory modality in memory, etc. As regards analyses of retrieval, several studies of the similarity of "stimulating conditions" (i.e., context) at storage and retrieval are considered, as are several studies of successive recalls; but the largest number of studies concerned with recall are found under the heading of "Relationships between different measures of retention" (McGeoch, 1933, p. 57). These studies, best exemplified by Luh's (1922) work, reflect the common attitude of investigators at the time towards the issue of retrieval: It is viewed as a problem of *measurement*, rather than as a psychological process that forms a crucial part of the memory system and that requires systematic theoretical analysis. Serious theoretical consideration of retrieval and its role in the memory system was to emerge shortly in the work of Bartlett (1932), Köhler (1930), and Koffka (1935), before disappearing for the next 30 years; but with few exceptions (such as Hollingworth, 1926, 1928; Meumann, 1913; Selz, 1913, 1922; and to some extent, Myers & Myers, 1916) the problem was treated in an almost uniformly atheoretical fashion in the years preceding and following Semon's work.

Additional evidence on this point can be adduced by sampling general theoretical statements made about memory in the period under consideration. For instance, there was William James' (1890, p. 653) view that " . . . *the cause both of retention and of recollection is the law of habit in the nervous system, working as it does in the 'association of ideas'*." Kennedy, in his 1898 review, reduced memory to two factors: " . . . the conditions which govern the chances that a certain object be remembered depend, first, upon the depth and clearness of the impression which that object made on me in my experience of it, and second, upon the transformation which my image undergoes in the temporal flow" (p. 485). Thorndike's (1913) proclamation provides a typical textbook view of memory around Semon's time: "Goodness of memory depends upon the permanence of impressions, the permanence of connections, their number and their nature or arrangement" (p. 25). The neglect of retrieval factors in the above formulations is clear, and these statements are quite typical of memory theory at the time. We will refer to some of the individual experiments and ideas that were directed at retrieval phenomena in the next section of the paper. The major purpose of the present section, in addition to providing a general characterization of research interests between 1885 and 1935, has been to demonstrate the relative lack of theoretical concern for the problem of retrieval throughout this period.

SEMON'S THEORY IN HISTORICAL PERSPECTIVE: A DETAILED ANALYSIS

We now proceed to a more fine-grained exposition of Semon's theory. As we consider the various aspects of Semon's theoretical position, we will relate his formulations to the theories of his contemporaries, and will also juxtapose Semon's views with those advanced by modern students of human memory.

Biological Perspective

We initiate the discussion by considering the *substrate* of engraphy: how did Semon conceptualize the representation of engrams? It may be advisable first to remind the reader that, in the early part of the 20th century, the question of whether memories are represented in the brain (that is, physically) or in the mind (that is, psychically) was a hotly debated issue. Eminent thinkers such as Bergson (1911) and McDougall (1911) argued at great length that memories are not physically represented in the brain but rather in some nonphysical, "psychical" form. Semon's view on the matter reflected his biological training; he unequivocally took the position that engrams are stored via physiochemical processes in the brain. However, Semon declined to hypothesize about the precise form of this biological storage, arguing that in the limited state of then contemporary physiology, such speculation was unwarranted. Semon did go on to raise the question of whether memory storage is neurologically distributed or localized, and offered a surprisingly modern view (see, for example, Luria, 1973):

> We seem . . . to be placed in the dilemma of having either to reject altogether
> a localization theory which imagines that each single engram can be stored
> up in a single cell—or in a comparatively small complex of cerebral cells
> . . . or to admit that in the human organism a special interdependence exists
> between definite regions of the cerebral cortex and the ecphory or, as perhaps
> we ought to say, the possibility of the ecphory of distinct individually-acquired
> engrams. The latter admission, implies, however, the recognition of a certain
> localization, although it need not be the kind which makes each nerve-cell of
> the brain a repository for a specific engram (1921, p. 120).

It is interesting to note the manner of criticism directed toward these views. On the one hand, Semon was grossly misinterpreted and accused of one of the worst scientific sins of the day: the advocacy of vitalism. Since he did not construct a model which specified the precise nature of biological memory storage, and because he did not adhere to a strict localizationist view, various critics (e.g., Kostyleff, 1911) attached the vitalistic label to Semon's position. To these critics, Semon gave an incisive reply which merits close attention even today:

> I should be as able as anyone else to turn out some sort of schematic representation on the model of the diagram of Mendelian determinants in which engrams would be naively represented, schematized as tiny particles and conveniently packed together. This would meet the views of those readers whose thirst for causality requires such schematic representation, and who cannot resign themselves to leaving such questions open for the time being. My own conception of inductive science is a different one, and I attribute more value to an honest note of interrogation than to constructions which are only representable through an effort of imagination (1923, p. 329).

On the other hand, avowedly vitalistic writers such as Bousefield (1928)—who advanced the theory that memories are not physically represented in "protoplasm" but rather are psychically represented in "psychoplasm"—accused Semon of erring by reverting to crass mechanistic reductionism. Thus, Semon was criticized by both mechanists and vitalists for espousing general hypotheses concerning the biological nature of memory storage that today seem both perfectly reasonable and appropriate to the state of physiological knowledge at the time.

Relation of Perception to Memory

Returning to Semon's view of engraphy, an important point to note is that Semon's analysis of memory was directly related to his analysis of perception:

> . . . the very expression "mnemic sensation" necessarily implies that such a sensation has been preceded by an original one. The nature of this dependence will be fully explained later. The bare fact of its existence, however, makes it a precondition for the study of mnemic sensations that we should closely follow the orientation of certain aspects of original sensations, because the former depend on the latter as inevitable predecessors (1923, pp. 69–70) . . .

Indeed, the first part of *Mnemic Psychology* is devoted to an analysis of sensation and perception, upon which Semon's analysis of memory is based. In Semon's time, the analysis of perception was largely divorced from the analysis of memory, and with few exceptions (e.g., Külpe, 1895), explicit theoretical realization of the interrelatedness of perception and memory was not manifested until the appearance of the work of Bartlett (1932), Gibson (1929), and the Gestaltists (Köhler, 1930; Koffka, 1935). The interrelatedness of perception and memory is, of course, a major theme in contemporary research, forming an important part of numerous theories.

In order to understand the relation between perception and memory in

Semon's theory, we must first briefly consider his analysis of perception. In contrast to atomistic conceptualizations of sensation and perception that were dominant in experimental psychology around the turn of the century (e.g., Külpe, 1895; Titchener, 1911: Wundt, 1902), Semon stressed the unity and wholistic nature of "sensation-complexes": " . . . what we experience immediately are not single sensations but connected complexes of sensation, forming at any given moment the whole content of consciousness" (1923, p. 65). Semon preferred to speak of "fields of sensation" rather than "sensation-elements," emphasizing the "primary unity" of such fields, and he ascribed an important role to the "reciprocal influence" of the components of a field of sensation. In so doing Semon anticipated Gestalt analyses of perception and the context and contrast effects that the Gestalt theory was based upon. Similar views concerning "reciprocal influence" can be found in Höffding (1891, p. 114), and other early wholistic, Gestalt-like analyses of perception were offered by Mach (1959); but these were exceptions to the prevailing atomistic views (Boring, 1942).

Semon's conceptualization of the engram follows directly from his wholistic analysis of perception. The memory trace is to be regarded as a unified complex, reflecting the unitary nature of perceptual experience. The essence of this idea is captured in Semon's law of engraphy. However, Semon stressed that the engram is comprised of "emergent components" that could to some extent be dissociated from each other. This view, similar to recent multicomponent theories of the memory trace (Bower, 1967; Underwood, 1969), was elaborated further by Semon and will be discussed shortly. At this point the reader may rightly ask if all Semon has done is to offer another "literal-copy" theory of memory stated in Gestalt-like terms: engram complexes are simply faithful recordings of perceptual experience, and when we remember we have access to this stored "snapshot" of the world. It turns out that Semon was saying no such thing; he in fact directly addressed the question of why the output from the memory system is so different from the input, and his answers to this question form some of the most interesting parts of his theory.

First, Semon argued that distortion is introduced into the memory trace at the time of storage. This is because every act of storage, in Semon's view, involves some retrieval: the new input acts as a retrieval cue which operates ecphorically on the principle of "partial return" described in Semon's second law. Hence, what is stored is not just a faithful recording of perceptual experience; rather " . . . nearly every complex of original sensations has grouped around it numerous mnemic sensations which are evoked by it and work engraphically in the grouping . . . every simultaneous complex of sensations is composed of original and mnemic sensations which are closely connected with one another, and thus form a whole; and this whole—regarded from its energetic side—works engraphically" (1923, p. 168).

Semon also considered the problem of why only fragments of this whole (however different from a literal "snapshot" it might be) can be remembered. Semon argued that these memory fragments are not isolated links in a semi-intact associative chain; rather, reflecting his multicomponent orientation, he suggested that " . . . a conception much more in accordance with our meaning leads us to regard such fragments not as associated, but as *integral components, as emergent points of a connected simultaneous complex of sensations*" (1923, p. 164). Semon's concern with memory fragments foreshadowed the recent systematic work of Jones (1976), whose "fragmentation hypothesis" of memory holds that memories are *stored* as fragments of a perceived situation. Semon offered three explanations of fragmentation, two of these reflecting his view that fragmentation arises at retrieval. First, Semon argued for the importance of retrieval conditions in fragmentation. The direction of attention at the time of ecphory influences which fragments of the trace are "noticed:" "The fixing of attention on specific points in the simultaneous complex acts as a dissolvent and dissociates these parts from the rest of the connection" (1923, p. 165). Second, Semon suggested that homophony, or resonance, between the ecphoric stimulus and certain components of the retrieved engram-complex might accentuate some fragments at the expense of others. Third, he noted that mnemic sensations are "less vivid" than original sensations; hence, only the "peaks of sensation" may emerge during ecphory.

In outlining Semon's position on the input-output discrepancies, it is clear that in most respects his approach to the problem was quite different from that of his contemporaries. The major theoretical emphasis in explanations of input-output discrepancies at the time Semon wrote was on the role of unconscious processes in changing, distorting, or weakening the memory trace over time (Kennedy, 1898); this notion also played a large role in subsequent Gestalt analyses of memory (c.f., Koffka, 1935). Semon's notion that the fading of mnemic sensations contributes to fragmentation is similar to these traditional views. Exceptions to the prevailing hypothesis are found in the work of Bentley (1899) and Kuhlmann (1906), who attached importance to associations formed at storage as major determinants of input-output discrepancies. This position is in some ways similar to Semon's point that each new engram-complex is comprised of "original" and "mnemic" sensations, although Semon's conception of this process is quite different from the mechanisms envisaged by Bentley or Kuhlmann. It was not until the work of Crosland (1921) and the later monograph by Bartlett (1932) that serious consideration of retrieval conditions as causes of input-output discrepancies is found. These authors placed major emphasis on the subjects' "attitude" at the time of recall in developing accounts of distorted and fragmentary remembering. In modern studies of input-output discrepancies, the "unconscious transformation" hypothesis so popular in Semon's time has been abandoned, and research has been directed at processes of generalization, fragmentation, and abstraction occurring at both storage and retrieval (Bransford & Franks, 1971; Frederiksen, 1975; Jones, 1976; Loftus, Miller, & Burns, 1978). Additionally, the notion of "implicit associative responses" advanced by Underwood (1965) to account for false recognition data resembles Semon's idea that both incoming stimulus information and information from the memory store are represented in each new memory trace; however, the mechanisms of this process postulated by Semon and by Underwood are quite different. Thus, it seems clear that the thrust of Semon's position on the problem of input-output discrepancies was more in accord with the modern approach than was the popular theory of his era.

The Acoluthic Phase and Temporal Organization

Closely related to the perception-memory issue is Semon's distinction between the *synchronous* and *acoluthic* phases of sensation. The synchronous phase lasts only as long as a physical stimulus is present, whereas the acoluthic phase persists for some time after the cessation of the stimulus. Semon distinguished two components of the acoluthic phase: a period of short-lived oscillating activity (less than a second) which " . . . manifests itself regularly in sensations above the threshold of consciousness . . . " (1923, p. 140); and a longer lasting activity of unspecified duration that is not always manifested in consciousness. At first glance, it is tempting to say that Semon was simply talking about after-images that were the subject of some research during this time (Boring, 1942). However, closer consideration of Semon's treatment of the acoluthic phase reveals that he assigned it an important *functional* role in the overall memory process. As we shall see shortly, Semon's concern for the mnemonic functions of the acoluthic phase sharply distinguishes this conception from that of the static afterimage that was not studied as a functional component of the memory system during this time.

Before describing the functional use to which Semon put the acoluthic phase, we must first outline his conception of the temporal arrangement of the memory store, for it is in his analysis of temporal relations that Semon makes use of the acoluthic phase. Semon hypothesized that the engram-store is organized primarily along temporal dimensions, and that engram-complexes are deposited in "chronological strata:"

> Every simultaneous complex which may be figuratively described as one "layer" of an engram-store is joined to the layer immediately preceding it and, in its turn, bears the same relation to the next most recent layer. Owing to the uninterrupted laying down of these 'layers' the components of each layer are in immediate contact with those of its nearest predecessor and nearest successor (1923, p. 327).

Again it is worth noting that Semon concerned himself with an issue that was not of prime importance to his contemporaries. Galton (1879), James (1890), and Ribot (1882) did talk about the temporal organization of memory, but the problem was clearly not of major concern in Semon's time, as can be verified by examining the review papers we cited earlier. Semon's interest in temporal organization anticipated modern theories such as Landauer's (1975), in which time is viewed as the principal dimension of organization in memory, and experimental work such as that reported by Crovitz and Schiffman (1974), Guenther and Linton (1975), and Underwood (1977), in which various aspects of temporal factors in memory are explored. Semon's ideas on temporal organization also bear a striking resemblance to the general theory of temporal organization put forward in Murdock's (1974) conveyer belt model.

Having exposed Semon's views on the "chronological stratification" of memory, we now return to a consideration of the functional role of the acoluthic phase in the genesis of temporal organization. Semon proposed that memory traces of successive events are temporally linked by the co-occurrence of the synchronous phase of event N with the acoluthic phase of event N–1. Thus, the persisting acoluthic excitation provides the "temporal glue" permitting the establishment of unique engram-complexes comprised of the synchronous phase of one stimulus and the acoluthic phase of a preceding one. The critical point to note is that Semon did not view this process as one of "horizontal" association between successive events. Rather, the *simultaneous* conjoining of synchronous and acoluthic phases establishes a unique engram-complex. The nature of this distinction is best illustrated by Semon's explanation of Ebbinghaus' finding that remote associations exist between nonadjacent nonsense syllables in his classic study. Rather than positing a direct "horizontal" association between, say, Event X and Event Y, Semon suggested that X and Y form a new engram-complex by virtue of the simultaneous occurrence of the synchronous phase of Y and the fading acoluthic phase of X. Then, when there occurs partial return of this complex (let us say Event X as a retrieval cue) memory for the whole complex follows. Thus, in contrast to the traditional associative account of remote association, Semon offered a novel explanation based on the functional role of the acoluthic phase and on his redintegrative principle of ecphory through partial return of the conditions of engraphy.

This theory led Semon to adopt the view that all association is simultaneous; apparent cases of successive association arise through the simultaneous occurrence of the acoluthic phase of Event X and the synchronous phase of Event Y. Semon's provocative position on this matter led directly to some of the earliest experimental work explicitly concerned with simultaneous vs. successive association in human memory, reported by Wohlgemuth (1915). Although Wohlgemuth claimed that his results strongly supported Semon's theory, inspection of his method and data suggest extreme caution in interpretation of his results. It is interesting to note, though, that this is the only instance we have found in which one of Semon's theoretical positions on human memory was put to direct experimental test. There are, clearly, serious deficiencies in Semon's conceptualization of the acoluthic phase that hinder meaningful experimental investigation of it, for example, it is unclear how long the acoluthic phase lasts, and how one obtains independent evidence of its existence. Accordingly, it would be fruitless to attempt to evaluate Semon's hypothesis in the light of the subsequent experimental literature (Carr, 1919: Froeberg, 1918: see also Robinson, 1932).

However, there are two senses in which Semon's conception of the acoluthic phase anticipated modern research and theory. First, Semon's ideas would fit well with recent experimental demonstrations of long-persisting visual memory traces (e.g., Kroll, Parks, Parkinson, Bieber, & Johnson, 1970). Second, the conception of the acoluthic phase is in some ways quite similar to modern conceptions of short-term memory. The acoluthic phase constitutes a preliminary *stage of processing* which temporally precedes a more permanent engraphic representation, and it plays an important *functional role* in the memory system, as does the short-term memory envisaged in recent theories (e.g., Atkinson & Shiffrin, 1968: Baddeley & Hitch, 1974). Of course, there are numerous ways in which Semon's conception of the acoluthic phase has little in common with modern conceptions of short-term memory: but at a time when the major interest in short-term memory concerned individual differences in memory span (Binet & Henri, 1894; Hawkins, 1897) and the effects of varying materials on span length (Kennedy, 1898), the similarities are impressive.

The Law of Ecphory

We have already described Semon's law of ecphory, and have outlined his application of it to two problems of memory, namely, input-output discrepancies and simultaneous vs. successive association. We now discuss Semon's conception of ecphory in greater detail and describe further applications of this concept to problems of memory.

As noted earlier, a key notion embodied in the law of ecphory is that of redintegration, the reinstatement of a whole via one of its parts. The classical historical reference is, of course, to Sir William Hamilton, who argued for a redintegrative position in 1859. Semon did not cite Hamilton in either *The Mneme* or *Mnemic Psychology*, and was most likely unaware of Hamilton's redintegrative position. Somewhat similar redintegrative views can be found in Höffding (1891) and Selz (1913, 1922). The most prolific exponent of redintegration in the period just following publication of Semon's work was Hollingworth (1926, 1928); more recently, Horowitz and Prytulak (1969) have refamiliarized modern students with the notion of redintegration.

Although the basic redintegrative position taken by Semon was similar to the positions of his contemporaries Höffding, Hollingworth, and Selz, there are two distinguishing characteristics of Semon's approach to redintegration. First, Semon's elaboration of his position sounds much like modern theories of retrieval in which feature overlap between retrieval cue and memory trace is granted a critical role in the retrieval process (Kintsch, 1974; Tulving, 1976): "Resemblance, that is to say, partial coincidence between the components of an actual group of excitations and those of any previous engram-complex, causes ecphory of the latter through the former" (Semon, 1923, p. 326). Although Selz advanced similar notions, none of the other redintegrationists have taken such a position. Second, Semon directly applied his law of ecphory to a variety of specific problems in the study of memory. Hollingworth did apply his redintegrative principle to various problems in psychology, especially those involving pathology, but he did not relate it specifically to memory.

Contiguity vs Similarity and the Engraphic Role of Ecphory

One of Semon's most striking and innovative applications of redintegrative ecphory to a problem of memory concerned the question of association by contiguity vs association by similarity. This problem has a long history in psychology and philosophy, with some authors arguing that all association is by similarity, others that all association is by contiguity, and others that both forms of association occur (see Warren, 1921; Robinson, 1932). Semon took the position that all association is developed through contiguity, which in itself was nothing new; but his manner of reaching the conclusion was quite interesting, and merits close attention for two reasons. First, it again highlights the important role of retrieval processes in Semon's theory; second, it brings to light an important distinction that was largely overlooked at the time.

In order to account for apparent association by similarity (that is, the case in which Stimulus X evokes a semantically, visually, acoustically, etc., similar Memory Trace Y) Semon invoked his principle of partial return. Owing to shared components between Stimulus X and Trace Y, Y is ecphorized in the presence of X, just like in any other ecphory via partial return. It is only at this point that the two events are associated, through contiguity, and the new engram-complex is then stored. Thus Semon argued that association by similarity is due to:

> . . . an ecphory based on the partial recurrence of certain components of an excitation-complex. When departing, it leaves behind a new engram-complex in which the two images are associated, but *this consecutive association is a typical simultaneous association* (1923, p. 189).

Semon went on to state that, "In fact 'association' through resemblance does not exist. What is taken for it is ecphory due to the partial return of a complex which has previously left its engram" (1923, p. 189).

There are two critical points to be extracted from this analysis. First, it led Semon to make an important distinction between *ecphory* and *association*. Association can be revealed through ecphory, but it cannot be equated with the process of ecphory. Here Semon was challenging the common assumption of his era that association *is* the *mechanism* of recall. Semon rejected this notion, preferring to think of association as a descriptive concept which should be logically distinguished from the mechanism of retrieval. By disentangling these two concepts, Semon was able to offer a novel analysis of association by similarity: " . . . the essential gain from our investigation is that the notion of association through likeness was based on a confusion of two concepts: association and ecphory" (p. 189). Semon's analysis is closer in spirit to modern conceptions such as encoding specificity (Tulving & Thomson, 1973) than to the theories of his time.

The second point that is brought into bold relief by this analysis concerns one of the important *functions* of retrieval in Semon's theory: the establishment of new engram-complexes. Semon argued that every act of ecphory results in the establishment of a unique engram-complex comprised of the retrieved information and information in the present context: " . . . each ecphory of an engram-complex produces not only a mnemic sensation . . . but through this creates a new engram which adheres to the new engram-stratum" (1923, p. 178). He utilized this notion in his explanation of association by similarity presented above, and also invoked it in his consideration of how engrams from different "chronological strata" are combined. Semon suggested that when a particular engram-complex has been ecphorized, it can then act as a cue for engrams in other chronological strata with which it shares common components, and hence can be retrieved via partial return; this new juxtaposition is then stored as a unique engram-complex.

Semon's conceptualization of ecphory as a generator of novel engram-complexes was unique in its time. There was some concern with the functions of recall in the years following publication of Semon's two books, but little before. Abbott (1909) compared the memorial effects of extra recall time and study time, finding that time spent recalling is more beneficial than additional study time; Trow (1928) and Raffel (1934) came to similar conclusions. In a slightly different vein, Bartlett (1928) and Whitely and McGeoch (1927) investigated the effect of one recall on a subsequent recall. With these few exceptions, however, the functional significance of the act of retrieval was rarely treated in a theoretical manner during Semon's time. Indeed, this characterization can be accurately applied to the period extending into the 1960s at which point serious theoretical concern with the function of the act of recall began to emerge. This concern has manifested itself in several ways. The memorial consequences of recall trials vs. study trials have been pursued in a systematic manner (eg., Izawa, 1969; Tulving, 1967); the facilitating effects of retrieval on subsequent retrieval have been the object of both experimental and theoretical attention (e.g., Darley & Murdock, 1971; Modigliani, 1976); and inquiries into the inhibiting effects of the act of recall have been made (e.g., Roediger, 1974; Rundus, 1973). Thus it would appear that Semon's early interest in the functions of ecphory anticipated a number of current research trends. It should be noted, though, that in the above studies, facilitating effects of recall are almost invariably attributed to some sort of "strengthening" process: The accessibility of an existing memory trace is increased via the strengthening effect of recall. Semon, on the other hand, suggested that what emerges after recall is not a strengthened version of an already existing trace, but rather a new, unique constellation of information in the present context plus information in the retrieved trace. The modern research closest in spirit to Semon's approach is the recent work on memory for remembered events reported by Gardiner and Klee (1976; Klee & Gardiner, 1976). These authors posit that "Each act of remembering itself . . . constitutes a new event in episodic memory" (Klee & Gardiner, p. 471), and provide evidence to support this hypothesis. Further research in this area might well profit from serious consideration of Semon's ideas on the engram-establishing capacities of the act of recall.

Internally-Generated Stimuli

We noted earlier that Semon specifically allowed for representation of internal stimuli in the formation of engram-complexes, and suggested that these internal stimuli function as potent ecphoric cues. First let us consider the notion that internally-generated stimuli are stored as components of an engram-complex. This notion, which forms part of the law of engraphy, is one that very few investigators of Semon's time explicitly formulated. The notable exception is Hollingworth (1926, 1928) who in his various expositions of redintegration ascribed considerable mnemonic import to internally-generated stimuli. Research and theory explicitly concerned with the representation of internal stimuli in memory is still scant in modern times. Anderson and Bower (1973) specifically allowed for the representation of internally-generated stimuli in HAM, the mnemonic significance of inner or experiential contexts has been suggested by McGeoch (1939) and Reiff and Scheerer (1959), and experimental investigation of memory for internally-generated stimuli has recently been reported by Dosher and Russo (1976). It is clear, though, that serious research on this topic of concern to Semon is just getting under way.

Consider next Semon's position on internal stimuli as ecphoric cues: " . . . ecphory can arise without any recurrence of an original stimulus through the mere partial return of the inner energetic situation which was present at the formation of the engram-complex" (1923, p. 180). It is exceedingly difficult to find any experimental or theoretical work bearing on this issue in Semon's time; exceptions are found in Hollingworth (1926), and to some extent, in Ribot's (1882) book. Also, concern for the relation between internal states and memory was manifested in the clinical work of Freud (1913), Janet (1928), and Prince (1916); but the emphasis here was on exploiting the relation between internal states and mnemonic processes for therapeutic purposes rather than on developing a theoretical analysis of memory per se that would account for the ecphoric efficacy of internal states.

One particularly interesting manifestation of Semon's interest in internal states as ecphoric stimuli is his anticipation of modern research on state-dependent retrieval (Eich, 1977). Although one can spot the outlines of this anticipation in the quotation cited above, Semon developed this position far more explicitly, noting that " . . . in cases where the energetic condition has greatly changed . . . not even the recurrence of the original stimulus suffices for the ecphory of the corresponding engram" (1921, p. 144). This led Semon to suggest that, "Alcoholic intoxication may, under certain circumstances, create an energetic condition whose engrams are ecphorable in the next state of intoxication, but not in the intervening state of sobriety" (1921, p. 144). Semon followed this remarkably prescient statement with one that even modern students of state-dependence would have difficulty in addressing satisfactorily: "Only in cases where by virtue of the experience of years the engrams are deeply fixed and frequently ecphorized may we expect ecphory independent of abnormal or contrasting conditions" (p. 145). Does repetition attenuate state-dependent effects? Can we find evidence of state-dependence in semantic memory? Are frequently retrieved memories less susceptible to state-dependent effects than rarely retrieved memories? These issues, barely touched upon in present-day research, are intriguing and important questions about state-dependence that emerge directly from consideration of Semon's analysis.

Homophony, Repetition and Recognition

Earlier in the paper we briefly described Semon's conception of homophony as a resonance metaphor that Semon employed to describe the way in which information from different sources is combined. The following is a general characterization of homophony:

> At the ecphory of a combination of engrams . . . what is given is not a single indissoluble blend of mnemic excitations—"coalescence" some physiologists call it—but a unisonant chorus in which the single components of an apparently uniform combination of engrams, distinct indeed from each other as to their time of origin, may be individually discerned (1921, p. 165).

Semon emphasized that the contributors to homophony (be they original or mnemic sensations) run a "side-by-side" course and are superposed much in the manner of individual transparencies containing different information that are placed on top of each other. He went on to distinguish two subtypes of homophony, a "nondifferentiating" homophony, in which there is a combination of the components, and a "differentiating" homophony, which is " . . . always the result of an antagonism between two components or two groups of components" (1923, p. 248). Whether a differentiating or nondifferentiating homophony occurs depends largely on the conditions of ecphory.

In order to further clarify Semon's conception of homophony, let us briefly consider his use of the idea in an analysis of generic vs. temporally specific memory imagery. Semon argued that the ecphory of generic images (e.g., a particular house) occurs when " . . . all the engrams belonging to my view of the house are allowed to act homophonously" (1923, p. 277). However, with different retrieval demands, specific temporally dated images of the house may be ecphorized: "When I wish to ecphorize the images of this house I can do so by fixing my attention on a definite, temporally determined engram of the same . . . " (p. 276). Thus, the information from the individual engrams is combined via homophony; and whether or not homophonous resonance occurs depends on the intentions of the rememberer and the conditions of ecphory. It would be tempting to suggest that Semon was here anticipating the distinction between episodic and semantic memory (Tulving, 1972) as a utilization phenomenon; but since he did not explicitly discuss such a distinction, such a statement would probably reveal more about our own theoretical dispositions than about Semon's thoughts on the matter. In any case, Semon's conception of homophony, although admittedly somewhat vague, again reflects his intimate concern with the nature of retrieval processes, and stands out as a unique conception in its time. There are few ideas in the memory literature of his day that bear even the remotest resemblance to Semon's conception of homophony, as noted by Becher (1910) in a review of *Die mnemischen Emfindungen*; perhaps Selz's notion of "pattern completion" (Kintsch, 1974) or Loeb's idea of association by resonance (Loeb, 1901) are the closest. Also, the notion of homophony bears a strong resemblance to the resonance metaphors of retrieval recently adopted by Lockhart, Craik, and Jacoby (1976), Moeser (1977), and by Ratcliff (1978).

What is most interesting about Semon's conception of homophony is the use to which he put it in the analysis of various memory problems. Let us specifically consider Semon's position on the problem of repetition. The dominant theoretical approach to repetition effects during Semon's time was the *strengthening* view: Repetition exerts its beneficial effects on memory by strengthening the representation of the repeated item. This paradigmatic theory of repetition effects was stated clearly by Ebbinghaus: " . . . as the number of repetitions increases, the series are engraved more and more deeply and indelibly . . . " (1885, p. 53). In almost all studies of repetition during the time period we have considered, strengthening is assumed to be *the* mechanism of repetition effects. Of all the questions asked about repetition at the time [which include the problem of massed vs distributed repetitions (Browning, Brown, and Washburn, 1913; Perkins, 1914), rate of repetition (McGamble, 1916), and number of repetitions (Calkins, 1894)], questions and hypotheses concerning the *mechanism* of repetition effects are conspicuously absent. One exception to this prevailing trend is found in Ward's (1893) paper, in which he explicitly distinguished between "functional" (strengthening) and "atomistic" (multiple-trace) views of repetition in the context of a discussion concerning recognition and association. However, debate examining the relative merits of strengthening and multiple-trace points of view did not emerge in the subsequent experimental or theoretical literature.

It is against this background that we introduce Semon's theory of repetition effects: "Every repetition of a stimulus and, consequently, of an original excitation deposits a new engram which, if by nothing else, is distinguishable from all its predecessors by the important difference of its being an integral element of an engram-complex belonging to a new layer" (1923, p. 254). In contrast to the dominant strengthening theory of the time, Semon hypothesized a mechanism of repetition effects much closer to the recently advanced multiple-trace views of repetition (Bernbach, 1969; Bower, 1967; Hintzman & Block, 1971). Like Semon, these theorists have argued that each repetition of a stimulus creates a separate, unique memory trace. Recent critical reviews contrasting multiple-trace and strength theories have concluded that the bulk of the experimental evidence currently favors the multiple-trace hypothesis (Hintzman, 1976; Howell, 1973). However, while most modern multiple-trace theories suggest some sort of read-out of the number of stored traces as the vehicle of repetition effects, Semon had something quite different in mind. He ventured that although multiple traces are stored, the output from the memory system could be in the form of separate traces or of some amalgam of the separate traces via homophony, depending upon the conditions of retrieval. So while repetitive input to the memory system is always in the form of multiple traces, output varies, depending upon retrieval conditions and consequent homophony. Semon was quite explicit in juxtaposing his theory with the strength theory, noting that " . . . if the formation of an engram through excitation were a question of mere facilitation of channels, the repetition of an excitation would, at best, only enlarge the engram, but could not create a new, distinct, isolatedly ecphorable engram . . . " (1923, p. 255) and stating emphatically that:

REPETITION OF A STIMULUS DOES NOT STRENGTHEN AN ALREADY EXISTING ENGRAM, BUT GENERATES A NEW ENGRAM, AND THE MNEMIC EXCITATIONS RESULTING FROM ANY SUBSEQUENT ECPHORY ARE IN HOMOPHONY (1921, p. 169).

These statements leave little room for doubt about Semon's position on repetition effects; they also illustrate the functional use to which Semon put the concept of homophony.

In Semon's analysis of recognition, we find the notion of homophony being put to a slightly different use, and again encounter Semon's distaste for "strengthening" views of memory. By the time Semon published his two books, there already existed a substantial literature, both experimental and theoretical, on the problem of recognition (Woods, 1915).

Many different analyses of recognition had been put forward in this literature [Woods (1915) was able to distinguish between 13 theories] and debate among theorists of different persuasions often reached highly emotional levels. Among the popular theories of the time were notions that recognition depends upon the reactivation of images associated with the recognized object (Hollingworth, 1913; Lehmann, 1889): the theory that recognition is a subprocess of recall (Müller, 1913); the view that recognition results from a comparison of image and percept (Wolfe, 1886; Foucault, 1911); and the quite popular idea that recognition and the accompanying "feeling of familiarity" are caused by a facilitation in underlying neural processing when perceiving a stimulus for a second time (Allin, 1895; Dearborn, 1899; Höffding, 1893).

It was this last view that Semon emphatically disagreed with, and in contrast with which he developed his own theory of recognition, a *comparison theory* which relied heavily on the process of differentiating homophony.

Semon distinguished two kinds of recognition. Simple recognition of a previous event is " . . . the manifestation of differentiating homophony between an original and a mnemic sensation . . . " (1923, p. 283) and does not entail conscious awareness of the difference between the original and newly perceived stimuli. To the contrary, in recognition accompanied by the "sensation of difference" the differentiating homophony gives rise to a "differential of sensation" (that is, a discrepancy between original and reencountered stimuli that is large enough to be consciously perceived by the rememberer). Semon characterized both of these modes of recognition as products of "homophonous comparison." Consistent with his earlier position that new engrams are established by each ecphory, Semon posited that both kinds of recognition, which he viewed as subtypes of ecphory, deposit new engrams in the memory system.

Semon professed no special concern with the problem of recognition, commenting that " . . . it is interesting to us only as the manifestation of differentiating homophony and in its capacity of a differential of sensation" (1923, p. 288). Semon did make a special effort to criticize Höffding's (1893) theory that recognition results from the "greater ease" of neural transmission of a second encounter with a stimulus relative to the first, noting that this theory was in direct opposition to his own "homophonous comparison" view. In terms of modern theories of recognition, Semon's ideas seem close in spirit to those of modern researchers who posit a continuity between recognition and recall (Lockhart, Craik, & Jacoby, 1976, Tulving & Watkins, 1973). Semon, like these theorists, drew no sharp distinctions between recognition and other forms of ecphory. However, Semon did not offer specific comparisons of recognition and recall; hence we must be cautious in contrasting his ideas on this topic to modern theories.

Miscellaneous Phenomena

We have now presented the body of Richard Semon's theory of human memory. While there are numerous other points in Semon's work that we will not discuss, two ideas do merit at least some mention.

The first concerns Semon's analysis of "competition" between stimulus input and output from the memory store. Semon was interested in whether original and mnemic sensations are processed in the same channels or regions of sensation-fields. Semon based his discussion upon an analysis of binocular rivalry (that is, competition between two original sensations) and concluded that original and mnemic sensations do in fact compete with each other, and hence must share common mechanisms. Semon specified four consequences of such competition, but deferred their further discussion to future work:

> (1) Mnemic sensations already present lose in vividness; (2) or are extruded; (3) the ecphory of new sensations is hampered; (4) or altogether prevented according as other original or mnemic sensations are already present or simultaneously ecphorized (1923, p. 312).

Here again we find Semon concerned with a problem of little interest to his contemporaries. With the exception of Baxt's early work on masking effects (see Murray, 1976), there is little to be found in the literature of Semon's time concerning interference or competition between perceptual and mnemonic information. Several modern experimenters have investigated various aspects of this problem (e.g., Chow & Murdock, 1975; Doost & Turvey, 1971, Johnston, Griffith, & Wagstaff, 1972), but research on this topic is just getting under way.

The second idea, related to the first, is Semon's interest in serial vs. parallel processing in memory. Semon noted that the sort of competition between perceptual and mnemonic information he had previously discussed exemplified *spatial* interactions. He then initiated his analysis of serial vs. parallel processing by remarking that, "Instead of two simultaneous states of sensation, we are now dealing with two temporally parallel chains of sensation in competition . . ." (1923, p. 313). The issue of interest to Semon had to do with the question of what takes place when two engram-complexes are related equally to a particular ecphoric cue. In such cases, are the two candidate complexes retrieved in parallel, or only through "alternately ecphorizing," that is, serially processing the two complexes? In *The Mneme*, Semon concluded that in all such cases, serial processing is the rule; apparent parallel processing could be attributed to rapidly alternating ecphory. However, in *Mnemic Psychology*, Semon modified this position:

> It is not *altogether* impossible to produce side by side and simultaneously two manifestations of ecphorized verbal engrams and to let two series of such engrams run their course simultaneously side by side . . . side by sideness undoubtedly exists, if for a very short time, and therefore I have to abandon my first contention as to the impossibility of any simultaneous manifestation of two different chains of excitation ecphorized from verbal engrams (p. 315).

Here we find Semon clearly anticipating the issues arising from Sternberg's (1969) pacesetting work that initiated interest in serial vs. parallel processing in memory. This question was simply not part of memory research in Semon's day; but for Semon, interest in serial vs. parallel ecphory is just another manifestation of his theoretical concern with the process of retrieval.

FLAWS IN THE THEORY

We have now outlined Semon's theory of memory and have contrasted it with the theories of his time and with those of today. We have been impressed by Semon's original and incisive thinking and by the remarkable degree to which his various theoretical postulates accurately forecast many problems and theories of modern memory research. However, we do not wish to imply that Semon's theory was free of problems or inconsistencies: as with any psychological theory of his time, or of the present time, Semon's analysis was incomplete in several important respects.

The most conspicuous omission from Semon's theory is any attempt to specifically deal with the problem of *forgetting*; in fact, it is extremely difficult to find the word "forgetting" in either of Semon's books. A second problem, related to the first, is that Semon did not assign a functional role to interference phenomena in his account of memory. As mentioned earlier, he did offer some discussion of "competition" and interference as regards perceptual and mnemonic information: but he did not systematically integrate this into his theory of memory. Given his lack of concern with forgetting, it is hardly surprising that interference phenomena did not play a functional role in Semon's theory.

A third conspicuous gap in Semon's analysis is his failure to specify the role of attention in memory storage. Semon did attribute some importance to attentional processes occurring at *retrieval*, as noted several times, but he never considered its possible role as a determinant of memory storage. As it stands, Semon's theory suggests that *all* perceptual events are given permanent engraphic representation; there is no mechanism for emphasizing relevant and for ignoring irrelevant information at the time of study. The role of attention in memory had been given experimental and theoretical consideration in the years preceding Semon's work (e.g., Gordon, 1903): it is difficult to understand why he did not address this issue.

A final noticeable drawback of Semon's position is that it leaves little room for active encoding processes, that is, transforming and recoding of input. Semon's remembering organism is fundamentally a passive one, incapable of changing or directing the flow of information into the memory system. His theory would have great difficulty accounting for modern research on the coding and transformation of sensory input. Of course, almost every theory of his time would have an identical problem; but this is clearly one area in which Semon's work did not anticipate modern trends.

WHY IS SEMON'S WORK UNKNOWN TODAY?

In the light of the points made in the previous section, it would perhaps be easiest to answer the above question by simply noting that Semon's theory was clearly imperfect, and that its subsequent obscurity befits such a flawed theory. However, such a line of argument would not take us very far, since all other theories of memory put forward in the period we have considered had at least as many gaps as Semon's theory. Indeed, comprehensive theories of memory were conspicuously absent from the literature during the time that Semon wrote; it is no exaggeration to say that Semon's theory attempted to unify and explain more phenomena and problems than almost any other theory of his time. Why, then, has such a theory, so close in spirit to many modern positions, remained virtually unknown to contemporary researchers?

We will suggest four factors that may have contributed to the obscurity which characterized Semon's theory then and has continued to this day. First, consider the heavy emphasis placed on the conditions, functions, and processes of retrieval in Semon's theory. As noted earlier, there were few studies of retrieval in Semon's time compared to the large number of studies directed at other features of human memory. More important, the few studies of retrieval were divorced from any theoretical superstructure that would have accounted for retrieval phenomena in a systematic manner. With the exception of Selz and possibly Hollingworth, systematic theoretical concern for retrieval phenomena was rare in Semon's time. Why, then, *should* anyone have paid attention to Semon's views? Semon's problems and those of his contemporaries were very different; retrieval phenomena were of the greatest importance to Semon and of the least importance to his contemporaries. Toulmin (1961, p. 57) captured the essence of such a state of affairs in the domain of science:

> Men who accept different ideals and paradigms have really no common theoretical terms in which to discuss their problems. They will not even *have* the same problems: events which are "phenomena" in one man's eyes will be passed over by the other as "perfectly natural."

Given Semon's "aparadigmatic" stature with respect to the rest of the field, it is not surprising that his theories were never noticed and passed down to succeeding generations.

A second, and probably less important, factor contributing to Semon's obscurity is his invention of terminology. As discussed earlier, Semon created his own scientific terms in order to avoid the misleading connotations inherent in the everday language typically used to describe human memory. Others had commented on the problem (Bentley, 1899: Ebbinghaus, 1885: Hamilton, 1859), but only Semon did something about it. Unfortunately, his usage of admittedly strange terms such as "engraphy" and "ecphory," which led to potentially intimidating chapter titles such as "Ecphoric Quantivalence of Components" (1923, Chap. 11), may have served to create a barrier to the uninitiated reader. Additionally, it became easy to focus upon Semon's terminological creations rather than concentrating on the substance of his work. For instance, Campion and Smith (1934, p. 105) noted rather harshly that, "It is held by many that Semon's 'engrams' have no neurological significance and should be dismissed with others of the uncouth terms in which he enshrined his psychological tenets." Thus, in his quest for purity and precision of expression, Semon may have unwittingly contributed to the isolation of his own work.

A third and more important reason why Semon's theory of memory has not received its due acknowledgment is related to the memory-heredity issue mentioned earlier. Semon's Lamarckian views, and his thesis that the mechanisms of heredity and memory are identical, received considerable harsh criticism (e.g., Weismann, 1906). Consequently, his name became closely tied with the "wrong" views on the memory-heredity problem which lessened considerably the impact of his views on human memory in general. Numerous authors cite Semon for his ideas on heredity but nowhere mention the bulk of his theory of human memory; Brett (1921), Edgell (1924), Moore (1939), and Rignano (1926) exemplify this tendency.

A fourth factor that we propose to account for the lack of recognition of Semon's theory is that he provided no original experimental evidence to support his theory. Semon often cited the experimental literature of the time, and attempted to incorporate experimental findings into his analysis of various memory problems: he commented explicitly that " . . . the results of experimental psychology must be reckoned with" (1923, p. 57). However, Semon offered no original evidence other than his own introspection in support of his theory. Accordingly, one is in no way *driven* to agree with Semon or take his radical, strange-sounding notions very seriously at all.

These conjectures may or may not be valid; they are, admittedly, educated speculations. We also do not know if progress in memory research would have been accelerated had Semon's ideas been accepted in their time. But we do know that Semon's work on memory has been ignored for over half a century, and there must have been some reasons for it.

In her introduction to *Mnemic Psychology*, Vernon Lee lamented that Semon devoted so much of his time to the "hopeless" Lamarckian thesis, but expressed optimism concerning Semon's psychological theory of memory:

> The psychological part of his work remains, however highly elaborated, a fragment—a fragment, however, whose shape and substance are so suggestive that I cannot but think that a part of Semon's importance may consist in what will be added by others to the work he left unfinished (1923, p. 27).

It is perhaps sad that Semon's work never did exert the influence that Vernon Lee hoped it would. But it is ironic that modern students of memory have been concerned with so many of the issues dealt with in his theory without being aware of it. Sixty years after his death, Semon's rich theoretical constructs and novel conceptualizations not only deserve full recognition; they are also potential sources of insight to those of us who continue to be intrigued by the phenomena of memory that Richard Semon studied with such penetrating vision.

REFERENCES

Abbott, E. E. On the analysis of the factor of recall in the learning process. *Psychological Monographs*, 1909, *11*, 159–177.

Allin, A. The recognition theory of perception. *American Journal of Psychology*, 1895, *7*, 236–248.

Anderson, J. R., & Bower, G. H. *Human associative memory*. Washington, DC: Winston, 1973.

Atkinson, R. C., & Shiffrin, R. M. Human memory: A proposed system and its control processes. In K. W. Spence & J. T. Spence (Eds.), *The psychology of learning and motivation* (Vol. 2). New York: Academic Press, 1968.

Baddeley, A. D., & Hitch, G. Working memory. In G. H. Bower (Ed.), *The psychology of learning and motivation* (Vol. 8). New York: Academic Press, 1974.

Ballard, P. A. Obliviscence and reminiscence. *British Journal of Psychology Monograph Supplements*. 1913, *1*, 1–81.

Bartlett, F. C. An experiment upon repeated reproduction. *Journal of General Psychology*, 1928, *1*, 54–63.

Bartlett, F. C. *Remembering*. Cambridge: University Press, 1932.

Becher, E. Review of *Die mnemischen Empfindungen. Archiv für Gesamte Psychologie*, 1910, *17*, 165–172.

Bentley, I. M. The memory image and its qualitative fidelity. *American Journal of Psychology*, 1899, *11*, 1–48.

Bergson, H. *Matter and memory*. New York: The Macmillan Company, 1911.

Bernbach, H. A. Replication processes in human memory. In G. H. Bower & J. T. Spence (Eds.), *The psychology of learning and motivation* (Vol. 3). New York: Academic Press, 1969.

Binet, A., & Henri, V. La memoire de mots. *L'Annee Psychologique*, 1894, *1*, 1–23.

Boring, E. G. *Sensation and perception in the history of experimental psychology*. New York: Appleton Century Crofts, 1942.

Bousefield, W. R. *The basis of memory*. London: Kegan Paul, 1928.

Bower, G. H. A multicomponent theory of the memory trace. In K. W. Spence & J. T. Spence (Eds.), *The psychology of learning and motivation* (Vol. 1). New York: Academic Press, 1967.

Bransford, J. D., & Franks, J. J. The abstraction of linguistic ideas. *Cognitive Psychology*, 1971, *2*, 331–350.

Brett, G. S. *A history of psychology*. London: George Allen & Unwin, 1921.

Browning, M., Brown, D. E., & Washburn, M. F. The effect of the interval between repetitions on the speed of learning a series of movements. *American Journal of Psychology*, 1913, *24*, 580–583.

Burnham, W. H. Memory, historically and experimentally considered. *American Journal of Psychology*, 1888–9, *2*, 39–90; 225–270; 431–464; 568–622.

Calkins, M. W. Association. *Psychological Review*, 1894, *1*, 476–483.

Campion, G. G., & Smith, E. G. *The neural basis of thought*. London: Kegan Paul, 1934.

Carr, H. Length of time interval in successive association. *Psychological Review*, 1919, *26*, 335–353.

Chow, S. L.. & Murdock, B. B. The effect of a subsidiary task on iconic memory. *Memory and Cognition*, 1975, *3*, 678–688.

Crosland, H. A qualitative analysis of forgetting. *Psychological Monographs*, 1921, *29*, Whole No. 130.

Crovitz, H. F., & Schiffman, H. Frequency of episodic memories as a function of their age. *Bulletin of the Psychonomic Society*, 1974, *4*, 517–518.

Darley, C. F., & Murdock, B. B. Effects of prior free-recall testing on final recall and recognition. *Journal of Experimental Psychology*, 1971, *91*, 66–73.

Dearborn, G. V. Recognition under objective rehearsal. *Psychological Review*, 1899, *6*, 395–406.

Doost, R., & Turvery, M. I. Iconic memory and central processing capacity. *Perception and Psychophysics*, 1971, *9*, 269–274.

Dosher, B. A., & Russo, J. E. Memory for internally generated stimuli. *Journal of Experimental Psychology: Human Learning and Memory*, 1976, *2*, 633–640.

Ebbinghaus, H. *Über das Gedächtnis*. Leipzig: Duncker & Humblot. 1885. (English translation. Dover Press, 1964).

Edgell, B. *Theories of memory*. Oxford: Clarendon Press, 1924.

Eich, J. E. State-dependent retrieval of information in human episodic memory. In I. M. Birnbaum & E. S. Parker (Eds.), *Alcohol and human memory*. Hillsdale, N.J.: Lawrence Erlbaum Associates, 1977.

Foucault, M. Etude expérimentale sur l'association de resemblance. *Archives de Psychologie*, 1911, *10*, 338–360.

Frederiksen, C. H. Acquisition of semantic information from discourse: Effects of repeated exposures. *Journal of Verbal Learning and Verbal Behavior*, 1975, *14*, 158–169.

Freud, S. *The interpretation of dreams*. London: George Allen & Unwin, 1913.

Froeberg, S. Simultaneous versus successive association. *Psychological Review*, 1918, *25*, 156–163.

Galton, F. Psychometric experiments. *Brain*, 1879, *2*, 148–162.

Gardiner, J. M., & Klee, H. Memory for remembered events: An assessment of output monitoring in free recall. *Journal of Verbal Learning and Verbal Behavior*, 1976, *15*, 227–234.

Gibson, J. J. The reproduction of visually perceived forms. *Journal of Experimental Psychology*, 1929, *12*, 1–39

Gordon, K. Meaning in memory and attention. *Psychological Review*, 1903, *10*, 267–283.

Guenther, R. K., & Linton, M. Mechanisms of temporal coding. *Journal of Experimental Psychology: Human Learning and Memory*, 1975, *1*, 182–187.

Hamilton, W. *Lectures on metaphysics and logic*. Edinburgh: William Blackwood & Sons, 1859.

Hawkins, C. J. Experiments on memory types. *Psychological Review*, 1897, *4*, 289–294.

Hintzman, D. L. Repetition in memory. In G. H. Bower (Ed.), *The psychology of learning and motivation* (Vol. 10). New York: Academic Press, 1976.

Hintzman, D. L., & Block, R. A. Repetition in memory: Evidence for a multiple-trace hypothesis. *Journal of Experimental Psychol-*

ogy, 1971, *88,* 297–306.

Höffding, H. *Outlines of psychology.* London: Macmillan. 1891.

Höffding, H. Zur Theorie des Wiedererkennens. *Philosophische Studien,* 1893, *8,* 86–96.

Hollingworth, H. L. Characteristic differences between recall and recognition. *American Journal of Psychology,* 1913, *24,* 532–544.

Hollingworth, H. L. *The psychology of thought.* New York: Appleton & Co., 1926.

Hollingworth, H. L. General laws of redintegration. *Journal of General Psychology,* 1928, *1,* 79–90.

Horowitz, L. M.. & Prytulak, L. S. Redintegrative memory. *Psychological Review,* 1969, 76, 519–531.

Howell, W. C. Representation of frequency in memory. *Psychological Bulletin,* 1973, *80,* 44–53.

Izawa, A. C. Comparison of reinforcement and test trials in paired-associate learning. *Journal of Experimental Psychology,* 1969, *81,* 600–603.

James, W. *Principles of Psychology.* New York: Henry Holt, 1890.

Janet, P. *L'evolution de la mémoire et de la notion du temps.* Paris: Chahine, 1928.

Johnston, W. A., Griffith, D., & Wagstaff, R. R. Speed, accuracy, and ease of recall. *Journal of Verbal Learning and Verbal Behavior,* 1972, *11,* 512–520.

Jones, G. V. A fragmentation hypothesis of memory: Cued recall of pictures and of sequential position. *Journal of Experimental Psychology: General,* 1976, *105,* 277–293.

Kennedy, F. On the experimental investigation of memory. *Psychological Review,* 1898, *5,* 477–499.

Kintsch, W. *The representation of meaning in memory.* Hillsdale. NJ: Lawrence Erlbaum Associates, 1974.

Klee, H., & Gardiner, J. M. Memory for remembered events: Contrasting recall and recognition. *Journal of Verbal Learning and Verbal Behavior,* 1976, *15,* 471–478.

Köhler, W. *Gestalt psychology.* London: G. Bell & Sons, 1930.

Koffka, K. *Principles of gestalt psychology.* New York: Harcourt, Brace, & Co., 1935.

Kostyleff, N. *Review of Die Mneme. Review Philosophique,* 1911, *71,* 749–753.

Kroll, N. E. A., Parks, T., Parkinson, S. R., Bieber, S. L., & Johnson, A. L. Short-term memory while shadowing: Recall of visually and of aurally presented letters. *Journal of Experimental Psychology,* 1970, *85,* 220–224.

Kuhlmann, F. On the analysis of the memory consciousness: A study in the mental imagery and memory of meaningless visual forms. *Psychological Review,* 1906, *13,* 316–348.

Kuhlmann, F. The present statues of memory investigation. *Psychological Bulletin,* 1908, *5,* 285–293.

Külpe, O. *Outlines of psychology.* New York: Macmillan, 1895.

Laird, D. A., Remmers, H., & Peterson, L. J. An experimental study of the influences of organization of material for memorizing upon its retention. *Journal of Experimental Psychology,* 1923, *6,* 69–81.

Landauer, T. K. Memory without organization: Properties of a model with random storage and undirected retrieval. *Cognitive Psychology,* 1975, 7, 495–531.

Lashley, K. S. In search of the engram. In F. A. Beach, D. O. Hebb, C. T. Morgan, & H. W. Nissen (Eds.), *The neuropsychology of Lashley.* New York: McGraw-Hill, 1960.

Lee, V. Introduction. Being notes on some applications of *mnemic* principle in recent psychological literature. In R. Semon, *Mnemic psychology.* London: George Allen & Unwin, 1923.

Lehmann, A. Über Wiedererkennen. *Philosophische Studien,* 1889, *5,* 96–156.

Lockhart, R. S., Craik, F. I. M., & Jacoby, L. Depth of processing, recognition, and recall. In J. Brown (Ed.), *Recall and recognition.* London: Wiley, 1976.

Loeb, J. *Comparative physiology of the brain and comparative psychology.* London: John Murray, 1901.

Loftus, E. F., Miller, D. G., & Burns, H. J. Semantic integration of verbal information into a visual memory. *Journal of Experimental Psychology: Human Learning and Memory,* 1978, *4,* 19–31.

Luh, C. W. The conditions of retention. *Psychological Monographs,* 1922, *31,* Whole No. 142.

Luria, A. R. *The working brain.* London: Penguin, 1973.

McDougall, W. *Body and mind.* London: Methuen, 1911.

Mach, E. *The analysis of sensations.* New York: Dover, 1959.

McGamble, E. A. Rate of repetition and tenacity of impression. *Psychological Monographs,* 1916, *22,* 101–151.

McGeoch, J. A. Memory. *Psychological Bulletin,* 1928, *5,* 513–549.

McGeoch, J. A. Memory. *Psychological Bulletin,* 1930, *27,* 514–563.

McGeoch, J. A. The psychology of human learning: A bibliography. *Psychological Bulletin,* 1933, *30,* 1–62.

McGeoch, J. A. Learning. In E. G. Boring, H. S. Langfeld, & H. P. Weld (Eds.), *Introduction to psychology.* New York: Wiley, 1939.

Meumann, E. *The psychology of learning.* New York: Appleton Company, 1913.

Modigliani, V. Effects on a later recall by delaying initial recall. *Journal of Experimental Psychology: Human Learning and Memory,* 1976, *2,* 609–622.

Moeser, S. D. Recognition processes in episodic memory. *Canadian Journal of Psychology,* 1977, *31,* 41–70.

Moore, T. V. *Cognitive psychology.* New York: Lippincott, 1939.

Müller, G. E. Zur Analyse der Gedächtnistätigkeit und des Vorstellungsverlaufes. III. Teil. *Zeitschrift für Psychologie, Ergänzungsband,* 1913, *8,* 1–567.

Müller, G. E., & Pilzecker, A. Experimentelle Beiträge zur Lehre vom Gedächtnis. *Zeitschrift für Psychologie, Ergänzungsband,* 1900, *1,* 1–300.

Müller, G. E., & Schumann, F. Experimentelle Beiträge zur Untersuchung des Gedächtnisses. *Zeitschrift für Psychologie,* 1894, *6,* 81–190.

Murdock, B. B., Jr. *Human memory: Theory and data.* Potomac, Md: Lawrence Erlbaum Associates, 1974.

Murray, D. J. Research on human memory in the nineteenth century. *Canadian Journal of Psychology,* 1976, *30,* 201–220.

Myers, A. G., & Myers, E. C. Reconstructive recall. *American Journal of Psychology,* 1916, *27,* 493–506.

Perkins, N. L. The value of distributed repetitions in rote learning. *British Journal of Psychology,* 1914, *7,* 253–261.

Prince, M. *The unconscious.* New York: Macmillan, 1916.

Raffel, G. The effect of recall on forgetting. *Journal of Experimental Psychology,* 1934, *17,* 828–838.

Ratcliff, R. A theory of memory retrieval. *Psychological Review,* 1978, *85,* 59–108.

Reiff, R., & Scheerer, M. *Memory and hypnotic age regression.* New York: International Universities Press. 1959.

Ribot, T. *Diseases of memory.* New York: Appleton, 1882.

Rignano, E. *Biological memory.* New York: Harcourt, Brace, & Co., 1926.

Robinson, E. S. Memory. *Psychological Bulletin,* 1924, *21,* 569–594.

Robinson, E. S. *Association theory to-day.* New York: Century, 1932.

Roediger, H. L. Inhibiting effects of recall. *Memory & Cognition,* 1974, *2,* 261–269.

Rundus, D. Negative effects of using list items as recall cues. *Journal of Verbal Learning and Verbal Behavior,* 1973, *12,* 43–50.

Russell, B. *The analysis of mind.* London: George Allen & Unwin, 1921.

Schrödinger, E. *My view of the world.* Cambridge: Cambridge University Press, 1964.

Selz, O. *Über die Gesetze des geordneten Denkverlaufs.* Stuttgart: Spemann, 1913.

Selz, O. *Zur Psychologie des producktiven Denkens und des Irrtums.* Bonn: Cohen, 1922.

Semon, R. *In the Australian bush and on the coast of the Coral Sea.* London: Macmillan, 1899.

Semon, R. *Die Mneme als erhaltendes Prinzip im Wechsel des organischen Geschehens.* Leipzig: Wilhelm Engelmann, 1904.

Semon, R. *Die mnemischen Empfindungen.* Leipzig: Wilhelm Engelmann, 1909.

Semon, R. *The mneme.* London: George Allen & Unwin, 1921.

Semon, R. *The mneme.* London: George Allen & Unwin, 1923.

Sternberg, S. Memory scanning: Mental processes revealed by reaction-time experiments. *American Scientist,* 1969, *57,* 421–457.

Thorndike, E. L. *The elements of psychology.* New York: A. G. Seller, 1913.

Titchener, E. B. *A text-book of psychology.* New York: Macmillan, 1911.

Toulmin, S. *Foresight and understanding.* New York: Harper & Row, 1961.

Trow, W. C. Recall vs. repetition in the learning of rote and meaningful material. *American Journal of Psychology,* 1928, *40,* 112–116.

Tulving, E. The effects of presentation and

recall of material in free-recall learning. *Journal of Verbal Learning and Verbal Behavior,* 1967, *6,* 175–184.

Tulving, E. Episodic and semantic memory. In E. Tulving & W. Donaldson (Eds.), *Organization of memory.* New York: Academic Press, 1972.

Tulving, E. Ecphoric processes in recall and recognition. In J. Brown (Ed.), *Recall and recognition.* London: Wiley, 1976.

Tulving, E., & Thomson, D. M. Encoding specificity and retrieval processes in episodic memory. *Psychological Review,* 1973, *80,* 352–373.

Tulving, E., & Watkins, M. J. Continuity between recognition and recall. *American Journal of Psychology,* 1973, *86,* 739–748.

Underwood, B. J. False recognition produced by implicit verbal responses. *Journal of Experimental Psychology,* 1965, *70,* 122–129.

Underwood, B. J. Attributes of memory. *Psychological Review,* 1969, *76,* 559–573.

Underwood, B. J. *Temporal codes for memories.* Hillsdale, NJ: Lawrence Erlbaum Associates, 1977.

Ward, J. Assimilation and association. *Mind,* 1893, *3,* 347–362.

Warren, H. C. *History of the association psychology.* London: Constable & Co., 1921.

Weismann, A. Semon's "Mneme" und die "Verebung erworbener Eigenschaften." *Archiv für Rassen- und Gesellschafts biologie,* 1906, *3,* 1–27.

Whitely, P. L., & McGeoch, J. A. The effect of one form of report upon another. *American Journal of Psychology,* 1927, *38,* 280–284.

Wohlgemuth, A. Simultaneous and successive association. *British Journal of Psychology,* 1915, *7,* 434–452.

Wolfe, H. K. Untersuchungen über das Tongedächtnis. *Philosophiche Studien,* 1886, *3,* 534–571.

Woods, E. L. An experimental analysis of the process of recognizing. *American Journal of Psychology,* 1915, *26,* 313–387.

Wundt, W. *Outlines of psychology.* Leipzig: Wilhelm Engelmann, 1902.

Young, J. Z. The organization of a memory system. *Proceedings of the Royal Society of London,* 1965, *163,* 285–320.

References

Aall, A. Zur Frage der Hemmung bei der Auffassung gleicher Reize. *Zeitschrift für Psychologie,* 1908, *47,* 1–114.

Aall, A. Ein neues Gedächtnisgesetz. *Zeitschrift für Psychologie,* 1913, *66,* 1–50.

Abbott, E. On the analysis of the factor of recall in the learning process. *Psychological Monographs,* 1909, *11,* 159–177.

Abrahamsen, D. *The mind and death of a genius.* New York: Columbia University Press, 1946.

Allin, A. Recognition. *American Journal of Psychology,* 1896, *7,* 249–273.

Alsberg, M. *Die Grundlagen des Gedächtnisses, der Vererbung und der Instinkte.* Munich: E. Reinhardt, 1906.

Anderson, J. R., & Bower, G. H. *Human associative memory.* Hillsdale, N.J.: Lawrence Erlbaum Associates, 1979. Originally published, 1973.

Baddeley, A. *The psychology of memory.* New York: Basic Books, 1976.

Bain, A. *The senses and the intellect.* London: Parker, 1855.

Bain, A. On 'association' controversies. *Mind,* 1887, *12,* 161–182.

Baird, J. Memory. *Psychological Bulletin,* 1911, *8,* 243–253.

Balaban, A. Über den Unterschied des logischen und des mechanischen Gedächtnisses. *Zeitschrift für Psychologie,* 1910, *56,* 356–377.

Baldwin, J. M., & Shaw, W. J. Memory for square size. *Psychological Review,* 1895, *2,* 236–239.

Balfour, M. *The kaiser and his times.* Great Britain: Pelican Books, 1975.

Barber, B. Resistance by scientists to scientific discovery. *Science,* 1961, *134,* 596–602.

Barclay, J. R., Bransford, J. D., Franks, J. J., McCarrell, N. S., & Nitsch, K. Comprehension and semantic flexibility. *Journal of Verbal Learning and Verbal Behavior,* 1974, *13,* 471–481.

Barlow, W. (Ed.). *The autobiography of Charles Darwin.* New York: W. W. Norton, 1958.

Barnes, S. R. *Sociology of science.* London: Penguin, 1972.

Barnett, M. Sadi Carnot and the second law of thermodynamics. *Osiris,* 1958, *13,* 327-357.

Barrett, C. *An Australian animal book.* Melbourne: Geoffrey Cumberlege, 1947.

Bartlett, F. C. *Remembering.* Cambridge: Cambridge University Press, 1932.

Bartlett, J. C. Effects of immediate testing on delayed retrieval: Search and recovery operations with four types of cue. *Journal of Experimental Psychology: Human Learning and Memory,* 1977, *3,* 719–732.

Barzun, J. *Darwin, Marx, Wagner. Critique of a heritage.* New York: Doubleday & Co., 1958.

Bateson, W. Heredity and variation in modern lights. In A. C. Seward (Ed.), *Darwin and modern science.* Cambridge: University Press, 1910.

Bateson, W. *Problems of genetics.* New Haven: Yale University Press, 1913.

Baxter, M. F., Yamada, K., & Washburn, M. F. Directed recall of pleasant and unpleasant experiences. *American Journal of Psychology*, 1917, *28*, 155–157.

Bean, C. H. The curve of forgetting. *Archives of Psychology*, 1912, *3*, No, 21.

Becher, E. Review of *Die mnemischen Empfindungen*. *Archiv für die Gesamte Psychologie,* 1910, *17*, 165–172.

Bell, E. T. *Men of mathematics.* London: Victor Gollancz, 1937.

Ben-David, J., & Collins, R. Social factors in the origin of a new science: the case of psychology. *American Sociological Review*, 1966, *31*, 451–465.

Berg, E. J. *Heaviside's operational calculus.* New York: McGraw-Hill, 1936.

Bergson, H. *Matter and memory.* New York: Macmillan, 1911.

Bergstrom, J. A. Experiments upon physiological memory by means of the interference of associations. *American Journal of Psychology*, 1893, 5, 356–369.

Bergstrom, J. A. The relation of the interference to the practice effect of an association. *American Journal of Psychology*, 1894, *6*, 433–442.

Bernbach, H. A. Replication processes in human memory. In G. H. Bower & J. T. Spence (Eds.), *The psychology of learning and motivation* (Vol. 3). New York: Academic Press, 1969.

Biddiss, M. *The age of the masses.* Great Britain: Penguin Books, 1977.

Binet, A., & Henri, V. La memoire des mots. *Année Psychologique*, 1894, *1*, 1–23.

Binswanger, L. *Sigmund Freud; reminiscences of a friendship.* New York: Grune & Stratton, 1957.

Birkhoff, G. Galois and group theory. *Osiris*, 1937, *3*, 260–268.

Blüh, O. The value of inspiration. *Isis*, 1952, *43*, 211–220.

Boadella, D. *Wilhelm Reich: The evolution of his work.* London: Vision Press, 1973.

Boadella, D. (Ed.). *In the wake of Reich.* London: Coventure Ltd., 1976.

Bölsche, W. *Haeckel: His life and work.* (J. McCabe, trans.). London: T. Fisher Unwin, 1906.

Bolton, T. L. The growth of memory in school children. *American Journal of Psychology*, 1892, *4*, 362–380.

Boltzmann, L. The recent development of method in theoretical physics. *The Monist,* 1901, *11*, 226–257.

Boltzmann, L. *Theoretical physics and philosophical problems* (B. McGuiness, Ed.). Boston: D. Reidel, 1974.

Boring, E. G. *A history of experimental psychology.* New York: The Century Co., 1929.

Bower, G. H. A multicomponent theory of the memory trace. In K. W. Spence & J. T. Spence (Eds.), *The psychology of learning and motivation.* New York: Academic Press, 1967.

Brannigan, A. The reification of Mendel. *Social Studies of Science*, 1979, *9*, 423–454.

Bransford, J. D., & Franks, J. J. The abstraction of linguistic ideas. *Cognitive Psychology*, 1971, *2*, 331–350.

Broda, E. *Ludwig Boltzmann.* Vienna: Franz Deuticke, 1955.

Brome, V. *Freud and his early circle.* New York: William Morrow, 1967.

Broughton, M. M., & Freeman-Moir, D. J. (Eds.), *The cognitive-developmental psychology of James Mark Baldwin.* Norwood, N.J.: Ablex, 1981.

Brown, T. *Lectures of the philosophy of the human mind.* Edinburgh: Tait and Longman, 1820.

Browning, M., Brown, D. E., & Washburn, M. F. The effect of the interval between repetitions on the speed of learning on a series of movements. *American Journal of Psychology*, 1913, *24*, 580–583.

Brush, S. G. The development of the kinetic theory of gases. II. Waterston. *Annals of Science*, 1957, *13*, 273–282.

Brush, S. G. John James Waterston and the kinetic theory of gases. *American Scientist*, 1961, *49*, 202–214.

Brush, S. G. (Ed.). *Lectures on gas theory.* Berkeley: University of California Press, 1964.

Burkhardt, R. W., Jr. *The spirit of system.* Cambridge: Harvard University Press, 1977.

Butler, H. The development of mammalian dural venous sinuses with especial reference to the post-glenoid vein. *Journal of Anatomy*, 1967, *102*, 33–56.

Butler, S. *Evolution, old and new.* London: Hardwicke and Bogue, 1879.

Butler, S. *Life and habit.* London: A. C. Fifield, 1910.

Calkins, M. W. Association. *Psychological Review*, 1896, *3*, 32–49.

Campion, G. G., & Smith E. G. *The neural basis of thought.* London: Routledge and Kegan Paul, 1934.

Cannan, G. *Samuel Butler; a critical study.* London: Martin Secker, 1915.

Challey, J. G. Nicholas Leonard Sadi Carnot. In P. Cahanis & H. von Dechen (Eds.), *Dictionary of scientific biography* (Vol. 3). New York: Charles Scribner's Sons, 1971.

Claparède, E. La question de la memoire affective. *Archives de Psychologie*, 1911, *10*, 361–377.

Clark, R. W. *Einstein. The life and times.* New York: Avon Books, 1971.

Clerf, L. H., & Baltzell, W. H. Re-evaluation of Semon's hypothesis. *Laryngoscope*, 1953, *63*, 693–699.

Cohen, I. D. *The Newtonian revolution.* Cambridge: Cambridge University Press, 1980.

Cohn, J. Experimentelle Untersuchungen über das Zusammenwirken des akustischmotorischen und des visuellen Gedächtnisses. *Zeitschrift für Psychologie*, 1897, *15*, 161–183.

Conrad, H. E., & Arps, G. F. An experimental study of economical learning. *American Journal of Psychology*, 1916, *27*, 507–529.

Cole, J. R., & Cole, S. *Social stratification in science.* Chicago: University of Chicago Press, 1973.

Cole, S. Professional standing and the reception of scientific discoveries. *American Sociological Review*, 1970, *76*, 286–306.

Coley, N. G. The physico-chemical studies of Amedeo Avogadro. *Annals of Science*, 1964, *20*, 195–210.

Conklin, E. G. *Heredity and environment.* Princeton: University Press, 1915.

Cope, E. D. *The origin of the fittest.* New York: D. Appleton and Co., 1887.

Cope, E. D. On inheritance in evolution. *American Naturalist*, 1889, *23*, 1058–1071.

Cope, E. D. *Primary factors of organic evolution.* Chicago: Open Court Publishing, 1904.

Coper, R. *Failure of a revolution.* Cambridge: Cambridge University Press, 1955.

Coulson, T. *Joseph Henry.* Princeton: Princeton University Press, 1950.

Craig, G. A. *Germany. 1866–1945.* New York: Oxford University Press, 1978.

Crosland, H. A. A qualitative analysis of forgetting. *Psychological Monographs*, 1921, *29* (Whole No. 130).

Crosland, M. P. Amedeo Avogadro. In C. C. Gillispie (Ed.), *Dictionary of scientific biography* (Vol. I). New York: Charles Scribner's Sons, 1970.

Crovitz, H. F. *Galton's walk.* New York: Harper & Row, 1970.

Crowder, R. G. *Principles of learning and memory.* Hillsdale, N.J.: Lawrence Erlbaum Associates, 1976.

Dallenbach, K. M. The relation of memory error to time interval. *Psychological Review*, 1913, *20*, 323–337.

Dana, C. L. The study of a case of amnesia or double consciousness. *Psychological Review*, 1894, *1*, 570–580.

Darley, C. F., & Murdock, B. B. Effects of prior free-recall testing on final recall and recognition. *Journal of Experimental Psychology*, 1971, *91*, 66–73.

Darwin, C. *The variation of animals and plants under domestication* (Vol. II). New York: Appleton and Co., 1897.

Darwin, F. *The life and letters of Charles Darwin* (Vol. 1). New York: Appleton, 1908.

Darwin, F. Presidential Address. *Report of the British Association for the Advancement of Science, Sept. 1908, Dublin.* London: John Murray, 1909.

Dawidowicz, L. *The war against the Jews 1933–1945.* Great Britain: Penguin Books, 1977.

De Camp, J. E. A study of retroactive inhibition. *Psychological Monographs*, 1915, *19* (Whole No. 84).

Decker, H. S. *Freud in Germany.* New York: International Universities Press, 1977.

Deffner, K. Die Aehnlichkeitsassociation. *Zeitschrift für Psychologie*, 1898, *18*, 218–249.

DeGrazia, A. *The Velikovsky affair.* New York: University Books, 1966.

DeGroot, A. *Thought and choice in chess.* The Hague: Mouton, 1965.

DéLage, Y. Review of Die Mneme. *L'Année Biologique*, 1904, *9*, 479–482.

DéLage, Y., & Goldsmith, M. *The theories of evolution.* New York: B. W. Huebsch, 1913.

Dendy, A. *Outlines of evolutionary biology.* London: Constable & Co., 1938.

Detto, C. Über den Begriff des Gedächtnisses in seiner Bedeutung für die Biologie. *Naturwissenschaftliche Wochenschrift*, 1905, *4*, 657–667.

Dolby, R. G. A. What can we usefully learn from the Velikovsky affair? *Social Studies of Science*, 1975, *5*, 164–175.

Donaldson, W., & Bass, M. Relational information and memory for problem solutions.

Journal of Verbal Learning and Verbal Behavior, 1980, *4*, 592–604.

Dosher, B. A., & Russo, J. E. Memory for internally generated stimuli. *Journal of Experimental Psychology: Human Learning and Memory*, 1976, *2*, 633–640.

Dowd, D. A. The carotid body-carotid sinus complex in monotremes. *Acta Anatomica*, 1966, *65*, 353–380.

Driesch, H. *The science and philosophy of the organism*. Aberdeen: University Press, 1908.

Dulsky, S. G. The effect of a change of background on recall and relearning. *Journal of Experimental Psychology*, 1935, *18*, 725–740.

DuMont, C. De la ressemblance et de la contiguité dans l'association des idées. *Revue de Metaphysique et de Morale*, 1895, *3*, 285–307.

Duncan, S. S. The isolation of scientific discovery: indifference and resistance to a new idea. *Science Studies*, 1974, *4*, 109–134.

Dunn, L. C. *A short history of genetics*. New York: McGraw-Hill, 1965.

Ebbinghaus, H. *Über das Gedächtnis*. Leipzig: Duncker & Humblut, 1885 (English translation, Dover Press, 1964).

Ebbinghaus, H. *Psychology*. Boston: D. C. Heath, 1908.

Ebert, E., & Meumann, E. Über einige Grundfragen der Psychologie der Übungsphänomene im Bereiche des Gedächtnisses. *Archiv für die Gesamte Psychologie*, 1904, *4*, 1–232.

Eich, J. E. The cue-dependent nature of state-dependent retrieval. *Memory and Cognition*, 1980, *8*, 157-173.

Eichhorn, G. *Vererbung, Gedächtnis und transzendentale Erinnerungen vom Standpunkte des Physikers*. Stuttgart: Julius Hoffmann, 1909.

Eiduson, B. T. *Scientists: Their psychological world*. New York: Basic Books, 1962.

Eimer, G. H. T. *Organic evolution* (J. T. Cunningham, trans.). London: Macmillan and Co., 1890.

Eisley, L. *Darwin's century*. New York: Doubleday, 1961.

Ellenberger, H. F. *The discovery of the unconscious*. New York: Basic Books, 1970.

Ephrussi, P. Experimentelle Beiträge zur Lehre vom Gedächtnis. *Zeitschrift für Psychologie*, 1905, 37, 56–103.

Esper, E. Max Meyer: The making of a scientific isolate. *Journal of the History of the Behavioral Sciences*, 1966, *2*, 341–356.

Esper, E. A. Max Meyer in America. *Journal of the History of the Behavioral Sciences*, 1967, *3*, 107–131.

Fabre, A. *The life of Jean Henri Fabre*. New York: Dodd, Mead & Co., 1921.

Feingold, G. A. Recognition and discrimination. *Psychological Monographs*, 1915, *18* (Whole No. 78).

Feuchtwanger, E. J. *Prussia: Myth and reality*. London: Oswald Wolff, 1970.

Feuer, L. *Einstein and the generations of science*. New York: Basic Books, 1974.

Finkenbinder, E. O. The curve of forgetting. *American Journal of Psychology*, 1913, *24*, 8–32.

Fisher, R. P., & Craik, F. I. M. Interaction between encoding and retrieval operations in cued recall. *Journal of Experimenral Psychology: Human Learning and Memory*, 1977, *3*, 701–711.

Flexser, A. J., & Tulving, E. Retrieval independence in recognition and recall. *Psychological Review*, 1978, 85, 153–171.

Forbes, E. G. Tobias Mayer (1723–62): A case of forgotten genius. *British Journal for the History of Science*, 1970, 5, 1–20.

Forel, A. *Das Gedächtniss und seine Abnormitäten*. Zurich: Orell Füssli, 1885.

Forel, A. *Ants and some other insects*. Chicago: Open Court, 1904.

Forel, A. Richard Semons *Mneme als erhaltendes Prinzip im Wechsel des organischen Geschehens*. *Archiv für Rassen-und Gesellschafts-Biologie*, 1905, *2*, 169–197.

Forel, A. *Hygiene of nerves and mind in health and disease*. London: John Murray, 1907.

Forel, A. *The sense of insects*. London: Methuen 1908.

Forel, A. Richard Semon's Weiterentwicklung seiner Theorie über die Mneme. *Archiv für Rassen-und Gesellschafts-Biologie*, 1910, 7, 11–34.

Forel, A. *Der hypnotismus*. Stuttgart: Enke, 1918.

Forel, A. H. *Out of my life and work*. New York: W. W. Norton, 1937.

Fothergill, P. G. *Historical aspects of organic evolution*. London: Hollis and Carter, 1952.

Frankfurter, W., & Thiele, R. Über den Zusammenhang zwischen Vorstellungstypus und sensorischer Lernweise. *Zeitschrift für Psychologie*, 1912, *62*, 96–131.

Franz, V. Review of *Die Mneme. Zeitschrift für Psychologie*, 1909, *54*, 227–231.

Frederiksen, C. H. Acquisition of semantic information from discourse: effect of repeated exposures. *Journal of Verbal Learning and Verbal Behavior*, 1975, *14*, 158–169.

Freud, E. (Ed). *Letters of Sigmund Freud*. New York: Basic Books, 1960.

Freud, S. *The origins of psycho-analysis: Letters to Wilhelm Fliess*. M. Bonaparte, A. Freud, & E. Kris (Eds.). London: Imago, 1954.

Freud, S. The psychopathology of everyday life. In J. Strachey (ed.), *The standard edition of the complete psychological works of Sigmund Freud*. London: The Hogarth Press, 1960.

Freud, S. *The history of the psychoanalytic movement*. New York: Collier Books, 1963.

Freud, S. Review of August Forel's *Hypnotism* (1889). In J. Strachey (Ed.), *The standard edition of the complete psychological works of Sigmund Freud* (Vol. I). London: The Hogarth Press, 1966.

Frings, B. Über den Einfluss der Komplexbildung auf die effektuelle und generative Hemmung. *Archiv für die Gesamte Psychologie*, 1914, *30*, 415–479.

Fromm, E. *Sigmund Freud's mission*. New York: Harper and Row, 1959.

Führinger, M. Schlussübersicht über den gesamten Inhalt von Professor Semons Zoologischen Forschungsreisen. In R. W. Semon, *Zoologische Forschungen in Australien und dem maylischen Archipel*. Jena: G. Fischer, 1913.

Gardiner, J. M., & Klee, H. Memory for remembered events: An assessment of output monitoring in free recall. *Journal of Verbal Learning and Verbal Behavior*, 1976, *15*, 227–234.

Gardner, M. The hermit scientist. *Antioch Review*, 1950, *10*, 447–457.

Gardner, M. *Fads and fallacies in the name of science*. New York: Dover, 1957.

Gardner, M. Quantum theory and quack theory. *New York Review of Books*, May 17, 1979, 39–41.

Gasking, E. Why was Mendel's work ignored? *Journal of the History of Ideas*, 1959, *20*, 60–84.

Gasman, D. *The scientific origins of national socialism: Social Darwinism in Ernst Haeckel and the German Monist League*. London: Macdonald, 1971.

Gates, A. I. Recitation as a factor in memorizing. *Archives of Psychology*, 1917, *6*, No. 40.

Gay, P. *Freud, Jews, and other Germans*. New York: Oxford University Press, 1978.

Glaser, B. G. *Organizational scientists*. New York: Bobbs-Merrill, 1964.

Glass, B. The long neglect of a scientific discovery: Mendel's laws of inheritance. In *Studies in intellectual history*. Maryland: Johns Hopkins University Press, 1953.

Goblet, E. Sur la theorie physiologique de l'association. *Revue Philosophique*, 1898, *46*, 487–503.

Gode-Von Asch, A. G. F. *Natural science in German romanticism*. New York: Columbia University Press, 1941.

Gomulicki, B. R. The development and present status of the trace theory of memory. *British Journal of Psychology Monograph Supplements*, 1953, *29*.

Gordon, K. Meaning in memory and attention. *Psychological Review*, 1903, *10*, 267–283.

Gorczynski, R. M., & Steele, E. J. Inheritance of acquired immunological tolerance to foreign histocompatibility antigens in mice. *Proceedings of the National Academy of Sciences*, 1980, *77*, 2871–2875.

Gould, S. J. Zealous advocates. *Science*. 1972, *176*, 623–625.

Gould, S. *Ontogeny and phylogeny*. Cambridge: Harvard University Press, 1977.

Gould, S. J. Exultation and explanation. *New York Review of Books*, May 17, 1979.

Gratarolo, G. *The castel of memorie*. London, 1562 (New York: Da Capo Press, 1971).

Green, H. G. Biography of George Green, mathematical physicist of Nottingham and Cambridge. In M. F. A. Montagu (Ed.), *Studies and essays in the history of science and learning*. New York: Henry Schuman, 1946.

Grunberger, R. *Red rising in Bavaria*. London: Arthur Baker, 1973.

Gruneberger, F. J. A measure for crackpots. *Science*, 1964, *145*, 1413–1415.

Haeckel, E. *Generelle Morphologie der Organismen*. Berlin: Georg Reimer, 1866.

Haeckel, E. *Natürliche Schöpfungsgeschichte*. Berlin: Georg Reimer, 1868.

Haeckel, E. *Anthropogenie*. Leipzig: W. Englemann, 1874.

Haeckel, E. *Die Perigenesis der Plastidule oder die Wellenzeugung der Lebenstheilchen*. Berlin: Georg Reimer, 1876.

Haeckel, E. *The evolution of man* (2 Vols.). New York: Appleton & Co., 1879.

Haeckel, E. *India and Ceylon.* New York: J. W. Lovell, 1883.

Haeckel, E. *Die Welträtsel.* Bonn: E. Strauss, 1899.

Haeckel, E. *The confession of faith of a man of science. Monism as connecting religion and science.* London: Adam and Charles Black, 1903.

Haeckel, E. *The wonders of life.* London: Watts & Co., 1904.

Haeckel, E. Charles Darwin as an anthropologist. In A. C. Seward (Ed.), *Darwin and modern science.* Cambridge: University Press, 1910.

Haeckel, E. *Eternity: World-war thoughts on life and death, religion, and the theory of evolution.* New York: The Truth Seeker Co., 1916.

Haeckel, E. *The riddle of the universe.* London: Watts and Co., 1929.

Hagstrom, W. O. *The scientific community.* New York: Basic Books, 1965.

Halacy, D. S. *Man and memory.* New York: Harper & Row, 1970.

Haldane, J. S. Memoir of J. J. Waterston. In J. S. Haldane (Ed.), *The collected scientific papers of John James Waterston.* London: Oliver & Boyd, 1928.

Hall, I. S., & Colman, B. H. *Diseases of the nose, throat and ear.* Edinburgh: Churchill Livingstone, 1973.

Hamerow, T. S. *The social foundations of German unification 1858–1871.* Princeton: Princeton University Press, 1969.

Hamilton, W. *Lectures on metaphysics and logic.* Edinburgh: William Blackwood & Sons, 1859.

Harris, J. F. *Samuel Butler, author of Erewhon.* London: Grant Richards, 1916.

Hartley, D. *Observations on man, his frame, his duty and his expectations.* London: S. Richardson, 1749.

Hartog, M. Introduction. In S. Butler, *Unconscious memory.* London: Jonathan Cope, 1920.

Hasher, L., & Griffin, M. Reconstructive and reproductive processes in memory. *Journal of Experimental Psychology: Human Learning and Memory*, 1978, *4*, 318–330.

Haugeland, J. The nature and plausibility of cognitivism. *Behavioral and Brain Sciences*, 1978, *2*, 215–226.

Hawkins, C. J. Experiments on memory types.

Psychological Review, 1897, *4*, 289–294.

Hellwig, L. Über die Natur des Erinnerungsbildes. *Zeitschrift für Psychologie*, 1899, *21*, 45–46.

Henderson, E. N. Do we forget the disagreeable? *Journal of Philosophy, Psychology, and Scientific Methods*, 1911, *8*, 432–437.

Hering, E. Memory as a universal function of organized matter. In S. Butler, *Unconscious memory.* London: Jonathan Cope, 1920.

Herivel, J. *Joseph Fourier.* Oxford: Clarendon Press, 1975.

Hilgard, E. R. *Divided consciousness.* New York: John Wiley and Sons, 1977.

Himmelfarb, G. *Darwin and the Darwinian revolution.* New York: W. W. Norton, 1968.

Hintzman, D. L. Repetition in memory. In G. H. Bower (Ed.), *The psychology of learning and motivation* (Vol. 10). New York: Academic Press, 1976.

Hintzman, D. L., & Block, P. A. Repetition in memory: Evidence for a multiple trace hypothesis. *Journal of Experimental Psychology*, 1971, *88*, 297–306.

Höffding, H. *Outlines of psychology.* London: Macmillan, 1891.

Höffding, H. Zur Theorie des Wiedererkennens. *Philosphische Studien*, 1893, *8*, 86–96.

Hollingworth, H. L. Characteristic differences between recall and recognition. *American Journal of Psychology*, 1913, *24*, 532–544.

Hollingworth, H. L. *The psychology of thought*, New York: Appleton & Co., 1926.

Holton, G. *The scientific imagination. Case studies.* Cambridge: Cambridge University Press, 1978.

Howell, W. C. Representation of frequency in memory. *Psychological Bulletin*, 1973, *80*, 44–53.

Huizinga, F. Sir Felix Semon. *Archives of Otolaryngology*, 1966, *84*, 473–478.

Hyatt, A. Bioplastology and the related branches of biologic research. *Proceedings of the Boston Society of Natural History*, 1893, *26*, 59–125.

Iltis, H. *Life of Mendel.* London: Allen & Unwin, 1932.

Izawa, C. Comparison of reinforcement and test trials in paired-associate learning. *Journal of Experimental Psychology*, 1969, *81*, 600–603.

Jacobi, J. *Complex, archetype, symbol in the psychology of C. G. Jung.* Princeton: Princeton University Press, 1959.

Jacobs, J. Experiments on "prehension." *Mind*, 1887, *12*, 75–79.

Jacoby, R. *Social amnesia*. Boston: Beacon Press, 1975.

James, W. *Principles of psychology*. New York: Henry Holt, 1890.

Jessen, P. W. *Versuch einer wissenschaftlichen Begründung der Psychologie*. Berlin: Veit & Co., 1855.

Johannsen, W. L. *Elemente der Exakten Erblichkeitslehre*. Jena: G. Fischer, 1913.

Johansen, K., Lenfant, C., & Grigg, G. C. Respiratory properties of blood and responses to diving of the platypus, *Ornithorhynchus Anatinus* (Shaw). *Comparative Biochemistry and Physiology*, 1966, *18*, 597–608.

Jones, E. *The life and work of Sigmund Freud*. New York, Basic Books, 1961.

Jones, G. V. A fragmentation hypothesis of memory: cued recall of pictures and sequential position. *Journal of Experimental Psychology: General*, 1976, *105*, 277–293.

Jones, H. F. *Samuel Butler*. London: Macmillan, 1919.

Joravsky, D. *The Lysenko affair*. Cambridge, Mass.: Harvard University Press, 1970.

Jost, A. Die Assoziationsfertigkeit in ihrer Abhängigkeit von der Verteilung der Wiederholungen. *Zeitschrift für Psychologie*, 1897, *14*, 436–472.

Judd, C. H. *Psychology*. New York: C. Scribner's Sons, 1907.

Judson, H. F. *The eighth day of creation*. New York: Simon & Schuster, 1979.

Jung, C. G. *Memories, dreams and reflections*. New York: Random House, 1961.

Kahn, L. *Mirrors of the Jewish mind*. New York: Thomas Yoseloff, 1968.

Kammerer, P. *The inheritance of acquired characteristics*. New York: Bons and Liveright, 1924.

Katchalsky, A., & Neumann, E. Hysteresis and the molecular memory record. *International Journal of Neuroscience*, 1972, *3*, 175–182.

Katzaroff, D. Contribution à l'étude de la récognition. *Archives de Psychologie*, 1911, *11*, 2–78.

Kellogg, V. L. *Darwinism to-day*. New York: Henry Holt & Co., 1907.

Kennedy, F. On the experimental investigation of memory. *Psychological Review*, 1898, *5*, 477–499.

Kintsch, W. *The representation of meaning in memory*. Hillsdale, N.J.: Lawrence Erlbaum Associates, 1974.

Kirkpatrick, E. A. An experiment in memorizing versus incidental learning. *Journal of Educational Psychology*, 1914, *5*, 405–42.

Kirkpatrick, G. A. An experimental study of memory. *Psychological Review*, 1894, *1*, 602–609.

Klee, H., & Gardiner, J. Memory for remembered events: contrasting recall and recognition. *Journal of Verbal Learning and Verbal Behavior*, 1976, *15*, 471–478.

Knors, C. Experimentelle Untersuchungen über den Lernprozess. *Archiv für die Gesamte Psychologie*, 1910, *17*, 297–361.

Koening, F. O. On the history of science and the second law of thermodynamics. In H. Evans (Ed.), *Men and moments in the history of science*. Seattle: University of Washington Press, 1959.

Koestler, A. *The sleepwalkers*. London: Hutchinson, 1959.

Koestler, A. *The case of the midwife toad*. London: Hutchinson, 1971.

Koffka, K. *Principles of Gestalt psychology*. New York: Harcourt, Brace, & Co., 1935.

Köhler, W. *Gestalt psychology*. London: B. Bell & Sons, 1930.

Köhler, W. *Gestalt Psychology*. New York: Liveright, 1947.

Kohn, H. *The mind of Germany*. New York: Charles Scribner's Sons, 1960.

Kolby, M. N., & Haugen, L. K. Attempts at evaluation of the function of various laryngeal muscles in the light of muscle and nerve stimulation experiments in man. *Acta Oto-Laryngologica*, 1970, *70*, 419–427.

Kostyleff, N. Review of *Die Mneme* and *Die mnemischen Empfindunge*n. *Revue Philosophique*, 1911, *71*, 745–753.

Kris, E. Introduction to *The origins of psychoanalysis*. New York: Basic Books, 1954.

Kubie, L. Some unsolved problems of the scientific career. *American Scientist*, 1953, *41*, 596–613.

Kubie, L. Some unsolved problems of the scientific career. *Science*, 1954, *42*, 104–112.

Külpe, O. *Outlines of psychology*. New York: Macmillan, 1895.

Kuhlmann, F. The present status of memory investigation. *Psychological Bulletin*, 1908, *5*, 285–293.

Kuhn, T. S. *The structure of scientific revolutions*. Chicago: University of Chicago Press, 1962.

Kuhn, T. S. *The essential tension*. Chicago:

University of Chicago Press, 1977.

Lakatos, I., & Musgrave, A. (Eds.). *Criticism and the growth of knowledge*. Cambridge: Cambridge University Press, 1970.

Lamberti, M. *Jewish activism in imperial Germany*. New Haven and London: Yale University Press, 1978.

Landauer, T. K. & Bjork, R. A. Optimum rehearsal patterns and name learning. In M. M. Gruneberg, P. E. Morris, & R. N. Sykes (Eds.), *Practical aspects of memory*. New York: Academic Press, 1978.

Lashley, K. S. In search of the engram. In F. A. Beach, D. O. Hebb, C. T. Morgan, & H. W. Nissen (Eds.), *The neuropsychology of Lashley*. New York: McGraw-Hill, 1960.

Laudan, L. *Progress and its problems*. Berkeley: University of California Press, 1977.

Laycock. T. A chapter on some organic laws of personal and ancestral memory. *Journal of Mental Science*, 1876, *21*, 155–187.

Learned, W. S. *The Oberlehrer*. Cambridge: Harvard University Press, 1914.

Lee, Sir S. *King Edward VII* (Vol. II). London: Macmillan, 1927.

Lee, V. Introduction to R. Semon, *Mnemic psychology*. London: George Allen & Unwin, 1923.

Lee, V. *Proteus*. New York: E. P. Dutton, 1925.

Lehmann, A. Über Wiedererkennen. *Philosophische Studien*, 1889, *5*, 96–156.

Levinson, D. J. *The seasons of a man's life*. New York: Ballantine Books, 1978.

Lewin, K. *Resolving social conflicts*. New York: Harper and Brothers, 1948.

Lewy, W. Experimentelle Untersuchungen über das Gedächtnis. *Zeitschrift für Psychologie*, 1895, *5*, 231–292.

Light, L. L., & Carter-Sobell, L. Effect of changed semantic context on recognition memory. *Journal of Verbal Learning and Verbal Behavior*, 1970, 9, 1–11.

Lindsay, R. B. *Julius Robert Mayer*. Oxford: Pergamon Press, 1973.

Lipmann, O. Die Wirkung der einzelnen Wiederholungen auf verschieden starke und verscheiden alte Assoziationen. *Zeitschrift für Psychologie*, 1904, *35*, 195–233.

Lobsien, M. Experimentelle Untersuchungen über die Gedächtnissentwickelung bei Schulkindern. *Zeitschrift für Psychologie*, 1902, *37*, 34–76.

Lockhart, R. S. The facilitation of recognition by recall. *Journal of Verbal Learning and Verbal Behavior*, 1975, *14*, 253–258.

Lockhart, R. S., Craik, F. I. M., & Jacoby, L. Depth of processing, recognition, and recall. In J. Brown (Ed.), *Recall and recognition*. London: Wiley, 1976.

Loftus, E. F., Miller, D. G., & Burns, H. J. Semantic integration of verbal information into a visual memory. *Journal of Experimenral Psychology: Human Learning and Memory*, 1978, *4*, 19–31.

Lord Rayleigh. *Collected scientific papers, Vol. III: 1887–1892*. New York: Dover, 1964.

Lubarsch, O. Einleitung. In Semon, R. Bewusstseinsvorgang und Gehirnprozess. Wiesbaden: J. F. Bergmann, 1920.

Luh, C. W. The conditions of retention. *Psychological Monographs*, 1922, *31* (Whole No. 142).

Lutz, R. H. *Fall of the German empire: 1914–1918*. Stanford: Stanford University Press, 1932.

MacBride, E. W. *The idea of memory in biology*. Oxford: University Press, 1928.

MacGregor, J. H. Semon on the montremes. *Science*, 1897, *5*, 643–645.

McDonagh, E. L. Attitude changes and paradigm shift: social psychological foundations of the Kuhnian thesis. *Social Studies of Science*, 1976, *6*, 51–76.

McDougall, W. *Body and mind*. London: Methuen, 1911.

McGamble, E. A. A study in memorising various materials by the reconstruction method. *Psychological Monographs*, 1909, *10* (Whole No. 43).

McGamble, E. A. Rate of repetition and tenacity of impression. *Psychological Monographs*, 1916, *22*, 101–151 (Whole No. 96).

McGeoch, J. A. The psychology of human learning: A bibliography. *Psychological Bulletin*, 1933, *30*, 1–62.

Mahoney, M. J. *Scientist as subject*. Cambridge, Mass.: Bellinger, 1976.

Mandler, G., & Mandler, J. M. *Thinking: From association to Gestalt*. New York: Wiley, 1964.

Marshall, J. C., & Fryer, D. M. Speak, memory: An introduction to some historic studies of remembering and forgetting. In M. M. Gruneberg & P. Morris (Eds.), *Practical aspects of memory*. London: Methuen, 1978.

Martin, L. Zur Begründung und Anwendung

der Suggestionsmethode in der Normal-psychologie. *Archiv für die Gesamte Psychologie*, 1907, *10*, 321–402.

Marwick, A. *The deluge*. London: Macmillan, 1978.

Masterman, M. The nature of a paradigm. In I. Lakatos & A. Musgrave (Eds.), *Criticism and the growth of knowledge*. Cambridge: Cambridge University Press, 1970.

Masur, G. *Imperial Berlin*. New York: Basic Books, 1970.

Matthew, P. *On naval timber and aboriculture*. London: Longman, Rees, Orne, Brown, Green, 1831.

Maudsley, H. *The physiology and pathology of mind*. London: Macmillan, 1867.

Mauskopf, S. H. The atomic structural theories of Ampére and Gaudin: molecular speculation and Avogardro's hypothesis. *Isis*, 1969, *40*, 61–74.

Mauxion, M. La vraie memoire affective. *Revue Philosophique*, 1901, *51*, 139–150.

Mead, M., & Metraux, R. The image of the scientist among high-school students. *Science*, 1957, *126*, 384–390.

Meinecke, F. *The German catastrophe*. Boston: Beacon Press, 1950.

Meinhard, J. E. Chromatography: a perspective. *Science*, 1949, *110*, 387–392.

Meldrum, A. H. *Avogadro and Dalton*. Aberdeen: Aberdeen University Press, 1904.

Mendoza, E. Contributions to the study of Sadi Carnot and his work. *Archives Internationales D'Histoire des Sciences*, 1959, *12*, 377-396.

Merton, R. K. *The sociology of science*. Chicago: University of Chicago Press, 1973.

Meumann, E. Über Bekanntheits-und Unbekanntheitsqualität. *Archiv für die Gesamte Psychologie*, 1911, *20*, 36–44.

Meumann, E. *The psychology of learning*. New York: Appleton Co., 1913.

Meyer, H. V. Bereitschaft und Wiedererkennen. *Zeitschrift für Psychologie*, 1915, *70*, 161–211.

Meyer, M. *How we hear*. Boston: C. T. Branford, 1950.

Meyer, S. *Übung und Gedächtnis*. Wiesbaden: Bergmann, 1904.

Meyer, S. Gedächtnis und Vererbung. *Archiv für Rassen-und Gesellschafts-Biologie*, 1906, *3*, 629–645.

Middleton, W. E. K. P. H. Maille, a forgotten pioneer in meteorology. *Isis*, 1965, *56*, 320–326.

Mill, J. *The analysis and the phenomena of the human mind*. London: Baldwin and Cradock, 1829.

Mill, J. S. *A system of logic*. (1843) London: Longmans and Green, 1900.

Mitchell, A. *Revolution in Bavaria 1918–1919*. Princeton: Princeton University Press, 1965.

Mitroff, I. I. *The subjective side of science*. New York: Elsevier, 1974.

Modigliani, V. Effects on a later recall by delaying initial recall. *Journal of Experimental Psychology: Human Learning and Memory*, 1976, *2*, 609–622.

Moede, W. Gedächtnis in Psychologie, Physiologie und Biologie. *Archiv für die Gesamte Psychologie*, 1912, *72*, 312–389.

Moeser, S. D. Recognition processes in episodic memory. *Canadian Journal of Psychology*, 1977, *31*, 41–70.

Montgomery, W. M. Germany. In T. F. Glick (Ed.), *The comparative reception of Darwinism*. Austin: University of Texas Press, 1974.

Morgan, C. L. *Habit and instinct*. New York: E. Arnold, 1896.

Morris, C. D. Bransford, J. D., & Franks, J. J. Levels of processing versus transfer appropriate processing. *Journal of Verbal Learning and Verbal Behavior*, 1977, *16*, 519–533.

Mosse, G. *The crisis of German ideology*. New York: Grosset and Dunlap, 1964.

Mulkay, M. J. *The social processes of innovation*. London: Macmillan, 1972.

Müller, F. Zur frühen Evolution der Säuger-Ontogenesetypen. *Acta Anatomica*, 1969, *74*, 297–404.

Müller, G. E. Zur Analyse der Gedächtnistätigkeit und des Vorstellungsverlaufs. III Teil. *Zeitschrift für Psychologie, Ergänzungsband*, 1913, *8*, 1–567.

Müller, G. E., & Pilzecker, A. Experimentelle Beiträge zur Lehre vom Gedächtnis. *Zeitschrift für Psychologie, Ergänzuungsban*, 1900, *1*, 1–300.

Müller, G. E. & Schumann, F. Experimentelle Beiträge zur Untersuchung des Gedächtnisses. *Zeitschrift für Psychologie*, 1894, *6*, 81–190.

Müller-Freienfels, R. Studien zur Lehre vom Gedächtnis. *Archiv für die Gesamte Psychologie*, 1915, *34*, 65–105.

Münsterberg, H., & Bigham, J. Memory: Studies from the Harvard Psychological Laboratory. *Psychological Review*, 1894, *1*, 34–38.

Murdock, B. B. *Human memory: Theory and data*. Hillsdale, N.J.: Lawrence Erlbaum Associates, 1974.

Murray, D. J. Research on human memory in the nineteenth century. *Canadian Journal of Psychology*, 1976, *30*, 201–220.

Murray, R. H. *Science and scientists in the nineteenth century*. London: The Sheldon Press, 1925.

Myers, F. W. H. *Human personality and its survival of bodily death*. New York: Longmans, Green, & Co., 1903.

Myers, G. C. A comparative study of recognition and recall. *Psychological Review*, 1914, *21*, 442–456.

Myers, G. C., & Myers, C. E. Reconstructive recall. *American Journal of Psychology*, 1916, *27*, 493–506.

Nagel, F. Experimentelle Untersuchungen über Grundfragen der Assoziationslehre. *Archiv für die Gesamte Psychologie*, 1912, *23*, 156–253.

Nash, L. K. The atomic-molecular theory. In J. B. Conant (Ed.), *Harvard case histories in experimental science, Vol. I*. Cambridge, Mass: Harvard University Press, 1957.

Nordenskiöld, E. *The history of biology: A survey*. New York: Tudor Publishing Co., 1929.

Obermeier, S. *Münchens goldene Jahre*. München: C. Bertelsmann, 1976.

Offner, M. *Das Gedächtnis*. Berlin: Reuther & Reichard, 1913.

Ogden, R. M. Memory and the economy of learning. *Psychological Bulletin*, 1904, *1*, 177–184.

Orr, H. B. *A theory of development and heredity*. New York: Macmillan, 1893.

Packard, A. *Lamarck, the founder of evolution*. New York: Longmans, Green, & Co., 1901.

Palermo, D. Is a scientific revolution taking place in psychology? *Science Studies*, 1971, *1*, 135–155.

Pan, S. The influence of context upon learning and recall. *Journal of Experimental Psychology*, 1926, *9*, 468–491.

Patten, C. J. *The memory factor in biology*. London: Balliere, Tindall, and Cox, 1926.

Perkins, M. L. The value of distributed repetitions in rote learning. *British Journal of Psychology*, 1914, *7*, 253–261.

Peters, W. Gefühl und Erinnerung. *Psychologische Arbeiten*, 1911, *6*, 197–260.

Peterson, H. A. On the influence of complexity and dissimilarity on memory. *Psychological Monographs*, 1909, *12* (Whole No. 49).

Pfeifer, E. J. The genesis of American neo-Lamarckism. *Isis*, 1965, *56*, 156–167.

Pflanze, O. *Bismarck and the development of Germany*. Princeton: Princeton University Press, 1963.

Pièron, H. La question de la mémoire affective. *Revue Philosophique*, 1902, *54*, 612–615.

Pilet, P. E. Auguste-Henri Forel. In E. Fischer & G. Haberlandt (Eds.), *Dictionary of scientific biography* (Vol. 5). New York: Charles Scribner's Sons, 1972.

Pillon, F. La mémoire affective: Son importance theorique et pratique. *Revue Philosophique*, 1901, *51*, 113–138.

Pillsbury, W. B. *Essentials of psychology*. New York: Macmillan, 1911.

Pohlmann, A. *Experimentelle Beiträge zur Lehre vom Gedächtnis*. Berlin: Gerdes und Hödel, 1906.

Polanyi, M. *Personal knowledge*. London: Routledge, Kegan & Paul, 1958.

Polanyi, M. The potential theory of adsorption. In M. Greene (Ed.), *Knowing and being*. Chicago: University of Chicago Press, 1969.

Poliakov, L. *The Aryan myth*. New York: Basic Books, 1974.

Poppelreuter, W. Über die Ordnung des Vorstellungsverlaufes. *Archiv für die Gesamte Psychologie*, 1912, *25*, 209–349.

Popper, K. *The logic of scientific discovery*. New York: Harper and Row, 1959.

Popper, K. *Conjectures and refutations*. New York: Harper and Row, 1963.

Pribram, K. H., & Gill, M. *Freud's project reassessed*. New York: Basic Books, 1976.

Price, D. J. S. *Little science, big science*. New York: Columbia University Press, 1963.

Price, G. M. Cranks and prophets. *Catholic World*, 1930, *132*, 44–51.

Prince, M. *The unconscious*. New York: Macmillan, 1916.

Pyle, W. H. Retention as related to repetition. *Journal of Educational Psychology*, 1911, *2*, 311–321.

Pyle, W. H. Concentrated versus distributed practice. *Journal of Educational Psychology*, 1914, *5*, 247–258.

Radossawljevitch, P. R. *Die Behalten und Vergessen bei Kindern und Erwachsenen nach Experimentellen Untersuchungen*. Leipzig: Nemnich, 1907.

Raffel, G. The effect of recall on forgetting. *Journal of Experimental Psychology*, 1934, *17*, 828–838.

Ranschburg, P. Über Hemmung gleichzeitiger Reizwirkungen. *Zeitschrift für Psychologie*, 1902, *30*, 39–86.

Ranschburg, P. Über die Bedeutung der Ähnlichkeit beim Erlernen, Behalten und bei der Reproduktion. *Journal für Psychologie und Neurologie*, 1905, *5*, 93–127.

Ransom, C. P. *The age of Velikovsky*. Glassboro: N.J.: Kronos Press, 1976.

Rapaport, D. *Emotions and memory*. New York: International Universities Press, 1950.

Ratcliff, R. A theory of memory retrieval. *Psychological Review*, 1978, *85*, 59–108.

Ravetz, J. R. *Scientific knowledge and its social problems*. England: Penguin, 1973.

Reich, I. O. *Wilhelm Reich: A personal biography*. New York: St. Martin's Press, 1969.

Reich, W. *The mass psychology of fascism*. New York: Farrar, Straus, & Giroux, 1970.

Reich, W. *Listen, little man*. New York: Farrar, Straus, & Giroux, 1971.

Reich, W. *The function of the orgasm*. New York: Farrar, Straus, & Giroux, 1973.

Reinharz, J. *Fatherland or promised land. The dilemma of the German Jews, 1893–1914*. Ann Arbor: University of Michigan Press, 1975.

Reuther, F. Einige Bemerkungen über die Methoden und über gewisse Sätze der Gedächtnisforschung *Psychologische Studien*, 1906, *2*, 89–114.

Ribot, T. *Diseases of memory*. New York: D. Appleton, 1882.

Ribot, T. *Heredity*. New York: D. Appleton & Co., 1889.

Ribot, T. Le role latent des images motrices. *Revue Philosophique*, 1912, *73*, 248–268.

Rich, J. *The doctor who saved babies*. New York: Doubleday, 1961.

Rignano, E. *Biological memory*. New York: Harcourt, Brace, & Co., 1926.

Ringer, F. K. *The decline of the German mandarins. The German academic community, 1890–1913*. Cambridge, Mass.: Harvard University Press, 1969.

Roediger, H. L. Inhibiting effects of recall. *Memory and Cognition*, 1974, *3*, 261–269.

Romanes, G. J. *Darwin, and after Darwin*. Chicago: Open Court Publishing Co., 1895.

Rosenthal, I. Review of *Die Mneme. Biologisches Centralblatt*, 1905, *25*, 365–368.

Ross, B. M., & Kerst, S. M. Developmental memory theories: Baldwin and Piaget. In H. W. Reese & L. P. Lipsitt (Eds.), *Advances in child development and behavior* (Vol. 12). New York: Academic Press, 1978.

Rukeyser, M. *Willard Gibbs*. New York: Doubleday, Doran & Co., 1942.

Rundus, D. Negative effects of using list items as recall cues. *Journal of Verbal Learning and Verbal Behavior*, 1973, *12*, 43–50.

Russell, B. *The analysis of mind*. London: George Allen & Unwin, 1921.

Sahakian, W. S. *History and systems of psychology*. New York: Schenkman, 1975.

Sakodynsky, K. M. S. Tswett—his life. *Journal of Chromatography*, 1970, *49*, 2–17.

Sarton, G. *The history of science and the new humanism*. New York: Henry Holt & Co., 1931.

Sarton, G. Evariste Galois. *Osiris*, 1937, *3*, 241–259.

Sarup, G. Historical antecedents of psychology: The recurrent issue of old wine in new bottles. *American Psychologist*, 1978, *33*, 478–485.

Sayre, A. *Rosalind Franklin and DNA*. New York: W. W. Norton & Co., 1975.

Schacter, D. L., Eich, J. E., & Tulving, E. Richard Semon's theory of memory. *Journal of Verbal Learning and Verbal Behavior*, 1978, *17*, 721–743.

Schacter, D. L., & Tulving, E. Amnesia and memory research. In L. S. Cermak (Ed.), *Human memory and amnesia*. Hillsdale, N.J.: Lawrence Erlbaum Associates, 1982.

Schatzmann, J. *Richard Semon und seine Mnemetheorie*. Zurich: Juris Druck, 1968.

Scheffler, I. *Science and subjectivity*. New York: Bobbs-Merrill, 1967.

Schmidt, H. (Ed.), *Was wir Ernst Haeckel verdanken*. Leipzig: Verlag Unesma, 1914.

Schorsch, I. *Jewish reactions to German antisemitism 1870–1914*. New York: Columbia University Press, 1972.

Schrödinger, E. *My view of the world*. Cambridge: Cambridge University Press, 1964.

Schwalbe, G. The descent of man. In A. C. Seward (Ed.), *Darwin and modern science*. Cambridge: University Press, 1910.

Sedgwick, A. On the influence of sex in hereditary disease. *British and Foreign Medico-Chirurgical Review*, 1863, *32*, 159–197.

Segal, J. Über den Reproduktionstypus und das

Reproduzieren von Vorstellungen. *Archiv für die Gesamte Psychologie*, 1908, *12*, 124–235.

Selz, O. *Über die Gesetze des geordneten Denkverlaufs*. Stuttgart: Spemann, 1913.

Selz, O. Zur Psychologie des producktiven Denkens und des Irrtums. Bonn: Cohen, 1922.

Semon, F. On the proclivity of the abductor fibres of the recurrent laryngeal nerve to become affected sooner than the adductor fibres. *Archives of Laryngology*, 1881, *2*, 197–215.

Semon, F. *The autobiography of Sir Felix Semon*. H. C. Semon & T. A. McIntyre (Eds.). London: Jarrolds, 1926.

Semon, R. *Beitlräge zur Naturgeschichte der Synaptiden des Mittelmeeres*. Leipzig: Breitkopf & Härtel, 1887.

Semon, R. *Die Entwickelung der Synapta digitata und die Stammgeschichte der Echinodermen*. Jena: G. Fischer, 1888.

Semon, R. *Studien über den Bauplan des Urogenitalsystems der Wirbeltiere*. Jena: G. Fischer, 1891.

Semon, R. *In the Australian bush and on the coast of the Coral Sea*. London: Macmillan, 1899.

Semon, R. *Die Mneme als erhaltendes Prinzip im Wechsel des organischen Geschehens*. Leipzig: Wilhelm Engelmann, 1904.

Semon, R. Beweise für die Vererbung erworbener Eigenschaften. *Archiv für Rassen-und Gesellschafts-Biologie*, 1907, *4*, 1–46. (a)

Semon, R. Kritik und Antikritik der Mneme. *Archiv für Rassen-und Gesellschafts-Biologie*, 1907, *4*, 201–211. (b)

Semon, R. *Die mnemischen Empfindungen*. Leipzig: Wilhelm Engelmann, 1909.

Semon, R. *Das Problem der Vererbung 'Erworbener Eigenschaften.'* Leipzig: Wilhelm Engelmann, 1912.

Semon, R. Aus Haeckels Schule. In H. Schmidt (Ed.), *Was wir Ernst Haeckel verdanken*. Leipzig: Verlag Unesma, 1914.

Semon, R. *Beweisteinsvorgang und Gehirnprozess*. Wiesbaden: J. F. Bergman, 1920.

Semon, R. *The mneme*. London: George Allen & Unwin, 1921.

Semon, R. *Mnemic psychology*. London: George Allen & Unwin, 1923.

Shryock, R. The strange case of Wells' theory of natural selection. In M. F. A. Montagu (Ed.), *Studies and essays in the history of science and learning*. New York: Henry Schuman, 1946.

Sinclair, W. S. *Semmelweis. His life and his doctrine*. Manchester: University Press, 1909.

Singer, C. *A history of biology*. London: Abelard-Schuman, 1959.

Slamecka, N. J., & Graf, P. The generation effect: Delineation of a phenomenon. *Journal of Experimental Psychology: Human Learning and Memory*, 1978, *4*, 592–604.

Slaughter, F. G. *Immortal Magyar*. New York: Henry Schuman, 1950.

Sleight, W. G. Memory and formal training. *British Journal of Psychology*, 1911, *4*, 386–457.

Smith, S. M., Glenberg, A. M., & Bjork, R. A. Environmental context and human memory. *Memory and Cognition*, 1978, *6*, 342–353.

Smith, W. G. The place of repetition in memory. *Psychological Review*, 1896, *3*, 21–31.

Snyder, L. L. *German nationalism: The tragedy of a people*. New York: Kennikat Press, 1969.

Sorabji, R. *Aristotle on memory*. London: Duckworth, 1972.

Spear, N. E. *The processing of memories: Forgetting and retention*. Hillsdale, N.J.: Lawrence Erlbaum Associates, 1978.

Spencer, H. *The factors of organic evolution*. New York: Appleton and Co., 1887.

Spencer, H. *Principles of psychology* (Vol. 1). New York: D. Appleton and Co., 1888.

Starch, D. Periods of work in learning. *Journal of Educational Psychology*, 1912, *3*, 209–213.

Steffens, L. Experimentelle Beiträge zur Lehre von ökonomischen Lernen. *Zeitschrift für Psychologie*, 1900, *22*, 321–382.

Steinmetz, M. (Ed.). *Geschichte der Universität Jena*. Jena: Gustav Fischer, 1958.

Stern, B. J. *Society and medical progress*. Princeton: Princeton University Press, 1941.

Stern, F. *The politics of cultural despair*. Berkeley: University of California Press, 1961.

Sternberg, S. Memory scanning: Mental processes revealed by reaction-time experiments. *American Scientist*, 1969, *57*, 421–457.

Stevens, A. *The dispossessed*. Great Britain: Clark, Doble, & Brendon, 1975.

Stillman, C. G. *Samuel Butler: A mid-Victorian modern*. New York: The Viking Press, 1932.

Stocking, G. W. Lamarckianism in American social science. *Journal of the History of Ideas*, 1962, *23*, 239–256.

Stout, G. F. *Analytic psychology*. London: Allen & Unwin, 1896.

Strong, E. K. The effect of time-interval upon recognition memory. *Psychological Review*, 1913, *20*, 339–372.

Strong. E. K. The factors affecting a permanent impression developed through repetition. *Journal of Experimental Psychology*, 1916, *1*, 319–338.

Strong, M. H., & Strong, E. K. The nature of recognition, memory and of the localization of recognitions. *American Journal of Psychology*, 1916, *27*, 341–362.

Sulloway, F. *Freud, biologist of the mind*. New York: Basic Books, 1979.

Tal, U. *Christians and Jews in Germany*. Ithaca: Cornell University Press, 1975.

Talbot, E. B. An attempt to train the visual memory. *American Journal of Psychology*, 1896, *8*, 414–417.

Taton, R. Evariste Galois. In E. Fischer & G. Haberlandt (Eds.), *Dictionary of scientific biography* (Vol. 5). New York: Charles Scribner's Sons, 1972.

Taylor, A. J. P. *Germany's first bid for colonies 1884–1885*. New York: W. W. Norton and Co., 1970.

Taylor, A. J. P. *The course of German history*. London: Methuen & Co., 1976.

Taylor, R. B. Lamarckist revival in immunology. *Nature*, 1980, *286*, 837–838.

Thomson, J. A. *Heredity*. London: John Murray, 1926.

Thomson, D. M., & Tulving, E. Associative encoding and retrieval: Weak and strong cues. *Journal of Experimental Psychology*, 1970, *86*, 255–262.

Thorndike, L. *History of magic and experimental science. Vol. V. Sixteenth Century*. New York: Columbia University Press, 1941.

Titchener, E. B. Affective memory. *Philosophical Review*, 1895, *4*, 65–76.

Tomkeieff , S. J. The mnemic theories of evolution. *Scientia*, 1923, *34*, Series 2, 159–172.

Toulmin, S. *Foresight and understanding*. New York: Harper and Row, 1961.

Tuchman, B. W. *The proud tower*. New York: Macmillan, 1966.

Tulving, E. The effects of presentation and recall of material in free-recall learning. *Journal of Verbal Learning and Verbal Behavior*, 1967, *6*, 175–184.

Tulving, E. Ecphoric processes in recall and recognition. In J. Brown (Ed.), *Recall and recognition*. London: Wiley, 1976.

Tulving, E., & Pearlstone, Z. Availability versus accessibility of information in memory for words. *Journal of Verbal Learning and Verbal Behavior*, 1966, *5*, 381–391.

Tulving, E., & Thomson, D. M. Encoding specificity and retrieval processes in episodic memory. *Psychological Review*, 1973, *80*, 352–373.

Tulving, E., & Watkins, M. J. Continuity between recognition and recall. *American Journal of Psychology*, 1973, *86*, 739–748.

Turner, R. S. Julius Robert Mayer. In A. T. Macrohius & K. F. Naumann (Eds.), *Dictionary of scientific biography* (Vol. 9). New York: Charles Scribner's Sons, 1974.

Tversky, B. Eye fixations in prediction of recognition and recall. *Memory and Cognition*, 1974, *2*, 275–278.

Underwood, B. J. Attributes of memory. *Psychological Review*, 1969, *76*, 559–573.

Ungar, G. (Ed.), *Molecular mechanisms in memory and learning*. New York: Plenum Press, 1970.

Urban, W. M. The problem of a 'logic of the emotions' and affective memory. I. *Psychological Review*, 1901, *8*, 262–278.

Uschmann, G. *Geschichte der Zoologie und der zoologischen Anstalten in Jena 1779–1919*. Jena: G. Fischer, 1959.

Velikovsky, I. *Earth in upheaval*. New York: Dell Publishing, 1968.

Vellar, I. D. A. Thomas Peel Dunhill, the forgotten man of thyroid surgery. *Medical History*, 1974, *18*, 22–50.

Venable, F. P. *The development of the periodic law*. Easton, Pa.: Chemical Publishing Co., 1896.

Verworn, M. *Irritability*. New Haven: Yale University Press, 1913.

von Kries, L., & Schattelius, E. Beitrag zur Lehre vom Farbengedächtnis. *Zeitschrift für Sinnes-Physiologie*, 1908, *42*, 192–209.

von Sybol, A. Über das Zusammenwirken verschiedener Sinnesgebiete bei Gedächtnisleitungen. *Zeitschrift für Psychologie*, 1909, *53*, 257–360.

Wallace, A. R. *Darwinism*. London: Macmillan and Co., 1901.

Ward, J. *Heredity and memory*. Cambridge: University Press, 1913.

Warren, N. Is a scientific revolution taking place in psychology?—doubt and reservations. *Science Studies*, 1971, *1*, 407–413.

Watson, J. D. *The double helix.* New York: Atheneum, 1968.

Watt, H. J. Review of *Die Mneme. Archiv für die Gesamte Psychologie*, 1905, *5*, 127–130.

Weber, M. Science as a vocation. In H. H. Gerth & C. W. Mills (Eds.), *Essays in sociology.* New York: Oxford University Press, 1946.

Weimer, W. B. The history of psychology and its retrieval from historiography: I. The problematic nature of history. *Science Studies*, 1974, *4*, 235–258. (a)

Weimer, W. B. The history of psychology and its retrieval from historiography. II. Some lessons for the methodology of scientific research. *Science Studies*, 1974, 367–396.(b)

Weimer, W. B., & Palermo, D. S. Paradigms and normal science in psychology. *Science Studies*, 1973, *3*, 211–244.

Weiner, B. Effects of motivation on the availability and retrieval of memory traces. *Psychological Bulletin*, 1966, *65*, 24–37.

Weingart, P. On a sociological theory of scientific change. In R. Whitley (Ed.) *Social processes of scientific development.* London: Routledge & Kegan Paul, 1974.

Weismann, A. Semons 'Mneme' und die "Vererbung erworbener Eigenschaften." *Archiv für Rassen-und Gesellschafts-Biologie*, 1906, *3*, 1–27.

Weismann, A. *Essays upon heredity.* E. B. Poulton, S. Schönland, & A. E. Shipley (Eds.), Oxford: Clarendon Press, 1889.

Weismann, A. *The germ-plasm.* New York: Charles Scribner's Sons, 1893.

Whipple, G. M. An analytic study of the memory image and the process of judgment in the discrimination of changes and tones. *American Journal of Psychology*, 1901, *12*, 409–457.

Whitehead, A. N. *The principles of natural knowledge.* Cambridge: Cambridge University Press, 1919.

Whitehead, L. G. A study of visual and aural memory processes. *Psychological Review*, 1896, *3*, 258–269.

Whitely, G. P. *The fishes of Australia: Part I.* Sydney: Royal Zoological Society of New South Wales, 1940.

Whitten, W. B. Initial-retrieval 'depth' and the negative recency effect. *Memory and Cognition*, 1978, *6*, 590–598.

Whitten, W. B., & Bjork, R. A. Learning from tests: effects of spacing. *Journal of Verbal Learning and Verbal Behavior*, 1977, *16*, 465–478.

Wilkie, J. S. Some reasons for the rediscovery and appreciation of Mendel's work in the first years of the present century. *British Journal for the History of Science*, 1962, 7, 5–18.

Willey, B. *Darwin and Butler.* London: Chatto and Windus, 1960.

Witasek, S. Über Lesen und Rezitieren in ihren Beziehungen zum Gedächtnis. *Zeitschrift fürPsychologie*, 1907, *44*, 161–185.

Wohlgemuth, A. Simultaneous and successive association. *British Journal of Psychology*, 1915, *7*, 434–452.

Wolfe, H. K. Untersuchungen über das Tongedächtniss. *Philosophische Studien*, 1886, *3*, 534.

Woltmann, L. *Politische Anthropologie.* Jena: Eugen Diederichs, 1906.

Woods, E. L. An experimental analysis of the process of recognizing. *American Journal of Psychology*, 1915, *26*, 313–387.

Wundt, W. *Outlines of psychology.* Leipzig: Wilhelm Engelmann, 1907.

Wyke, B. D., & Kirchner, J. A. Neurology of the larynx. In R. Hinchcliffe & D. Harrison (Eds.), *Scientific foundations of Oto-laryngology.* Chicago: William Heinemann Medical Books, 1976.

Yates, F. *The art of memory.* Chicago: University of Chicago Press, 1966.

Young, J. Z. The organization of a memory system. *Proceedings of the Royal Society of London*, 1965, *163*, 285–320.

Zechmeister, L. Mikhail Tswett—the inventor of chromatography. *Isis*, 1946, *36*, 108–109.

Ziehen, T. *Introduction to physiological psychology.* New York: Macmillan, 1899.

Zirkle, C. Natural selection before the 'Origin of Species'. *Proceedings of the American Philosophical Society*, 1941, *84*, 71–123.

Zirkle, C. Mendel and his era. In R. M. Nardone (Ed.), *Mendel centenary: Genetics, development and evolution.* Washington: Catholic University Press, 1965.

Author Index

Numbers in italics denote pages with complete bibliographic information.

291

Subject Index